0800 496 5

D1138338

PX
PCC ID/309300114
A

'But I Say to You'.

amazon. co.UK/
Kendle support

Back of router.

security PIN.

20927448.

orange.

'But I Say to You'

Exploring the Gospel of Matthew

Leith Fisher

Foreword by
PROFESSOR JOHN BARCLAY
Lightfoot Professor of Divinity, University of Durham

SAINT ANDREW PRESS
Edinburgh

First published in 2009 by
SAINT ANDREW PRESS
121 George Street
Edinburgh EH2 4YN

ISBN 978 0 7152 0873 1

British Library Cataloguing in Publication Data
A catalogue record for this book is available from the British Library

It is the publisher's policy to only use papers that are natural and recyclable and that have
been manufactured from timber grown in renewable, properly managed forests. All of
the manufacturing processes of the papers are expected to conform to the environmental
regulations of the country of origin.

Typeset by Waverley Typesetters, Fakenham
Printed and bound by Bell & Bain Ltd, Glasgow

CONTENTS

v

FOREWORD

For most of Christian history, the gospel of Matthew has stood as the gateway into the New Testament and as the definitive gospel. Its opening genealogy forms the bridge from the Old Testament to the New, and its towering portrait of Jesus as teacher, healer and controversialist demands and keeps our attention right up to the climactic ending, when he departs with the promise to be with his disciples to the end of history. Matthew has carefully organised his gospel around five great blocks of Jesus' teaching, beginning with the stunning 'Sermon on the Mount' (chapters 5–7), in which Jesus both evokes and surpasses the law of Moses. This arrangement makes this gospel almost a 'manual' of discipleship, and the explicit references to 'the church' in this gospel (unique to Matthew) indicate that this discipleship is to be pursued not in individualistic isolation, but in community. When Jesus says 'But I say to you', the 'you' is plural and communal.

In these respects, Matthew's gospel perhaps speaks more than any other gospel directly and accessibly to the church, and fittingly finds some of its best and most acute commentators among those who have spent their lives in that simultaneously frustrating and glorious community we know as the present-day church. But it speaks to us, in many respects, from a rather different place from the church today. As Leith Fisher rightly notes throughout this excellent new reading of the gospel, Matthew's is the gospel most obviously indebted to its Jewish heritage, and also most vehemently in conflict with its contemporary Jewish rivals, the Judaism reforming its identity and its boundaries after the devastation of the Judean War (AD 66–70). That conflict gives this gospel a shrill edge in its harsh polemics against 'the scribes and Pharisees' and its appallingly fateful presentation of the Jerusalem crowd calling out to Pilate: 'his blood be upon us and upon our children'. It is also deeply concerned about fake discipleship, those who talk the Christian talk (calling Jesus 'Lord, Lord') but fail to walk the Christian walk. Fighting on both fronts, Matthew has Jesus speak rather often of 'outer darkness' where there is 'weeping and gnashing of teeth' – language we find hard to reproduce today.

Among the many merits of this highly valuable commentary is Leith Fisher's willingness and ability to wrestle with such issues in the text – neither to bypass them nor to pretend they are not a problem. That is just one symptom of the chief hallmark of this commentary – its theological and pastoral maturity. Making judicious use of his wide reading in theology and New Testament studies, Leith opens up dimensions of this text in a way no popular commentary can match. But this is no purely academic treatise: ever down to earth, Leith consistently relates the gospel to the everyday and the ordinary, with all its ambiguities, not least through a wonderful selection of poems and other aids to reflection. Throughout, his ear is attuned to the quirky, the unsettling and the surprising elements in this reputedly conservative gospel – the scandalous women in the genealogy, the magi of dubious origin, the daring Canaanite woman, and the parables that unsettle our picture of the world. Like Matthew, Leith Fisher keeps asking us: 'What would it be like to be a church that lives by grace?' We are challenged here by Jesus' 'I say to you' not only in the Sermon on the Mount, with its insistence on loving our enemies, but also in the parable of the sheep and goats (Matthew 25:31–46), when as king he points to the weak, the hungry, the foreigner and the prisoner: 'Truly, I say to you, as you did it (or did it not) to the least of one of these …'. There could be no clearer or more urgent statement to the church today, and I warmly commend to readers this accessible, engaging and deeply enriching study of Matthew, adaptable to both individual and group study. And, if you haven't yet read the earlier ones on Mark and Luke, when you have finished this I have little doubt you will want to get hold of them as well!

As this book was being prepared for publication, to our enormous loss its author, Leith Fisher, died suddenly on 13 March 2009. His family and huge circle of friends mourn his passing very deeply, but it is some comfort to know that, through this book, as through his hymns and other publications, we will continue to hear his strong compassionate voice – the voice of a man deeply attuned to the gracious beckoning of God and to the hope that draws us, in Christ, beyond darkness into light.

PROFESSOR JOHN BARCLAY
Durham University

INTRODUCTION

Welcome to an exploration of the gospel of Matthew. As John Barclay notes in his Foreword, Matthew's gospel, with its emphasis on and concern for the church as community of faith, has been the insider's gospel, much used and studied by the church down through the Christian centuries. Paradoxically, it is written by an outsider, probably a Greek-speaking Jewish Christian from Syrian Antioch post-70 CE. The writer is doubly an outsider, on the one hand battered and bruised by the rupture between the young church and its Jewish origins, on the other seeking to come to terms with an increasingly Gentile church with its growing influx of stranger Gentiles into its ranks and counsels. It is therefore written against a background of both pain and change – realities not unknown in our Christian lives today.

Matthew is a great teacher, and he seeks to show his readers both Jesus as teacher and the content of his teaching – the medium and the message. He does so with painstaking thoroughness, and not a few tricks of the teacher's trade, particularly in the way he subtly reinforces his main themes throughout his story. His concern for order does not shut the door on his capacity to surprise – and there are plenty surprises in store in wrestling with his witness. His twin passions are to show his readers Jesus as Lord and to lay out for them the way of humble, faithful discipleship in the midst of a bruising and confusing world. Matthew's gospel remains a gospel for today for serious disciples.

Two issues in writing this exploration are worthy of initial comment. As in my earlier explorations of Mark and Luke, I have used the Good News Bible (GNB) text throughout on the basis that its purpose was to render the biblical text in simple, accessible English. Jesus' words to his original audience of the Galilean and Judean 'crowd' were characterised by simplicity and directness. On occasions, however, and particularly in the Beatitudes of the Sermon on the Mount (Matthew 5), I have used the text of the New Revised Standard Version (NRSV) either to clarify or to amplify the GNB translation.

The second issue concerns the amount of material in Matthew which is common also to Mark or Luke, or sometimes both. The largely accepted supposition is that Matthew knew Mark's gospel when he wrote his own, and he also had access to a source common to himself and Luke. The Mark/Matthew relationship poses the larger problem. Not only does Matthew use a great deal of Mark's content, he largely follows his chronology of events in Jesus' life, though not without alteration in the light of his own concerns. The commentator's dilemma is to what extent he should let the Matthew text stand on its own as opposed to continually cross-referencing with Mark. I have tried to tread a middle path of cross-referencing with Mark when the change Matthew makes is of interest or substance, though refraining from comment on each and every occasion.

This introduction, coupled with John Barclay's excellent Foreword, is a long enough preliminary. What matters is our engagement with the text itself. Happy 'learning' with Matthew the teacher, witness to a greater teacher.

How to use this book – some suggestions

Any book has a life of its own once it finds itself in the hands of a reader or a group of readers. This book is offered both for personal and group reading. It can be read either at a sitting, or in smaller doses over a period of a month or a year. It could form the basis for a year's preaching through Matthew or for a series of group studies. Its forty sections also make it suitable for the days of Lent.

After each section in the book, some stimulus for personal reflection is suggested. Keeping your own journal of your thoughts as you journey through the gospel will deepen your study and reflection. Another aid to reflection is to read over the text for each section and mark it thus:

- with a question mark against anything which puzzles you
- with a cross against anything you find difficult or don't agree with
- with an exclamation mark against anything you find surprising or see in a new light
- with a tick against anything that makes you want to cry out 'Yes!'

Material for group work is also offered for around half of the sections. These can be picked and mixed. Do them all, or simply pick out a few. Some require more 'homework' than others; it will be a good idea to look at what 'homework' is needed in advance.

Before you begin reading, you might jot down your answers to this question. What do I know about Jesus which excites, scares, perplexes, challenges, reassures me? Ask yourself the same question when you come to the gospel's end.

ACKNOWLEDGEMENTS

Once again, I am greatly indebted to Professor John Barclay of Durham University, both for his judicious if too generous Foreword and for acting as my mentor throughout this exploration's writing. He has both kept me from (some) errors and often pointed and inspired me on the way. Part of this material was used with either the Evening Service Group or the Questions of Faith Group at Wellington Church, Glasgow: I thank their members for their patience and encouragement. The book was begun during a period of study leave under the Church of Scotland's scheme for ministers and completed in the early months of my 'retirement'. My thanks are due to Nonie, my spouse, for coping with not only a removal and retirement but also a book-writing husband who fled upstairs to the study rather than hang the curtains. Her life has exemplified one of Matthew's main themes: 'mercy, not sacrifice'. Harold Reid and Elspeth Kelman undertook a painstaking reading of the text which removed not a few typographical howlers and grammatical clangers. Thanks to Michael Given for his proofreading. Finally, grateful thanks go to Ann Crawford of Saint Andrew Press for enabling me to continue with the series begun with the Scottish Christian Press, now amalgamated, and for her skill, along with Richard Allen, in seeing the book through to publication.

COPYRIGHT
ACKNOWLEDGEMENTS

The author gratefully thanks the following for their kind permission to use extracts from their work.

Page 5 and throughout, extracts from Carter, Warren (2000), *Matthew and the Margins: a Socio-political and Religious Reading*, Sheffield: Sheffield Academic Press. © 2000 by Warren Carter.

Page 18, extract © Donald McIlhagga 2004. Taken from *The Green Heart of the Snowdrop* by Kate McIlhagga, published by Wild Goose Publications, www.ionabooks.com

Page 18 and throughout, extracts from Bonhoeffer, Dietrich (1959), *The Cost of Discipleship*, London: SCM Press; and (1967), *Letters and Papers from Prison*, 3rd edn, London: SCM Press.

Pages 46 and 246, extracts from Herzog, William II (2000), *Jesus, Justice and the Reign of God*, Louisville: Westminster John Knox Press. Used with permission.

Page 77, extract from *The Economics of Innocent Fraud* by John Kenneth Galbraith (Penguin Books 2004, 2009). Copyright © John Kenneth Galbraith, 2004.

Pages 80–1, extract from Søren Kierkegaard, *Fear and Trembling*, Princeton University Press. Used with permission.

Page 82, extract from 'S.K.', R. S. Thomas, *Collected Later Poems: 1988–2000* (Bloodaxe Books, 2004).

Page 93, and on several pages thereafter, excerpts from LEARNING TO DANCE, copyright © 2001 by Darton, Longman & Todd, Ltd.

Page 94, 'We Alone', from Alice Walker, *Horses Make a Landscape Look More Beautiful*, Harcourt Brace Jovanovich. Used with permission.

Pages 147 and 359, extracts taken from *Christ on Trial: How the Gospel Unsettles our Judgement* by Rowan Williams © Rowan Williams 2000. Used by permission of Zondervan.

Pages 178–9, 'The Other' by R. S. Thomas, from *Collected Poems* (JM Dent, an imprint of the Orion Group). Copyright © 1993 R. S. Thomas.

Page 230, extract © Ian M. Fraser, 2006. Taken from *The Way Ahead: Grown Up Christians*, published by Wild Goose Publications, www.ionabooks.com

Page 233 and others, extract from Holloway, Richard (2002), *On Forgiveness*, Edinburgh: Canongate Books.

Pages 234–5, extract from Bornkamm, G. (1995), 'The authority to "bind" and "loose" in the church of Matthew's Gospel', in G. M. Stanton (ed.), *The Interpretation of Matthew*, Edinburgh: T&T Clark. By kind permission of Continuum International Publishing Group.

Page 285, extract from *A Season in the Desert* by W. Paul Jones © 2000 W. Paul Jones.
Used by permission, Paraclete Press, www.paracletepress.com

Page 315, extract from Herzog, William II (1994), *The Parables as Subversive Speech: Jesus as Pedagogue of the Oppressed*, Louisville: Westminster John Knox Press. Used with permission.

Pages 317–18, extract from Romero, Oscar (1988), *The Violence of Love*, Robertsbridge: Plough Publishing House; © Chicago Province of the Society of Jesus. Used with permission of the Chicago Province, all rights reserved.

Pages 318–19, extract from Sacks, Jonathan (2005), *To Heal a Fractured World: The Ethics of Responsibility*, London: Continuum. By kind permission of Continuum International Publishing Group.

Chapter 1

BEGINNINGS AND BIRTH

Matthew 1
The Ancestors of Jesus Christ
(*Luke 3:25–38*)

This is the list of the ancestors of Jesus Christ, a descendant of David, who was a descendant of Abraham.

From Abraham to King David, the following ancestors are listed: Abraham, Isaac, Jacob, Judah and his brothers; then Perez and Zerah (their mother was Tamar), Hezron, Ram, Amminadab, Nahshon, Salmon, Boaz (his mother was Rahab), Obed (his mother was Ruth), Jesse and King David.

From David to the time when the people of Israel were taken into exile in Babylon, the following ancestors are listed: David, Solomon (his mother was the woman who had been Uriah's wife), Rehoboam, Abijah, Asa, Jehoshaphat, Jehoram, Uzziah, Jotham, Ahaz, Hezekiah, Manasseh, Amon, Josiah, and Jehoiachin and his brothers.

From the time after the exile in Babylon to the birth of Jesus, the following ancestors are listed: Jehoiachin, Shealtiel, Zerubbabel, Abiud, Eliakim, Azor, Zadok, Achim, Eliud, Eleazar, Matthan, Jacob, and Joseph, who married Mary, the mother of Jesus, who was called the Messiah.

So then, there were fourteen generations from Abraham to David, and fourteen from David to the exile in Babylon, and fourteen from then to the birth of the Messiah.

The Birth of Jesus Christ

(*Luke 2:1–7*)

This was how the birth of Jesus Christ took place. His mother Mary was engaged to Joseph, but before they were married, she found out that she was going to have a baby by the Holy Spirit. Joseph was a man who always did what was right, but he did not want to disgrace Mary publicly; so he made plans to break the engagement privately. While he was thinking about this, an angel of the Lord appeared to him in a dream and said: 'Joseph, descendant of David, do not be afraid to take Mary to be your wife. For it is by the Holy Spirit that she has conceived. She will have a son, and you will name him Jesus – because he will save his people from their sins.'

Now all this happened in order to make what the Lord had said through the prophet come true: 'A virgin will become pregnant and have a son, and he will be called Immanuel (which means, "God is with us").'

So when Joseph woke up, he married Mary, as the angel of the Lord had told him to do. But he had no sexual relations with her before she gave birth to her son. And Joseph named him Jesus.

Where does he come from?

Matthew's gospel begins with the 'begats'. The opening seventeen verses of the gospel have been called, somewhat irreverently, 'the begat chapter' in the light of the King James translation, which reads: 'Abraham begat Isaac; and Isaac begat Jacob; and Jacob begat Judas and his brethren ... etc.' 'Where do you come from?' is a frequently posed question. In today's world, we ask one another about our geography and genealogy; tracing the family tree has become a flourishing leisure pastime. In the world of Jesus' time, questions of origins were highly significant; a person's list of antecedents established their identity and credentials. It has been said of Matthew's gospel: 'Matthew will speak to those who value order and history'. It's no great surprise therefore to find this gospel beginning with a highly ordered and structured list which traces the ancestry of Jesus back to two of the great founding fathers of the

2

faith of Israel, David and Abraham. Abraham is important not only as a father of Israel but also as the father of many nations, one in and through whom God's promise of salvation would be delivered to the Gentile world also. The gospel's beginning hints at what will be made clear by its end – that the one whose story is here told is for both Jew and Gentile.

Take a closer look

I doubt if many of us have heard many sermons on these first seventeen verses or indeed heard the list of names foreign to our culture read as gospel in our worship. Writers of many kinds, however, sweat over their introductory lines out of the knowledge that first words matter; and the writer of this gospel considers the ordered listing of Jesus' ancestors to be a fitting start to his story. A key resource for the study of the infancy narratives in Matthew and Luke is the big book by the distinguished American biblical scholar Raymond Brown, *The Birth of the Messiah*. One of his students has said that at his seminary in New York, Brown carried out a one-man campaign to encourage his students to preach from these verses during the Advent season. And the Roman Catholic scholar Brown quoted as one of his authorities for his campaign the sixteenth-century Swiss reformer Zwingli, who said that these seventeen verses of tongue-twisting names gave eloquent testimony to the reality of the grace of God. Raymond Brown's book is greatly helpful in unweaving the strands of the minutiae of these verses and indeed of Matthew's first two chapters. Here we have to content ourselves with a few broad brush-strokes, beginning by taking a look at the first names on the list.

'Abraham was the father of Isaac; and Isaac was the father of Jacob; and Jacob was the father of Judah and his brothers, and Judah was the father of Phares and Zareh (their mother was Tamar).' There is something slightly odd about most of these names. Abraham was the father of Isaac, but in Hebrew society it was the first-born son who carried on the line and held the privileges of inheritance – and, before Abraham was the father of Isaac, he was the father of the blameless Ishmael. Isaac was the father of Jacob, but Jacob was the twin brother of Esau, who was the first-born. Jacob cheated his brother out of his inheritance, but the line continues through Jacob, the twister, and not through Esau. Jacob was the father of Judah and his brothers, but Judah and his brothers were stained with the blood of their most famous brother, Joseph, whom they sold into slavery. The line goes on through Judah, and not through the gifted and far-sighted brother Joseph.

The earlier quotation 'Matthew will speak to those who value order and history' continues: 'and sow subversive seeds of the Kingdom'. All through Matthew's gospel, in and through his ordered account, there is the possibility of being surprised and ambushed by the unexpected. In these opening lines, there is the reminder that God chooses whom God will choose to be his instruments, servants, agents of his purpose. And God can, does and will use those who seem to us to be quite odd, inappropriate or, to make more of a value judgement, simply not good enough. Even old Abraham himself, from the biblical record, has some pretty real skeletons rattling around in his cupboard; what of the great and blessed David, who may have given us some beautiful psalms but was also the stealer of wives and the murderer of rivals? God chooses whom God will choose, and God blesses whom God will bless. The hymn is right to say 'for the love of God is broader than the grasp of mortal mind' (*Church Hymnary 4*, no. 187) – and the ways of God are more mysterious and surprising, as this story of the Good News of Jesus Christ will go on to reveal. In these opening verses, there are more surprises in store. Look at the women who are here mentioned.

The women

'Judah was the father of Phares and Zerah by Tamar' (1:3 NRSV). Here's the first of the women, Tamar. The others are Rahab, Ruth, Bathsheba (though she is not named, only called 'the one who had been the wife of Uriah') and, at the end, Mary herself, the mother of Jesus. Matthew mentions five women, and they are truly an extraordinary collection. Consider Tamar. She was Judah's daughter-in-law. Widowhood was a great affliction in the ancient world, and, when Tamar's husband died, she was promised in marriage to his younger brother. But Judah, her father-in-law, didn't keep the promise, and so Tamar did an extraordinary, courageous and resourceful thing. She disguised herself as a prostitute and slept incestuously with Judah, who made her pregnant. When her pregnancy became known, and as a widow unlawfully pregnant she should have been punished by death, she revealed to Judah that he was the father of her future twins. And Judah recognised that it was he, and not she, who was in the wrong. 'She is more righteous than I', he said (Genesis 28:36).

First comes Tamar, the Canaanite who played the prostitute. She is followed by Rahab, the Canaanite prostitute from the walls of Jericho, commended for her faith (Hebrews 11:31). Next is Ruth, the Moabite woman, another outsider, cuddling up to Boaz in the barn, yet the great-grandmother of David himself (Ruth 1:1ff.). (The relationship of Israel with the Canaanites was uneasy; with the Moabites it was frequently murderous.) Then there is Bathsheba, wife of Uriah the Hittite, who slept with David unlawfully if not unwillingly (2 Samuel 11) before becoming the mother of David's successor, Solomon. Last is Mary herself, pregnant in circumstances which had her future husband Joseph wanting quietly to call the whole thing off (1:19). Each of the five has some kind of scandal or doubt connected with them, three of them are clearly outsiders in a society where the purity of the racial bloodline was a deeply held value, yet they're all in their different ways commended. Some of them indeed come down to us as very models of faith.

'Subversive seeds of the Kingdom.' These five women are in their different ways outsiders, whether by birth, by their Gentile origins, or through their actions – what they do or what is done to them is not the norm, not according to the rules, not culturally approved. Through them, we are invited to scan a wider horizon, to look and find God at work on the margins, beyond the familiar, the known, the acceptable, the tribe. Warren Carter writes: 'God's actions are not contained by or bound to these structures. God breaks them open to work on the margins. The margins are not God-forsaken or cursed, but crucial to God's purposes' (2000 p. 60). At the very start of Matthew's story, in the listing of Jesus' human pedigree, there are strong hints that the one who comes will be a breaker of the bounds.

From Solomon to Joseph

Last comes the long list of names from Solomon to Joseph the father of Jesus. The list divides into two sections, from the time of Solomon to the time of exile in Babylon and from the exile to Joseph. The first section comprises a list of kings. The record of their reigns is recorded in 2 Chronicles, and the chronicler is distinctly unimpressed by most of them. Of the list of names in the final section, most of us would be pretty hard pressed to recognise any of them. Maybe that's just the point. They are little or unknown figures of faith, a bit like us. We don't expect to find our names up in lights anywhere in the roll of honour of the saints. The truth is that faith goes on, and is passed on through countless hosts of ordinary people, people like you and me, who very often have a quite limited awareness of the ways in which God uses us and will continue to use us. There's something both comforting and challenging in this last section of names. The comfort and the challenge are the same: that today, as yesterday, God uses and calls each one of us, with all our flaws and hesitations, to be his witnesses and instruments in the world of today.

Let's put it this way:

> Matthew's genealogy is showing us how the story of Jesus Christ contained – and would continue to contain – the flawed and inflicted and insulted, the cunning and the weak-willed and the misunderstood. His is an equal-opportunity ministry for crooks and saints. And this is where the message settles directly upon us ... *isn't Matthew's list of sinner, saint and obscure* ... a pretty hopeful testament that God is using us, with our individual flaws and gifts, in all manner of peculiar and unexpected ways? (Godwin, *Evensong*, 1999)

Matthew's gospel begins by drawing our attention to this list of the human origins of Jesus, his forefathers and mothers. Here is the human 'before' of Jesus. What about the 'after'? What about the ways in which the story and the life of Jesus go on through human history? Raymond Brown suggests that the story goes on something like this: 'Jesus called Peter and Paul ... Paul called Timothy ... someone called you ... and you must call someone else'. The story of the 'after' is a continuing story; it's our story, now.

6

Joseph's dream

Matthew and Luke are the two gospels which tell the story of the birth of Jesus at Bethlehem. In contrast with Luke's story of the events around Jesus' birth in the stable at Bethlehem (Luke 2:1–20), Matthew's account of the actual birth is extremely spare and lacking in any detail. Where Luke's pre-birth narrative concentrates on mother Mary at some length, Matthew's focus is on father Joseph. The gospel tells us that Joseph is Jesus' legal rather than natural father since Mary is pregnant by the exclusive agency of the Holy Spirit – which adds another twist to the genealogy of the previous verses. The arguments for and against the virgin birth of Jesus continue to rage, often generating more heat than light. Matthew's gospel simply assumes its truth rather than seeking to prove it.

It does seem clear, however, that the question of Jesus' origins was of some concern to Matthew and his readers. It is quite likely that the synagogue opponents of the new Jewish Christian community were spreading rumours and innuendo about the circumstances of Jesus' birth. The story of Joseph's dream is told to set the record straight. Dreams feature prominently in the early chapters of Matthew as means of divine communication. Here, Joseph, the good man who wants to do the decent and charitable thing when he learns the embarrassing fact of his betrothed's pregnancy, is confronted in a dream by a divine messenger who tells him not to be afraid to marry Mary, who has 'conceived by the Holy Spirit'. Joseph is also told to name the child Jesus.

Two great names

This passage gives two hugely significant names for the child who is to be born, 'Jesus' (1:21) and 'Immanuel' (1:23). 'Jesus' is the Greek translation of the Hebrew name Joshua, the leader who, as Moses' successor, led his people to the freedom of the promised land after their deliverance from slavery in Egypt and their wilderness wanderings. The very name means 'the one who saves', 'God will save'. Jesus means 'Saviour'. The angel continues: 'Name him Jesus – because he will save his people from their sins' (1:21). In slavery in Egypt, in exile in Babylon, the Jewish people had known the reality of oppression and the need for a saviour, a liberator. They also had known of God coming to their rescue and bringing them deliverance. Such was part of their history and a lively part of their tradition and hope. What is new in the words of the gospel is the linking of sins to salvation. Central to the gospel is the reality of the forgiveness of sins; watch as this motif appears again and again.

Matthew tells also of a second name for Jesus. He says that the coming of Jesus is the fulfilment of a prophecy about a son being born whose name is 'Immanuel' – which means 'God is ever with us'. The reference is to Isaiah 7:14. The claim that, in Jesus, God is with us always, brackets this gospel. It is here at the beginning, and it appears in the gospel's final words when Jesus says: 'I will be with you always, to the end of the age' (28:20b). How central to our faith is the reality that, in Jesus, we receive the presence of God with us who never leaves us! These words and this promise had a very special meaning for Matthew's original readers. They were living in the years after the destruction of the great Temple of Jerusalem. The Temple was seen as the place where God dwelt on earth; its destruction led to the strong feeling among the Hebrew people that God had left and abandoned them. At the start of the gospel, Matthew is saying: 'Look again, don't lose faith, for in the life of this special person, son of Abraham, son of David, here is the new Temple, the continuing and continual presence of God with his people, the sign and seal of God ever with us'.

Study

By yourself

Read the beginnings of all four gospels: Matthew 1–2, Mark 1:1–39, Luke 1–2, John 1:1–18.

Make a note of anything which strikes you about each one.

Putting them together, what do they tell you about Jesus?

Chapter 2

INTERRUPTION – A CLASH OF KINGS

Matthew 2
Visitors from the East

Jesus was born in the town of Bethlehem in Judea, during the time when Herod was king. Soon afterwards, some men who studied the stars came from the east to Jerusalem and asked, 'Where is the baby born to be the king of the Jews? We saw his star when it came up in the east, and we have come to worship him.'

When King Herod heard about this, he was very upset, and so was everyone else in Jerusalem. He called together all the chief priests and the teachers of the Law and asked them, 'Where will the Messiah be born?'

'In the town of Bethlehem in Judea', they answered. 'For this is what the prophet wrote:

> "Bethlehem in the land of Judah,
> you are by no means the least of the leading cities of Judah;
> for from you will come a leader
> who will guide my people Israel".'

So Herod called the visitors from the east to a secret meeting and found out from them the exact time the star had appeared. Then he sent them to Bethlehem with these instructions: 'Go and make a careful search for the child, and when you find him, let me know, so that I too may go and worship him'.

And so they left, and on their way they saw the same star they had seen in the east. When they saw it, how happy they were, what joy was theirs! It went ahead of them until it stopped over the place where the child was. They went into the house, and when they saw the child with his mother Mary, they knelt down and worshipped him. They brought out their gifts of gold, frankincense, and myrrh, and presented them to him.

Then they returned to their country by another road, since God had warned them in a dream not to go back to Herod.

The Escape to Egypt

After they had left, an angel of the Lord appeared in a dream to Joseph and said, 'Herod will be looking for the child in order to kill him. So get up, take the child and his mother and escape to Egypt, and stay there until I tell you to leave.'

Joseph got up, took the child and his mother, and left during the night for Egypt, where he stayed until Herod died. This was done to make what the Lord had said through the prophet come true, 'I called my Son out of Egypt'.

The Killing of the Children

When Herod realized that the visitors from the east had tricked him, he was furious. He gave orders to kill all the boys in Bethlehem and its neighbourhood who were two years old and younger – this was done in accordance with what he had learned from the visitors about the time when the star had appeared.

In this way, what the prophet Jeremiah had said came true:

> 'A sound is heard in Ramah,
> the sound of bitter weeping.
> Rachel is crying for her children;
> she refuses to be comforted,
> for they are dead.'

The Return from Egypt

After Herod died, an angel of the Lord appeared in a dream to Joseph in Egypt and said, 'Get up, take the child and his mother, and go back to the land of Israel, because those who tried to kill the child are dead'. So Joseph got up, took the child and his mother, and went back to Israel.

But when Joseph heard that Archelaus had succeeded his father Herod as king of Judea, he was afraid to go there. He was given more instructions in a dream, so he went to the province of Galilee and made his home in a town named Nazareth. And so what the prophets had said came true: 'He will be called a Nazarene'.

A little background to a familiar story

The story of the visit of the 'wise men' to the new-born child at Bethlehem is thoroughly well known through a multitude of nativity plays with children draped in garish dressing-gowns or cut-down curtains to represent the 'three kings' from the east. We can begin this section by noticing that the gospel itself nowhere says that the eastern visitors were three in number nor that they were either wise men or kings. These are later traditions which have grown around the bare bones of Matthew's narrative.

If it can easily be seen that later tradition has embroidered this incident, there are also a number of interesting questions to be asked about where Matthew got the raw material for this infancy story. The question of the sources for the composition of the story of Matthew's infancy narrative from 1:18 to 2:23 is extensively explored in Raymond Brown's book, *The Birth of the Messiah* (pp. 96–232). It is commended to those who wish to work through a piece of painstaking detection. Here, we simply note that three Old Testament passages are central to the background: the story of Joseph in Egypt in Genesis 39ff., the story of the birth of Moses in Exodus 1–2, and the story of Balaam, the foreign magus, in Numbers 22–4.

The Balaam reference is the least familiar. Numbers tells of how Balak, king of Moab, fearing that the Israelites on their journey to the Promised Land were out to destroy him, enlisted the services of Balaam, a renowned soothsayer, against Israel. The Gentile Balaam, however, does not play ball with Balak; rather, he issues prophetic utterances which foretell Israel's future greatness. Brown argues that, in writing this story, the gospel writer used both the written biblical material and the oral traditions which had grown up around it and that the writer was also familiar with stories about the birth of Jesus which were already circulating in the young Christian community. From these various sources, Matthew skilfully weaves the narrative we know today ...

... which raises the question: how much of this story is fabricated by Matthew and how much is history as we understand it? Scholars caution scepticism in view of both the Old Testament allusions and the lack of good corroborating evidence about the star, the magi or the killing of the children at Bethlehem. We do need to remember that no one in the time of Jesus was writing academic history as it is understood today. It was common practice to embellish the birth of a great man. About the early years of Jesus we know precious little because, in a real sense, the significance of his life comes back to front. It is around the events of the years of his public ministry and, above all, the mystery of his highly public death that the gospel is formed. Whatever its claim to history as reportage of actual events, Matthew's story here speaks volumes of the significance of Jesus and forms a fitting prologue for what is to come after. Let Raymond Brown have the last word on the question of the worth of this chapter:

> There are preachers who are uneasy about the popularity of this story, feeling that it serves as a palliative for the true Gospel. But this is to neglect the fact that the infancy narrative contains both the cross and the God-given triumph. Herod stalks the trail of the magi, a menacing reminder that, while the star of the newborn King has shone forth in purity and simplicity, there are those who will seek to blot out that light. If the infancy story is an attractive drama that catches the imagination, it is also a substantial proclamation of the coming of the kingdom and its possible rejection. The dramatis personae may be exotically costumed as Eastern potentates and as a Jewish king and priests, and for that reason they are not easily forgotten. But beneath the robes one can recognise the believers of Matthew's time and their opponents. And, indeed, a perceptive reader may even recognise some of the drama of the Christian proclamation and its fate in all times. (Brown 1993 p. 232)

Start with the star

Having looked at the background, we turn to the story itself and begin with that not inconsiderable heavenly body, the star. The ancient world of the time of Jesus had a great interest in the movement of the stars. People genuinely thought that they could see signs in the heavens which followed or predicted important events of triumph or disaster, weal or woe here on earth. The Latin poet Virgil reported that a star led the wandering Aeneas of Troy to the spot where the city of Rome should be founded. The Jewish historian Josephus speaks of a star which stood over Jerusalem and of a comet that continued for a year at the time of the fall of the city. We're still at the beginnings of Matthew's gospel. We've seen the listing of the genealogy of Joseph, the father of Jesus, establishing his pedigree as son of Abraham, son of David, and heard of the visit of the angel to Joseph in a dream. Both angelic visitations and dream communications were well-known ways by which God spoke to human beings. From the story of Joseph and the angel, we were given two of the great names of the child who is born: 'Jesus, the one who saves' and 'Emmanuel, God is with us'. With the appearance of the star, we learn that the very heavens proclaim the significance of this new birth. So, is this the climax of these opening chapters of Matthew? Impressive genealogy, angelic announcement, signs and wonders in the heavens — all these bear witness that the one who is born is special indeed, but it's the gospel itself which suggests, with a number of subtle hints in sundry different places, that this whole panoply of conventional heavenly power is not quite to be taken at its face value; throughout the narrative there are rumblings of subversion.

We have seen the ambiguities of the genealogy and its hints about the significance of those who are outsiders to the exclusive society of Israel. The angel's presence here is occasioned by the unusual circumstance of Mary being with child. It's all very well for us to read this story casually and take it at face value after years of familiarity, but what, in the original state of affairs, did Mary say to Joseph? 'I met an angel who tells me I'm pregnant'? Joseph's obvious disquiet shows that he, good man, found it all a bit much to swallow.

Dubious outsiders

The star also raises questions. For every ancient writer like Virgil and Josephus who found confirmation for the events on earth in the movements of the heavens, we can find someone of equal reputation but opposite view who thinks that this star-gazing and the interpretation thereof are largely a matter of tosh. Such a view would be particularly strong within the community of Israel. It would have a healthy suspicion of the principal human characters here, the magi. The two English words which clearly relate to 'magi' are 'magic' and 'magician'. The magi could be described as old-world new-agers. Like many new-agers today, they laid claim to the possession of arcane and esoteric knowledge beyond the grasp of mere ordinary mortals or believers. Just as there is evidence today that many of the rich and powerful in our world have their own private gurus, magi frequently had the ear of the powerful, just in case their soothsaying might have some element of truth in it. Here, they get ready access to King Herod, about whom the verdict of history is that he ruled by fear but was also ruled by his fears. Magi, however, were also treated with a good deal of scepticism, particularly then (as now) by those with a more orthodox faith. Such would certainly be the attitude towards them which comes from the pages of the Old Testament.

So, while the events in the heavens may seem clear enough, the events and characters here on earth are somewhat more opaque. The gospel story of the coming of the magi is traditionally heard on 6 January, the Feast of the Epiphany, also known as the Manifestation of Christ to the Gentiles. It confronts us with the reality that the ones who are led by the star to greet the new-born child are, from the perspective of Matthew's original audience of Jewish Christians, both ideologically suspect and foreigners, representatives of lesser breeds outside the law. Once again, at the very start of the gospel we are being introduced to a Messiah who is significantly other than his people's expectations. The key significance of the magi is that they are outsiders, Gentiles – racially, religiously and culturally different from Jesus' own people. At the outset of the life of Jesus, we are given to see that he has come to make known the truth and glory of God, not to some little exclusive group but for and to all, regardless of caste and race and religion and culture. The one the magi bow down before, and to whom they are led to offer their gifts, this little child, is Christ, the light of the world, in the words of the prologue of John's gospel, 'the light of humanity'. In that we rejoice, for this is the very gospel. But we're left with a question. The outsiders, these strangers, for all their suspect knowledge recognise the Christ in the life of this child. Will the insiders like us do likewise?

'Rachel weeping for her children'

There are murkier waters yet for us to explore. As Matthew tells the story, the coming of the magi not only allows them to pay their homage to Jesus, it also puts the life of Jesus in mortal danger and it leads inadvertently to the killing of the baby boys of Bethlehem. This story ends with no angelic voices but with the sound of women weeping. The strangers, for all their knowledge of the stars, don't quite get it right. At the very least, they show great naivety in going to the present king of the Jews in his seat of power to ask him where the new king will be born.

Matthew says that, in the killing of the boys of Bethlehem, some words of the prophet Jeremiah are fulfilled. The question arises sharply: does God intend or will the killing of these children? 'No' is the answer. Matthew is often interested in Jesus as the fulfilment of the words of the Old Testament. Very often, Jesus is shown as saying or doing something 'to fulfil the words of the prophet'. Here, the verb is passive not active; it says: 'Thus was fulfilled, what had been spoken of by the prophet Jeremiah'. It describes the significance of what happened, rather than ascribing the agency to God.

The larger question remains: 'Where is God in this act of murderous cruelty, this moment of appalling pain?' What Matthew's gospel does show from beginning to end is the life of Jesus intertwined with the pain and suffering of the world. The infant Jesus escapes Herod here, but the man Jesus does not flinch from the cross. He is not divorced, separated from the weeping of the women of Bethlehem, then or now, for we know there are many weeping women in Bethlehem today.

John Miller, in a short meditation on television for the beginning of the year, used a picture called *The Beggar's Gift*. It showed on the bottom left-hand side an obviously poor woman with a child at her breast. On the right is a small boy with one hand outstretched upward. In the centre is a tall gaunt beggar figure. He has an arm outstretched downwards, almost touching the hand of the little boy.

The meeting of the two hands compels attention. The beggar is handing over to the boy a small coin. It is the picture of a poor man moved to share what he has with someone in similar straits. John Miller said that the picture illustrated one of his key understandings of the gospel, namely that out of suffering can come compassion and hope. In his life's work in a parish which has known more than its share of poverty, he had learned and been humbled by the way those who have known pain and suffering can and do share with those who suffer. It was one of the main grounds for his hope for the future. The gospel says we are all wounded healers, flawed like the magi, burdened like the women of Bethlehem. But, through our very wounds, if we remain open to others and open to the hope of the gospel, there can and does flow the healing balm of grace. Where is God? God is with us, in us, among us.

Epiphany today: its challenge

In December 2001, Bill Clinton delivered on BBC TV the Dimbleby Lecture for the year. Not unnaturally, September 11th was much in his thoughts. He called his lecture 'The Struggle for the Soul of the Twenty-first Century'. He portrayed the struggle as between those who had a closed world view where they thought that they, and they alone, were right, and those whose view of the world was more open and who were prepared to seek and listen to the truth and needs of the other. The contest is between the fanatics and those who believe in a more open society. About those of us who live in the open society, he said:

> Now most of us believe that no one has the absolute truth. Indeed, in our societies, the most religious among us sometimes feel that most strongly, because we believe as children of God we are by definition limited in this life, in this body, with our minds ... believe that life is a journey toward truth, that we have something to learn from each other, and that everybody ought to have a chance to make the journey.

He continued by describing the way we now live in a global village which has brought the western world enormous benefits but which leaves us with a huge and continuing task in tackling the remaining poverty and inequalities of the village. The modern temptation for all of us is to live our lives in little boxes, surrounding ourselves with like-minded people who affirm us and our values. One of the greatest challenges we face today is the age-old one of coming to terms with difference, overcoming our fear of, our prejudice against, our dismissal and denial of the stranger. (From a different perspective, Jonathan Sacks, the Chief Rabbi for Britain and Ireland, has also written most perceptively on the challenges of globalisation in *The Dignity of Difference: How to Avoid the Clash of Civilisations*.) Bill Clinton ended his lecture by saying he was an optimist, and that we can make the world of our dreams for our children, but 'since it's a world without walls, it will have to be a home for all our children'.

Bill Clinton lays down the challenge and the context for Epiphany and for our lives. A 'Church without Walls' has been a powerful and energising slogan within the Church of Scotland in recent years. The main reason for pursuing the challenge of a Church without Walls is seeing and hearing God, the living God, calling us to build and live in a world without walls, because we have seen and known the light that lightens all humanity. At Epiphany, we see the challenge that the glittering star and the angels' song, and the poverty of the birthplace and the sound of women weeping, are all conjoined, intertwined, as the Christ is made known to the most unlikely of people, these suspect strangers, and the way stretches before us, to find Christ our light, not just in the little boxes of our holy huddles, but shining clear, out before us, in the pain and hopes of all people, hidden at the very heart of the world he came to save.

Escape to Nazareth

This chapter ends by following the journey of the infant Jesus and his parents as they escape to the safety of Egypt until word comes to them that Herod, who had sought the child's life, is dead. Herod's death is mentioned three times (2:13, 19, 20), perhaps to remind us that all things come to an end, even the lives of powerful tyrants. Yet another dream warns father Joseph that Galilee would be a safer place for the family than Judea under Archelaus, who was an even worse ruler than his late father Herod. The family settle in Nazareth; Matthew ends the chapter with a quotation (2:23) which

17

echoes the first verse of Isaiah 11: 'There shall come forth a shoot from the stump of Jesse, and a branch shall grow out of his roots' (RSV). The Hebrew word *nazir* means 'branch'.

Study

By yourself

A meditation for Epiphany:

> Epiphany is a jewel
> multifaceted,
> flashing colour and light.
> Epiphany embraces
> the nations of the world,
> kneeling on a bare floor
> before a child.
> Epiphany shows
> a man
> kneeling in the waters of baptism.
> Epiphany reveals
> the best is kept for last
> as water becomes wine
> at the wedding feast.
>
> O Holy One
> to whom was given
> the gifts of power and prayer,
> the gift of suffering,
> help us to use
> these same gifts
> in your way
> and in your name.
>
> McIlhagga (2004 p. 94)

For group work

'God is the beyond in the midst of our life. The church stands, not at the boundaries where human powers give out, but in the middle of the village' (Bonhoeffer 1967 p. 155).

The significance of Epiphany is to make plain that the event of Christ's birth at Bethlehem is for all the world in a twofold sense: it is not for some, but for all people, and it is not a religious event, but a happening in history which has implications for every area of life. In that sense, we can say that Christianity is the most worldly of all the world's major faiths in requiring us to see our daily lives in the world as the place where faith is born, tested and grown. Yet the story of the magi, the outsiders, coming after a false detour to learn of the light of Christ, reminds us that life in the world always has its ambiguities and compromises.

How does the group understand the famous quotation of Bonhoeffer?

What does it mean to say that the church stands at the centre of life?

Should the church also be at the margins, and with the marginalised?

Pause

Introducing the opposition

The story of the killing of the male children under two years of age in Bethlehem by order of Herod indicates that Jesus as prophet of God's Kingdom coming near faced serious and powerful opposition. This can be listed under the following four headings.

- The house of Herod. It is significant that neither the name of Herod nor of his ancestors appears in the genealogy of 1:1–17. The explanation is simple: the so-called royal house of Herod consisted of late-coming intruders as rulers in the Hebrew territories. They were from Idumea (Old Testament Edom), and Idumeans had an ambiguous relationship with the Jewish people – the Jewish historian Josephus refers to Herod as a 'half-Jew' (*Antiquities* XIV, xv, 2). Herod's family had come to power through the patronage of Rome and remained in power only as long as they succeeded in doing Rome's bidding. Two Herods appear in the gospel. It is Herod the Great who died in 4 BCE who is the perpetrator of the atrocity at Bethlehem in Matthew 2; his son, Herod Antipas, ruler of Galilee, is the one who imprisons and kills John the Baptist (4:12, 14:1–

12). The reigns of the two Herods were marked by plotting, ruthlessness and capriciousness: as those who sought to carry out the orders and impositions of alien Roman rule, they were unpopular rulers. They further alienated their subjects by adopting and advancing Greek rather than local culture and by their scant regard for the hard lot of those they ruled. The kingdoms of the Herods were far from the Kingdom of heaven which Jesus came to proclaim.

- The Empire of Rome. In Matthew's gospel, there is little reference to the Roman power apart from the highly significant event at its climax: Jesus died on a Roman cross. He was killed as an enemy of and a threat to the Roman Empire. The all-embracing power of Roman rule, however, stands in the background to the whole gospel. The probability is that this gospel was written in Antioch late in the first century of the Christian era. Antioch was one of Rome's provincial capitals where its power and influence were all-pervasive and would have direct effects on the daily lives of Matthew's first readers. An implicit tension runs through the gospel between Rome as the supreme example of the kingdoms of this world and the new word and ways of the Kingdom of heaven which Jesus announced had come near.

- Scribes and Pharisees. All four gospels witness to the struggle between Jesus and the representative officers of his people's faith: high priests, scribes, Pharisees and Sadducees. In a number of different ways, Matthew heightens and deepens the extent of the controversies of Jesus with his people's religious leaders and particularly with the scribes. These instances will be picked up on the way through the gospel. Warren Carter argues that Matthew's stance 'reflects the community's experiences of a bitter conflict within at least part of the Jewish community in Antioch. The present situation reflects some distance and hostility. The intensity of the hostility in the gospel suggests recent and bitter conflict' (Carter 2000 p. 33). Behind the gospel lies the tragedy of the fall of Jerusalem and the destruction of the Temple in AD 70. After this catastrophe, there was huge disruption and debate within the Jewish community about the future shape of their faith. The young church of Jewish Christians was embroiled in the argument about which path Judaism should take to continue its life. Its vision of the future was rejected and the Jewish Christians ejected from the synagogue. Matthew writes in the aftermath of that rejection and the resultant painful division.

• Satan. There is one final power to be noted, quite different in character to the obvious earthiness of the previous three. In Matthew's gospel, Jesus clearly does battle with the devil, Satan, together with his subsidiary demonic powers, the spiritual representations of the power of evil. Beginning with the story of Jesus' temptations in the next chapter, Matthew portrays Jesus as being involved in an intense battle with the forces of evil personified by the devil and his agents. Sometimes that agency will be simply demonic, at others Satan will work through human agencies. Jesus does battle with the powers of hell; the battle is of apocalyptic stature, coming to its climax and resolution around the cross and the events of Easter. We move now to see the battle joined with the following story of Jesus' baptism and temptation.

Chapter 3

BAPTISM

Matthew 3
The Preaching of John the Baptist
(Mark 1:1–8, Luke 3:1–18, John 1:19–28)

At that time, John the Baptist came to the desert of Judea and started preaching. 'Turn away from your sins', he said, 'because the Kingdom of heaven is near!' John was the man the prophet Isaiah was talking about when he said:

> 'Someone is shouting in the desert.
> "Prepare a road for the Lord;
> make a straight path for him to travel!"'

John's clothes were made of camel's hair; he wore a leather belt round his waist, and his food was locusts and wild honey. People came to him from Jerusalem, from the whole province of Judea, and from all the country near the River Jordan. They confessed their sins, and he baptized them in the Jordan.

When John saw many Pharisees and Sadducees coming to him to be baptized, he said to them, 'You snakes – who told you that you could escape from the punishment God is about to send? Do these things that will show that you have turned from your sins. And don't think you can escape punishment by saying that Abraham is your ancestor. I tell you that God can take these stones and make descendants for Abraham! The axe is ready to cut down the trees at the roots; every tree that does not bear good fruit will be cut down and thrown in the fire. I baptize with water to show that you have repented, but the one who will come after me will baptize you with the Holy Spirit and fire. He is much greater than I am; and I am not good enough even to carry his sandals. He has his winnowing shovel with him to thresh out all the grain. He will gather his wheat into his barn, but he will burn the chaff in a fire that never goes out.'

The Baptism of Jesus
(Mark 1:9–11, Luke 3:21–2)

At that time Jesus arrived from Galilee and came to John at the Jordan to be baptized by him. But John tried to make him change his mind. 'I ought to be baptized by you', John said, 'and yet you have come to me!'

But Jesus answered him, 'Let it be so for now. For in this way we shall do all that God requires.' So John agreed.

As soon as Jesus was baptized, he came up out of the water. Then heaven was opened to him, and he saw the Spirit of God coming down like a dove and alighting on him. Then a voice said from heaven, 'This is my own dear Son, with whom I am pleased'.

The wild voice from the wilderness

Enter John the Baptist. John is a bruiser, a spiritual heavyweight, in the best traditions of the prophets of Israel – 'the voice crying in the wilderness'. For 'crying' substitute 'shouting'. Shouting usually implies a measure of complaint or warning. Our parents shouted at us when we wouldn't get out of our beds in the morning, our teachers shouted at us when we were being noisy or dim. We've all heard the words, 'Look out!' ring in our ears. John shouts, because he has a complaint to make and a warning to give.

Everything about him suggests a single-minded devotion. He makes his home in the desert so that he won't be seduced by the pleasures and distractions of town and city. His dress, echoing that of his predecessor Elijah, is a dress of rude simplicity. His minimalist diet, like a permanent detox regime, is the food of one for whom meat and drink are a distraction; he knows that his real food and drink are to carry out the mission God has given him. Out from the margins of his society he comes, a loud voice shouting his complaints and warnings to any of his contemporaries who will hear.

His complaint is that his people have strayed far from the kingdom of heaven, from the rule of God. John has now been sent with a word from God that the Kingdom of heaven, the rule and reality of God, has come near and is close at hand. And it's time to 'Repent'. Repent! To satisfied and sophisticated ears, the very word jars. Maybe these ears are ours. For 'repent' is a wild word, offensive, shocking. To be called to repent is to be summoned to change our life. 'Repent' at its root means turning. 'Change the direction of your living' is the call of John the Baptist: 'instead of the relentless pursuit of your own agenda, turn to the God who is coming very near'.

Something in the message of John strikes a chord with his people. His call to repentance is addressed to people's personal lives but is also about the life of his nation. The life of John's nation was deeply unhappy. People lived in fear, oppression, subjugation, poverty. Many respond to his words, flocking to receive his baptism in the River Jordan, which for centuries has been a living symbol of God's promises and the people's freedom.

A curious thing happens. A group of Pharisees and Sadducees from Jerusalem, the power centre of the nation, come out to this wilderness prophet, this wild man from the margins. Pharisees and Sadducees were far from being habitual allies; the Pharisees, representing the religious elite of Israel, were suspicious of the Sadducees as a bunch of rich time-servers; the Sadducees, connected with the high priest's family, represented the political and social elite and probably saw the Pharisees as too pious by half. Both were linked by seeing themselves as superior classes, the Pharisees religiously and the Sadducees socially. John's response to them is pungent. 'A bunch of snakes', he calls them. After the complaint comes the warning. 'Don't think, don't for a moment think, that your past, pedigree or position mean anything at all in the sight of God, whose presence is drawing near. Changing your life, now, turning your face to God and following his ways, is all that matters.'

John shouts. Maybe if you're coming from the margins, you have to shout to make yourself heard. Two of the questions the story of John the Baptist raises for us are: 'Who are today's prophets?' and 'Where do we hear the call of God to us to repent, to consider and change our way of life?'

We can make our own lists of those who have challenged our assumptions and our way of life in a creative and costly way; in the struggles against injustice and discrimination in many forms, in movements like the Women's movement, the Peace movement, the Ecology movement. Within our churches, there have been prophetic and perceptive voices questioning whether, as churches, we haven't accepted much too easily the structures and values of the secular society. Does our ecclesiastical order and mindset simply mimic the values of the world? Many of these voices and these people have brought radical change to us and to our world; many of them speak of a still unfinished agenda.

Where do we hear God's call to us to change our lives? In our western culture, there are crucial questions to be faced. We sense straws in the wind, blowing from many different directions, asking us to consider our way of life. How, at every level of our lives from the personal to the global, can we work towards embracing the world without walls that Bill Clinton envisaged? John the Baptist specifically calls a nation to reconsider and repent. We live in interesting days; old debates about the relationship between the common weal and individual freedom and responsibility outcrop in new ways. Questions of what makes for the common weal and how we can build public services which are valued, fair and adaptable need selfless and creative thought, attention and effort. What are our responsibilities as a nation in today's global village? These are questions not just for politicians but for all concerned with civic society and our nation's place on the world stage. On our own ecclesiastical doorstep, there is the continuing agenda to wrestle with how we can better be a truly open church – a church in, of and for the community.

The affirming voice from heaven

John, by his own admission, is but the preparer of the way for the one who is to come. Jesus arrives at the banks of Jordan. Act 2 of this passage begins with a conversation between friends. Matthew shows John as reluctant to baptise Jesus, the one greater than he. 'Jesus', says John, 'this is all the wrong way round. I need to be baptised by you, not you by me.' Jesus insists on his baptism: 'Let it be so', he says. And so, Jesus is baptised by John in the River Jordan.

It's curious and significant that, at the beginning and end of Jesus' life, things are done to him rather than his being the actor and initiator. At the end of his life, terrible things are done to him by his enemies and by some of his erstwhile friends. Here, it is his friend and relative John who is the human actor. Jesus submits to baptism by John. It's interesting the way this key incident is portrayed. We've just met John the Baptist, full of fire and fury, and he prepares us for the entry of Jesus into the story by saying: 'the one coming after me is more powerful than I, ... he will baptise with the Holy Spirit and with fire. His winnowing fork is in his hand, and he will clear his threshing floor and will gather his wheat into the granary: but the chaff he will burn with unquenchable fire' (3:11–12 NRSV).

John's introduction leads us to expect and await the arrival of a yet more turbulent figure. Instead, we see Jesus approaching John, saying: 'Please, John, will you baptise me?' Jesus not only submits to baptism by John, he is also submitting to the will of God. It is God who is the principal actor in this scene, as will become clear at its end. As the gospel proceeds, we will indeed see Jesus as one who is able to do all manner of signs and wonders. At the outset of Jesus' ministry, we see Jesus receive from God. It is also true of us, as people of faith, that we are primarily receivers. We are always receivers before we are doers or actors. Jesus' openness to God makes possible his life of faithful witness, and it is our openness to God which enables our life of faith and witness. The still moment when we are open to receive, the attitude to life and faith which sees and acknowledges that our own lives and the life of the world are in the end in the mysterious and yet sure hands of God, are what's primary in Jesus and what comes first for us.

There remains the final, precious moment when the heavens open, the Spirit descends and the voice is heard. The heavens open. The open heavens were to Jesus' people a sign of God's presence and activity. This is an important symbolic moment. In Jesus' time, many believed that the heavens were closed, that God had stopped speaking to his people, drawing near to them. The open heavens are a potent sign of the nearness of the Kingdom of which John has spoken, a portent and a promise that God in Jesus is about to do a new thing.

The dove descends. The Spirit rests on Jesus with power. Here is a special moment of communion, where Father, Son and Holy Spirit are one in a dynamic unity of grace and love. The unity is confirmed in the words of the voice: 'This is my Son, the Beloved, with whom I am well pleased' (3:17). These are tender, affirming words of grace. Jesus' ministry, again like ours, begins by hearing God's 'Yes'. Who hears this voice from heaven? Well, there's no indication that anyone present at the baptism of Jesus hears it except Jesus himself. This is a moment of precious intimacy between Jesus and the Father alone. But that's not quite accurate, is it? We, the hearers of the gospel, know of it. It is disclosed to us. And it's disclosed to us for two reasons. The mundane reason is so that we can know as we read on in the gospel that Jesus is the one on whom God's favour rests. Those who heard and read these words when the gospel was written would hear in them many echoes of Old Testament passages where God speaks tenderly of his servants (e.g. Psalm 2:7, Isaiah 49:5).

There's another, deeper reason why it matters that we hear these words. The deepest reason is that these words of God are spoken not just to Jesus; they are also, in a real sense, spoken, through Jesus, to us. For, in Jesus' baptism and through his baptism we see, not only that he is blessed by God, but that all are blessed by God. Jesus' baptism is a sign of two things. It's a sign of his humanity, his humanness, his love from below, his sharing of our human way and lot. And it's the sign of the love of God, that love which always comes first; 'prevenient' is the big word for it. It's the sign of God's love flowing out in blessing to all his people without any partiality. To rest and to rise in that love is the beginning and end of our hope and our calling.

Study

By yourself

Martin Luther suffered more than a little from times of depression. One of his antidotes when the dark mood fell upon him was to repeat again and again: 'I am baptised, I am baptised, I am baptised'.

27

Repeat Luther's phrase, envisaging yourself washed in the love of God and reborn into newness of life.

Chapter 4

PREPARATION

Matthew 4
The Temptation of Jesus
(*Mark 1:12–13, Luke 4:1–13*)

Then the Spirit led Jesus into the desert to be tempted by the Devil. After spending 40 days and nights without food, Jesus was hungry. Then the Devil came to him and said, 'If you are God's Son, order these stones to turn into bread'.

But Jesus answered, 'The scripture says, "Human beings cannot live on bread alone, but need every word that God speaks."'

Then the Devil took Jesus to Jerusalem, the Holy City, set him on the highest point of the Temple, and said to him, 'If you are God's Son, throw yourself down, for scripture says:

"God will give orders to his angels about you;
they will hold you up with their hands,
so that not even your feet will be hurt on the stones."

Jesus answered, 'But scripture also says, "Do not put the Lord your God to the test."'

Then the Devil took Jesus to a very high mountain and showed him all the kingdoms of the world in all their greatness. 'All this I will give you', the Devil said, ' if you kneel down and worship me.'

Then Jesus answered, 'Go away, Satan! The scripture says, "Worship the Lord your God and serve only him!"'

Then the Devil left Jesus; and angels came and helped him.

Jesus Begins His Work in Galilee

(Mark 1:14–15, Luke 4:14–15)

When Jesus heard that John had been put in prison, he went away to Galilee. He did not stay in Nazareth, but went to live in Capernaum, a town by Lake Galilee, in the territory of Zebulun and Naphtali. This was done to make what the prophet Isaiah had said come true:

> 'Land of Zebulun and land of Naphtali,
> on the road to the sea, on the other side of the Jordan,
> Galilee, land of the Gentiles!
> The people who live in darkness will see a great light.
> On those who live in a dark land of death the light will shine.'

From that time Jesus began to preach his message: 'Turn away from your sins, because the Kingdom of heaven is near!'

Jesus Calls Four Fishermen

(Mark 1:16–20, Luke 5:1–11)

As Jesus walked along the shore of Lake Galilee, he saw two brothers who were fishermen, Simon (called Peter) and his brother Andrew, catching fish in the lake with a net. Jesus said to them, 'Come with me, and I will teach you to catch people'. At once they left their nets and went with him.

He went on and saw two other brothers, James and John, the sons of Zebedee. They were in their boat with their father Zebedee, getting their nets ready. Jesus called them, and at once they left the boat and their father, and went with him.

Jesus Teaches, Preaches, and Heals

(Luke 6:17–19)

Jesus went all over Galilee, teaching in the synagogues, preaching the Good News about the Kingdom, and healing people who had all kinds of disease and sickness. The news about him spread through the whole country of Syria, so that people brought to him all those who were sick, suffering from all kinds of diseases and disorders: people with demons, and epileptics, and paralytics – and Jesus healed them all. Large crowds followed him from Galilee and the Ten Towns, from Jerusalem, Judea, and the land on the other side of the Jordan.

Into the wilderness

'Then Jesus was led up by the Spirit into the wilderness to be tempted by the devil' (4:1). Immediately after the high point of the great moment of revelation and affirmation which is Jesus' baptism comes the story of his temptation in the wilderness. After the high comes the low; after the vision, the struggle; after the moment of certainty, the wrestling with questions. How often such is the rhythm of our lives. This time of testing is sandwiched between the moment of affirmation at Jesus' baptism and the start of his mission in Galilee. The location of the testing is the desert into which Jesus is led by the Spirit.

The wilderness, the desert place, is to be thought of at two levels, physical and symbolic. Beginning with the latter, for Jesus and his people the desert was rich in association and symbolism. It was in the desert of Sinai that Moses fasted for forty days before he received the second set of the tablets of the Law, the Covenant from God. So, the desert was seen as a place of prayer and devotion. It was in the desert over forty years after their deliverance from Egypt's slavery that the people of Israel learned of the faithful provision of the divine presence, feeding and guiding God's people, in spite of their waywardness at times of testing. The desert was seen as a place of both discipline and freedom. In thinking of the symbolism of the desert testing, it's not just the place that's significant; there's also the time. Here are some of the significant forty-day periods of the Old Testament:

- Forty days: the length of Noah's flood, time of judgement, covenant and new creation (Genesis 6–9).
- Forty days: the length of time that Ezekiel, that strangest of prophets, lay on his right side, portraying the punishment of Judah as a judgement on their sins (Ezekiel 4:6–8).

- Forty days: the time given to the citizens of Nineveh to repent of their sins and change their lifestyle in the story of Jonah (Jonah 3:4).

Themes of judgement and testing were much associated in people's minds with the forty days. The whole wilderness experience of sifting and testing, finding the real among the distractions, the gold among the dross was part of the people's tradition – a tradition continued in the church's observance of Lent.

What of the physical place, the desert itself? In the desert, it is hard even to survive, physical comforts are lacking and the normal stimuli of everyday life are missing. The landscape is monotonous and boring, its emptiness magnified by a lack of signs of life. It is the place of aloneness, solitariness where all the outer voices of the world, the stimuli and the distractions which are part and parcel of our living are stilled.

What happens to us, in the quiet place, the dark place, the place where we are alone, where we are deprived of movement and action, where we are without the normal signals from our senses? What do we meet in the lonely place, in the long watches of the night? Are we still, quiet, content, at peace, or do we find, when the outer voices are stilled, the inner voices, the voices from deep within us, the voices of our questions, angers, fears, loves, memories, dreams come flooding to the surface? The story of Jesus' temptation is presented to us in the form of a dialogue between Jesus and the devil; it is also helpful to see this time of conflict as a time of Jesus' wrestling not just with the devil, but with himself. Here he struggles with himself as he seeks to work out what being faithful does and does not mean as he prepares to begin his outer work.

I had a conversation with a young man thinking about becoming a monk. He spoke of the attractions of a life built around a daily routine of work and prayer and the singing and saying of the Psalms. My young friend had already experienced a good deal of the monastic life to begin the testing of his vocation. In the course of our conversation, he said something like this: 'It's only when you spend time in a community like that, following the rule of worship and prayer, you realise the extent to which we live in a modern very secular world, and are affected in all sorts of ways, unconsciously and consciously, by it'.

To use the current fashionable phrase, he was saying that the monastic experience, which we should remember had its Christian origins in the deserts of Egypt around 1,700 years ago, is like a course of spiritual detoxification, or a life of the same. It's a time of conscious and concentrated waiting upon God, and, as such, it has much in common with the time of Jesus in the wilderness. In the rhythm of our lives, the wilderness time, the desert experience is very important to us, thoroughly secular people though we are. The place of retreat and silence becomes more important in the busy, noisy world we live in. That place can be found or made in our lives in many different ways, and what suits one of us won't necessarily suit another, and it would be wrong to be definitively prescriptive. But a time to be alone with God, a time when, in the words of the Psalmist, 'On God alone, I wait silently' (Psalm 62), a time when we affirm: 'O God, you are my God alone, eagerly I seek you' (Psalm 63) – making that time and space is vital to our lives.

It's good too that there are people who are being called today into monastic vocations, so that monasteries and places like them can continue their witness to another set of values, another kingdom if you like, in the midst of the clamour of the kingdoms, dominions and regimes of this world. But most of us are not monks, nor called to be monks. We're called to live our lives in the rhythm of engagement and withdrawal which we see in the life of Jesus himself. He doesn't remain in the wilderness; he returns to live his life and bear witness to that other Kingdom in the very midst of the hustle, bustle and hurly-burly of everyday life. It's fair to assume that, after the experience of his temptation, when Jesus re-enters the tumults, testings and distractions of life in the world, he does so with a renewed sense of focus 'On God alone'; in other words, that God is first and last in his life. Matthew's gospel would say with a new sense of the primacy of the Kingdom, the rule of heaven.

The temptations

Let's stop there for a moment. Jesus emerges from his testing with a deeper awareness of God first, the primacy of the Kingdom, living

33

life out of the rule of heaven. A strong case can be made for saying that the phrase 'the Kingdom of heaven' is totally central to the teaching of Jesus in Matthew's gospel. Again and again, we meet Jesus saying: 'The Kingdom of heaven is, the Kingdom of heaven is like ...'. A similarly strong case can be made out for saying that the life and death of Jesus exemplify the rule of the Kingdom, Kingdom reality. One way to interpret Jesus' temptations is that they are a testing of his commitment to the way of the Kingdom, to the primacy, the priority of the rule of God in his life.

The temptations themselves are beguiling in their superficial attractions; two of them are even dressed up in the language of religious clothing. The first temptation is basic and physical. 'If you are the Son of God ... then ... make these stones bread. Come on, you're hungry; eat, satisfy your own physical needs. Don't be daft, starving yourself like this.' Jesus replies: 'There's more to life than bread, much more; before there's the bread, there's the giver of the bread, the warden of the loaf. God comes first' (4:3–4). The second is the temptation to Jesus to prove his credentials by a demonstration of the miraculous. All the gospels bid us be wary of 'signs and wonders'; they are not at the root of the miracle of who Jesus is. The devil says: 'If you are the Son of God ... then ... Throw yourself off the temple pinnacle. Everyone will see this wonder and believe in you. Doesn't scripture even say that God will send his angels to protect you?' Here is the temptation of the instant miracle, to be the wonder-worker, to draw attention to himself, not the Kingdom. Jesus replies: 'I'm here to do God's will; that's first, not to make God submit to my demands' (4:5–7). Finally, Jesus is taken to the mountain top, traditionally a place of divine disclosure, here become the place of a beguiling secular vision. Jesus is shown a vision of this world's kingdoms, spread before him. 'Just say yes, to me', says Satan; 'settle for less, you can serve two masters. Live according to my worldly wisdom, let your life be shaped by that, and you can have it all.' Jesus answers: 'God first, God alone' (4:8–10).

When we look closely at this temptation story, imagining this time as one of real, costly, deadly struggle for Jesus, mortal combat, make-or-break time, there's something very interesting about its beginning and end. The first words are: 'The Spirit led him into the wilderness' (4:1), and the last: 'and angels came and waited on him' (4:11). These words say that Jesus went into his battle with the reality and the resource of the Kingdom already with him. He doesn't go unprotected and unarmed. It's the Kingdom reality, his awareness of God's primacy and God's presence which enables him to win this battle, to reaffirm his commitment to putting God first now, in the ministry to come, and in his final battle at the end. We are invited to give space so that the same Kingdom reality can grow in us, through our prayers, our study, our fellowship, our decisions and our actions.

Our lives are now the battleground. It's in our lives that the Kingdom reality, the truths and values of heaven, are to grow: we are called to be witnesses to that reality in the face of formidable forces. Apart from the claims of our needs and desires, the power of our instincts, we live in a world where all around us are potent earthly powers, the media, money, the marketplace, advertising, public opinion, government, the scientific world view, the pervasive influence of technology. Among such a welter of forces, a loud and cacophonous clamour of voices, how are we to discern the Kingdom and to put God first? It is a matter of discernment, for it's not as if the Kingdom is not there; here in this world, God is working his purpose out, but we've got to find it in among very different powers and values around us. We find it hidden in the field, for the sake of which we sell all else to find it (13:44). We've got to seek it … single-mindedly. We too gain our single-mindedness through making time in our own desert place, and through our prayers, our study, our fellowship and our decisions and, not least, our commitments and our actions.

The story of Jesus in his temptations dramatises a conflict, a battle which continues for all those who seek to put God first and follow the Kingdom way. Read this story as Jesus holding up here a mirror to ourselves, showing what human life is like, what faith life is like for us all. We can see it as Jesus battling with us, alongside us. In the church's tradition, beginning with St Paul and specifically in Hebrews 4:14–16, this story has also been read as Jesus battling for us, and winning for us a victory over the powers of sin and death which we could not and cannot win for ourselves. In that sense, the temptation story, which is so often read at the start of Lent, is but a forerunner of the greater, final battle which is the story of the cross, the victory of grace.

One of the challenges we face as Christians today is in the asking and answering of the question: how we can become a church which lives by grace? How can our church life be formed by more than rules and regulations, form and custom, use and wont; how can it overcome divisions between insider and outsider, believer and unbeliever? How can our church life be ruled by grace, by the knowledge that the values of God are not our values, and *the* Kingdom reality is that while we were yet sinners, Christ struggled, battled, suffered, died for us, so that we might know we are caught in God's free and loving embrace? – and, in the catching, are set free of all these forces and worldly powers within and without which would claim us. Like Jesus himself, although the ultimate freedom is given and secured, for us also, freedom only comes through struggle.

The strange thing is this. In his ministry, Jesus battled with two particular sets of worldly powers. On the one hand, he was up against the worldly power represented by King Herod and the Roman Empire, and these forces can be clearly seen as thoroughly active in our lives and the life of our world. His second battle, equally committed and engaged, was with the worldly powers represented by the ruling elite of his own people's religion, the Scribes and Pharisees. Remembering this second conflict gives a timely reminder that religious rules, habits and customs can be very worldly indeed. They can so easily be the clothing of self-justification, the means we use to satisfy our cravings for meaning and order, to feel secure and to reckon ourselves righteous. To enthrone our own religious beliefs and practices as idols rather than trusting, relying on God alone, putting God first, is to deny the first and second commandments (Exodus 20:3–4). The gospel in the story of the temptations is that Jesus does put God first, no matter the cost – and so, in St Paul's words, he becomes God's 'Yes and Amen' to us (2 Corinthians 1:20). Beyond and before our battles and our struggles, our faith life begins with gratitude for the one who has joined and endured the costliest of battles for us. Grace and gratitude live in the same hedgerow; a faith rooted in genuine thankfulness swells into praise and grows minds and hearts that are generous.

The ministry of Jesus begins

'From that time Jesus began to preach his message: "Turn away from your sins, because the Kingdom of heaven is near!"' (4:17). We've arrived at the beginning of Jesus' ministry in Galilee. It begins in unpromising circumstances. The time of the start of Jesus' ministry is given as 'when he heard that John had been arrested' (4:12). The story of John's arrest and its grisly aftermath is told in 14:1–12. John falls victim to Herod – not the Herod of the slaying of the children at Bethlehem in chapter 2, but one of his sons, Herod Antipas, whom the Roman overlords had installed as ruler of Galilee. As one prophet is silenced, another prophetic voice continues the message. When the empire of Herod, with its rule of brute force and capricious power, strikes God's messenger and silences the Baptist, Jesus' public work begins.

The second half of chapter 4, telling of the inception of Jesus' ministry, is liberally peppered with place names: 'Galilee, Nazareth, Capernaum, the territory of Zebulun and Naphtali, Jordan, Syria, Decapolis, Jerusalem, Judea, from beyond the Jordan'. Some of them are very familiar, some less so. Some are familiar as key names in the gospel narrative; others are familiar or indeed notorious in terms of the world of the present day. Here's a short note about them.

- Galilee (4:12) was the locus of the first half of the ministry of Jesus. Well to the north of the metropolitan heartland of Jesus' nation around Jerusalem, it was looked upon by the heartland people with a fair bit of suspicion, a bit like the way Lowland Scotland regarded the Gaelic-speaking Highlands before the 1745 Rebellion. It's called here 'Galilee of the Gentiles' (4:15). It was home to a large number of non-Jewish incomers, and in places its way of life had become Hellenised rather than Jewish, but it got its name of 'Galilee of the Gentiles' because it was very firmly under Roman rule. Herod Antipas, one of the notorious family dynasty of Herod, was the titular ruler, but the power behind the throne was Rome. Indeed, by the time this gospel was written, Rome had taken a yet firmer grip on Galilee and taken much of its land from its original tenants to hand over to Rome's own friends – to the considerable resentment of the native population, much as the Israeli settlements in the Occupied Territories do today with their contribution to the continued slow smouldering of a sense of injustice and resentment among the Palestinian population.

- Nazareth (4:12) was the town of Jesus' upbringing. In the eyes of some, it was just another sleepy little rural village, except that there are no sleepy little rural villages in a land under occupation. It was also only a hilltop away from the crossroads of the main trade routes through the land of Israel.

- Capernaum (4:13) was a fishing village of around 1,000 inhabitants on the Sea of Galilee. It was a community of ordinary, pretty poor, native working people, not having an easy time under the exactions of foreign rule.

- With the territory of Zebulun and Naphtali (4:15), the reference here is backwards to the allotting of land to the original twelve tribes of Israel when they entered the Promised Land (Joshua 19). The area of Galilee was allocated to the members of these two tribes, and the reference speaks of the people to whom this land originally belonged.

- Jordan (4:15) was the site of Jesus' recent baptism. In the memory of Jesus' people, as the borderland it was symbolic as the place of promise and freedom.

- Syria (4:24) does not simply refer to the modern boundaries of the state we know today. The significance of the mention of Syria is that it clearly included Gentile territory, as do the next reference to the Decapolis (4:25), the ten Greek towns in and around the borderlands of Galilee, and also the last reference, 'from beyond the Jordan' (4:25). Remember the coming of the magi (2:1–11) which indicated that Jesus' mission and purpose are not for his people alone; Jesus will stretch out to touch and include not only those who are different from, but also those who are the long-standing enemies of, his own people.

- Mention of Jerusalem and Judea (4:25), the heartland of Israel, show that the prophetic voices from the wilderness have reached the very centre of the nation. Whether this is an unmixed blessing is to be doubted; John the Baptist's encounter with the Pharisees and Sadducees from Jerusalem and Judea was distinctly abrasive (3:7–12). This new voice from the wilderness will also cause more than a little offence in high places.

Behind the geography lies a complex human landscape. On the one hand, there's the heritage of Jesus' own people with its proud and exclusive tradition, though not without its vision of something wider and greater at the edges. On the other, these same people are now living in a situation of poverty and powerlessness, aware of their traditions and life being under attack from powers beyond. It's in a landscape of political subjection, economic exploitation and cultural turmoil that Jesus begins his ministry – a world which contains many echoes of our world, if we have ears to hear.

The Kingdom announced, the call issued, the work of healing and including begun

'Jesus began to preach his message: "Turn away from your sins, because the Kingdom of heaven is near!"' (4:17). What is it that we see and hear Jesus doing as his ministry begins? He announces, he calls and he heals, and in his healing he includes. First, he announces. 'Turn away from your sins, because the Kingdom of heaven has come near.' Are these words familiar? They should be; they are the very same words which summarise the preaching of John the Baptist (3:2). 'Turn your life round', they say, 'take a new direction, for the Kingdom of heaven, the reign of God, has come near.' 'The Kingdom of heaven, the reign, the rule of God has come near.' Let's look at these words a little more closely in the light of the realities of life for the people to whom Jesus first spoke them.

Those who made up the great majority of the population of Galilee in the time of Jesus, the rural poor, lived their lives between a rock and a hard place, burdened under the weight of earthly rulers and powers. Politically, they were pretty much under the thumb of Rome or Rome's vassal monarch, Herod. Daily life was one of economic hardship and oppression, with people suffering under all manner of petty abuses, punctuated by incidents of savage cruelty. The well-documented cruelties of Herod and the ill repute of collaborating tax collectors in the gospel record are obvious witnesses to this. The burdens of the rural poor were not all of alien origin. The poor also suffered under the exactions of the rich of their own society, in particular from the indifference and rapaciousness of an absentee landlordism. In addition, for many of the ordinary people, the poor of the land, their faith had become a mixed blessing. They were burdened by a sense that God had deserted them, and deserted them as a result of their own failure to keep covenant with God. They therefore laboured under a sense of their own lack of self-worth which was compounded by the condemnation of the 'unco guid' of their own society.

Jesus' announcement of the imminence and nearness of the Kingdom of heaven to folk's ordinary lives challenges the powers which burden. He will describe and embody, as his ministry unfolds, the lineaments and substance of the Kingdom reality; much of it can be seen in the description of the healing ministry with which this passage ends (4:23–5). 'Kingdom of heaven, rule of God' is not a precise term. It defies too easy definition, and Jesus often points to its reality by way of parable, inviting the imagination of his hearers to go to work. The Kingdom encompasses the three dimensions of past, present and future. Grasping the reality of this different, other Kingdom is about knowing that God is real, active, present, though hidden in the day-to-day life of the world. God is not remote, indifferent, uncaring, inactive; God is here and God is now. That living reality can be heard and seen in Jesus' own words and life. 'The kingdom of heaven, the alternative empire, the presence and rule of God is very near' (4:17). To those who sat sad, sullen, bent and oppressed in the darkness of their times, the light of a new reality dawned. The following prayer was produced for Homelessness Sunday in 2002. It points powerfully to what it means for the reality of the Kingdom to dawn in our lives.

'O Lord, even in the darkness, Your light shines.
Even in the squalor and desolation, Your gentle breath caresses.
Even in the emptiness and loneliness, You are there.

Even when I am cold and tired, You nourish me and give me rest.
Even when I have nowhere to go, in You I have my home.'

Jesus announces, and then he calls. He invites his first disciples to follow him from the business and concerns of their working life. The story is so familiar. The names of these disciples are still commonplace in our world of today: Peter, Andrew, James and John. What about the story's meaning? This calling of the disciples: is this the birth of the church, or is it something else? It could be the birth of the church, depending on how we understand 'church'. The disciples are called to a task; they are to be bridge-builders, agents of Jesus' purpose under God in his mission to the world. In terms of what has just gone before, they are to be fellow-bearers and announcers of the reality of the Kingdom. What does the story of the call of the disciples have to say to us about the way of discipleship today?

Can we say that, for us as Christians, there are but two primary great realities, God and the world? Perhaps there are three: God, the world *and* our Christian discipleship, our response to the call. The church only exists to be an instrument, a source of mediation, a conduit, between the great realities of God, and the rule and presence of God, and his world. So often, we make the church an end in itself, and we end up thinking in ways which are fundamentally and small-mindedly selfish. At every turn of the road, in every waking hour, these first disciples, Peter, Andrew, James and John, knew the reality of the rule and presence of God, because they lived with Jesus. For them it was inescapable, though in their stories we see that they too backslide and make mistakes. How good it would be, and also how essential, to catch again that reality and to live out of it, that as a church we only exist to make known the rule, presence and love of God to the world. It is to that, single-mindedly, that we are called ... and, of course, called together.

This chapter ends with a summary picture of Jesus healing (4:23–5). Matthew's picture of people from many different places and backgrounds flocking to Jesus makes very clear that, in his healing, he includes. There isn't space to do justice to the scope, depth and significance of Jesus' healing ministry here; the subject will come up again in the gospel through particular healing stories.

41

Let it be enough to say now that Jesus' healings were diverse and particular; they are about the changes he brought to real, personal, human lives. Some were mainly physical; many were in the realm we would now call either mental or psychosomatic. Of these, in not a few instances, people's illness would be caused by the totality of the conditions they lived under, an environment of want, fear, denigration, oppression. It was one of the common expectations of the Messiah that, with his coming, people would be liberated from all that harmed them – physical, mental, economic and political. In his ministry of healing, Jesus fulfils that expectation. Thanks to a good deal of recent scholarship, we are able to see and understand today much better the complexities of the world in which Jesus lived, and of how he addressed people living in that complexity at every level. In particular, we understand much better today just how often in biblical times illness went hand in hand with abject poverty and very real social exclusion, how it often led to people being reduced by these realities. When Jesus heals people, so often what he does is not merely something physical or mental; he restores people to their place in family and society; he restores them in face of all the powers within and without which would keep them burdened and chained.

One striking feature in this description of Jesus' healing ministry here is how indiscriminate it is. He heals those who come to him. He doesn't ask: 'Are you a worthy person?' 'Are you a church member?' 'Are you a native or an incomer?' 'Are you rich, poor, wise, simple, employed, unemployed?' He simply is at work among those who are brought to him, no matter what their ailment is, no matter where they come from, no matter what their background, their race, their personal history – at work bringing hope and healing, welcome and acceptance. The call to continue such an indiscriminate ministry of Jesus remains, and the church is at its best when Christians hear and heed that costly call. It's all part of the battle for the Kingdom against all the powers which reduce, paralyse, silence or demean our brothers and sisters. The battle continues. In every place where people suffer, where folk live in darkness, from the margins of Galilee to the heartland of Jerusalem, from the divisions in our cities to the poverty of our world, Jesus Christ is waiting. He announces, he calls and he heals, in face of all that obscures the reality of the coming, near, present rule of God. He waits for our response.

Study

By yourself
A prayer:

> Jesus Christ,
> vulnerable and alone,
> in the desert
> you faced the force of evil
> yet withstood temptation.
> Be with us
> in our struggles with temptation
> that by your strength
> we may reject the devil
> in whatever form he comes.   Amen
>
> *Common Order* (1994 p. 433)

For group work
Divide your time in half; for the first half of your meeting, discuss Jesus' temptations. How do you understand each of the three in terms of your own life today?

For the second half of your meeting, look at the call of the first four fishermen disciples. Have someone read the story (very slowly, with plenty of pauses) and imagine yourself present at the encounter. Share with one another whatever has struck you in the story's hearing. What questions does it raise for the group members?

Pause

The sources and structure of Matthew's gospel
The material in the first two chapters of Matthew's gospel appears nowhere else in the gospels. Perceptive readers of chapter 3 will have noticed in the stories of Jesus' baptism and temptation and of the start of his ministry considerable convergences with the accounts contained in the gospels of Mark and Luke. The general scholarly

consensus remains that Mark's gospel was written first and that, when Matthew came to write his account, he had the material of Mark available to him. He uses Mark's material and in large part accepts Mark's sequence of events. In chapters 3–4 and 12–28, Matthew follows Mark largely without exception. While he uses Mark's pattern, within it he inserts other material. He also often significantly shortens Mark's narrative, particularly in the healing stories.

The considerably greater length of Matthew compared to Mark raises the question as to where the additional material in Matthew comes from. Much of it is shared with Luke, though again the common material is often subtly altered. With less unanimity, the weight of scholarly opinion would continue to favour Matthew and Luke having access to an additional source of the sayings of Jesus, called Q. We have already seen in Chapters 1–2 that there is material in Matthew which is peculiarly his own. In part, this material may have come from another source or sources circulating in the early church while some of it may have originated from the gospel editor's own hand.

Turning to the structure of the gospel, chapters 1–2 have already been referred to as Matthew's own account of Jesus' origins. As mentioned above, chapters 3–4 follow Mark, as do the chapters from 12 to the end. What is also significant in terms of Matthew's structure is the collection of five distinct blocks of Jesus' teaching, found at chapters 5–7 (The Sermon on the Mount), 10, 13, 18 and 24–5. Matthew has a strong emphasis on Jesus the teacher, though he makes it abundantly clear that this teacher certainly does not operate by words alone but by the integrity of words and action. We move now into the first and arguably the most famous and significant of the blocks of teaching, the Sermon on the Mount.

Chapter 5

STRANGE BLESSINGS

Matthew 5:1–16

The Start of the Sermon on the Mount

Jesus saw the crowds and went up a hill, where he sat down. His disciples gathered round him, and he began to teach them:

True Happiness

(*Luke 6:20–3*)

'Happy are those who know they are spiritually poor; the Kingdom of heaven belongs to them!

Happy are those who mourn; God will comfort them!

Happy are those who are humble: they will receive what God has promised!

Happy are those whose greatest desire is to do what God requires; God will satisfy them fully!

Happy are those who are merciful to others; God will be merciful to them!

Happy are the pure in heart; they will see God!

Happy are those who work for peace; God will call them his children!

Happy are those who are persecuted because they do what God requires; the Kingdom of heaven belongs to them!

Happy are you when people insult you and persecute you and tell all kinds of evil lies against you because you are my followers. Be happy and glad, for a great reward is kept for you in heaven. This is how the prophets who lived before you were persecuted.'

Salt and Light

(Mark 9:50, Luke 14:34–5)

'You are like salt for the whole human race. But if salt loses its saltiness, there is no way to make it salty again. It has become worthless, so it is thrown out and people trample on it.

You are like light for the whole world. A city built on a hill cannot be hidden. No one lights a lamp and puts it under a bowl; instead he puts it on the lampstand, where it gives light for everyone in the house. In the same way your light must shine before people, so that they will see the good things you do and praise your Father in heaven.'

Up and down

'The Kingdom of heaven is near!' (4:17) were the words of proclamation with which Jesus, the herald of God and God's Kingdom, began his work in Galilee. William Herzog comments:

> In expansion of his basic formula, Matthew includes a triad of activities associated with Jesus' appearance as herald of the reign of heaven. He taught in the synagogues, proclaimed the good news of the kingdom, and healed diseases and infirmities (4:23). The role of this herald was more than announcing; he articulated the meaning of the coming reign of God, and he mediated its power. (Herzog 2000 p. 203)

News of the presence and power of Jesus spread like wildfire, far beyond the confines of the lakeside towns and villages. Now, as the crowds gather round Jesus, Matthew pictures him sitting down to give extended teaching about what it means in personal terms to enter the Kingdom. Here is the first of the five big blocks of Jesus' teaching in this gospel. We prepare ourselves well to sit, concentrate, listen. We are about to be shaken by the explosive force of the Sermon on the Mount.

This is no ordinary 'sermon'. The words here recorded and collected by Matthew tower like a great rock in the history of the world's literature. Profound has been their effect on countless people and many societies. In the twentieth century, both Gandhi and Martin Luther King bore witness to the place of the Sermon in shaping their thought and action. In the Sermon, Jesus assumes the roles familiar within his people of both teacher of wisdom and radical prophet, yet the meaning and the impact of the Sermon cannot be wholly contained within the categories of tradition. Part of the Sermon's genius lies in its enigmatic character. While its meaning is often plain and the challenge it poses is the doing of it, it also frequently acts more as a stimulus to thought and reflection, asking deep questions of its hearers rather than providing any easy ready-made answers. Certainly, the 'beatitudes' (5:1–12) with which the Sermon begins can be thought of as profound paradoxical provocations, designed to stir the hearer into faith's restlessness. The question remains: 'What is the Sermon on the Mount?' It's a question which each person can better answer once Jesus' own words have been heard, studied and pondered. Here are some of the many attempts to capture in a few words the Sermon's essence. There's truth in each of them, yet all of them together do not exhaust the Sermon's truth. The Sermon has been described as: an extended summons to faith, a picture of the outlines of the good life, an impressionistic portrayal of the new Law which fulfils and surpasses the old Law of Moses, a morality for every day based not on mere command but on the bedrock of grace, the life of heaven brought to earth in the here and now. Remembering that it is Jesus who brings the life of heaven to earth in the words and actions of his Kingdom announcement alerts us to the dangers of divorcing the Sermon's words from the Sermon's speaker. Word and speaker are 'wedded' to one another. They inform and complement each other, particularly in the promises the Sermon contains; these promises would remain mere empty and facile words apart from the reality of the one who utters and fulfils them.

Before turning to the Sermon itself, it is worth noting its setting. Jesus goes up to the 'mountain'. In practical terms, in face of the crowd, taking the high ground simply increases his visibility. In symbolic terms, the mountain, the high place, long seen as the place of holiness and vision, the home of the gods, has deep significance. The Sermon's hearers would readily associate Jesus' assuming the high place both with the Temple mount of Zion and even more with Mount Sinai, Moses and the giving of the Law. Is this the new Law given by the new Moses? Having climbed to the high place, the teacher sits down to instruct. Israel's teachers sat to teach;

this one begins teaching about the Kingdom of heaven. Not just teachers but rulers also sat to give judgement; is there also an echo of divine kingly authority here?

Upside down

Jesus begins: 'Happy are those ...'. Not a few modern Bible versions translate the Greek word 'makarioi' as 'happy' rather than the older, more familiar 'blessed'. 'Happiness' in the sense of deep contentment is part of the original meaning, but it far from exhausts it. The original meaning also contained the sense of being favoured by God. In the Bible, those who were favoured by God were enabled to bring forth fruit, in other words to live a productive life. It's worth exploring 'happiness' a little longer. The American Constitution's declaration of 'life, liberty and the pursuit of happiness' as universal human rights has become something of a truism. Behind the truism lurks a question. Can we pursue happiness directly, or do we only achieve or receive happiness as a by-product of the pursuit of something else, like the way of love and justice or the service of God and our fellows? The beatitudes point to this tangential way, this road of indirectness. Indeed, at first sight, they invite us into some very strange 'blessings' which contrast sharply with the received opinions of what happiness means today. To the natural person, they may appear most peculiar and paradoxical, puzzling riddles at best. They may also be too easily dismissed as empty promises of 'pie in the sky when we die'. With their frequent mention of heaven, they do have a reference to the future and the beyond. The gospel, however, proclaims that this is a future and a beyond which has come near. Tom Wright says the clue is in the petition of the Lord's Prayer which asks: 'your kingdom come, your will be done on earth as it is in heaven' (6:10). He says:

> The life of heaven – the life of the realm where God is already king – is to become the life of the world, transforming the present 'earth' into the place of beauty and delight that God always intended. *And those who follow Jesus are to begin to live by this rule here and now.* That's the point of the Sermon on the Mount and these 'beatitudes' in particular. They are a summons to live in the present in the way that will make sense in

God's promised future; because that future has arrived in the present in Jesus of Nazareth. It may seem upside down, but we are called to believe, with great daring, that it is in fact the right way up. Try it and see. (Wright 2002 p. 38)

Inside out

The beatitudes are nine in number, and they show considerable correspondence with the four 'blessings' and four 'woes' in Luke's Sermon on the Plain (Luke 6:20–6). Matthew is using here a form familiar to his original audience. 'Blessings' are found in sayings among the wisdom literature of the Old Testament and in the Psalms and also, significantly, in the proclamation of the Law in Deuteronomy (27:15, 28:1ff., 15ff.). In the earlier Old Testament references, the blessing relates to earthly happiness; in those later, the promise is for a coming future time of salvation. What is new and distinctive about the beatitudes of the Sermon is that they take a future blessing of what shall be and declare it to be present here and now.

Omitting the ninth and last beatitude for a moment, the preceding eight form two groups of four, each with exactly the same number of words. The first four have the characteristic of each beginning with the Greek letter 'pi'; they could be called roughly in English 'the poor, the plaintive, the powerless, those who pine for righteousness'. More significantly, this quartet speaks of those whose situation will be reversed, overturned in the coming Kingdom. It also describes the inner attitudes formed by outward circumstances, whereas the second quartet describes the qualities and actions which will make manifest the Kingdom. The movement is from the inside out, a characteristic of Matthew's gospel which frequently stresses integrity and is consistently at pains to expose any hypocrisy. The final beatitude, which moves from the third to the second person – 'happy are you when people insult you …' – reiterates and amplifies its immediate predecessor. It clearly belongs to the time of Matthew's writing of the gospel, speaking as it does of the young church suffering pains and persecution in its now irreparable breach with the synagogue.

'He began to teach them'

There's one other question to consider before turning to the beatitudes themselves. Who is Jesus speaking to throughout the Sermon? Gathered before him are both the crowd and an inner group of disciples (5:1). The two groups, crowd and disciples, are linked together; the disciples who have already begun to make their commitment to Jesus and the crowd, a gathering of those drawn together in varying degrees of curiosity and hunger. Jesus speaks to the disciples, in the context of the crowd. It's as if, with each one of the beatitudes, there's an invitation to step out of the crowd and become a disciple, a learner on the Jesus way, a pupil of the Kingdom. Each beatitude calls for a change of vision and a transformation of values. They invite a movement in our lives away from what is cherished by the way of the world to a new way of being God's people in the midst of the world which, in spite of all human waywardness, God cherishes. We turn now to the beatitudes themselves (using the words of the NRSV).

Blessed are the poor in spirit, for theirs is the kingdom of heaven.

'The poor in spirit', sometimes helpfully paraphrased as 'those who know their need of God', form the subject of the first blessing. Luke's version of this beatitude says simply 'Blessed are the poor' (Luke 6:20), while Matthew adds 'in spirit'. Matthew's addition has led to the accusation that he has spiritualised what was in origin a reference to material poverty. Poverty as such is no blessing, though it can yield precious insights. Looked at positively, what Matthew does is to internalise one great lesson which poverty can teach. It can make people aware of the inadequacy of their own resources and their dependence on both other human beings and on God. In his little book of *Reflections* John Miller expresses the reality of this beatitude:

> It was from a Franciscan, Albert Gelin, that I learned this interpretation: 'Blessed are those who have the spirit of the poor'. The poor are like this: they have no resources outside themselves. They have no wealth to spend, no property to sell, no bought house, nothing set aside for a 'rainy day'. They search down the sides of chairs for pennies for the

children's bus fares. They have no slippers or dressing-gown if they are taken into hospital, no money to buy birthday or Christmas presents unless they go into debt. If they come into money, they know what friendship means; and they will often give all they have to others. The poor often think of God, because there is no other help.

And *the spirit of the poor* is found in others, others whose material circumstances may be quite different. All kinds of events can bring us face to face with our own fragility, our mortality, our utter dependence on the One who has given us life ... And Jesus affirms that those who have the spirit of the poor keep company with God. (Miller 2002 pp. 9–10)

To be 'poor in spirit' is to be stripped of our pretensions and illusions, to know our need of God and to seek God with empty hands and an open heart and mind. Seeking, we find, or are found, for it is God who takes the initiative. We then become the bearers of the paradox in our own lives of which Paul speaks when he talks of 'having nothing, yet possessing all things' (2 Corinthians 6:10). When we come to life with the inner attitude of 'knowing we are poor', we see the world and we see people in a very different light; we see them with the compassion and hope which God gives. We see with Kingdom eyes and know ourselves 'blessed'.

Blessed are those who mourn, for they will be comforted.

There is little that is more shattering to us than the pain of loss. Poverty of spirit speaks of a sense of emptiness, and in the experience of loss we know emptiness very acutely. It can make us turn in on ourselves and cut us adrift from others in a desert of isolated desolation. How can it be 'blessed'? Mourning, like poverty, is a great stripper of illusions; it stops us pretending that life is other than it is. In a paradoxical way, when we mourn, our tears are not only for ourselves, they are also for those we have lost. We not only turn in on ourselves; we are also taken out of ourselves in our remembering of the ones who have gone from us. As a minister over many years, I have been privileged to share in many situations of loss and bereavement. In these situations, I have often seen death as the occasion of profound truth and a deep humanness from which spring the beginnings of comfort.

In the years following the rise of Hitler and the coming to power of the National Socialists in Germany, Dietrich Bonhoeffer wrote his powerful exposition of the Sermon on the Mount, translated into English as *The Cost of Discipleship*. In his commentary on this beatitude, out of his own life situation, Bonhoeffer puts 'mourning' into a larger context, saying:

> By 'mourning' Jesus, of course, means doing without what the world calls peace and prosperity: he means refusing to be in tune with the world or to accommodate oneself to its standards ... Why does the Christian Church so often have to look on from the outside while the nation is celebrating? ... Nobody loves his fellow-men better than the disciple, nobody understands his fellow-men better than the Christian fellowship, and that very love impels them to stand aside and mourn. It was a happy and suggestive thought of Luther, to translate the Greek word here by the German *Leidtragen* (sorrow-bearing). For the emphasis lies on the *bearing* of sorrow. The disciple-community does not shake off sorrow as though it were no concern of its own, but willingly bears it. And in this way they show how close are the bonds which bind them to the rest of humanity. (Bonhoeffer 1959 p. 98)

Bonhoeffer moves us from being grief-stricken to sorrow-bearing. He reminds us of the call to live in sympathy – 'suffering with' – others; to share with them in a common human solidarity. Thus do we offer comfort to one another. But how do we receive comfort? One of the main thrusts of Bonhoeffer's book is the linking of the Sermon on the Mount at the beginning of Jesus' ministry to the cross at its end and fulfilment. It's as we stand beneath the cross that we receive that mysterious comfort which only a suffering God who suffers with and for us can give. And the cross is but three days away from an empty tomb, and the revealing of that love which comes again, and again, and again ...

Blessed are the meek, for they will inherit the earth.

There is a problem. The word 'meek' is no longer adequate to carry the meaning of this beatitude. 'Meekness' today too often suggests a kind of fearful, grovelling timidity, which is not what this beatitude is about. It's about humility, a genuine humility. Let's say it's about 'knowing our place' – but our place not in the human pecking order or the rat race, but our place in the created order, before the immensity and intricacy of the universe, our place before the face of God, 'with whom one day is as a thousand years and a thousand years but as one day'. For those who do know their place as 'frail children of dust', there is a rich promise: 'they will inherit the earth'. Inheriting the earth immediately raises questions about two huge contemporary hot potatoes: the environment and land-ownership. It is becoming increasingly clear in Christian circles that the environment and land distribution are faith issues.

In terms of the environment, there is more and more an awakening to the reality that the race to which we belong, the race of nasty little bipeds with massively overlarge feet, has planted a huge and destructive ecological footprint in the creation that God, for a time, lends us. Global warming, melting ice fields, rising sea levels, growing weather instability, massively increasing waste and pollution all point to the dire results of our careless lack of sensitive and informed humility in our treatment of the earth and its resources. An increasingly damaged and defiled earth is the heritage we pass on to our children. Somehow, in our headlong rush to exploit and consume, we forgot that the root meaning of 'humility' is about being close to the earth itself and learning to respect the rhythms of the natural world. Our conversion is long overdue.

The struggle for just and equitable ownership and distribution of land is both highly contemporary and as old as biblical times, as we will see later in this gospel as we study some of Jesus' parables. In biblical times, land rather than money was the principal measure of wealth – and, in some less developed economies, the same is true today. An unwelcome ironic connection between biblical times and our own is the continuing dispute over land in the Occupied Territories between Israeli and Palestinian where the unjust and unsanctioned seizure of Palestinian land keeps stoking the fires of bitterness and conflict.

In the Highlands and islands of Scotland, the disintegration of the clan system and the Clearances of the nineteenth century, with the resultant forming of big estates often with largely absentee landlords, has left its imprint on Scotland's psyche to the present day. One manifestation of this has been the strength of opposition to the privatisation of the water industry, which still remains in public hands north of the border. In part, that opposition has theological roots, springing from the conviction that 'The earth is the Lord's' (Psalm 24:1) and that the water God provides in plenty in our somewhat damp land belongs to everybody, for the common good, rather than to some company for the making of profit. (Of course, the water industry has a point when it argues that it is not the water it owns but its means of harvesting and distribution; but this is not simply a utilitarian argument.)

What does it mean to 'inherit the earth?' The poet Norman MacCaig, with his roots deep in Gaeldom, asks the question thus (1990 p. 214, 'A Man in Assynt'):

> Who possesses this landscape? –
> The millionaire who bought it or
> the poacher staggering downhill in the early morning
> with a deer on his back?
>
> Who possesses this landscape? –
> The man who bought it or
> I who am possessed by it?

'I who am possessed by it' sounds like the song of a free man, filled with a joyful humility as he is enraptured and enthralled by the world around him. 'To inherit the earth' as God's gift to us while we are pilgrims upon it is to forsake the notions of grasping, owning, possessing, trampling, organising, bleeding dry which have been so disastrous both for the poor and the earth itself, and to be possessed by the poet's vision of appreciating, cherishing, enjoying, respecting the mystery of the world around us, even on a wet day in Assynt in February.

Blessed are those who hunger and thirst after righteousness, for they will be filled.

> 'As a deer longs for flowing streams,
>   so my soul longs for you, O God.
> My soul thirsts for God,
>   for the living God.' (Psalm 42:1–2)

The theme of emptiness and need, of our human dependence on the resources which God alone provides, is persistent in the first quartet of beatitudes. The sense of hungering and thirsting, of a visceral longing, frequently appears in the Old Testament and particularly in the Psalms. In this beatitude, the hunger is for 'righteousness', which has both a personal and a societal dimension. Just a few verses later at 5:20, Jesus says: 'Unless your righteousness exceeds that of the scribes and the Pharisees, you will never enter the kingdom of heaven' (NRSV). In personal terms, 'righteousness' could be translated as 'integrity', bearing in mind Matthew's frequent strong condemnation of 'hypocrisy'. To long for righteousness is to seek the gift of a life where there is no division between thought and action, no contradiction between word and deed. The beatitude acknowledges that such a life of integrity is the gift of God; it is not achievable solely by our own efforts. In the end, it is God alone who makes righteous.

At the level of community and wider society, 'righteousness' is well rendered as 'justice', not in any mere juridical sense, but in the sense of right relations of fairness and equity. The Bible's witness is constant and consistent that God's will is for an end of oppression and poverty and that God's people have a holy obligation laid upon them to care for those in any society who are powerless or oppressed, forgotten or rendered invisible. In today's world of intercommunication and interdependence, the call for the people of God to hunger and thirst for justice has local, national and international dimensions. On the one hand, it is heartening to see churches becoming more involved in issues of justice at all levels and, in their involvement, making common cause with people of good will from a wide variety of backgrounds and commitments. Campaigns for debt relief and fair trade, and the Make Poverty History Campaign, provide good examples. On the other hand, growing knowledge and understanding of how our world really works in economic terms confirms our belief that the task of doing justice will be a never-ending one which requires great reserves of hope, imagination, resolve and patience. The justice tank will always be in need of filling, hence the necessity of the daily prayer: 'your kingdom come, your will be done on earth as it is in heaven' (6:10).

The promise is that those who grow lean in the passionate pursuit of integrity and justice will be filled. The filling comes from following the pattern and example of Jesus as he himself found his strength renewed throughout his ministry of compassion and justice. And, of course, for the hungry and thirsty, there is nothing like an invitation to sit down to eat and drink. From the vision of the Messianic banquet in Isaiah 25:6–10 to the marriage feast of the Lamb in the book of Revelation (19:9), the Bible issues many such invitations. As Christians, we are fed at the table of the Lord's Supper, the Eucharist, where in the breaking and sharing of the bread we both have a foretaste of that final feast and here and now are bound together in the remembering of the wonder of Christ's sacrifice and the reality of his continuing presence with us through the Spirit. Here is our food for the constant struggle and continuing journey. 'O taste and see that the Lord is good; happy are those who take refuge in him' (Psalm 34:8).

Blessed are the merciful, for they will receive mercy.

Being merciful, showing mercy is one of the major themes of Matthew's gospel. It outcrops again and again as a sure sign of the reign of God. Mercy is first of all a gift which we receive. Jesus is the bearer of the mercy of God to the world and its people. But those who receive mercy in turn are bidden to show it to others and thus become Kingdom signs in themselves. As in today's judgemental times, so in the world of Jesus to be 'merciful' was to act against the prevailing spirit of the age. The merciful lived out a countersign. Warren Carter provides the references:

> Those who encounter God's reign are to be merciful. They provide the destitute with necessary economic resources (5:42, 6:2–4, 25:31–46). Mercy forgives (6:12, 14–15) and extends love to enemies (5:38–48) and other marginals, foreigners and women (15:22). It marks God's empire. Jesus' healings (9:27, 17:15, 20:30–1) and exorcisms (15:22) demonstrate mercy (cf. 4:23–5 and 9:36), as do his meals with social outcasts (9:13) and his allowing the hungry to eat (12:7) when religious leaders disapprove. (Carter 2000 p. 134)

Bonhoeffer, in *The Cost of Discipleship*, writes of the merciful with great power:

These men, without possessions or power, these strangers on earth, these sinners, these followers of Jesus, have in their life with him *renounced their own dignity*, for they are merciful. As if their own needs and their own distress were not enough, they take upon themselves the distress and humiliation and sin of others. They have an irresistible love for the down-trodden, the sick, the wretched, the wronged, the outcast and all who are tortured with anxiety. They go out and seek all who are enmeshed in the toils of sin and guilt. No distress is too great, no sin too appalling for their pity. If any man falls into disgrace, the merciful will sacrifice their own honour to shield him, and take his shame upon themselves. They will be found consorting with publicans and sinners, careless of the shame they incur thereby. In order that they may be merciful, they cast away the most priceless treasure of human life, their personal dignity and honour. For the only honour and dignity they know is their Lord's own mercy, to which alone they owe their very lives. He was not ashamed of his disciples, he became the brother of mankind, and bore their shame unto the death of the cross. This is how Jesus, the crucified, was merciful. (1959 p. 101)

It is no light thing to be truly 'merciful'. The reward can be that, through a self-forgetful and inclusive concern for others, the merciful create around them, quite unselfconsciously, a community of grace and mutual acceptance. The ultimate mercy is God's, and that is sure; but have we not met those who by their selflessness radiate a generosity of spirit which brings its own reward?

Blessed are the pure in heart, for they will see God.

Once again, this word of Jesus builds on the familiar traditions of his people. The 'pure in heart' awake many echoes in the Old Testament, the words of Psalm 24 (3–4) offering a good example:

> Who shall ascend the hill of the Lord?
> And who shall stand in his holy place?
> Those who have clean hands and pure hearts,
> who do not lift up their souls to what is false,
> and do not swear deceitfully.

This psalm is clearly for use in an entry procession at the Temple. In its stress for the need for more than mere outward, ritual purity, it fits well with Matthew's emphasis on integrity and purity of motivation. 'Clean hands' are not enough. Bonhoeffer comments on this beatitude: 'Purity of heart is here contrasted with all outward purity, even the purity of high intentions' (1959 p. 101). The final words of that sentence are arresting: 'even the purity of high intentions'. We all recognise the struggle against our 'base desires'; what is not so obvious is that the pursuit of high ideals can also get in the way of the integrity of vision here asked for and promised. Our idealism and even our service of others can serve as a subtle cloak for our egoism, our self-justification; our relentless pursuit of the good can narrow our vision and blind us to the truth of realities and needs staring in our faces. Remember the poet's prayer and warning: 'O Lord, deliver me from the man of excellent intention and impure heart: for the heart is deceitful above all things and desperately wicked' (Eliot 1969 p. 158).

Where then are we to find true 'purity of heart'? Once again, we are being invited into a struggle which is renewed day by day. Søren Kierkegaard, the Danish thinker, said: 'Purity of heart is to will one thing'. In other words, the requisite for a pure heart is single-mindedness, but it is single-mindedness with a particular object in mind. The object is to let the mind of Christ form and reform our minds. Hymns say it much better than mere prose. Both the following verses offer much to ponder and pray. The first simply prays that the mind of Christ live in us, constantly:

> 'May the mind of Christ my Saviour
> live in me from day to day,
> by his love and power controlling
> all I do or say.'
>
> (Katie Barclay Wilkinson (1859–1928)
> in *CH4* 1994 no. 536 v. 1)

The second, from deep in the Celtic tradition, is the very familiar prayer for singleness of sight:

> 'Be thou my Vision, O Lord of my heart;
> naught be all else to me, save that thou art;

thou my best thought in the day or the night,
waking or sleeping, thy presence my light.'

(Irish, eighth century, translated Mary Elizabeth Byrne,
revised Eleanor Henrietta Hull in *CH4* 1994 no. 465 v. 1)

For Jesus' people, seeing God in this life was impossible. From
the time of Moses, it was firmly held that to see God was to die;
before his majesty and power the fate of humans was annihilation.
Certainly then, Jesus' words here would be heard as a future
promise for the life to come. There's more, however. In Jesus
himself, we see the face of God. By concentrating on him, following
him, living with him on the way of discipleship which he will reveal
as his gospel story continues, the disciple comes to 'see God'. The
promise remains, and is ours, and so we can make the words of
Charles Wesley's great hymn our own:

'No condemnation now I dread;
Jesus, and all in him, is mine!
Alive in him, my living Head,
and clothed in righteousness divine,
bold I approach the eternal throne,
and claim the crown, through Christ, my own.'

(*CH4* 1994 no. 396 v. 5)

Does the search for 'purity of heart' carry the danger of slipping
into an other-worldly piety? It can, but an honest focusing single-
mindedly on Christ the way throws us immediately back into
following him in the midst of the challenges and ambiguities of the
real world. Once again, Bonhoeffer can help us. He was sustained
through the darkest days of his struggles against Hitler by what he
called his 'secret discipline' of prayer, devotion and attention to the
scriptures. It fed him through the worst. As Ronald Gregor Smith
wrote: 'The real strength and significance of this secret discipline,
however, is its persistent pushing of the believer back into the world'
(1956 p. 105).

Blessed are the peacemakers, for they will be called the children of God.

In this fallen world, it seems as if the desire for and the absence of 'peace' are well nigh universal. Peace is longed for in every arena of our lives, from the personal, through the domestic, the neighbourhood, society, the nation, to peace between and among the nations. Yet restlessness, anxiety, despair, hostility and conflict stalk every sector of our living. The search for peace is both comprehensive and elusive, yet the promise remains of 'the peace of God, beyond our understanding ...' (Philippians 4:7).

In the background to this beatitude is just such a promise, rooted in the Old Testament development of the *shalom* of God, God's peace. For Israel, true peace was much more than the absence of conflict. God's *shalom* promised not only a people living in reconciliation and plenty but also a world with its original harmony restored and with violence and the roots of violence banished. Some of the most compelling pictures of such a world come from the words of the prophet Isaiah, and in particular these passages long associated with the season of Advent, Isaiah 2, 9 and 11. Let one verse stand for many. 'They shall not hurt or destroy on all my holy mountain: for the earth will be full of the knowledge of the Lord as the waters cover the sea' (*Isaiah 11:9*).

While this beatitude builds on the heritage of *shalom*, there is another contrasting piece of background. The dominant political reality of the world of both Jesus and Matthew was that of the Roman Empire, which made the proud boast of having brought to the nations it had conquered the *pax Romana*, Rome's peace. Throughout the gospel, there is a clear interplay and tension between Rome's empire and the reign of God. Both promised peace, but the peace which Rome brought was ultimately based on force of arms and worked from the top down, and therefore primarily to the advantage of those at the top. In contrast, God's peace is furthered in this world by those who are in themselves peaceable and who take the way of conscious peacemaking and reconciliation. We are reminded of the saying: 'Ask not what is the way to peace, peace is the way'. Living in God's peace is about knowing of peace received and out of that knowledge becoming peacemakers. This is a revolution from below; it is the poor, humble, hungry disciples who are called to be peacemakers, at every level of our lives.

The reward is to be called 'children of God'. The 'children of God' were God's chosen ones, and the people of Israel understood such a calling to belong to them. Here, Jesus loosens the bonds of ethnicity; he says that all who work for peace are worthy of the title 'God's children' as they all further God's purposes of peace, here on earth, as it is in heaven (6:10).

Blessed are those who are persecuted for righteousness' sake, for theirs is the kingdom of heaven.

Blessed are you, when people revile you and persecute you and utter all kinds of evil against you falsely on my account. Rejoice and be glad, for your reward is great in heaven, for in the same way they persecuted the prophets who were before you.

The last two beatitudes form a doublet and belong together, with the second reinforcing the first. The final beatitude becomes more pointed as it moves from the third to the second person and so becomes a word of direct address to the assembled disciples: 'Blessed are you ...'. While in terms of Matthew's narrative these words are spoken to the original disciples, their primary purpose was that they should be heard by the community of Matthew's young church, bruised and battered in its conflicts with the synagogue. Matthew offers these words of encouragement to a community which had known in its own personal life and experience that the cost of discipleship was indeed not cheap. He reminds them that they enter into an ancient and honourable tradition and company of those who have suffered for the sake of faithfulness to God's word. In George MacLeod's words, true prophets are as liable to be pelted as praised.

In the preceding beatitude, all who 'are persecuted for righteousness' sake', those who suffer in the cause of right living and the doing of justice, are promised entry into the reign of God, the kingdom of heaven. As in the case of the peacemakers, the promise is universalised. It is not only Christians who suffer in the cause of the right, and it is not Christians alone who through their pains receive a vision of the ways of God. Here we have to confess that, all too often, Christians have locked themselves away in their own self-satisfied and seemingly self-sufficient citadel – and, like Elijah before the still small voice (1 Kings 19:18), have failed to recognise and honour those of different commitments and confessions who are one with them in a common struggle. In the day-to-day struggles for peace and justice in situations large or small, local or international, Christians are called and challenged to work together with those of many faiths and none for the coming of the right. Raymond Fung, sometime secretary of the World Council of Churches' Commission on World Mission and Evangelism, in his energising little book *The Isaiah Vision*, suggests that making such common cause and sharing in partnership with those who are different is both a potent and an authentic way of evangelism and a Kingdom task.

Suffering persecution because of our allegiance to Jesus Christ is largely remote from the experience of western Christians of my generation. There have been occasional instances of verbal abuse, and there is the constant drip of a smug, sneering and superior hostility to faith from many sections of the popular media who trumpet their deliverance from our primitive superstition. By no stretch of the imagination can it be called persecution. It is salutary therefore to remember that it has been said that there have been more Christian martyrs in the twentieth century than in any other since the first century of the Christian era. We remember and honour them as we continue to pray for the persecuted church, sadly still a reality in not a few places in our world today.

Retrospect

Writing about the beatitudes in Luke's gospel, Richard Rohr says: 'There is an almost Zen-like quality to these statements: riddles given by the master to make us redefine our reality. He praises what we would normally avoid – hunger and mourning – so that we need a new life paradigm to understand what he is saying' (1997 p. 111). The beatitudes are a shaking of our foundations, a radical call to a new way of life, a new way of both attitude and action. May we continue to be struck and challenged by their heady amalgam of passion and detachment, blending together to call us out, greatly daring, on the royal road of faith, the discipleship road.

Before we leave them, it is worth asking what they tell us about Matthew's community. There is nothing grand and triumphalist about it. On the contrary, it is a community whose members have experienced poverty and powerlessness and who have been bruised and buffeted for their faith. They sound very like the young Christian community at Corinth of whom Paul writes. 'Consider your own call, brothers and sisters: not many of you were wise by human standards, not many were powerful, not many of noble birth' (1 Corinthians 1:26). Let a final word from Bonhoeffer reiterate the link between the call to faith of the beatitudes early in the gospel with the dénouement at the gospel's end:

> Having reached the end of the beatitudes, we naturally ask if there is any place on this earth for the community which they describe. Clearly, there is one place, and only one, and that is where the poorest, meekest, and most sorely tried of all men is to be found – on the cross at Golgotha. The fellowship of the beatitudes is the fellowship of the Crucified. With him it has lost all, and with him it has found all. From the cross there comes the call, 'blessed, blessed'. The last beatitude is addressed directly to the disciples, for only they can understand it. 'Blessed are you when ...' (Bonhoeffer 1959 p. 103)

Salt and light

Finally in this opening section of the Sermon comes the call to the disciples to be salt for the earth and light to the world. The metaphors of salt and light have considerable pedigrees in the history of faith. Salt appears quite frequently in the Old Testament, while light is a pervasive symbol throughout the world's religions. The effective work of salt, like yeast, is both hidden and out of all proportion to its small size. It works unseen to give taste and to preserve. But it can lose its savour and become useless. To be salt to the earth suggests a universal calling, taking 'earth' as a synonym for the world; 'earth' also suggests being close to the ground and that this work of salting is humble as well as hidden work. Remaining salty, keeping savour depends on the disciple's use of the resources of faith and prayer to remain faithful to the mission of humble service in the world. It is worth noting that Jesus says: 'You *are* the salt'. Being salt isn't a demand; it is simply a corollary of being called to be a disciple, something which permeates the follower's whole being.

Light is visible and makes other things visible; more than that, it is inseparable from sight, growth and indeed life itself. It is so vital to life that it is no accident that the Genesis story says the creation of light was the first of God's actions in the work of Creation (Genesis 1:3–5). Scripture is full of references to God and light: 'God is light, and in him is no darkness at all' (1 John 1:5). Jesus claims the title: 'I am the light of the world' (John 8:12). The surprising, awesome claim that Jesus makes here is that you and I – very ordinary disciples – are light to the world. And we would never do anything as silly as to cover up a light! Jesus' injunction to us is to let the light of our actions shine bright in the world. Remember the words of Luther that only a church which is inconveniently visible will ever truly be the invisible church.

Study

By yourself
Learn the Beatitudes (Matthew 5:1–16) by heart. Carry them with you, always.

Group work
Ask each member of the group to identify two beatitudes each; first, one which puzzles them, second, one which attracts them. Get the group members to share first of all their puzzlement with the others in the group and, second, their attraction. You may be in for a long night!

Chapter 6

'BUT I SAY TO YOU'

Matthew 5:17–48
Teaching about the Law

'Do not think that I have come to do away with the Law of Moses and the teachings of the prophets. I have not come to do away with them, but to make their teachings come true. Remember that as long as heaven and earth last, not the least point nor the smallest detail of the Law will be done away with – not until the end of all things. So then, whoever disobeys even the least important of the commandments and teaches others to do the same, will be least in the Kingdom of heaven. On the other hand, whoever obeys the Law and teaches others to do the same, will be great in the Kingdom of heaven. I tell you, then, that you will be able to enter the Kingdom of heaven only if you are more faithful than the teachers of the Law and the Pharisees in doing what God requires.'

Teaching about Anger

(Luke 12:57–9)

'You have heard that people were told in the past, "Do not commit murder; anyone who does will be brought to trial." But now I tell you: whoever is angry with his brother will be brought to trial, whoever calls his brother, "You good-for-nothing!" will be brought before the Council, and whoever calls his brother a worthless fool will be in danger of going to the fire of hell. So if you are about to offer your gift to God at the altar and there you remember that your brother has something against you, leave your gift there in front of the altar, go at once and make peace with your brother, and then come back and offer your gift to God.

'If someone brings a lawsuit against you and takes you to court, settle the dispute with him while there is time, before you get to court. Once you are there, he will hand you over to the judge, who will hand you over to the police, and you will be put in jail. There you will stay, I tell you, until you pay the last penny of your fine.'

Teaching about Adultery

'You have heard that it was said, "Do not commit adultery." But now I tell you: anyone who looks at a woman and wants to possess her is guilty of committing adultery with her in his heart. So if your right eye causes you to sin, take it out and throw it away! It is much better for you to lose a part of your body than to have your whole body thrown into hell. If your right hand causes you to sin, cut it off and throw it away! It is much better for you to lose one of your limbs than for your whole body to go to hell.'

Teaching about Divorce

(Matthew 19:9, Mark 10:11–12, Luke 16:18)

'It was also said, "Anyone who divorces his wife must give her a written notice of divorce." But now I tell you: if a man divorces his wife, for any cause other than her unfaithfulness, then he is guilty of making her commit adultery if she marries again; and the man who marries her commits adultery also.'

Teaching about Vows

'You have also heard that people were told in the past, "Do not break your promise, but do what you have vowed to the Lord to do." But now I tell you: do not use any vow when you make a promise. Do not swear by heaven, for it is God's throne; nor by earth, for it is the resting place for his feet; nor by Jerusalem, for it is the city of the great King. Do not even swear by your head, because you cannot make a single hair white or black. Just say "Yes" or "No" – anything else you say comes from the Evil One.'

Teaching about Revenge

(Luke 6:29–30)

'You have heard that it was said, "An eye for an eye, and a tooth for a tooth." But now I tell you: do not take revenge on someone who wrongs you. If anyone slaps you on the right cheek, let him slap your left cheek too. And if someone takes you to court to sue you for your shirt, let him have your coat as well. And if one of the occupation troops forces you to carry his pack one kilometre, carry it two kilometres. When someone asks you for something, give it to him; when someone wants to borrow something, lend it to him.'

Love for Enemies

(Luke 6:27–8, 32–6)

'You have heard that it was said, "Love your friends, hate your enemies." But now I tell you: love your enemies, and pray for those who persecute you, so that you may become the children of your Father in heaven. For he makes his sun to shine on bad and good people alike, and gives rain to those who do good and those who do evil. Why should God reward you if you love only the people who love you? Even the tax collectors do that! And if you speak only to your friends, have you done anything out of the ordinary? Even the pagans do that! You must be perfect – just as your Father in heaven is perfect!'

A matter of interpretation

There are questions and there are questions. If the provocation of the beatitudes was to raise questions for us about our attitudes and understandings, we now meet the provocation of questions of another sort. The questions which follow are about our actions. Jesus speaks plainly enough, it's just that what he asks of us here is so difficult to practise faithfully. Jesus lists six examples of what is required of those whose righteousness should exceed that of the scribes and Pharisees, those who would live out the values of the reign of God. Carter summarises them as: about anger and relationships, about adultery and male lust, about divorce and male mistreatment of women, about integrity of word and action, about non-violent resistance to evil, about love for enemies (Carter 2000 p. 143).

Before turning to the examples, the short significant opening section of verses 17–20 needs to be considered. It raises the issue of the understanding of Jesus' and Matthew's relationship to the existing Law of Moses, and its interpretation is difficult but important. Keep in mind the background situation of the original hearers of Matthew's gospel. Matthew writes for a community of Jewish Christians who have recently experienced a serious break with their fellow Jews in the synagogue. For them, the issue of the keeping of the Law of Moses was important as a link of continuity which authenticated Jesus as the fulfilment of God's promises to Israel. Matthew's community also lived in the situation of a growing Gentile church whose new members did not have the historical and emotional ties to the Law which characterised the Jewish Christians. Indeed, there is clear evidence in the New Testament of a serious antinomian strain in the Gentile church which Matthew would be concerned to counter. The influences on Matthew suggest that his position on the relation of Jesus to the Law would be conservative – and so, with qualification, it is here.

The passage begins with Jesus' statement that he has come not to destroy but to fulfil the Law and the prophets. His first statement is then strengthened and reinforced by a second where he says 'as long as heaven and earth last, not the least point nor the smallest detail of the Law will be done away with – not till the end of all things' (5:18 GNB). 'Least point' and 'smallest detail' is the GNB rendering of the AV's 'one jot and one tittle', the 'jot' being a reference to iota, the smallest letter in the Greek alphabet, the 'tittle' referring to the little ornamental embellishments added to a manuscript by Jewish scribes. Sharp eyes will have noticed that there are two qualifications to Jesus' declaration of the unchanging nature of the Law, viz. 'as long as heaven and earth last' and 'not till the end of all things'. For the first, the NRSV translation, 'until heaven and earth pass away', is much more accurate and helpful. There was a general expectation that heaven and earth would pass away at the end time, the end of this age. Is Jesus the bringer of the new age? For the second, again the NRSV translation is more accurate where it replaces 'the end of all things' with 'until all is accomplished' or 'fulfilled'. Again, it is more than possible to interpret these words as pointing to the Law's fulfilment in the coming of Jesus himself. He will build upon the foundations of the Law of Moses, but his interpretation will rest on the key Kingdom values of the justice and mercy of God which he has come to announce. Eduard Schweizer's summary is helpful:

> The crucial point of this section is not to misunderstand Jesus' message: it is a call to take the Law seriously, to take God's will seriously. The Pharisees practised a magnificent obedience: in addition to all their taxes, they donated ten percent of their income, down to the last penny, to charity; they let themselves be butchered defencelessly rather than make light of God's gift of the Sabbath; they suffered the most horrible forms of martyrdom not to surrender their Bible; they know that life is truly human only when God is more important than anything else. Nothing is said to ridicule their obedience. Obedience must not be made easy, God must not be devalued. But what is expected of Jesus' disciples is something even more: the mighty, luminous, unmistakable discipleship referred to in verses 13–16. (1975 p. 109)

It was indeed true that the Pharisees' obedience to the Law was formidable. Yet Matthew's gospel will complain that, for all its dedication, it had become static and over-concerned with the minutiae of externals and had lost touch with the overflowing stream of the mercy and justice of God. It had become self-regarding and self-referential; turned in on itself, it denied the call to be light to the world. Jesus has come to announce and embody that overflowing dynamic and transforming mercy and justice; as his disciples do likewise, so they too embody the greater 'righteousness'.

About anger and relationships

Jesus begins: 'The old law says, "Don't kill, don't murder" ... I say to you, "Anger is murder".' His first example comes from the Ten Commandments, where he starts by moving back one stage from the act itself to the motivation for the act. Much violence springs from anger, therefore learning to temper and control our anger is an important step to take. The boiling, poisonous bitterness of soul is as deadly in its own way as the swinging fist or the savage knife blow. It both corrupts the one who is angry and destroys the relationship with the person who is the object of anger. Anger displayed in public will result in appearance before the local court (6:22).

Jesus continues by instancing two particular outcrops of overflowing anger, both of which result in verbal abuse. They remind us of the dangers of an unbridled tongue (see James 3:1–12) and of the damage to others that an angry tongue can inflict. In the world of New Testament times, codes of honour and shame were very powerful; to insult someone in public was to expose them to humiliation and probably to provoke an equally damaging response, thus continuing or escalating the cycle of violence. Such a public insult, says Matthew, would result in an appearance before the 'council', probably the Sanhedrin, the supreme court of the land. The second example is to call someone 'a fool'. 'Fool' in the Old Testament is associated with godlessness: it involves arrogantly assuming powers which belong to God alone. There is therefore a huge jump in the penalty for such speech – nothing less than the threat of fiery hell!

Back from the flames, there comes next the wonderfully humane advice about the respective priorities of worship and reconciliation (5:23–4). Make peace with your brother and sister before you make praise. Here is another variation of the consistent theme of this gospel – mercy before sacrifice. Finally, Jesus offers a piece of good advice: in the case of a dispute, settle differences with anyone who accuses you as fast as you can out of court; legal processes are tortuous, lawyers are not cheap, and jail is to be avoided. It can be ruinous (5:25–6). When we look closely, there's a certain unevenness about the words attributed to Jesus in this section. There is clearly a common theme, but there's a strong impression that a number of different sayings have been gathered together from different sources into the one place. Blame the editor – and remember, editors are powerful people.

About adultery and male lust

The second example also has its roots in the Decalogue, specifically in the commandment forbidding adultery, but also in the commandment forbidding covetousness (Exodus 20:14, 17). Once again, Jesus bids us look behind our actions to the wellsprings of action in our feelings and motivations. Jesus' words are spoken in the context of a society which was heavily patriarchal and where power within a marriage resided almost entirely with the male. Attitudes to adultery were ambivalent, but the Law itself was strongly biased in favour of the male. Jesus here seeks a new way of understanding and conducting male/female relationships based on a new respect for a woman's dignity and integrity. She is not to be regarded as the object of male desire, and men are to deal forcefully and decisively with their basic instincts.

A word of caution is needed about the drastic remedies proposed for the curbing of male lust, i.e. plucking out eyes and cutting off hands. The use of hyperbole was part of the stock-in-trade linguistic tools of the Jewish teacher; and Jesus uses it not infrequently, and clearly here. Hyperbole is a dangerous substance for literalists to handle. Beware!

About divorce and male mistreatment of women

The third example is closely linked to its predecessor. The link is made clear not just in the content but also through the brevity of the introduction, 'It was also said ...'. Once again, Jesus is speaking about the breaking of the most crucial of relationships, between husband and wife, at the very centre of family life. In the society of his times, rules for divorce were also heavily weighted in favour of the male. The Law from Deuteronomy 24:1–4 gave licence for a man to divorce his wife for virtually any cause, although by the time of Jesus there was real debate within rabbinic circles about what grounds were permissible. While the school of Hillel held to the more lax and traditional view, that the wife could be 'put away' for something as trivial as burning the toast, the school of Shammai took a position virtually identical with that here proposed by Jesus: to restrict male power to divorce except in the case of a wife's 'unchastity'. Jesus' proposal is that any man who divorces his wife would make her and her new husband guilty of adultery on remarriage. The economic pressure on the divorced wife to remarry was enormous; where, without a husband or the less likely alternative of a return to her own family, would she find means of support? Jesus' proposal means that the divorcing husband shares in the guilt of exposing his ex-wife to commit adultery. He makes the playing field between husband and wife more level, but it's still a tough view. It still offers no opportunities for a woman to escape from an exploitative or violent relationship, and, with its refusal to permit remarriage, condemned her to a life of poverty or at least economic insecurity.

Huge volumes of words have been written around this difficult example, in part because of the difficulty of understanding the exact background and situation the example refers to, in part also because, of all Jesus' teaching in this section, divorce alone carries the force of law. A. M. Hunter writes wisely and compassionately when he says:

> The truth seems to be that Jesus was not laying down a binding law about marriage but stating the divine ideal. (If this saying is a piece of legislation, it stands alone in the Sermon!) Marriage, in Jesus' view, is a God-given institution, having for its aim the life-long union of a man and a woman, and divorce is a declension from the divine will for them. But if Jesus stated the ideal, he did not go into the casuistry of the matter. (Hunter 1965 p. 54)

The truth is that it is extremely difficult to extract from the Bible's pages any set of binding rules for issues of marriage and divorce today, given that people's life situations in general, and their views and experiences of the male/female relationship in the context of family, are so completely different. Rather than trying to construct a set of rules for today covering every situation, or, even worse, taking refuge behind a blanket prohibition, are we not better to rest content on the wider ethical sweep of the gospels with their emphasis on relationships of trust, faithfulness and genuine mutuality – and, of course, mercy and forgiveness?

About integrity of word and action

In the time of Jesus, the swearing of oaths was extremely widespread. While the purpose of swearing an oath was to create a binding word, various chicaneries and evasions were practised to render sworn oaths unbinding. In the background to the words of Jesus here is the commandment against taking the Lord's name in vain (Exodus 20:7). In his forbidding of swearing by heaven, earth, Jerusalem or even the hairs of your own head, Jesus is warning against co-opting and binding God – for behind heaven, earth, Jerusalem and our own selves is God the Creator – for the furtherance of our purposes. 'Forget about dramatic and pretentious swearing of oaths', says Jesus; 'let your "Yes" mean "Yes" and your "No" be "No"'.

George MacLeod often used to talk about righteousness as 'right relations', and about the Kingdom that Jesus announced as the Kingdom of right relations. This whole section of the Sermon is about right relations. So far, we have seen that the outworking of our angers disrupts right relations, as do failures and evasions of trust, loyalty and respect within the family and male/female relationships. What builds right relations? Nothing more than letting your 'Yes' be 'Yes' and your 'No' mean 'No', in other words being a person of your word, of integrity, who doesn't go in for the extravagant and the high-flown but is simply honest and reliable through and through.

About non-violent resistance to evil

Around the final two examples, Jesus' words come to a climax as the heat gets turned up. 'You have heard it said, An eye for an eye and a tooth for a tooth' – in other words, if you are wronged, you may retaliate in proportion, same again, but no more (see Exodus 21:4, Leviticus 24:20, Deuteronomy 19:21). 'But I say to you, Don't resist the person who wrongs you.' This is certainly not the reaction of the natural man in us. How fascinating are the examples Jesus gives us. 'If someone hits you on the right cheek, offer him the other also.' If someone hits us, which fortunately hasn't happened to me for quite some time, we are not only hurt, we are humiliated. What do we do if we turn and offer the other cheek? We refuse to be humiliated. 'If someone takes your coat, offer them your cloak as well.' The coat was the outer garment, the cloak the inner; if you gave away both, you had very little left indeed. How would someone take your coat? They could hold you up, rob you, but it would be much more likely, the coat would be taken in payment of a debt of some kind. Again, to have your coat taken means humiliation; if you offer the taker of your coat your cloak also and are prepared to stand before them in your loincloth, you refuse to accept being humiliated, you regain the initiative, without violence. 'If anyone forces you to go one mile, go a second.' The 'anyone' would almost certainly be a soldier, probably a foreign soldier, who had the right to conscript one of the natives to carry their pack for a mile. Humiliation again. If, at the end of the mile, you say 'Let me carry your pack a bit further', the initiative becomes yours again. Something very strange is happening here in terms of human worth and dignity. An oppressive force gets turned back on itself without any more force being used. These moves beyond retaliation open up all sorts of new possibilities. Of course, there's no certainty that they'll be taken up; we may just get our other cheek slapped or be left nearly naked. That's not the point, is it? One of the more promising aspects of life today is that there are quite a number of groups now working away at training others in how to resist violent and threatening situations non-violently. It's taken society and church a long time to learn that there is deep wisdom here in Jesus' teaching.

About love for enemies

Finally, we come to: 'Love your enemies and pray for those who persecute you [*and every word counts here*] so that you may be sons and daughters of your Father in heaven (children of the heavenly kingdom); for he makes his sun rise on the evil and the good, and sends his rain on the righteous and the unrighteous'. 'What would it be like to be a church which lived by grace?' We've asked that question already – it's such a good question that we'll return to it again and again. Love of our enemies, the love which breaks out of the charmed circle of family, friends, tribe, nation, birds of a feather, that's a distinguishing mark; easy to say, hard to practise. But what an important act of faith and witness it is. When we are asked to give account of our faith, the questions that will matter most will be not doctrinal but practical, such as: 'Do you practise love of your enemies and pray for those who misuse you?'

After the invitation to love our enemies, Jesus says by way of explanation of this considerable request: 'If you greet only your brothers and sisters, what *more* are you doing than the others?' (5:46). The word (*perisson*) translated into English as 'more' means a lot more than 'more'. It means 'extra', 'greater than', 'beyond all that'. What makes our lives special, distinctive? Jesus teaches here that it's the way we treat those who are very different from us, who are indeed our enemies one way or another. We only love our enemies by the strength of grace. So often, the church itself has baulked at this; it has let the voice of the natural man drown out the still small voice of the claims of grace. Bonhoeffer saw this very clearly. In *The Cost of Discipleship*, he wrote of the church of the nineteenth and early twentieth centuries. 'There was a fatal flaw in a false Protestant ethic which diluted Christian love into patriotism, loyalty to friends and industriousness, which in short, perverted the better righteousness into mere civic justice' (p. 137). Writing as he was at the start of an elemental struggle against his enemies and the forces of evil in the Hitler regime, he also saw clearly what the 'more' is. He says:

> What is this 'more', this 'extraordinary'? It is the unreserved love for our enemies, for the unloving and the unloved, love for our religious, political and personal adversaries. In every case it is the love which was fulfilled in the cross of Christ. For the 'more' is the love of Jesus Christ himself, who went patiently and obediently to the cross – it is in fact the cross itself. The cross is the differential of the Christian religion, the power which enables the Christian to transcend the world and to win the victory. The passion, the suffering, the endurance in the love of the Crucified is the supreme expression of the 'extraordinary' quality of the Christian life. (1959 p. 137)

In the unconditional love revealed on the cross, we see more clearly the face of God who 'makes his sun rise on the evil and the good, and sends rain on the righteous and on the unrighteous' (5:45 NRSV). As Schweizer says (p. 129), 'Jesus does not erase all distinctions between those who are good and those who are evil; what he does is reject the stance that will only show love to those who are considered good'. For the sun and rain which the Father sends on the good and bad alike can be taken as much more than just the ordinary elements with which we are so familiar. They can stand for the light that shines from the cross, and the food which is our salvation. For, at the foot of the cross, we are found to be enemies, but this is the glory of the gospel of grace. 'While we were yet sinners, Christ died for us' (Romans 5:8).

Back to the beginning

As we come to the end of this important passage, let's reconsider its beginning. Jesus' opening words are: 'Don't think that I've come to abolish the law or the prophets; I have come to fulfil' (5:17). Matthew's is the most Jewish of the four gospels. He writes in a context where many people doubt whether Jesus really is a prophet from within the traditions of Israel, of Moses and the Law. Matthew wants to settle that argument early. The answer is 'Yes', Jesus is firmly rooted within the faith of his fathers. In this specific answer there is also a general truth, that the genuine reformer never starts from scratch, with a blank page and an empty memory. The genuine reformer is steeped in memory – steeped in, not shackled by; it's out of memory and the honouring of the tradition that hope and the new comes to birth.

Jesus does stand in the traditions of his ancestors, yet out of that tradition he brings something radically new. The key sign of his new teaching is in the formula which begins his examples: 'You have heard it said in the past, i.e. in the Law's traditions, ... but I say to you'. Jesus here does offer new teaching, new ways of seeing and new ways of doing, and in his 'but I say to you' he makes clear his intention to do so. His 'but' does not stand in simple contradiction to the old Law, the Law of Moses; often it's an amplification, though towards the end it becomes a radical reinterpretation indeed. Remember that all this teaching from the Mount is set in the context of Jesus setting out his vision of the Kingdom of heaven come near. Let's hear these words as an invitation to walk further into the Kingdom. Remember also that behind all these words at the gospel's beginning looms the cross at the gospel's ending. Let's hear these words also as an invitation to sit and learn at a strange, wonderful and surprising new school of love.

Study

By yourself

'But I say to you?' Where do you hear Jesus saying something different, fresh, new to you?

For group work

Discuss together what you think Jesus' 'new law of love' means in terms of personal relationships, church life, the life of your community, and relationships between the nations. What part have we to play as individuals and as faith communities in each of these spheres?

In the light of Jesus' teaching about the love of our enemies, ask what response group members have to the following quotation. Why do we continue to tolerate the institutional violence which is war?

> We cherish the progress in civilisation since biblical times and long before. But there is a needed and, indeed, accepted qualification ...
>
> Civilisation has made great strides over the centuries in science, health-care, the arts, and most, if not all, economic well-being. But it has also given a privileged position to the development of weapons and the threat and reality of war. Mass slaughter has become the ultimate civilised achievement.
>
> The facts of war are inescapable – death and random cruelty, suspension of civilised values, a disordered aftermath. Thus the human condition and prospect is now supremely evident. The economic and social problems ... can, with thought and action, be addressed. So they have already been. War remains the decisive human failure.
>
> (Edited extract in the *Guardian*, 15 July 2004, the day after
> the presentation of the Butler Report, from
> J. K. Galbraith, *The Economics of Innocent Fraud:
> Truth for Our Time*, Allen Lane)

Chapter 7

INSIDE OUT

Matthew 6:1–18
Teaching about Charity

'Make certain you do not perform your religious duties in public so that people will see what you do. If you do these things publicly, you will not have any reward from your Father in heaven.

'So when you give something to a needy person, do not make a big show of it, as the hypocrites do in the houses of worship and on the streets. They do it so that people will praise them. I assure you, they have already been paid in full. But when you help a needy person, do it in such a way that even your closest friend will not know about it. And your Father, who sees what you do in private, will reward you.'

Teaching about Prayer
(Luke 11:2–4)

'When you pray, do not be like the hypocrites! They love to stand up and pray in the houses of worship and on the street corners, so that everyone will see them. I assure you, they have already been paid in full. But when you pray, go to your room, close the door, and pray to your Father, who is unseen. And your Father, who sees what you do in private, will reward you.

'When you pray, do not use a lot of meaningless words, as the pagans do, who think that their gods will hear them because their prayers are long. Do not be like them. Your Father already knows what you need before you ask him. This, then, is how you should pray:

"Our Father in heaven,
May your holy name be honoured;
may your Kingdom come;
may your will be done on earth
as it is in heaven.
Give us today the food we need.
Forgive us the wrongs we have done,
as we forgive the wrongs that
others have done to us.
Do not bring us to hard testing,
but keep us safe from the Evil One."

'If you forgive others the wrongs they have done to you, your Father in heaven will also forgive you. But if you do not forgive others, then your Father will not forgive the wrongs you have done.'

Teaching about Fasting

'And when you fast, do not put on a sad face like the hypocrites do. They neglect their appearance so that everyone may see that they are fasting. I assure you, they have already been paid in full. When you go without food, wash your face and comb your hair, so that others cannot know that you are fasting – only your Father, who is unseen, will know. And your Father, who sees what you do in private, will reward you.'

Behind the door

We've seen already that Jesus in Matthew's gospel is much concerned with 'inwardness', with what goes on inside us; matters of motive and heart. He is concerned with the springs of our action, what gives us motivation, and also about the congruence between our outside and our inside, our integrity, the matching of what we feel and believe with what we do. We know that all of us have an outside and an inside – a face we present to the world, and an inner life known only to ourselves. And the two can be very, very different. There can be all the difference in the world between the 'me' of my daylight actions and the 'me' of the night watches, though of course they're connected; and it's that connection which we want to explore.

The common thread of this passage, about in turn almsgiving, prayer and fasting, is about performing all three without any show of our piety. With the insertion into the middle of the passage of the Lord's Prayer, we can say that it is mainly about prayer; and prayer belongs largely but not exclusively to the inner life, to the place of silence and heart choices, the place of questions, fears, desires, imaginings, hopes, longings, motivations; that place which lies deep in all of us. Here's a strange thing. In our world, there are many who would be very sceptical and doubtful about both the theory and the practice of regular prayer, yet, as a society, we remain fascinated by the inner life; analysts, psychotherapists, counsellors, gurus abound. One of the architects of this modern world of our self-examination and self-concern, long before Freud, is the Danish nineteenth-century thinker Søren Kierkegaard.

Kierkegaard, in many ways a tortured soul, rebelled against the formal religion of the Danish Lutheran State Church which he saw as conventional, insincere and ineffectual. Against such a faith, he asserted passionately that truth is inwardness; real truth wells up from the inner springs of motive, passion and commitment. Indeed, he says that faith is so much a matter of the inner springs that there is nothing in the outward appearance of a person which gives any hint of that secret wellspring. He tells a famous story to try to illustrate this. He talks of looking endlessly for the person whom he calls the knight of faith. He asserts that his search has been fruitless – but, if he ever discovered such a person:

> I have never discovered a knight of faith, but I can easily imagine one. Here he is. I make his acquaintance, I am introduced to him. And the moment I lay eyes on him, I push him away and leap back suddenly, clap my hands together and say half aloud: 'Good God! Is this really he? Why, he looks like an Inspector of Taxes.' But it is really he. I draw closer to him, I watch every movement that he makes to see whether he shows any sign of the least telegraphic communication with the infinite, a glance, a look, a gesture, an air of melancholy, a smile to betray the contrast of infinity and the finite. But no! ... He is completely solid. How does he walk? Firmly. He belongs wholly to the finite; and there is no townsman dressed in his Sunday best, ... who treads the earth more firmly than he; he belongs altogether to the earth.... He takes pleasure in all things,

takes part in everything, and everything he does, he does with the perseverance of earthly men whose souls hang fast to what they are doing … On Sundays he takes a holiday. He goes to church. No heavenly glance … betrays him; and without knowing him it would be impossible to distinguish him from the rest of the congregation, for his healthy bellowing of the psalms proves only that he has got a sound pair of lungs …' (Kierkegaard 1946 pp. 41–2)

Kierkegaard goes on in that vein, showing how firmly the feet of the knight of faith are rooted in this world with nothing outward to indicate that this person has taken what Kierkegaard calls the leap of faith and made the commitment, in the depths of the soul, of saying 'yes' to God. There's something very appealing in the picture of the knight. It reminds us of the deep, secret and intimately personal dimension of faith and prayer. It's a picture too which finds a more modern echo in Bonhoeffer's talk about the Christian's secret discipline as the counterpoint to Christian living unreservedly in the world as Christ did, the world as the place God loves … that discipline well described as 'a kind of humorous, humble, self-effacing secrecy of devotion and hope, which finds no counterpart in the visible world, but which works … in persistently pushing the believer back into the world' (Smith 1969 pp. 104–5). Just as an aside, is it not because we recognise the truth that integrity is more than skin-deep, and any kind of show of religion soon lays us open to the dangers of hypocrisy, that the church is so poor at publicity in this world of relentless advertising and self-promotion? We have a gut distrust of it.

But there's another side to this. We have to ask: 'Is the Christian life quite as invisible as Kierkegaard suggests?' Is the picture of the knight of faith not much too individualistic? Is it not dangerously and perhaps arrogantly dismissive of communication and communion with other people? Kierkegaard, in his own life, broke off his engagement to the woman he loved and in many ways shut himself off from the society around him. He was in danger of getting lost in the labyrinths of self and ending up, for all his passion, talking to nobody but himself, with no real 'other' – whether people or God. R. S. Thomas, the Welsh poet, recognised the tortured genius of Kierkegaard. In one of his late poems, he asks aloud if the Dane's emphasis on inwardness was not his temptation, like meeting the serpent in the garden (Genesis 3). He says:

> How do we know his study
> was not the garden
> over again, where his mind
> was the serpent, insinuator
> of the heresy of the self
> as God? The difficulty
> with prayer is the exchange
> of places between I and thou,
> with silence as the answer
> to an imagined request.
> Is this the price genius
> must pay, that from an emphasis
> on the subjective only
> soliloquy remains? Is prayer
> not a glass that, beginning
> in obscurity as his books
> do, the longer we stare
> into the clearer becomes
> the reflection of a countenance
> in it other than our own?

> (S. K., from *No Truce with the Furies*
> in Thomas 2004 p. 221)

The poem's final question is an answer and a promise. 'Is prayer not a glass that, beginning in obscurity ... the longer we stare into, the clearer becomes the reflection of a countenance in it other than our own?' Prayer in the secret place is valid. The promise is that, on the inward journey, in the hidden place, if our hearts are still, we move beyond the chatter of our hopes and hurts, fears and desires, past the endless conversations with our self until on the inward journey we meet the other; through the glass darkly, we begin to see the face of God. What we see on the journey inward is also shown to our eyes in the journey outward. It is well caught in Kenneth Steven's short poem called 'Prayer', inspired by the experience of being on the west coast of Scotland:

> If you do not believe in God
> Go on a blue spring day across these fields:
> Listen to the orchids, race the sea, scent the wind.
>
> Come back and tell me it was all an accident
> A collision of blind chance
> In the empty hugeness of space.

> (2000 p. 26)

All that's just a rather long way of saying that in this world we are condemned to live neither within the prison of ourselves nor in the vast emptiness of a meaningless universe. There is another reality. On our journey through Matthew's gospel, we have learned the name Jesus gives to this other reality; it is the Kingdom of heaven, the presence, claim, way, reality of God drawn near to us, clarified for us in the whole event of Jesus Christ.

'Pray then in this way'

At the centre of this passage is the prayer we call the Lord's Prayer. It's a prayer which should never be far from our consciousness, a constant part of our inner resource. Isn't it striking the way it turns us inside out? Jesus gives full weight to our inner reality, but his teaching about prayer is that the inner life should be shaped, formed and informed by our concentration on what lies beyond ourselves, the reality of God, the reality of other people, the reality of heaven's Kingdom, touching, claiming, filling our lives now. What does the prayer say?

> Give praise, honour, glory to the Maker of all things, hidden source of love and life, whose being is always beyond us. Pray and work for the coming of God's ways to become real in the life of this world, pray and work with others for that which feeds body and soul and leaves enough for all. Live the reconciled life with God and the community around you, forgive and know you are forgiven, and pray that the burdens of the day be not more than we can bear.

Let's have a brief look at the outlines of this prayer for all seasons, the everyday prayer which turns us outwards, inviting us, in a strength from beyond us, to live and pray with patience and perseverance, the Kingdom way in the midst of this world.

- **Our Father in heaven:** Luke's version (Luke 11:1–4) begins simply 'Father'. Matthew's beginning with 'Our' makes clear the communal nature of the prayer, while the addition of 'heaven' keeps us from any trivialising of the name of God. It is the heavenly Father to whom we pray. 'Father' is a major word for the naming of and approach to God in Matthew's gospel. It denotes both an intimacy of relationship and a providential care.

- **May your holy name be honoured:** this first petition reinforces the meaning of the 'Father in heaven'. It speaks of giving due honour and respect to the otherness, the 'beyondness' of God; it acknowledges the reality that when we pray we dare to approach the mystery before and behind all life.

- **May your kingdom come; may your will be done on earth as in heaven:** the two petitions powerfully reinforce one another. At the heart of the Lord's Prayer is this prayer for the Kingdom. The coming of the Kingdom is in the hands and by the will of God, and we pray and wait, wait and pray for it. Part of the way the Kingdom comes is in and through our doing of God's will here on earth. Here, prayer and action are linked very closely together.

- **Give us today the food we need:** here is the prayer for our 'daily' bread. Scholars are unclear about how to translate 'daily'. It could mean simply 'bread for today' or alternatively 'bread for tomorrow'. It could also mean 'the bread which is necessary', 'bread for our needs', 'the bread of necessity'. The prayer is for bread, not cakes; it's about having enough to live on. It's about 'our' not 'my' bread, about enough for the community, enough for all people. It's a prayer we as Christians pray on behalf of our world, in confidence, to a just and generous God. Again it's a prayer linked to action; we don't just pray for bread, we share it.

- **Forgive us the wrongs we have done, as we forgive the wrongs others have done to us:** more accurately, 'the wrongs we have done' should be translated as 'debts', i.e. the whole burden of what we owe to God and to our neighbours. Undergirding this prayer for forgiveness is the central gospel theme of the promise that we shall be forgiven. 'As we forgive others...' introduces a theme which is prominent in Matthew (see particularly 18:21–35) – that true forgiveness operates like the expanding circles of a wave in a pond as those who are forgiven likewise forgive others who have wronged them. As those who know the forgiveness of God, so we are bidden heartily to forgive one another.

- **Do not bring us to hard testing, but keep us safe from evil/the evil one:** there is unhappiness over the older, more familiar translation, 'Lead us not into temptation', on two grounds. First, why would God ever wish to lead us into temptation? Second, 'testing' is a more comprehensive word than 'tempting'. We all know the reality of times of testing. 'Don't ask of us more than we can bear' catches well the meaning, as does the second half of this doublet, 'keep us safe from evil/the evil one'. Matthew sees evil as personified in the devil; whether we believe in a personalised devil or not, anyone living in these times has seen the face of evil.

At this point, some later manuscripts of Matthew add in a form of doxology: 'For the Kingdom, the power and the glory are yours, evermore, Amen'. It is generally agreed that this did not form part of the prayer which Jesus originally taught, but that, early in the life of the young church, doxologies came to be used widely at the conclusion of prayers. Its addition here represents early practice within the young church. Significantly, what Matthew does add at the end of the prayer are more words of Jesus to reinforce the dynamic nature of forgiveness; is as we forgive one another, so our heavenly Father will also forgive us (6:14–15). Behind the prayer, we can glimpse the formation of a new community which honours God, is mutually concerned for the meeting of each other's material needs, and lives together in acceptance and forgiveness. Matthew's is the gospel most concerned with what we call 'church'.

Alms and fasting

On either side of Jesus' teaching on prayer are his words about almsgiving and fasting. In the Jewish world, almsgiving was part of what God required and would be assumed as proper by the disciples. Jesus is objecting not to the giving of alms *per se* but to their ostentatious giving. The picture of almsgiving to the sound of a trumpet (6:2) is slightly ridiculous, and indeed there is no evidence that this was a common practice. Is it another example of Jesus' poking fun by exaggeration? In all three examples in this passage, almsgiving, prayer and fasting, Jesus enjoins the disciples not to behave as the 'hypocrites'. The word 'hypocrite' originally comes from the theatre and describes an actor playing a part. In contrast to 'play-acting', throughout Matthew's gospel there is a consistent emphasis on simplicity being a characteristic of the lifestyle of discipleship. Matthew's gospel breathes a spirituality of the 'unshowy', of humbly getting on and doing things quietly and without fuss. It has been said that Matthew's hero is the unnoticed Christian who simply lives out his or her faith and obedience in a committed and disciplined way. Do the words about not letting your left hand know what your right hand is doing find their ultimate approbation in Matthew's final parable of the sheep and the goats (25:31–46), where recognition of humble service is not revealed until judgement day?

The final words about fasting reinforce the call to simplicity. The practice of fasting in Jewish society is again simply assumed by Jesus. The Jewish practice of fasting was so ubiquitous that it brought forth comments from the Gentile world. Within Israel, however, there were criticisms of the practice of fasting separated from the doing of justice, notably in the savage words of Isaiah 58: 'Is not this the fast I choose?' Jesus here takes aim at the practice of fasting producing an outward show of lugubrious piety. He has no time for long- and sour-faced religion. To the world, we bring our best face forward.

In the church today, we so often live with a confidence deficit, for times are a-changing, and in the European world the sea of faith seems ebbing and we don't know what the future holds for church or world. Underneath the call for simplicity, this passage with its emphasis on prayer should give us confidence in face of our immediate fears, a deeper confidence well able to face the troubles of our time – the confidence of a faith which is based on other than ourselves. It's a confidence in 'the face other than our own' we meet in the place of prayer, in the mute witness of the greening of the earth and its beauty, in the reality and presence of Jesus Christ and his Kingdom way and his Kingdom community. So we wait and work and pray and hope. And, as Jesus told us, we wash our face, groom our hair, smile at the world and face life with renewed vigour and boldness, for there is a reality beyond our reality, a face behind all our faces, a care beyond all our cares; a reality called 'Our Father', about whom we have learned and will learn more, through Jesus Christ our Lord.

Study

By yourself
For the next month, pray the Lord's Prayer in the morning, in the middle of the day and at night. Reflect on your prayer.

For group work
Take each of the petitions of the Lord's Prayer and share your thoughts on them in turn.

Pause

Our Father in heaven
In the three synoptic gospels, Matthew has by far the heaviest emphasis on God as heavenly father. For example, Matthew uses the word *pater* sixty-three times as compared to Mark's eighteen; forty-four of the sixty-three refer to God, while of Mark's eighteen only four have a God reference. For Matthew, God as father has great importance, reflecting in part Matthew's Jewish roots where God as heavenly father featured prominently in rabbinic prayer language. It is significant that Jesus speaks of God as father always in the presence of the disciples and never uses the word 'father' to describe God in his dealings with those who oppose him. 'Heavenly Father' evokes a certain secrecy and intimacy of relationship within

the believing community. 'Only the company of disciples, those in communion with Jesus, may witness Jesus' relationship with the father. Matthew's Jesus at no time exposes his or his community's special relationship with God-as-father to the gaze of enemies' (Sheffield 2001 p. 58).

As the gospel unfolds, it will be important to notice the way Matthew's emphasis on God as father interrelates with and influences his view of earthly fatherhood in this heavily patriarchal society. The effect is to weaken the significance of earthly fatherhood and to give much more importance to the new faith community that Jesus creates as a community of mutual nurture and support. As Sheffield says, Matthew's use of *pater* is carefully shaped both to emphasise the fatherhood of God and to displace the earthly father in favour of the father in heaven. 'This displacement of the human father in favour of God-as-father serves in turn to relativise patriarchy with respect to the relations of disciples to one another as well as to justify the replacement of the family of origin with a new kinship group' (Sheffield 2001 p. 52). The new kinship group is the community of those who would be disciples. Jesus says: 'Look! Here are my mother and my brothers! Whoever does what my Father in heaven wants him to do is my brother, my sister, and my mother' (12:49–50).

Chapter 8

TRUE TREASURE

Matthew 6:19–34
Riches in Heaven
(*Luke 12:33–4*)

'Do not store up riches for yourselves here on earth, where moths and rust destroy, and robbers break in and steal. Instead, store up riches for yourselves in heaven, where moths and rust cannot destroy, and robbers cannot break in and steal. For your heart will always be where your riches are.'

The Light of the Body
(*Luke 11:34–6*)

'The eyes are like a lamp for the body. If your eyes are sound, your whole body will be full of light; but if your eyes are no good, your body will be in darkness. So if the light in you is darkness, how terribly dark it will be!'

God and Possessions
(*Luke 16:13, 12:22–31*)

'No one can be a slave of two masters; he will hate one and love the other; he will be loyal to one and despise the other. You cannot serve both God and money.

'This is why I tell you not to be worried about the food and drink you need in order to stay alive, or about clothes for your body. After all, isn't life worth more than food? And isn't the body worth more than clothes? Look at the birds: they do not sow seeds, gather a harvest and put it in barns; yet your Father in heaven takes care of them! Aren't you worth much more than birds? Can any of you live a bit longer by worrying about it?

'And why worry about clothes? Look how the wild flowers grow: they do not work or make clothes for themselves. But I tell you that not even King Solomon with all his wealth had clothes as beautiful as one of these flowers. It is God who clothes the wild grass – grass that is here today and gone tomorrow, burnt up in the oven. Won't he be all the more sure to clothe you? How little faith you have!

'So do not start worrying: "Where will my food come from? or my drink? or my clothes?" (These are the things the pagans are always concerned about.) Your Father in heaven knows that you need all these things. Instead, be concerned above everything else with the Kingdom of God and with what he requires of you, and he will provide you with all these other things. So do not worry about tomorrow; it will have enough worries of its own. There is no need to add to the troubles each day brings.'

Vision and values

A sadly contemporary story comes from a country in West Africa which has suffered that most terrible of wars, a civil war. As in too many wars in poor countries these days, much of the fighting was carried out by young soldiers little more than boys, recruited or coerced from their rural communities and very largely unaware of the wider world beyond them. This is a reported conversation between one of these youths and his officer. Youth: 'What is this war about? What are we fighting for?' Officer: 'We're fighting for control of the diamond fields. They bring great wealth.' Youth: 'How do they do that? What are diamonds for? What do people do with diamonds?' Officer: 'Well in other countries, people wear them as ornaments, on rings, bracelets, jewellery of different kinds.' Youth: 'Are you telling me that we're fighting and killing one another for *that*?' In this very familiar section of the Sermon, Jesus focuses the attention of his hearers on what we value, fear and long for. He asks some pointed questions about our attitudes to wealth and security – recurring themes in the gospel. He makes plain and explicit the dangers of worldly wealth distorting our vision and dividing our loyalties. In our world of multiple insurance policies and proliferating security measures, his words have a real contemporary edge to them. His challenge here to all would-be disciples and to us is very real. 'No one can serve two masters ... You cannot serve God and wealth' (6:24 NRSV).

The words of the Sermon up to this point have been sketching in for us a picture of the new alternative community which is being created by those who take Jesus' teaching to heart. It is a community of the poor, not great in the eyes of the prevailing dominant systems but with its own powerful commitments to the Kingdom ways of integrity and justice. These commitments are maintained by a new orientation of heart and eye (6:21–3). From the heart springs attachment to the true treasure which Jesus himself unfolds in his own person. The eye gives singleness of vision by its concentration on the things of light and not darkness.

Don't worry

Stress, anxiety and worry form a trinity of words very familiar in today's culture. Pills, potions and techniques to help relaxation or gain peace of mind flood the marketplace. The irony is that our anxiety epidemic has broken out in a society whose members in general have more financial security, have better health and live longer lives than those of any previous generation. It seems to be true that having more is far from a recipe to cure our anxieties. The days when folk left their house doors open were days when most people had little in the way of material goods; it's the upwardly mobile today who have security gates on their houses and cars built like tanks. When Jesus uttered his famous words about not worrying, he was speaking to poor people who had very little and whose real anxiety could well have been about where their next meal was coming from. Worry is not confined to either rich or poor; it is universal, though for different reasons.

Jesus here invites the disciple to refocus vision with the help of the birds and the wild flowers (6:28–30). This is neither a philosophy of life nor a moral law; it is a gospel invitation, an invitation into the glorious freedom of the children of God, who know that they have a

Father in heaven who promises to provide. Once again, Bonhoeffer says it well:

> It is not more care that frees the disciples from care, but their faith in Jesus Christ. Only they know that we cannot be anxious … It is senseless to pretend that we can make provision because we cannot alter the circumstances of this world … But the Christian knows that he not only cannot and dare not be anxious, but that there is no need for him or her to be so. Neither anxiety nor work can secure his daily bread, for bread is the gift of the Father. (Bonhoeffer 1959 p. 159)

Look at the birds, consider the lilies. The birds soar and sing. The lilies in their beauty surpass the glories of Solomon. And if the glories of Solomon represent the height of human wealth, beauty and achievement, Solomon also stands for the hollowness of that achievement, for Solomon's glory was built 'on acquiring many wives, horses and great wealth by military conscription, forced labour, requisitioned property, heavy taxation, and slavery' (Carter 2000 p. 178). Solomon is a doer and a grabber, the epitome of human drivenness. The birds and the lilies neither do nor grasp, they simply are, and are provided for. They live, again in Bonhoeffer's words, out of 'a daily unquestioning of the Creator's gifts. Birds and lilies then are given as examples for the followers of Christ. In our godless self-sufficiency, we imagine there is a relation of cause and effect between work and sustenance, but Jesus explodes that illusion' (Bonhoeffer 1959 p. 159).

Birdwatching

Jesus' invitation to 'look to the birds' and 'consider the lilies' has attracted a huge response from poets, artists and people of prayer through the centuries. It will be good for us to pause for a moment to consider and contemplate the birds of the air. Michael Mayne's book of meditations, *Learning to Dance*, offers a rich seam of material for reflection and contemplation drawn from the worlds of both the arts and contemporary science. This next section is heavily indebted to his profound meditations on the rhythms of the natural world, our own lives and the Christian year. Here he invites us to 'look to the birds' and see behind the wonder of their reality the mystery of God who creates and provides. He begins with R. S. Thomas' poem 'Blackbird':

> Its eye a dark pool
> in which Sirius glitters
> and never goes out.
> Its melody husky
> as though with suppressed tears.
> Its bill is the gold
> one quarries for amid
> evening shadows. Do not despair
> at the stars' distance. Listening
> to blackbird music is
> to bridge in a moment chasms
> of space-time, is to know
> that beyond the silence
> which terrified Pascal
> there is a presence whose language
> is not our language, but who has chosen
> with peculiar clarity the feathered
> creatures to convey the austerity
> of his thought in song.

(Thomas (2000), quoted in Mayne 2001 pp. 56–7)

It is not only the poet who invites us to wait and wonder; the scientist also bids us contemplate a world which is simply amazing in its ordered complexity. Michael Mayne tells the mind-boggling story of the migrating red knots, birds which have a yearly migrating pattern that takes them from the southern tip of South America to the frozen islands of northern Canada and back again.

Each year they know exactly where to find food, leaving the sunny beaches of the south and timing their flight north just as horseshoe crabs are laying millions of eggs. Over a few weeks a single bird will eat over 100,000 such eggs; then, plump and re-energised, they continue the non-stop flight north. Here they meet and breed. By mid-July, the female adults head south again, followed a month later by the adult males. But only at the very end of August do the young red knots start the 9000-mile journey south, and without adult guides find their way along the old migration route, instinctively knowing at what points to

93

stop for the best feeding grounds, before rejoining their parents for the summer.

'"There is nothing", wrote John Donne in one of his sermons, "that God hath established in a constant course of nature, and which therefore is done every day, but would seem a miracle, and exercise our admiration, if it were done but once" (Sermon, Easter Day 1627)' (Mayne 2001 p. 101). Donne's wise words remind me of the poem 'We Alone', by Alice Walker, which could also serve as a commentary on Jesus' teaching here:

> We alone can devalue gold
> by not caring
> if it falls or rises
> in the market place.
> Wherever there is gold,
> there is a chain, you know,
> and if your chain is gold
> so much the worse
> for you.
>
> Feathers, shells
> and sea-shaped stones
> are all as rare.
> This could be our revolution;
> To love what is plentiful
> as much as
> what's scarce.
>
> (in Walker 1984)

Tomorrow

This whole passage about seeing and seeking the Kingdom with a singleness of vision and a single-minded commitment leading us into a world of wonder and freedom ends with some down-to-earth words from Jesus: 'Don't worry about tomorrow until tomorrow comes. Today's troubles are enough' (6:34). While Jesus bids us look, wonder and forget our cares in the contemplation of the birds and the flowers, in the words of the popular song he 'doesn't promise us a rose garden' in our daily lives in the world. Life in the world is tough, and particularly tough for the disciple who would be faithful. But there is always a vision to pursue and a promise to be realised – so, for the Kingdom, keep striving (6:33).

Study

By yourself

Here is another invitation into an exercise in contemplation, from one of our world's wise men, the Buddhist monk, Thich Nhat Hanh. This time, all you need is a blank white pristine piece of paper. Have a good look at it. Now read on.

If you are a poet, you see clearly that there is a cloud floating in this sheet of paper. Without a cloud, there will be no rain; without rain, the trees cannot grow; and without trees, we cannot make paper. The cloud is essential for the paper to exist. If the cloud is not there, the sheet of paper cannot be here either. So we can say that the cloud and the paper inter-are. 'Interbeing' is a word that is not in the dictionary yet, but if we combine the prefix 'inter-' with the verb 'to be', we have a new verb, inter-be. Without a cloud, we cannot have paper, so we can say that the cloud and the sheet of paper 'inter-are'.

If we look into this sheet of paper even more deeply, we can see the sunshine in it. If the sunshine is not there, the forest cannot grow. In fact, nothing can grow. Even we cannot grow without the sunshine. And so, we know that the sunshine is also in this sheet of paper. The paper and the sunshine inter-are. And if we continue to look, we can see the logger who cut the tree and brought it to the mill to be transformed into paper. And we can see the wheat. We know the logger cannot exist without his daily bread, and therefore the wheat that became his bread is also in this sheet of paper. And the logger's father and mother are in it too. When we look in this way, we see that without all of these things, this sheet of paper cannot exist.

Looking even more deeply, we can see that we are in it too. This is not difficult to see, because when we look at a sheet of paper, the sheet of paper is part of our perception. Your mind is here, and mine also. So we can say that everything is in here with this sheet of paper. You cannot point out one thing that is not here – time, space, the earth, the rain, the minerals in the soil, the sunshine, the cloud, the river, the heat. Everything co-exists with this sheet of paper. That is why I think the word inter-be should be in the dictionary. 'To be' is to inter-be.

95

You cannot just *be* by yourself alone. You have to inter-be with every other thing. This sheet of paper is because everything else is. (Nhat Hanh 1988 pp. 3–5)

For group work

Share together your thoughts from considering the birds, the lilies and the piece of white paper.

Chapter 9

OPEN TO OTHERS, OPEN TO GOD

Matthew 7:1–12

Judging Others

(*Luke 6:37–8, 41–2*)

'Do not judge others, so that God will not judge you, for God will judge you in the same way as you judge others, and he will apply to you the same rules you apply to others. Why, then, do you look at the speck in your brother's eye, and pay no attention to the log in your own eye? How dare you say to your brother, "Please, let me take that speck out of your eye," when you have a log in your own eye? You hypocrite! First take the log out of your own eye, and then you will be able to see clearly to take the speck out of your brother's eye.

'Do not give what is holy to dogs – they will only turn and attack you. Do not throw your pearls in front of pigs – they will only trample them underfoot.'

Ask, Seek, Knock

(*Luke 11:9–13*)

'Ask, and you will receive; seek, and you will find; knock, and the door will be opened to you. For everyone who asks will receive, and anyone who seeks will find, and the door will be opened to those who knock. Would any of you who are fathers give your son a stone when he asks for bread? Or would you give him a snake when he asks for a fish? Bad as you are, you know how to give good things to your children. How much more, then, will your Father in heaven give good things to those who ask him!

'Do for others what you want them to do for you: this is the meaning of the Law of Moses and of the teachings of the prophets.'

Measure for measure

'Don't judge, so that you may not be judged' is the way this section of the Sermon begins. Jesus' words here echo what we have already heard him say about forgiveness: 'forgive that you may be forgiven' (6:14) and anticipate the rule he will offer a few verses later: 'do to others as you would have them do to you' (7:12). One of the strands which runs through Matthew's gospel is a dynamic of reciprocity, connected both with Matthew's emphases on integrity, justice and right relations, and also with the view that, in dealings with others, disciples are called to copy or mirror the way in which God deals with us. In this passage, there is also a strong sense of humility, reticence almost, which stretches back to the beatitudes at the beginning of the Sermon.

When we make judgements on others, we have to recognise the persistent human tendency to judge others from the outside and ourselves from the inside. We are good at recognising our own complexity and making due allowances, and not so good at acknowledging the burdens which others are carrying. Jesus' words here take us back to his warnings in 5:22 not to bad-mouth, write off or condemn our brothers and sisters. Our relations with others are to be governed by a humble charity, and, in the matter of judging, we are not to take to ourselves powers which properly belong to God alone.

Of specks and planks

To ram the point home, Jesus offers the robust and ridiculous metaphor of comparing specks of dust and planks of wood in our neighbour's and our own eyes. The comparison is so gross, I'm sure we're meant to laugh ... and take the message to heart. The seriousness of Jesus' point is underlined when he brands our tendencies to be hard on our neighbour and soft on ourselves as the action of the hypocrite ... that word again. There's a reminder here of that favourite theme for talks with children that, when we point the finger at someone else, there are three fingers pointing back at ourselves! This section ends with another vivid double image about not giving what is holy to dogs or pearls to swine. Its meaning is somewhat obscure. 'Dogs' was a common derogatory Jewish reference to Gentiles, and swine of course were unclean animals. Schweizer suggests that this saying originated among the Jewish Christian community in its suspicions about the Gentile mission, although that is not how Matthew uses it here. Perhaps Matthew thought that Jesus' liberating words about not judging were fine as a principle but rather too broad when it came to dealing with seriously disruptive members in his own community. He therefore tacked on this saying which could be interpreted as saying there can be cases when someone is so unwilling to listen that it's pointless wasting your breath on them; they have to be treated simply as an outsider. But that's a case of last resort; remember the specks and planks!

Ask, seek, knock

Jesus turns once more to the practice of prayer. There's a connecting thread with what's gone before. The connection is the encouraging of disciples to trust in God's goodness, to know the heavenly Father who deals in good gifts for his children. The rhythm of asking, seeking, knocking is relevant not only to perseverance in prayer but also as the basic thrust of the disciple's faithful living before God in the day-to-day world. Once again, Jesus is not offering rules for the life of prayer; what Schweizer calls 'instructions for an unfailing magic ritual' (1975 p. 173). Jesus is offering a warm and enthusiastic invitation into the mystery of the life of prayer. Archbishop William Temple said: 'When I pray, coincidences happen. When I stop praying, they stop happening.' There is something deep within the life of prayer which simply feeds us, body, mind and soul. So, we are encouraged to keep asking, for ordinary things, like health and food and care for our close ones, and to ask for extraordinary things, like peace between the nations. We dare to keep asking, seeking ... and knocking, trusting in the Father's goodness. This is our prayer:

It is so simple, Lord,
yet I spend so much of my life
avoiding it.

I fret and worry,
        rather than ask;
I expect things to fall in my lap,
        rather than seek;
I stand with my hands behind my back,
        rigidly independent,
        rather than knock on heaven's door.

Teach me, Lord, to trust, to move,
        to lose my stubborn independence,
so that I can ask, seek, and knock,
as you intended.

(*Pray Now 1995–6*, p. 60)

Once again, Jesus reinforces his message with the use of a robust illustration. He invites us to compare the way we, fallible and sometimes malicious as we are, treat our own children, wanting to do the right thing by them, not sell them short, with the way God, who is infinitely better and wiser than we are, deals with us. 'Does God our Father not desire the best for all his children?' Jesus asks rhetorically. Perhaps today there is a question about what is best for our children. Here, Jesus speaks about faithfully giving our children their basic needs, like the right food on the table. Today, the danger is not that we give our children less than they need, but the wrong kind of more, as this prayer invites us to ponder.

I would like to think
that I would be the kind of parent
who gave good gifts,
        thoughtful gifts,
        appropriate gifts.

I would like to think
that I would never abuse a child's trust.

100

But spoil a child?
Give him a banquet
    when all he needs is a sandwich;
give her a toy shop
    when all she needs is a doll ...?
May I who never intend
to abuse a child's trust
never be guilty
of spoiling a child's appetite.

With deep gratitude,
let me remember with you, Lord,
those who, in my childhood,
gave me the best gifts ...
those who let me appreciate honesty,
    those who let me feel belonging,
    those who identified my hidden talents,
    those who rubbed my knees when I fell
        and dried my tears when I cried;
    those who made me want to sing 'Jesus loves me'
because those words so clearly
rang true for them.

(Pray Now 1995–6, p. 62)

Do to others ...

The section ends with Jesus' enunciation of what is often called 'The Golden Rule'. This 'rule' in a variety of forms and emphases appears in many societies. It takes two basic forms, the negative – 'Don't do to others what you would not have them do to you' – and the positive – 'Do to others as you would have them do to you'. It is said that the negative form can be reduced to a counsel of mere prudence, hopefully issuing in a quiet life. It's the positive form Jesus offers here. It is the best of what we wish for ourselves which we are to offer in our relations with others. Once again, it is easier said than done; how true that is of so much of the discipleship way.

We can see these words of the golden rule as a summary of all Jesus has said throughout the Sermon. Jesus' final words, 'for this is the law and the prophets', can point to such an interpretation. Carter offers this helpful conclusion:

> *this* refers to his teaching of a way of life in God's empire marked by indiscriminate love for all (cf. 5:43–8, 22:34–40) which is faithful to the scriptures. Disciples live this life, but they have been warned in the sermon (5:10–12, 38–48) that the imperial and synagogal powers will not always welcome their alternative structures and practices ... In these difficult circumstances, they must remain focused on God's empire, strengthened not only by the words of Jesus and the disciplines of prayer and fasting (6:1–18), but also one another. (2000 p. 185)

Study

By yourself

How can I offer the best of what I wish for myself in my relationships with others?

For group work

This passage speaks of generosity. We are encouraged to be generous in our judgements of others, and more generally generous in our relations with others. By our practice of generosity, we show we are the children of a generous God.

How would you speak of God's generosity to you?

How can we better practise generosity in our judgements?

How can we better practise generosity in our personal relationships?

Chapter 10

GOING THE DISTANCE

Matthew 7:13–29
The Narrow Gate
(*Luke 13:24*)

'Go in through the narrow gate, because the gate to hell is wide and the road that leads to it is easy, and there are many who travel it. But the gate to life is narrow and the way that leads to it is hard, and there are few people who find it.'

A Tree and its Fruit
(*Luke 6:43–4*)

'Be on your guard against false prophets; they come to you looking like sheep on the outside, but on the inside they are really like wild wolves. You will know them by what they do. Thorn bushes do not bear grapes, and briars do not bear figs. A healthy tree bears good fruit, but a poor tree bears bad fruit. A healthy tree cannot bear bad fruit, and a poor tree cannot bear good fruit. And any tree that does not bear good fruit is cut down and thrown in the fire. So, then, you will know the false prophets by what they do.'

I Never Knew You
(*Luke 13:25–7*)

'Not everyone who calls me "Lord, Lord" will enter the Kingdom of heaven, but only those who do what my Father in heaven wants them to do. When Judgement Day comes, many will say to me, "Lord, Lord! In your name we spoke God's message, by your name we drove out many demons and performed many miracles!" Then I will say to them, "I never knew you. Get away from me, you wicked people!"'

The Two House Builders

(Luke 6:47–9)

'So then, anyone who hears these words of mine and obeys them is like a wise man who built his house on rock. The rain poured down, the rivers overflowed, and the wind blew hard against that house. But it did not fall, because it was built on rock.

'But anyone who hears these words of mine and does not obey them is like a foolish man who built his house on sand. The rain poured down, the rivers overflowed, the wind blew hard against that house, and it fell. And what a terrible fall that was!'

The Authority of Jesus

When Jesus finished saying these things, the crowd was amazed at the way he taught. He wasn't like the teachers of the Law; instead, he taught with authority.

The narrow way

We come to the end of the Sermon, which Matthew concludes with two sayings he shares with Luke's Sermon on the Plain (Luke 6) and two other shared sayings from Luke 13:24–7. Together they serve to re-emphasise Jesus' strong words on motivation, commitment and action while warning the disciples of the tricky task of discerning the true from the false in their community and its leaders. Jesus begins by telling his hearers that entry into the Kingdom is by way of the narrow gate. The image is of a walled city, and probably Jerusalem is the city in mind. Jerusalem, at the heart of its people's faith, had many gates. Some were wide, and some were so narrow that they could only be entered singly, one person at a time. Entry by the wide gate, in contrast, was a bit like being carried along by a departing football crowd. The picture is clear enough and brings to mind a warning of Kierkegaard's. He often spoke of the crowd as 'untruth'. In the Denmark of his time, his concern was about those who were swept into church by the prevailing climate of the time, where churchgoing was 'the done thing' to do and attendance was largely perfunctory and unreflective. Today, in face of the power of our modern media, I suspect his warning would be about the danger of letting our views and judgements be formed by the popular currents of so-called 'public opinion'.

At the very least, Jesus here invites us to take responsibility for ourselves, to be our own person, in Scots 'oor ain man', and resist the temptation to be carried along by the crowd and manipulated by the gurus of the day. Of course, there's more. Jesus is also telling disciples, then and now, at the beginning of his ministry, that the discipleship way is a hard way, a way 'costing not less than everything'. It is the cross way, of self-forgetfulness and self-sacrifice. To enter through the narrow gate needs discipline and a discarding of encumbering baggage.

Discernment

There follows a warning about the dangers of false prophets – teachers who sow dissension in the faith community and have the potential to lead its members astray. Warnings about false prophets – those who claim to speak the Word of God but whose words are facile and bogus – are common in the Old Testament. Mention of them here indicates that dissension and division were problems within Matthew's young Christian community. Threats to its life of faith do not only come from without; they are present within. The problem, then and now, is how to discern the true from the false; wolves come in sheep's clothing. The acid test suggested is that we can judge people's character by the fruits of their living; with the aid of a couple of fruity metaphors, the gospel says that thorn bushes never bear grapes and a tree with poor roots never brings a bumper crop of fruit. Here, once again, is Matthew's stress on the consistency of word and action. There is a word of warning. 'It is important to note, especially in the light of the church's frequent use and oppressive misuse of this text, that the emphasis falls on discerning false prophets, not on condemning them (so 7:1–6). The gospel will subsequently provide a rehabilitation process for repentant members (18:15–17)' (Carter 2000 p. 190).

105

The theme of a consistency between word and action continues. 'Not everyone who calls me "Lord, Lord" will enter the Kingdom of heaven, but only those who do what my Father in heaven wants them to do.' Matthew here amplifies Jesus' terse question to his disciples in Luke's gospel: 'Why do you call me "Lord, Lord" and don't do what I tell you?' (Luke 6:46). 'Lord' is a title early attached to Jesus by the young church; with the reference to Judgement Day in 7:22, it here describes the risen and exalted Lord, sitting at the right hand of the Father. This is further emphasised by Jesus' speaking of 'my Father in heaven' in 7:21, the first occasion in the gospel when Jesus has spoken of God as 'my Father'.

Jesus here rejects not only those who claim to be his disciples through their words, 'Lord, Lord', but fail him in their actions; he also dismisses some whose actions – claiming to have performed exorcisms and miracles in his name (7:22) – appear thoroughly laudable. They too are set aside; more than the occasional miracle is required to prove allegiance to Jesus' Kingdom way. The demand once more is for a thorough-going consistency, an integrity of purpose. Paul's words in 1 Corinthians 13 come to mind: 'Though I speak with the tongues of men and of angels, and have not charity, I am nothing'. Jesus says of those whom he rejects: 'I never knew you' (7:23). 'Knowing' carries the weight of the Hebrew meaning of 'know' signifying a profound and comprehensive relationship.

A sure foundation

'The wise man built his house upon a rock and the rain came tumbling down.' Many of us will have early memories of this story, so easily dramatised for young children. This is much more than a children's story, forming as it does the final word of the Sermon. It sends the disciple out and on with a pointed reminder of two key activities on the Kingdom way with Jesus: 'Listen' and 'act'. The demand to 'listen to, concentrate on, attend to, take to heart' the words of Jesus is strong throughout the gospel, but listening by itself is never enough. We hear to be enabled to do. The tree is recognised by its fruits. 'Doing the Word' is just as vital as 'hearing' it. We know today the importance of learning by doing, of how strongly 'doing' reinforces the learning process. Jesus knew that a long time ago. To 'do' the Word has two consequences; it both reinforces the disciple's faith and it makes the gospel known to those around. Without hearing *and* doing, faith sits on sand.

The house of faith ... Perhaps when Matthew recorded these words he had in mind the old great house of faith, the Jerusalem Temple, recently fallen at the hands of Imperial Rome. Now there is a new house of faith, a new temple, the place where God lives. The new temple is built, not of stone and mortar, but out of the living material of the lives of faithful people who hear and do the Word. Against a house built on such foundations, the ill climate of the times, however strong and violent, will not prevail.

Moving on

'Now when Jesus had finished saying these things ...' (7:28). These words are used by Matthew at the conclusion of each of the five blocks of Jesus' teaching. They indicate to us that the Sermon is over and it's time to move on. Before we move, we pause to share in the astonishment of the crowd before the wonder of this teaching, old and new, and before the winsome authority of the teacher, who speaks with an authenticity and integrity which communicates a fresh power, and not as the scribes.

Study

By yourself

Reflect on the Sermon on the Mount as a whole. What parts do you particularly want to carry with you? With what parts do you continue to struggle?

For group work

Share your personal reflections with the group, using the two questions above.

Pause: Miracles and meaning

Matthew chapters 8 and 9 are dominated by a series of incidents which show Jesus' healing power. After the demonstration of the power of Jesus' words in the Sermon on the Mount, these next two chapters show the power of his actions to release people from their illness and bondage. In our reading of the gospels, however, there are few places where there is a greater gulf between our twenty-first-century world view and that of the first century than in our understanding of the miraculous. What would largely be taken for granted by the gospel's original readers as the accepted powers and potencies of a God-endowed healer have become seriously problematic for those living since the time of the Enlightenment and the rise of modern historical criticism. Our contemporary attitudes to the miracles range along a line from, at the one extreme, a dogged literalism – 'it must be true if the Bible says it' – to, at the other, a questioning scepticism – 'it may have happened but we can find a "natural" explanation'. Both are likely to miss the point. 'Why?' is a much more fruitful question than 'How?'

The evangelists are as one in their witness to Jesus as a healer, and all make the point that the healings they select and highlight as individual incidents are the merest fraction of the sum of Jesus' healing activity. The obvious question to ask is: why do they select these incidents from among the many? One obvious answer is simply that they are representative of the whole of Jesus' healing ministry; they are good examples. Did the evangelists have other criteria in mind? A very helpful introduction to the question 'Why?' is to be found in Jeffrey John's book, *The Meaning of the Miracles*. A brief summary could say that, while each gospel writer has his own emphasis, taken as a whole they attempt to speak not only to the religious context of their day but also to the wider social, political and cultural context. In the total context, they would emphasise Jesus as a healer sent from God, and also, particularly in the exorcism stories, Jesus as one who did battle in God's name with demonic powers, located both in evil spirits and in the forces of the religious elite of Israel and the political might of the Roman Empire.

In general, the miracle stories have considerable symbolic significance. Underneath the stories themselves, there is a wealth of allusion and symbolism. Often they refer backwards to incidents and values which come from the Old Testament, often they point forwards to the inbreaking of the Kingdom of Heaven. They point upwards to Jesus' divine authority; they also point downwards, the healing miracles can be seen as a litany of transformation and inclusion. So many of those whom Jesus heals belong to the poor and powerless, the disregarded and the marginalised in his society.

> The healing miracles seem to have been deliberately selected by the evangelists to show Jesus healing at least one of every category of persons who, according to the purity laws of Jesus' society, were specifically excluded and labelled unclean, or who were set at varying degrees of distance from worship in the inner temple. The list of those who suffered some degree of taboo and exclusion contains menstruating women, lepers, Samaritans, Gentiles, tax collectors, homosexuals, prostitutes, adulteresses, women in general, children, people with withered limbs, the deaf, the dumb, the blind, the lame and the dead. At least one representative from each of these categories is a subject of Jesus' healing in the miracle stories. (The inclusion of someone in the homosexual category is debatable, but we shall see that there is good reason to believe that the story of the centurion and his servant could be seen in this light.) (Jeffrey 2001 p. 10)

Chapter 11

HEALING AND PEACE

Matthew 8
Jesus Heals a Man
(*Mark 1:40–5, Luke 5:12–16*)

When Jesus came down from the hill, large crowds followed him. Then a man suffering from a dreaded skin disease came to him, knelt down before him, and said, 'Sir, if you want to, you can make me clean'.

Jesus stretched out his hand and touched him. 'I do want to', he answered. 'Be clean!' At once the man was healed of his disease. Then Jesus said to him, 'Listen! Don't tell anyone, but go straight to the priest and let him examine you; then in order to prove to everyone that you are cured, offer the sacrifice that Moses ordered.'

Jesus Heals a Roman Officer's Servant

(*Luke 7:1–10*)

When Jesus entered Capernaum, a Roman officer met him and begged for help: 'Sir, my servant is sick in bed at home, unable to move and suffering terribly'.

'I will go and make him well', Jesus said.

'Oh no, sir', answered the officer. 'I do not deserve to have you come into my house. Just give the order, and my servant will get well. I, too, am a man under the authority of superior officers, and I have soldiers under me. I order this one, "Go!" and he goes; and I order that one, "Come!" and he comes; and I order my slave, "Do this!" and he does it.'

When Jesus heard this, he was surprised and said to the people following him, 'I tell you, I have never found anyone in Israel with faith like this. I assure you that many will come from the east and the west and sit down with Abraham, Isaac, and Jacob at the feast in the Kingdom of heaven. But those who should be in the Kingdom will be thrown out into the darkness, where they will cry and grind their teeth.' Then Jesus said to the officer, 'Go home, and what you believe will be done for you'.

And the officer's servant was healed that very moment.

Jesus Heals Many People

(Mark 1:29–34, Luke 4:38–41)

Jesus went to Peter's home, and there he saw Peter's mother-in-law sick in bed with a fever. He touched her hand; the fever left her, and she got up and began to wait on him.

When evening came, people brought to Jesus many who had demons in them. Jesus drove out the evil spirits with a word and healed all who were sick. He did this to make what the prophet Isaiah had said come true, 'He himself took our sickness and carried away all our diseases'.

The Would-be Followers of Jesus

(Luke 9:57–62)

When Jesus noticed the crowd round him, he ordered his disciples to go to the other side of the lake. A teacher of the Law came to him, 'Teacher', he said, 'I am ready to go with you wherever you go'.

Jesus answered him, 'Foxes have holes, and birds have nests, but the Son of Man has nowhere to lie down and rest'.

Another man, who was a disciple, said, 'Sir, first let me go back and bury my father'.

'Follow me', Jesus answered, 'and let the dead bury their own dead.'

Jesus Calms a Storm

(Mark 4:35–41, Luke 8:22–5)

Jesus got into a boat, and his disciples went with him. Suddenly a fierce storm hit the lake, and the boat was in danger of sinking. But Jesus was asleep. The disciples went to him and woke him up. 'Save us, Lord!' they said, 'We are about to die!'

'Why are you so frightened?' Jesus answered. 'How little faith you have!' Then he got up and ordered the winds and waves to stop, and there was a great calm.

Everyone was amazed. 'What kind of man is this?' they said. 'Even the winds and the waves obey him!'

Jesus Heals Two Men with Demons

(Mark 5:1–20, Luke 8:26–39)

When Jesus came to the territory of Gadara on the other side of the lake, he was met by two men who came out of the burial caves there. These men had demons in them and were so fierce that no one dared to travel on that road. At once they screamed, 'What do you want with us, you Son of God? Have you come to punish us before the right time?'

Not far away there was a large herd of pigs feeding. So the demons begged Jesus, 'If you are going to drive us out, send us into that herd of pigs'.

'Go', Jesus told them; so they left and went off into the pigs. The whole herd rushed down the side of the cliff into the lake and was drowned.

The men who had been taking care of the pigs ran away and went into the town, where they told the whole story and what had happened to the men with the demons. So everyone from the town went out to meet Jesus; and when they saw him, they begged him to leave their territory.

From words to action

It's time to get on the move again. After the pause on the hillside to take time to hear, ponder, reflect upon the startling and stimulating words of the Sermon on the Mount, Jesus and his disciples move on. Matthew 8 is a chapter packed full of action, incident and movement. Already we have noticed Matthew's stress on the integrity of Jesus. He marries word and action. The incidents which follow put flesh and blood on Jesus' words in the Sermon; they stand as examples of the coming of the King and the breaking in of the new Kingdom and also of the way of discipleship and obedience which the King and the Kingdom summon forth and enable.

In this section comprising chapters 8 and 9, Matthew uses many of the stories found in Mark (and Luke), though he changes their sequence, subtly alters them and substantially shortens the descriptions of the healing miracles. Matthew is not particularly interested in the details of Jesus' healings, he is more concerned with them as demonstrations of Jesus' power and authority. At the outset of the chapter, the picture of the leper kneeling at Jesus' feet emphasises such divine authority.

Two stories of healing of outsiders

The chapter begins with two healing stories, of a leper (8:1–4) and the centurion's servant (8:5–13). While there are considerable contrasts between them, there is also a powerful link in that both describe the healing of those considered outsiders. Both would convey a strong sense of shock to the gospel's original hearers. Here, 'leper' is probably a generic term describing those suffering from a variety of skin diseases. In the society of Jesus' time, lepers were the great 'untouchables'. Because of leprosy's contagious nature, lepers were feared and shunned. There were rules for their segregation and rituals to be undergone before those who could give evidence of cure were accepted again into mainstream society. Lepers suffered not only from physical disability but also from social exclusion.

In the story of the healing of the leper, which is told briefly and baldly, it is Jesus reaching out to touch the man which would shock. To touch the afflicted was both risky and forbidden, but Jesus ignores the fear and taboo of society and religion to bring this man to health. After the healing is effected, Jesus is carefully correct in directing the healed man to observe the proper regulations of his faith so that he may become once more a fully participating member of his community. Although Matthew has already made mention of Jesus' healing ministry (4:23–5), the healing of the leper is the first description of the specific healing of a single person. The conversation between Jesus and the leper focuses on the issue of 'clean' versus 'unclean'. Suffering from leprosy carried the weight of ritual in addition to physical impurity. Does placing the story of the leper's healing in first place suggest symbolically that Jesus has come not just to heal but to cleanse the community of Israel?

Jesus and his disciples now enter Capernaum, the town on Lake Galilee at the centre of the Galilean ministry (4:12). He is met by a centurion of the Roman army. As a representative of Roman power, he is a figure both powerful and suspect. Unlike the version of this story in Luke 7:1–10, where it is a group of Jewish elders who come to Jesus and speak on the centurion's behalf, Matthew gives the picture of a direct conversation between the centurion and Jesus. The centurion, the man of obvious authority, approaches Jesus respectfully with his request for his servant's healing. He calls him 'Lord', the title usually given to Jesus by his disciples. He also acknowledges that Jesus, as a Jew, would have a scruple about entering the house of a Gentile. To Jesus' surprise, as much as ours, the centurion further acknowledges Jesus' powers by his statement that there is no need for Jesus to come to his house and make contact with his sick servant in person: 'Just give the order, and my servant will get well' (8:8).

The servant/slave is healed – a sign of the compassionate concern of both the centurion and Jesus? – and Jesus rejoices in the faith of this man from beyond the community of Israel's faith. He goes on to contrast the faith of this outsider with the lack of openness within his own people to what God is doing among them. A closed, inward and backward-looking faith is one of the greatest obstacles to the gospel; those who persist in such a view shut themselves out from the glad light of the wedding feast of the Kingdom (see Isaiah 25:6–9). They will be found skulking and sulking in the darkness of regret and remorse (8:12).

It is worth considering more closely the nature of the relationship between the centurion and his servant/slave, as one possible aspect of it relates to a contemporary and controversial issue in church and society. The concern of the centurion for his servant is obvious and commendable; certainly it goes beyond the normal expectations of the master/slave relationship. On the other hand, the general relationship between the local population and members of the Roman army was pretty poisonous. Jesus' home community largely regarded these powerful instruments of Rome with a mixture of fear and contempt. The word used to describe the centurion's servant is the Greek word, 'pais', which literally means 'boy'. Many Jews held suspicions about the nature of the relationship between some members of the Roman soldiery and their servants/slaves/boys. The local community may well have suspected that the centurion and his servant had homoerotic sex with one another. Most Gentile (and some Jewish) masters had sex with their slaves of either sex as a matter of routine. It is possible that the relationship between the centurion and his 'servant' was of this nature. It is likely that the surrounding crowd would hold such suspicions. It may well be that the original readers of the gospel would be shocked by this possibility. What is transparently clear is that Jesus both refuses to pry into the nature of the centurion's relationship with the servant and ignores the force of the suspicions of the crowd. He simply restores the servant to health. He refuses to hate; he does not condemn (Jeffrey 2001 pp. 155–64).

For us, the other tantalising ambiguity in this healing story is that while the servant/slave is restored to rude physical health, he still remains in the reduced condition of a slave. In terms of society, he is not 'free' from the structural power of slavery to diminish and demean, though of course it may well be that the attitude and relationship of his master tempered with humanity this inhumane system.

Home ...

Next, we find Jesus at home, not in his own home but in the home of the one who was to be his chief disciple, Peter. Peter's mother-in-law is not well; she has a fever. At the touch of Jesus, the fever leaves her, and she is able to take up again her tasks and serve the company in her house. What does that suggest to us? Very often, people's first encounter with Jesus is with one who brings healing, peace, release. Meeting with Jesus, we find our pain eased, our brokenness, our wounds bound up; we find peace from whatever troubles or harms us; we find a touch that heals. Meeting with Jesus, we hear words that speak to our hearts, open up our minds, excite our spirits.

My church had a series of services around the question 'What is it about Jesus that excites you?', which is another way of asking: 'How is Jesus alive for us today?' We agreed that the Jesus we meet in the gospels is attractive. He is winsome, he draws us to him.

Meeting Jesus is attractive, in the sense that to see him, hear him, encounter him is life-enhancing. He is forever doing and saying things which are both affirmative and challenging. The gospels keep giving us pictures of him meeting with very ordinary people, often folk carrying heavy burdens, folk whom life has seriously wounded, and for them he has time to listen to them, to speak with them, to address their needs directly. So often, discipleship begins when we find that Jesus speaks to us, touches us, welcomes us, says 'Yes' to us, ... heals, reassures, restores us, as he does with Peter's wife's mother.

But what happens next? The mother-in-law is restored, she's back to health again, she gives the company their tea; and, when it's over, she opens her front door and discovers waiting outside it half the sick population of Galilee. The discipleship paradigm is that the journey begins with our own personal encounter with Jesus, where he says 'Yes' to us and we say 'Yes' to him, but out of the closeness of that encounter he leads us to the door and says: 'I want you to meet my friends, I want you to be among those I have come to heal and help, serve and save'. The company consists of ill people, broken people, powerless people, the poor, the excluded, the dismissed. Here in verses 16–17 is terse anticipation of the very last parable in Matthew's gospel – the parable of the sheep and the goats (25:31–46). 'When did we see you hungry and thirsty, a stranger, naked, defenceless, sick, a prisoner?' 'Just as you served one of the least of my brothers and sisters, you did it to me.'

After this snapshot of Jesus outside the door of Peter's house, ministering individually to this crowd of sick, poor and broken folk, the gospel says a strange word. 'This was to fulfil what had been spoken through the prophet Isaiah, "He took our infirmities and bore our diseases"' (8:17). The reference is to Isaiah 53, the picture of the suffering servant, the one who takes the sins, wounds, griefs of others to himself, at real and awful cost, to bring healing, forgiveness and release to others. The picture originally referred to the remnant community of Israel, exiled in Babylon, but from the time of the gospels themselves it has come to stand as describing the cross and passion of Christ. Is Matthew saying to us: 'Look well, this healing ministry of Christ, this outgoing ministry to those on the margins is a ministry of real cost'? Is Matthew laying down a marker, a signpost on the discipleship way, saying: 'This is only the beginning, friend, there are many strange twists and turns in store. At the end there is the final revolution, of Jesus going into the ultimate margins of dishonour, disgrace and death, Jesus going to the place where we can hardly bear to look, that with his wounds we may be healed'?

... and away

Enter a scribe. Almost uniformly in this gospel, scribes get a bad press. They are opponents of Jesus, at the end complicit in his death. They are the custodians of the old Law who have taken privileges to themselves. It seems here as if we are about to meet a scribe who is serious about the discipleship way. 'Teacher, I will go wherever you go', says the scribe. In Matthew's gospel, it is those who do not, will not go with Jesus who call him 'Teacher'. Disciples call him 'Lord'. 'Teacher' should put us on our guard. Here's the opposition. 'Teacher, I will follow you wherever you go.' The scribe takes the initiative without waiting to be called, unlike the disciples. The obvious reply to him would be: 'Nobody asked you'. Jesus, however, is rarely reduced to the obvious. 'Foxes have holes, and the birds of the air their nests, but the Son of Man has nowhere to lay his head.'

'Are you serious?' asks Jesus, 'are you really serious? ... you with your very settled, comfortable, privileged lifestyle ... Are you really serious? Do you begin to know what it will mean to come with me? ... a different bed every night, life out on the margins with all sorts of folk you're never in the habit of meeting, challenge after challenge to your attitudes and ways of thinking, the complete rearranging of your mental and spiritual furniture ... Are you really serious?'

Next, if anything, it gets worse. A disciple this time, a genuine would-be disciple, says: 'Lord, ... right title ... Lord, first let me go and bury my father'. There could not be a more reasonable request on every count of sensitivity and the bonds of filial responsibility, so strong in the society of Jesus' time. One commentator says: 'Jesus' response is simply shocking'. Jesus says, 'Follow me, and let the dead bury their own dead'. The applecart of all the familiar traditional values is well and truly turned upside down. I suspect we're in a fair bit of trouble if we take this word of Jesus too literally, as we will be with the next story of the stilling of the storm. But the picture's clear enough. To take the way of Jesus is hard, uncompromising, demanding. It means looking at the world around us from a different perspective, from outside, from the margins, from the bottom up rather than the top down. It means setting loose the ties which have given us status and security and belonging.

Into stormy waters

It means living in the eye of the storm. Jesus now takes his disciples out across the sea of Galilee. They are heading for Gentile territory for the first time. A sudden storm breaks. The disciples, most of them hardened fishermen, fear that the boat is about to sink while Jesus is calmly asleep in the stern. In the Bible, the sea often represents the frightening forces of chaos which, however, God will subdue; stormy waters, then as now, stand for struggle, the encounter with forces in society which threaten and oppress, which again God will overcome. The disciples wake Jesus, 'Save us', they cry. 'Why are you frightened? What little faith you have', he says. The wind drops and the sea is calm again.

Some say that this is but the description of one of the sudden squalls which could be whipped up and calm down in a very short space of time in the inland lake of Galilee. Others will say that Jesus was so in tune with the mind of God and God's energies that he had an instinctive communication with the natural world around him. Once again, the story is a demonstration of Jesus' authority. It's also about discipleship, connecting with what has gone before in saying that following Jesus means getting into stormy waters, living in the eye of the storm ... but, the same Jesus who leads us into deeper water, into more dangerous encounters than we ever thought to experience, is always there with us. He brings peace, even out of the very eye of the storm.

A moment ago, the scribe who would follow Jesus has been asked: 'Do you really know what you're letting yourself in for if you come with me?' The disciples have at least come and gone with Jesus, they've let themselves be found with him over deep water in the eye of the storm. In the situation they sense as dangerous, they cry out: 'Lord, save us'; they recognise in whose hands their safety lies. Jesus' response, 'How little faith you have', is interesting. These words are both an affirmation and a gentle rebuke. Jesus doesn't say: 'Have you no faith?' or 'You have no faith'. It's just that the faith of the disciples is still too little, too small. There's more growing, learning, experiencing, suffering to be undergone, that the little faith may grow ... for them, for us, today's gospel readers.

Go away!

The last incident in this busy chapter sees Jesus and his disciples confronted by a different kind of storm. They come to land in Gentile territory where they are immediately confronted by two wild and dangerously deranged men, living in the local burial place, the site of death. The men are demon-possessed, and it was a commonly held belief of the time that the demon-possessed often had by-ordinary powers of discernment. This is true here: the men confront Jesus with the question: 'What do you want with us, you Son of God?' Remember, in face of the stilling of the storm, the disciples have just been moved to ask who Jesus is (8:27). The answer first comes from the forces of evil and opposition. Jesus exercises his authority over the demons as he exorcises the two men. The driven-out spirits enter the nearby herd of pigs, which then career in panic downhill and over the cliff edge into the lake. When the swineherds rush to the local town to tell what has happened, the population come *en masse* to confront Jesus and the disciple band and bid them leave the district. Matthew tells this story more tersely than the parallel accounts in Mark and Luke. There is no happy resolution to it. Jesus is seen by the Gentile population as threat rather than promise. This is part of Matthew's evidence and argument that, while Jesus is shown pushing out beyond the margins of his own people, the time for the Gentile mission is not yet. Discipleship work among the Gentiles entails struggle and conflict.

Symbolic swine

The presence of the pigs, unclean animals to the Jews, confirms that this incident is located in Gentile territory. Now and then, 'pigs', 'swine' have been long-standing epithets of abuse and denigration. As well as being generally abusive, there is a particular history of 'pigs' being used as an insulting term for authority figures. Today 'pigs' may be used to insult members of the police force; in Jesus' time, it was often used of the occupying forces of the Roman Empire. Just as the sea has considerable symbolic significance in the preceding story of the stilling of the storm, so also an argument can be made for the symbolic significance of the 'pigs' in this episode. Warren Carter writes:

> The conflict has multiple levels: *economic*, since the pigs are a source of food and income from sale and taxes; *political*, since Jesus has challenged their control and destroyed a symbol of Roman imperial power; *social*, since Jesus has taken the side of the expendables, at the expense of the elite; *ethnic*, since Jesus is a Jew asserting his authority among Gentiles; *religious*, since Jesus has destroyed an animal with important roles in religious rites. (Carter 2000 pp. 213–14)

On the discipleship road, Jesus has led his followers to a place and situation which is conflictual, multi-layered, ambiguous. That's life, as we know and live it.

'Through wind and waves and storm ...'

What does following Jesus look like? This chapter says it begins with attraction, to the Jesus who affirms us, heals us, says 'yes' to our lives. Jesus then leads us into the challenging company of those whom he came to serve and save. The way of the cross is introduced. The demands of discipleship intensify. Following Jesus has real cost. We will often end up in the eye of the storm ... where we will learn that the one to whom we were attracted in the first place, who called us in the first place, will never leave us and, in the storms of our life, will speak peace.

Study

By yourself

Take time to reflect on this chapter. Where are you in the story? Are you the scribe, who would like to follow, but it may cost too much, or the disciple, hesitant, fearful, still with growing to do, but still prepared to say 'yes' and knowing, albeit dimly, where real peace truly lies?

Where have you encountered stormy waters on the discipleship road?

Listen, and hear the voice which says: 'Peace, be still'.

Chapter 12

HEALING FROM
THE HEART

Matthew 9
Jesus Heals a Paralysed Man
(Mark 2:1–12, Luke 5:17–26)

Jesus got into the boat and went back across the lake to his own town, where some people had brought to him a paralysed man, lying on a bed. When Jesus saw how much faith they had, he said to the paralysed man, 'Courage, my son! Your sins are forgiven.'

Then some teachers of the Law said to themselves, 'This man is speaking blasphemy!'

Jesus perceived what they were thinking, so he said, 'Why are you thinking such evil things? Is it easier to say, "Your sins are forgiven," or to say, "Get up and walk"? I will prove to you, then, that the Son of Man has authority on earth to forgive sins.' So he said to the paralysed man, 'Get up, pick up your bed, and go home!'

The man got up and went home. When the people saw it, they were afraid, and praised God for giving such authority to people.

Jesus Calls Matthew

(Mark 2:13–17, Luke 5:27–32)

Jesus left that place, and as he walked along, he saw a tax collector, named Matthew, sitting in his office. He said to him, 'Follow me'.

Matthew got up and followed him.

While Jesus was having a meal in Matthew's house, many tax collectors and other outcasts came and joined Jesus and his disciples at the table. Some Pharisees saw this and asked his disciples, 'Why does your teacher eat with such people?'

Jesus heard them and answered, 'People who are well do not need a doctor, but only those who are sick. Go and find out what is meant by the scripture that says, "It is kindness that I want, not animal sacrifices." I have not come to call respectable people, but outcasts.'

The Question about Fasting
(Mark 2:18–22, Luke 5:33–9)

Then the followers of John the Baptist came to Jesus, asking, 'Why is it that we and the Pharisees fast often, but your disciples don't fast at all?'

Jesus answered, 'Do you expect the guests at a wedding party to be sad as long as the bridegroom is with them? Of course not! But the day will come when the bridegroom will be taken away from them, and then they will fast.

'No one patches up an old coat with a piece of new cloth, for the new patch will shrink and make an even bigger hole in the coat. Nor does anyone pour new wine into used wineskins, for the skins will burst, the wine will pour out, and the skins will be ruined. Instead, new wine is poured into fresh wineskins, and both will keep in good condition.'

The Official's Daughter and the Woman who Touched Jesus' Cloak
(Mark 5:21–43, Luke 8:40–56)

While Jesus was saying this, a Jewish official came to him, knelt down before him, and said, 'My daughter has just died; but come and place your hands on her, and she will live'.

So Jesus got up and followed him, and his disciples went along with him.

A woman who had suffered from severe bleeding for twelve years came up behind Jesus and touched the edge of his cloak. She said to herself, 'If I only touch his cloak, I will get well'.

123

Jesus turned round and saw her, and said, 'Courage, my daughter! Your faith has made you well'. At that very moment the woman became well.

Then Jesus went into the official's house. When he saw the musicians for the funeral and the people all stirred up, he said, 'Get out, everybody! The little girl is not dead – she is only sleeping!' Then they all laughed at him. But as soon as the people had been put out, Jesus went into the girl's room and took hold of her hand, and she got up. The news about this spread all over that part of the country.

Jesus Heals Two Blind Men

Jesus left that place, and as he walked along, two blind men started following him. 'Take pity on us, Son of David!' they shouted.

When Jesus had gone indoors, the two blind men came to him, and he asked them, 'Do you believe that I can heal you?'

'Yes, sir!' they answered.

Then Jesus touched their eyes and said, 'Let it happen, then, just as you believe!' – and their sight was restored. Jesus spoke sternly to them, 'Don't tell this to anyone!'

But they left and spread the news about Jesus all over that part of the country.

Jesus Heals a Man who could not Speak

As the men were leaving, some people brought to Jesus a man who could not talk because he had a demon. But as soon as the demon was driven out, the man started talking, and everyone was amazed. 'We have never seen anything like this in Israel!' they exclaimed.

But the Pharisees said, 'It is the chief of the demons who gives Jesus the power to drive out demons'.

Jesus has Pity for the People

Jesus went round visiting all the towns and villages. He taught in the synagogues, preached the Good News about the Kingdom, and healed people with every kind of disease and sickness. As he saw the crowds, his heart was filled with pity for them, because they were worried and helpless, like sheep without a shepherd. So he said to his disciples, 'The harvest is large, but there are few workers to gather it in. Pray to the owner of the harvest that he will send out workers to gather in his harvest.'

'Your sins are forgiven: walk on'

At the start of this chapter, we find the discipleship band with Jesus back in the home territory of Capernaum where the demands on him for healing continue. The first story tells of friends bringing to Jesus a paralysed man. Jesus is much impressed by the friends' faith and says to the man: 'Courage, my son! Your sins are forgiven.' Oops!! Should he have said that? We know that some kinds of physical paralysis are induced by feelings of guilt, real or neurotic; we know also that, in the time of Jesus, illness was very often seen as an affliction sent by God as a punishment for past misdeeds. 'Your sins are forgiven' is a sensitive and compassionate word of release. But by what authority does Jesus forgive sins? Lurking in the crowd around Jesus are some scribes, keepers and interpreters of the Law. Their interpretation of the Law was that only God could forgive sins. The scribes are angry and horrified at Jesus' words; they see him taking to himself a power they believe belongs to God alone.

Jesus has no intention of retracting. He repeats his words, and the paralysed man picks up his bedding and walks home. The people are awestruck, 'and praised God for giving such authority to human beings' (9:8 NRSV). This is an important passage. It marks the beginnings of Jesus' growing conflict with the religious authorities within his own people, Israel – a conflict mirrored in the story of Matthew's community some decades later. It also picks up the key theme of forgiveness which we have encountered before in the words of Jesus in the Sermon on the Mount and which we will meet again as the gospel unfolds. Central to the gospel is the promise that not only Jesus, but we also, can forgive like God. Forgiveness and acceptance are foundational to the forming of true Christian community.

Kindness, not sacrifice

That theme is repeated and reinforced in the next episode of the call of Matthew, the tax collector. One vivid human story follows another. Matthew is seated at his custom booth, collecting tolls from those who go in and out of the town and its market. Tax collecting was 'franchised': the collector had to pay a certain sum to the authorities for the taxes he was to gather in; he could then keep what he gathered over and above that sum. The system lent itself to extortion and malpractice, and tax collectors were more than socially ambiguous; they were despised as collaborators and swindlers. It's this dodgy character whom Jesus next bids join him on the discipleship road. Matthew tidies his desk, picks up his books and walks forward into a new life.

The scene changes. Jesus is now found in either Matthew's house or the house Jesus was using as his base, sharing a meal with a motley collection of folk collectively categorised as 'tax collectors and other outcasts' or 'publicans and sinners'. Jesus' table fellowship attracts the disapproval of a second group of religious authority figures, the Pharisees. Pharisaism had developed an elaborate purity code around meals, not only in terms of ritual washing, but also in terms of those with whom it was acceptable to sit at table and those beyond the pale. The latter far exceeded the former. In marked contrast to the Pharisees' fastidious exclusivism, Jesus and his disciples are shown as practising an open fellowship, intentionally regardless of the commonly held taboos of gender and status. Jesus overhears the Pharisees' question to the disciples: 'Why does your teacher eat with such people?' Their disdain is palpable. Cryptically, in reply Jesus says: 'Those who are well do not need a doctor, but only those who are sick'. He then reinforces these words with a quotation from Hosea 6:6: 'Go and learn what the scripture means which says, "I desire mercy and not sacrifice"' (9:12). 'Mercy not sacrifice' – not surprisingly, we will meet these words again; they stand as a succinct summary of a major theme which runs through the whole gospel.

The bridegroom is here, dance!

Enter a third set of questioners who raise a related issue with Jesus. This time, the questions come not from opponents but from likely allies, some of the followers of John the Baptist. John is an ascetic, severe, uncompromising figure; his followers would share the same mould. We can readily understand their uncertainties about Jesus, who appears to sit much more loosely with his people's religious exercises. Their doubts will resurface in their question in chapter 11:3. Here, their concern is that Jesus and his disciples appear insufficiently rigorous in the self-denying practice of fasting. Fasting, with its keynotes of denial and repentance, was part and parcel of religious life: Jesus assumes its legitimacy in the passage in the Sermon on the Mount (6:16–18). John's disciples query whether Jesus' followers fast sufficiently, and sufficiently obviously. Jesus' riposte is the cryptic saying about the inappropriateness of fasting in the presence of the bridegroom at a wedding feast. Obviously, the bridegroom is a reference to himself. Yet the bridegroom won't always be there: there is a hidden reference to the shadow of the cross falling across the disciples' path. The mourning time will come.

Torn and burst

Jesus continues with a couple of vigorous and explosive metaphors. He speaks of the havoc created by putting a patch of new, unshrunk cloth on an old cloak and the disaster of putting new wine into old wineskins. His appearance on the scene is not only an occasion for joy, a reason for a good party as in a wedding feast; it is also potentially highly disruptive, a shaking of the foundations and a radical calling into question of the ways things are. Jesus is obviously well aware that his presence on the public scene will be seen as a mixed blessing. He will know the force of opposition as much as the gladness of welcome. In his wisdom, he points to the more general truth that, while all change is difficult, growth and innovation are often more productive of stress and tension than steady decline. It's not only the people of Gadara who wish to see the back of the living Jesus. One New Testament commentator has said that the biggest threat to the church has always been, and is now, the presence of that same Jesus.

The two women

The sequence of healing stories is resumed. Matthew tells the story of the return to life and health of the two women, the young girl and the woman with the chronic bleeding, much more briefly than Mark (5:21–43) and Luke (8:40–56). He begins by stating quite baldly that a leader of the synagogue flung himself at the feet of Jesus with the announcement that his daughter is dead. Matthew's telling of the story therefore lacks the tension created in the other two gospels of the picture of Jesus' being delayed and distracted by the touch of the older woman while the young girl hovers between life and death. The symbolic parallels and contrasts between the twelve growing years of the young girl's age and the twelve wasting years of the older woman's haemorrhages are also lacking. The stress in Matthew's telling is on the power of Jesus to heal both the chronically sick and the untimely dead.

Breaking taboos

Jesus' amazing power remains firmly rooted in the things of earth. He ministers to the ambiguities of our flesh and among the disabling consequences of our social conventions. In this story of the healing and restoring to fullness of life of two women, Jesus breaks through two constricting conventions within his people's belief system. The story begins with a shock: not only does the ruler of the synagogue fall on his knees before Jesus, thereby acknowledging his authority, he also begs Jesus to come and lay hands on his dead daughter. As in the earlier story of the healing of the leper, touch is central here. To touch a corpse was to become unclean; Jesus, the holy one, is being invited by this representative of religious authority to become ritually unclean. Before he reaches the girl, however, Jesus is touched by the woman with the twelve years' bleeding. A bleeding woman was not only considered ritually unclean in herself, she also rendered all those who came into contact with her similarly unclean. The touch of the anonymous woman makes Jesus 'unclean'. Quite contrary to her expectation, Jesus praises and affirms her. From the moment of her touch, she is well.

The immediate consequence of the woman's touch is that it is an 'unclean' Jesus who, contrary to the ritual Law, enters the house of the ruler of the synagogue, and it's in his state of 'uncleanness' that he takes the young girl's hand and raises her to life. The wider consequence is that Jesus, by his actions of disregarding the ritual laws and conventions of his time, dissolves the taboos, not just for himself but for all those who will come after him. This is an important incident in the altogether too long story of women's liberation. There's a health warning here for all of us. Be on guard when church or society labels people 'unclean'. The issue is certainly 'live' today if we think of the history of the AIDS epidemic and the way in many places its sufferers have been stigmatised. The persistent homophobia which continues to accompany the debate about homosexuality speaks of a lingering taboo in urgent need of dissolution. Taboos are powerful, growing as they do in the fertile soil of our fears, real or neurotic. Some continue with good reason, as in our instinctive repulsion to rape or child abuse. Others are simply past their sell-by date. May God grant us the wisdom to know the difference.

'He makes the blind see, and the dumb speak'

The healing sequence concludes with the giving of sight to two blind men and speech to a dumb man. Interestingly, the blind men are taken by Jesus into a house where their healing is effected away from the crowd while the dumb man receives his speech in public, in face of the ever-present crowd. The story of the healing of the two blind men bears considerable similarities to the last healing miracle related by Matthew when Jesus, on the brink of his entry into Jerusalem at the start of the week which ends at the cross, heals two blind men as he and his disciples are leaving Jericho (20:29–34). In both stories, the men use the same words of greeting to call on Jesus: 'Son of David, take pity on us!' (9:27, 20:30). 'Son of David' was a well-known title for the longed-for Messiah; by the end of this sequence of healing miracles, Jesus will have performed and fulfilled all the healing miracles expected of the coming Messiah (see Isaiah 35:3–6). We, the readers of the gospel, will already have been given the answer to the question asked by the disciples of John the Baptist at the beginning of Matthew 11.

The incident of the healing of the blind men contains a number of features which recur in the healing stories.

- Those who are healed come from the poor and/or marginalised within Jesus' society.
- There is a strong emphasis on the faith of those who come for healing; faith to be understood as trust in Jesus and in his power to heal and restore.
- The story has more than a literal meaning; it is also powerfully symbolic. This story is not just about the healing of two blind men in a house in Capernaum, it is about Jesus' ability to open the eyes of all those who put their trust in him.

The exorcising of the dumb man which concludes this cycle of individual healing stories introduces another common element in the healings, namely that they produce opposition from the religious elite of scribe and Pharisee. In this case, it is the Pharisees who sneer at Jesus' power to exorcise, a sneer which Jesus will tackle head on in 12:22ff.

Healing from the heart

The chapter ends with a summary of Jesus' activity of teaching and healing within Galilee. It is only rarely that the gospels give any clues about Jesus' emotional motivation; here, it is significant to note the use of a strong Greek word in v. 36 which is variously translated 'he had pity on them' or 'he had compassion'. In the use of that word, we see that Jesus' motivation came not only from his single-minded devotion to his God-given calling but also from his deep sense of care for those he met.

'Sheep without a shepherd' (10:36) implies a lack of leadership, the loss of a sense of direction. The phrase is not surprising in the light of Matthew's scathing critique of the religious leadership of the time and the battles Jesus will have with that leadership. Ulrich Luz comments:

> At the end of the miracle cycle of Matthew 8–9, a split has occurred. The negative reaction of the Pharisees, for Matthew the most important and representative of the Jewish leaders who reject Jesus, stands in contrast to the neutral or positive reaction of the crowds to Jesus. Within the macrotext of the Gospel, the function of the miracles of chapters 8–9 is to bring about this split within Israel. They form the exposition of

the ensuing conflict. Given this, it is meaningful that Matthew more than once deliberately characterises the miracles reported in chapters 8–9 as miracles performed in Israel by Israel's Messiah. The three controversy discourses with the scribes, the Pharisees and John's disciples now have their meaningful place in chapters 8–9 in that they anticipate the split within Israel.... Here, as in other sections of his Gospel, Matthew harmoniously combines a conservative treatment of tradition with his own literary and theological purposes. This is Matthew's supreme literary achievement as an author. (Luz 2005 pp. 228–9)

Study

By yourself

Take any one of the healing stories from Matthew 8 and 9. Try to be present at the scene. Use your imagination to enter into it.

- What can you see, hear, smell, taste, feel, as you imagine yourself being present?

- How are you feeling? Curious? Attracted? Disturbed? Afraid? Excited?

- Do you want to speak to anyone in the incident in particular? What do you want to say? What do you hear being said to you?

- If any part of this story has particularly attracted you, go back to it. Without forcing anything, see if you can identify what is attracting you.

For group study

In the next chapter of Matthew (10), we will see Jesus giving to his disciples the task and ability to continue his ministry. Discuss together how you see the church's healing ministry today – you could make two lists, one of the similarities and one of the differences between the disciples' situation and ours.

The healing ministry is one where we all have a part to play – make a list/programme of the ways in which your church shares in this ministry and how it enables others to take part. Think broadly.

Jesus' ministry of healing involved breaking taboos and challenging conventional ways of thinking. It provoked controversy and opposition. Are there such clashes today?

(This study may well take more than one week – the subject deserves it.)

Chapter 13

THE HARD ROAD

Matthew 10
The Twelve Apostles
(Mark 3:13–19, Luke 6:12–16)

Jesus called his twelve disciples together and gave them authority to drive out evil spirits and to heal every disease and every sickness. These are the names of the twelve apostles: first, Simon (called Peter) and his brother Andrew; James and his brother John, the sons of Zebedee; Philip and Bartholomew; Thomas and Matthew, the tax collector; James son of Alphaeus, and Thaddaeus; Simon the Patriot, and Judas Iscariot, who betrayed Jesus.

The Mission of the Twelve
(Mark 6:7–13, Luke 9:1–6)

These twelve men were sent out by Jesus with the following instructions: 'Do not go into any Gentile territory or any Samaritan towns. Instead, you are to go to the lost sheep of the people of Israel. Go and preach, '"The Kingdom of heaven is near!" Heal the sick, bring the dead back to life, heal those who suffer from dreaded skin diseases, and drive out demons. You have received without paying, so give without being paid. Do not carry any gold, silver, or copper money in your pockets; do not carry a beggar's bag for the journey or an extra shirt or shoes or a stick. Workers should be given what they need.

'When you come to a town or village, go in and look for someone who is willing to welcome you, and stay with him until you leave that place. When you go into a house, say, "Peace be with you." If the people in the house welcome you, let your greeting of peace remain; but if they do not welcome you, then take back your greeting. And if some home or town will not welcome you or listen to you, then leave that place and shake the dust off your feet. I assure you that on the Judgement Day God will show more mercy to the people of Sodom and Gomorrah than to the people of that town!'

Coming Persecutions

(*Mark 13:9–13, Luke 21:12–17*)

'Listen! I am sending you out just like sheep to a pack of wolves. You must be as cautious as snakes and as gentle as doves. Watch out, for there will be those who will arrest you and take you to court, and they will whip you in the synagogues. For my sake you will be brought to trial before rulers and kings, to tell the Good News to them and to the Gentiles. When they bring you to trial, do not worry about what you are going to say or how you will say it; when the time comes, you will be given what you will say. For the words you will speak will not be yours; they will come from the Spirit of your Father speaking through you.

'Men will hand over their own brothers to be put to death, and fathers will do the same to their children; children will turn against their parents and have them put to death. Everyone will hate you because of me. But whoever holds out to the end will be saved. When they persecute you in one town, run away to another one. I assure you that you will not finish your work in all the towns of Israel before the Son of Man comes.

'No pupil is greater than his teacher; no slave is greater than his master. So a pupil should be satisfied to become like his teacher, and a slave like his master. If the head of the family is called Beelzebul, the members of the family will be called even worse names!'

Whom to Fear

(*Luke 12:2–7*)

'So do not be afraid of people. Whatever is now covered up will be uncovered and every secret will be made known. What I am telling you in the dark you must repeat in broad daylight, and what you have heard in private you must announce from the housetops. Do not be afraid of those who kill the body but cannot kill the soul; rather be afraid of God, who can destroy both body and soul in hell. For only a penny you can buy two sparrows, yet not one sparrow falls to the ground without your Father's consent. As for you, even the hairs of your head have all been counted. So do not be afraid; you are worth much more than many sparrows!'

Confessing and Rejecting Christ

(*Luke 12:8–9*)

'For those who declare publicly that they belong to me, I will do the same before my Father in heaven. But if anyone rejects me publicly, I will reject him before my Father in heaven.'

Not Peace, but a Sword

(*Luke 12:51–3, 14:26–7*)

'Do not think that I have come to bring peace to the world. No, I did not come to bring peace, but a sword. I came to set sons against their fathers, daughters against their mothers, daughters-in-law against their mothers-in-law; your worst enemies will be the members of your own family.

'Those who love their father or mother more than me are not fit to be my disciples; those who love their son or daughter more than me are not fit to be my disciples. Those who do not take up their cross and follow in my steps are not fit to be my disciples. Those who try to gain their whole life will lose it; but those who lose their life for my sake will gain it.'

Rewards

(*Mark 9:41*)

'Whoever welcomes you welcomes me; and whoever welcomes me welcomes the one who sent me. Whoever welcomes God's messenger because he is God's messenger, will share in his reward. And whoever welcomes a good man because he is good, will share in his reward. You can be sure that whoever gives even a drink of cold water to one of the least of these my followers because he is my follower, will certainly receive a reward.'

Discipleship – being church in the world

In Matthew 10, we come to the second block of teaching in the gospel. Unlike the Sermon on the Mount, which was addressed to disciples and the crowd, in this chapter Jesus is shown speaking only to disciples, indeed specifically to the 'twelve'. The subject of what it means to follow Jesus has already outcropped in the preceding two chapters; here, it is the dominant theme. This is an important block of teaching about being a disciple, belonging within the community of those who follow Jesus. To some extent, it has suffered from being overshadowed by the Sermon on the Mount and has not received overmuch attention by scholars through the years. Ulrich Luz suggests another reason why:

> The church should have every reason to show a particular interest in the mission discourse, yet it has received scant attention in interpretation history. The main reason may be that there is so much in the discourse that has contradicted and still contradicts church reality that the church exegetes have always had difficulty finding their own church addressed in it. (Luz 2005 p. 144)

This is a chapter full of tough words for a hard road, though it begins gently enough. It starts with the naming of the twelve disciples, representative of the leadership of the new community Jesus creates. The number is symbolic, calling to mind the names of the founding brothers of the old community of Israel with its twelve tribes. Like Israel of old, the new community lives out of a dynamic of mutual interdependence. The disciples are simply named, with four exceptions: Simon's given name, 'Peter', 'the rock' is added as befits the disciple who has a principal role; Matthew has his occupation appended, 'the tax collector', giving him a prominence as one particularly associated with this gospel; the second Simon is distinguished from Peter by reference to his allegiance to the Jewish nationalist movement of Zealots; and to the final name, Judas Iscariot, are appended the words, 'who betrayed Jesus' – an early pointer towards the cross.

Sent out

Next, Jesus sends his twelve named disciples out on their mission. In the first four verses of this chapter, the twelve have been called both 'disciples', *mathetes*, 'learners', and 'apostles', *apostoloi*, 'sent-out ones'. The two names are largely interchangeable as titles; their conjunction can serve as a reminder that, as Jesus' followers, learning is done on the way; action and learning belong together. In his description of the disciples, 'sending', while Matthew uses material from both Mark (6) and Luke (9–10), he shapes it to his own purposes. It is noteworthy that Matthew's account of the sending doesn't include any report of the return of the disciples from their mission, or any indication of its success or failure. By foregoing any neat ending or closure to this episode, Matthew conveys the impression that this is not simply about a past event – here is teaching for all 'disciples'. Indeed, the whole chapter is taken up with Jesus giving the twelve instructions. We can read it as a perennially relevant training manual. The impression of relevant preparation is enhanced in the second half of the chapter, where the words about persecutions and divisions (10:16–36) clearly relate very specifically to the situation of Matthew's community after the break with the synagogue and the onset of the Gentile mission.

However, Jesus' first instruction to the twelve is to concentrate their work within 'the lost sheep of Israel'. It is probably better to understand these words as referring to the plight of the nation as a whole rather than a particular group within it, though of course the gospel always shows Jesus with a special concern for the marginalised and ignored. Although from the very beginning of the gospel there have been strong intimations of Jesus' universal mission, its time is not yet; the work begins within Israel.

As to the disciples' task, it is striking that the instructions they are given are to mirror their master, in both word and action. They share his powers and his tasks. They are to proclaim the imminence of the Kingdom and in their works of healing make that nearness concrete (10:7–9). As they go, they are to be itinerant (10:11), poor (10:9), defenceless (10:10) and prepared to suffer for the one they serve (10:16–33). The manner and the marks of the disciples' going are closely related to the previous teaching in the Sermon on the Mount. Here, the Sermon's teaching is brought into sharp and concrete focus. Of course, the manner and marks of the disciples' way in the world are also the way of the master, Jesus, who teaches just as much by what he is and suffers as by what he says. For Matthew, the marks of the true church are to be located in the dynamic following of the disciple in the way of the Lord, out in the life of the world.

> Matthew achieves something remarkable: he places his marks of the church right at the centre of the concrete and at the same time ambiguous world.... In speaking of the disciples' itinerancy, poverty, defencelessness and love, Matthew focuses on the holiness given to the church in the midst of the world. In this way Matthew helps us to speak of the church in worldly, concrete and thus real terms. (Luz 2005 p. 163)

Matthew intends his readers to see Jesus' instructions to the twelve as he sends them out as a model for all who follow him, a template for being the church in the world. It's worth lingering on them. Those who are sent out go in his name and with his authority. That is enough. But they don't go alone; they go in pairs, in a shared collegiate ministry, relying on and supporting one another. As a sign of their Lord's sufficiency for them, they go in poverty and defencelessness. At the very least, Jesus' instructions demand that they make no money from their work of ministry; they are simply to receive enough for their basic needs. The demand is stronger than that. It's often said that Luke's is the gospel which stresses the vocation of poverty, not for some but for all Christians; the same emphasis is there in Matthew. One of Matthew's key words is 'perfect': 'You must be perfect – just as your Father in heaven is perfect' (5:48). Perfection is the goal for all disciples in their vocation of following, remembering always that it's God who makes perfect. The call to perfection appears again in the story of Jesus' encounter with the rich young man in 19:21: 'If you want to be perfect, go and sell all you have and give the money to the poor, and you will have riches in heaven; then come and follow me'.

The disciples go in poverty among poor people; they also go boldly with a courageous and unthreatening defencelessness.

To travel without staff and sandals was indeed to be defenceless as much against the animal kingdom as against potential human violence. When they come to a town or village, they are to look for a household which will welcome them. If they find such a house, they offer a peace blessing; if they can find no house and no welcome in the neighbourhood, they are simply to move on, shaking off the dust of the place as a sign of closure. Matthew, unlike Mark and Luke, adds at this point in his narrative verse 15: 'I assure you that on the Judgement Day God will show more mercy on the people of Sodom and Gomorrah [bywords for iniquity] than to the people of that town'. We hear these harsh words in the light of the bitter rift between synagogue and young church and of the pain it has brought to Matthew's community. They are another hint of the theme which runs throughout the gospel, that the mission of Jesus is in two stages – to his own people the Jews first, then to the Gentiles.

Trouble looming

Turning to the section from verses 16–25, the theme of defencelessness and vulnerability continues. The disciples are warned that their defencelessness leaves them open to pain and injury as they are sent out 'like sheep to a pack of wolves'. While their stance is one of consistent non-aggression – 'gentle as doves' – they are also to use all their intelligence and native cunning in their situation, like the proverbially wise serpent. They may well end up in court, which will be both a trial and an opportunity to bear witness to the powerful and the Gentiles. The Gentile reference presupposes the Gentile mission and makes clear that this passage speaks particularly to the situation of Matthew's hearers. In the intimidating atmosphere of the courtroom, they are not to worry about what to say; 'the Spirit of your Father' will prompt them and speak through them. Matthew's form of words and specific reference to 'your Father' indicates that Jesus is speaking to the disciples as part of the new household and family of God who know God as his Father and their Father.

The next section turns to relationships within immediate earthly families. Again, the reference is clearly to the situation of Matthew's church, where allegiance to Jesus and the split from the synagogue has caused pain, disruption and division within family circles. The pain will be felt particularly acutely within the closeness of family. The passage warns that the pain may be extreme and indeed terminal; disciples will need great resources of endurance to remain faithful. At the same time, they are not to seek martyrdom. If they meet trouble in one place, they have permission to run and seek to work in another while they wait for the return of 'the Son of Man'. The 'Son of Man' reference (10:22), difficult to interpret, may again point to the situation of the early church, which was waiting expectantly on Jesus' return post-Easter.

This section ends with Jesus' saying about the relation of pupil to teacher, servant to master (10:24–5). In the struggles and sufferings which come through our following in the way of Jesus, we have the opportunity and the privilege of imitating, becoming more like our Lord – a key and characteristic emphasis in this gospel. Jesus leavens this solemn statement about the living core of discipleship with a piece of wry humour: 'Don't worry if you get insulted and bad-mouthed. They call me "Beelzebul" – "the very devil" (12:24) – it will be your doubtful honour to be called even worse!'

'Do not be afraid'

Following the announcement of hard times ahead comes the offer to disciples of reassurance. Three times in the next few verses (10:26, 28, 31), Jesus counsels: 'Don't be afraid'. The words about uncovering what is now covered, and making known what is secret, have a reference to the time of judgement when all that is hidden will be revealed. They can also be read as referring to the completed life, death and rising of Jesus: what he is about and the ways and means of the Kingdom he announced are clarified and made plain by his life and passion. In face of their enemies and accusers, disciples are to witness boldly to the truth they now know. They are enjoined to be fearless in the face of their enemies and accusers; to be fearless even in the face of those who kill the body. There are worse fates than physical death. Apostasy, denying the truth and renouncing one's faith, was taken very seriously by the early church and condemned heavily. That is the negative side of the heavy words in this section. Positively, there is implicit here the faith that the death of the body is not the end. The end is in God's hands, for God alone is ultimate, and God can restore even that which has been destroyed by the death of the body.

'For only a penny you can buy two sparrows.' The message that our lives are ultimately in the hands of a God who cares for all he has made is illustrated by the gentle and unforgettable image of the sparrows, the smallest of birds, the cheap food of the poor. It is reinforced by the saying: 'even the hairs of your head are counted'. In the last analysis, our lives rest in the hands of a God whose knowledge and care of us is awesome (e.g. see Psalm 139). Sparrows will fall to the ground, and it will be the calling of some of God's faithful to suffer martyrdom; that is never the last word. It belongs to God who will vindicate his faithful people (10:33).

> This section derives its force from the fact that it does not try to sketch an illusory picture of a kindly God. Sparrows fall to the earth and disciples of Jesus are slain, and Jesus never says that it hardly matters. What these sayings assert is that God is indeed God, that he is above success and failure, help and isolation, weal and woe, holding them in hands that Jesus says are the hands of the Father. He can say this because he himself addresses God as his Father, and does so throughout his entire life and death. Therefore he knows and can say with authority that after the death of the body God, and fullness of life, await the disciple who confesses Jesus. (Schweizer 1975 p. 249)

More trouble

The narrative returns to the theme of strife and division, even within the family circle. Jesus' strong words about coming to bring not peace but a sword find two distinct echoes from the Old Testament tradition. On the one hand, Jesus evokes a continuing prophetic protest against those who promise a false peace, those who would paper over the cracks of their people's corporate sins with the unfounded reassurance that God would see them alright, regardless; on the other, he challenges the inference that, because the Messiah himself comes in peace, there will be no trouble. His ministry as announcer of God's presence and God's reign will mean division and trouble, though the sword will be in the hands of his enemies rather than his own or his disciples'. Referring back to

10:22, he makes clear that trouble and division will engulf even the closeness of family ties (echoing Micah 7:6). Elsewhere in the gospel, Jesus affirms the importance of family ties and obligations (5:27ff., 8:14–15, 15:4, 19:3ff.); here, he states that these obligations, however sacred and important, must not come before the disciple's primary and ultimate loyalty to himself.

He continues by making the first direct reference in the gospel to the cross. Here, he speaks of the cross of the disciple rather than his own cross. That will come later, at the end of chapter 16. Every time 'cross' is mentioned, we need to bear in mind just what a fearsome, terrifying and humiliating instrument of political power crucifixion was during the rule of the Roman Empire. The cost of discipleship is heightened indeed. Clearly, Matthew's construction of this discipleship narrative and his choice and arrangements of Jesus' sayings is largely influenced by the trials and sufferings being faced and endured by his 'church'. It is a mistake, however, to think of Jesus' words as restricted to the original first-century situation. It has been said that the twentieth century saw more Christian martyrs than any since the first. Some of the names are well known: Dietrich Bonhoeffer, Oscar Romero, Jani Lumum, Martin Luther King, Ita Ford, Dorothy Kazel, Maura Clarke, Rutillo Grande. They stand for and with many others. Some simply died for their faith. Others gave their lives through their faith commitments to various struggles for peace and justice against the powers and ambiguities of this world. All leave a memory and example to be pondered and cherished. They have their reward. It is the subject of rewards with which this key chapter ends. The theme of the disciples' mission returns. Those who welcome disciples and prophets are commended, as are those who 'hear' the prophetic word. No less worthy of commendation are those who simply give a drink of cold water to one of the 'little ones', the despised and the marginalised. They too have their reward.

Study

By yourself
Write a simple account of what following Jesus means to you.

Chapter 14

THE LIGHT BURDEN

Matthew 11

The Messengers from John the Baptist

(*Luke 7:18–35*)

When Jesus finished giving these instructions to his twelve disciples, he left that place and went off to teach and preach in the towns near there.

When John the Baptist heard in prison about the things that Christ was doing, he sent some of his disciples to him. 'Tell us', they asked Jesus, 'are you the one John said was going to come, or should we expect someone else?'

Jesus answered, 'Go back and tell John what you are hearing and seeing: the blind can see, the lame can walk, those who suffer from dreaded skin diseases are made clean, the deaf hear, the dead are brought to life, and the Good News is preached to the poor. How happy are those who have no doubts about me!'

While John's disciples were leaving, Jesus spoke about him to the crowds: 'When you went out to John in the desert, what did you expect to see? A blade of grass bending in the wind? What did you go out to see? A man dressed up in fancy clothes? People who dress like that live in palaces! Tell me, what did you go out to see? A prophet? Yes, indeed, but you saw much more than a prophet. For John is the one of whom the scripture says: "God said, I will send my messenger ahead of you to open the way for you." I assure you that John the Baptist is greater than anyone who has ever lived. But the one who is least in the Kingdom of heaven is greater than John. From the time John preached his messages until this very day the

Kingdom of heaven has suffered violent attacks, and violent men try to seize it. Until the time of John all the prophets and the Law of Moses spoke about the Kingdom; and if you are willing to believe their message, John is Elijah, whose coming was predicted. Listen, then, if your have ears!

'Now, to what can I compare the people of this day? They are like children sitting in the market place. One group shouts to the other, "We played wedding music for you, but you wouldn't dance! We sang funeral songs, but you wouldn't cry!" When John came, he fasted and drank no wine, and everyone said, "He has a demon in him!" When the Son of Man came, he ate and drank, and everyone said, "Look at this man! He is a glutton and a drinker, a friend of tax collectors and other outcasts!" God's wisdom, however, is shown to be true by its results.'

The Unbelieving Towns

(*Luke 10:13–15*)

The people in the towns where Jesus had performed most of his miracles did not turn from their sins, so he reproached those towns. 'How terrible it will be for you, Chorazin! How terrible for you too, Bethsaida! If the miracles which were performed in you had been performed in Tyre and Sidon, the people there would long ago have put on sackcloth and sprinkled ashes on themselves, to show that they had turned from their sins! I assure you that on the Judgement Day God will show more mercy to the people of Tyre and Sidon than to you! And as for you, Capernaum! Did you want to lift yourself up to heaven? You will be thrown down to hell! If the miracles which were performed in you had been performed in Sodom, it would still be in existence today! You can be sure that on the Judgement Day God will show more mercy to Sodom than to you!'

Come to Me and Rest

(*Luke 10:21–2*)

At that time Jesus said, 'Father, Lord of heaven and earth! I thank you because you have shown to the unlearned what you have hidden from the wise and learned. Yes, Father, this was how you wanted it to happen.

'My Father has given me all things. No one knows the Son except the Father, and no one knows the Father except the Son and those to whom the Son chooses to reveal him.

'Come to me, all of you who are tired from carrying heavy loads, and I will give you rest. Take my yoke and put it on you, and learn from me, because I am gentle and humble in spirit; and you will find rest. For the yoke I will give you is easy, and the load I will put on you is light.'

Are you the one?

This second block of narrative is ended by Matthew's stock phrase after a teaching: 'Now when Jesus had finished teaching ...'. It is well worth reflecting on the content Jesus has just given to his disciples: his authority, a corporate ministry, a road to follow of poverty, vulnerability and love, an invitation to become more and more like him, a warning of trials ahead coupled with the courage to face them, and the injunction to rest in the reassurance of the Father's ultimate care. These are the marks of the believing and following company, and it's interesting to note what is absent: there is no reference to doctrine, worship, hierarchy and structure. All these are secondary to following Jesus himself. The second half of 11:1 shows Jesus continuing on his way of strenuous mission.

Enter some disciples of the imprisoned John the Baptist, sent by him with a vital question for Jesus. 'Are you the one who is to come, or are we to wait for someone else?' We have already met disciples of John in 9:14ff. with their worry about the apparent laxity of Jesus' disciples with regard to fasting. We can understand John's doubts. Jesus points the questioning disciples to what they 'hear and see' (11:4) and goes on to list the many ways in which his ministry is freeing people from whatever binds and hinders them, climaxing in 'and the poor have the good news brought to them'. The list echoes the signs of the coming day of God announced by the prophets (see Isaiah 35:5–6). In Jesus, that day is not a mere future event, it is dawning in his work, here and now. To

Isaiah's list is added the cleansing of lepers and the resurrection of the dead, and good news to the poor, about which Schweizer comments: 'The emphasis on the greatest blessing brought by Jesus, the proclamation of joy to the poor (cf. Matthew 5:3), is unprecedented' (Schweizer 1975 p. 256).

The evidence is there, but a decision still has to be made in face of the evidence.

> For Jesus, however, miracles are not the point; what is most important in his ministry is what is least pretentious – his message of love and hope. Certainly his miracles are signs of authority ... But they are never unequivocal: they evoke faith, but also doubt and even total rejection. Thus it is clear that his deeds truly open their meaning only to the person who can hear. (Schweizer 1975 pp. 256–7).

Having pointed to the evidence, Jesus goes on to make his invitation: 'Blessed is anyone who takes no offence at me'. Always there is a decision to be made. Each must answer for themselves the question: 'Is he the one?'

After John's questions about the authenticity of Jesus as the one sent by God, Jesus speaks of John. He asks the crowd around him, with a rhetorical question, what they made of John. His answer, 'A reed shaken by the wind', sounds cryptic. Herod Antipas was symbolised by a reed on coinage. John's words were a challenge to the corrupt and oppressive rule of the likes of Antipas; by them he was shaken. There could be an older alternative reference, to the reeds of the Red Sea, blown back to allow the children of Israel to find their liberation from the slavery of Egypt. Is Jesus picturing John as the harbinger of a new exodus? The question is repeated with this time an ironic reply, 'A man dressed up in fancy clothes', bespeaking wealth, power and privilege. John's garb had been of the simplest. Jesus commends John with words from Malachi 3:1 which speak of the forerunning messenger sent to prepare the way of the Lord. John is 'the greatest' (11:11) until now. Jesus continues: 'But the one who is least in the Kingdom of heaven is greater than John'. One possible interpretation of this difficult verse is that, in the phrase 'the one who is least', Jesus is referring to himself and the upside-down, transforming values of the Kingdom where first are last, and last first, and the greatest the servant. The following verses are also difficult to interpret exactly; their general gist is concerning the violence from the powers that be to which John, Jesus and in turn disciples are exposed. The section ends with yet another commendation of John: Jesus says that those who truly 'hear' his words receive the words of a returning Elijah, preparing the way (the reference is to the intertestamental book of Ecclesiasticus [Sirach] 48:10).

Children's games

In his last word on himself and John, Jesus paints the vivid picture of a group of children squabbling among themselves about which street game they will play. Some want to play at weddings, others at funerals, and they can't agree. He likens his contemporaries and their views of himself and John to the children. Folk say that John is too severe, his asceticism opens him to the charge of being too serious by half, 'having a bit of the fanatic about him'; on the other, hand Jesus and the company he keeps make him appear altogether too lax. The word on the street is that the godly cannot consort with the ungodly. He can't be the one entrusted with the truth of God.

Jesus closes the matter with the cryptic saying: 'Yet wisdom is justified by her deeds'. The reader is referred back to the beginning (11:2) 'when John heard in prison about the deeds of Jesus'. Both the deeds of John and Jesus have their own validity. Once again, the challenge is to look and see what is being said and done and to decide. Throughout this chapter, Matthew has in mind the considerable weight of Old Testament wisdom literature. With its background help, he is asking his contemporaries: 'Do you discern in Jesus the hidden wisdom of God in person?' The signs are there, both for the disciples of John and the inhabitants of the unbelieving towns. Will they see? Will you, good reader, see? ... see, believe and follow the one who in his own person manifests the inclusive welcoming wisdom of God (11:28). Rowan Williams comments:

> Matthew's gospel is an appeal to the reader to learn how to look, to 'scan' the ambiguous world so as to read what it is truly saying. It is centred upon the belief that the identity of Jesus is what finally gives coherence to the history of God's dealings with his people – i.e. that he

> *is* Wisdom. It also prepares us gradually for a rejection of that Wisdom, which will show itself as a climactic moment of exclusion, an exclusion which will also be a *self*-destruction. (Williams 2000 p. 30)

The final sentence of Williams' quotation points us again to the mystery of the cross.

'Why can't you see?'

Jesus now turns to upbraid those who have seen and heard most of his ministry to date and have been unmoved. He mentions by name three of the lakeside towns where he has been most active, Chorazin, Bethsaida and Capernaum. The first two are compared with the nearby heathen towns of Tyre and Sidon, prosperous and wealthy communities who are frequently condemned by the prophets (see Isaiah 23, Jeremiah 47:4, Ezekiel 27–8 and Zechariah 9:1–4). They were bywords for uncaring luxury. Matthew adds a sting to the whole passage which is very similar to Luke 10:13–15. When he has Jesus name the third town Capernaum, 'home' for his Galilean ministry, he likens it to the proverbially wicked and condemned Sodom. It is not hard to feel the hurt and rejection Matthew has experienced in living through the rejection of Jesus and his followers by Jesus' 'home' people of Israel. The wider challenge of the preceding verses remains: see and believe.

Hidden from the wise

After these harsh words of condemnation, the tone changes to one of winsome appeal. Jesus has kind words of welcome and invitation for babes and the burdened. Three separate sayings are grouped together: 25–6, 27, 28–30. The first two sayings correspond with Luke 10:21–2 while the first and last lean heavily on the wisdom literature background of Ecclesiasticus [Sirach] 51. The subject which is common to all three is that of hidden things being revealed, and revealed to the unregarded and unlikely; life in the upside-down Kingdom seldom conforms to worldly expectations.

The first saying, which has no direct reference to Jesus, asserts the biblical theme that worldly wisdom and knowledge of God often clash. So-called wisdom can be a barrier to soul knowledge; the wise, like the rich, are potential victims of the limitations of the self-satisfied, self-contained life. Their smug assurance of their 'knowledge' can blind them to the truth beyond its limits. On the other hand, 'babes', 'the little ones', characterised by both their lack of knowledge and their powerlessness, are the potential recipients of the hidden truths of God and life. They are peculiarly open to the whisper of God's voice. Unlearned they may be, but they are well capable of learning; 'babes' is a metaphor for 'the lowly *and* the teachable, the beginner and the pilgrim, the righteous, the vulnerable child' (see Carter 2000 p. 257). While there is no direct reference to Jesus in this saying, it is clear that he is the medium through whom hidden things are revealed to the humble and lowly. Schweizer comments:

> A new note is struck, not heard in the opening words of the Sermon on the Mount; what was promised there to the poor is understood here as present fact in Jesus. In Jesus God breaks through into the world, the God before whom a man cannot be wise or rich, but also need not be, because he can dare to surrender himself totally to him, can expect everything from him, and live without anxiety. (1975 p. 270)

In the Hebraic world view, the gaining of true knowledge was not primarily by some detached, objective intellectual process, it was much more considered as coming via an intimate, personal, subjective relationship – the sexual act, related to the giving of life, was described as 'knowing'. It is in that profound light that we hear the words of the second saying about the relationship of the Son to the Father. The sequence of thought is that Jesus, the Son, is who he is through the knowing love of the Father; in turn, the intimacy of that relationship allows the Son to 'know' the Father and, through his 'knowing', impart that knowledge to those who hear and follow him.

Who are those who are invited to 'hear' and 'follow'? They are the weary and the heavy-laden, those suffering the burdens of unjust and unequal yokes. They would consist of the majority poor of the land, for whom life was a daily struggle on the margins of life and death; they would include all those who were marginalised, disregarded, rendered silent and powerless by the powers that be in their society. 'Easy' is not a good translation of Jesus' yoke; 'kindly' or 'gentle' would be better.

'Come to me, all who labour and are heavy-laden, and I will give you rest.' Jesus' words sound in the present tense to all those who carry heavy burdens in our world now, to the tired, to those with empty hands and hearts. The promise of a kindly yoke remains for all who have ears to hear. After so many tough words about discipleship, it is good to hear them. The road is not easy: Jesus would have those who would follow him suffer no illusions. But the road is with him; and, on the way, weary disciples will find the rest they need, and more than mere rest – the encouragement, enlightenment, love and laughter that comes from the company of the one who has taken the way of gentle lowliness to lift the disciple high, and put a spring in his step for the road ahead.

Study

By yourself

'Come to me, all who labour and are heavy-laden, and I will give you rest'.

Reflect on the times when you have found rest and refreshment in the company of Jesus, through his words, in the life of prayer, in communal worship or in other unexpected ways.

For group work

Share the above reflections together. Ask how your faith community can better issue Jesus' invitation today.

Chapter 15

UP AGAINST IT

Matthew 12
The Question about the Sabbath
(*Mark 2:23–8, Luke 6:1–5*)

Not long afterwards, Jesus was walking through some cornfields on the Sabbath. His disciples were hungry, so they began to pick ears of corn and eat the grain. When the Pharisees saw this, they said to Jesus, 'Look, it is against our Law for your disciples to do this on the Sabbath!'

Jesus answered, 'Have you never read what David did that time when he and his men were hungry? He went into the house of God, and he and his men ate the bread offered to God, even though it was against the Law for them to eat it – only the priests were allowed to eat that bread. Or have you not read in the Law of Moses that every Sabbath the priests in the Temple actually break the Sabbath law, yet they are not guilty? I tell you that there is something here greater than the Temple. The scripture says, "It is kindness that I want, not animal sacrifices." If you really knew what this means, you would not condemn people who are not guilty; for the Son of Man is Lord of the Sabbath.'

The Man with the Paralysed Hand
(*Mark 3:1–6, Luke 6:6–11*)

Jesus left that place and went to a synagogue, where there was a man who had a paralysed hand. Some people were there who wanted to accuse Jesus of doing wrong, so they asked him, 'Is it against our Law to heal on the Sabbath?'

Jesus answered, 'What if one of you has a sheep and it falls into a deep hole on the Sabbath? Will you not take hold of it and lift it out? And a human being is worth much more than a sheep! So, then, our Law does allow us to help someone on the Sabbath.' Then he said to the man with the paralysed hand, 'Stretch out your hand.'

He stretched it out, and it became well again, just like the other one. Then the Pharisees left and made plans to kill Jesus.

God's Chosen Servant

When Jesus heard about the plot against him, he went away from that place; and large crowds followed him. He healed all those who were ill and gave them orders not to tell others about him. He did this so as to make what God had said through the prophet Isaiah come true:

> 'Here is my servant, whom I have chosen,
> the one I love, and with whom I am pleased.
> I will send my Spirit upon him,
> and he will announce my judgement to the nations.
> He will not argue or shout,
> or make loud speeches in the streets.
> He will not break off a bent reed,
> or put out a flickering lamp.
> He will persist until he causes justice to triumph,
> and in him all peoples will put their hope.'

Jesus and Beelzebul

(Mark 3:20–30, Luke 11:14–23)

Then some people brought to Jesus a man who was blind and could not talk because he had a demon. Jesus healed the man, so that he was able to talk and see. The crowds were all amazed at what Jesus had done. 'Could he be the Son of David?' they asked.

When the Pharisees heard this, they replied, 'He drives out demons only because their ruler Beelzebul gives him power to do so.'

Jesus knew what they were thinking, so he said to them, 'Any country that divides itself into groups which fight each other will not last very long. And any town or family that divides itself into groups which fight each other will fall apart. So if one group is fighting another in Satan's kingdom, this means that it is already divided into groups and will soon fall apart! You say that I drive out demons because Beelzebul gives me the power to do so. Well, then, who gives your followers the power to drive them out? What your own followers do proves that you are wrong! No, it is not Beelzebul, but God's Spirit, who gives me the power to drive out demons, which proves that the Kingdom of God has already come upon you.

'No one can break into a strong man's house and take away his belongings unless he first ties up the strong man; then he can plunder his house.

'Anyone who is not for me is really against me; anyone who does not help me gather is really scattering. And so I tell you that people can be forgiven any sin and any evil thing they say; but whoever says evil things against the Holy Spirit will not be forgiven. Anyone who says something against the Son of Man can be forgiven; but whoever says something against the Holy Spirit will not be forgiven – now or ever.'

A Tree and its Fruit

(Luke 6:43–5)

'To have good fruit you must have a healthy tree; if you have a poor tree, you will have bad fruit. A tree is known by the kind of fruit it bears. You snakes – how can you say good things when you are evil? For the mouth speaks what the heart is full of. A good person brings good things out of a treasure of good things; a bad person brings bad things out of a treasure of bad things.

'You can be sure that on Judgement Day everyone will have to give an account of every useless word he has ever spoken. Your words will be used to judge you – to declare you either innocent or guilty.'

The Demand for a Miracle

(Mark 8:11–12, Luke 11:29–32)

Then some teachers of the Law and some Pharisees spoke up. 'Teacher,' they said, 'we want to see you perform a miracle.'

153

'How evil and godless are the people of this day!' Jesus exclaimed. 'You ask me for a miracle? No! The only miracle you will be given is the miracle of the prophet Jonah. In the same way that Jonah spent three days and nights in the big fish, so will the Son of Man spend three days and nights in the depths of the earth. On Judgement Day the people of Nineveh will stand up and accuse you, because they turned from their sins when they heard Jonah preach; and I tell you that there is something here greater than Jonah! On Judgement Day the Queen of Sheba will stand up and accuse you, because she travelled all the way from her country to listen to King Solomon's wise teaching; and I assure you that there is something here greater than Solomon!'

The Return of the Evil Spirit

(*Luke 11:24–6*)

'When an evil spirit goes out of a person, it travels over dry country looking for a place to rest. If it can't find one, it says to itself, "I will go back to my house." So it goes back and finds the house empty, clean, and all tidy. Then it goes out and brings along seven other spirits even worse than itself, and they come and live there. So when it is all over, that person is in a worse state than he was at the beginning. This is what will happen to the evil people of this day.'

Jesus' Mother and Brothers

(*Mark 3:31–5, Luke 8:19–21*)

Jesus was still talking to the people when his mother and brothers arrived. They stood outside, asking to speak with him. So one of the people there said to him, 'Look, your mother and brothers are waiting outside, and they want to speak with you.'

Jesus answered, 'Who is my mother? Who are my brothers?' Then he pointed to his disciples and said, 'Look! Here are my mother and my brothers! Whoever does what my Father in heaven wants him to do is my brother, my sister, and my mother.'

Sabbath stirrings

Ernst Käsemann, for many years the Professor of New Testament at Tübingen University, retells a story he was told in Amsterdam after the severe floods and storms which Holland suffered in 1952. It comes from a rural parish where people were extremely strict and conscientious about keeping the Sabbath holy in line with the fourth commandment. One Sunday, the dykes of the parish were under such pressure from storm and flood that they had to be strengthened if the whole area was not to be flooded and the lives of people and livestock threatened. The police notified the pastor, who found himself in a real dilemma. Should he call out the people to do the necessary work, in spite of the Sabbath prohibition of work of any kind, or should he leave them exposed to their possible destruction by their honouring the Sabbath law? He decided he shouldn't take the decision alone, and so he called the church council to debate and decide. The weight of the council debate was on obedience to the Sabbath law, regardless of the consequences. They would cast themselves on the mercy of Almighty God – and, if God willed to save them, he would save them. When the pastor pointed out examples from the gospels of Jesus himself breaking the Sabbath commandment, one venerable old man spoke up: 'I have always been troubled, Pastor, by something I have never yet ventured to say publicly. Now I must say it. I have always had the feeling that our Lord Jesus was just a bit of a liberal' (Käsemann 1969 p. 16).

At the start of Matthew 12, the temperature rises. Controversy is in the air. It begins with conflict over the keeping of the Sabbath Law. All of the first three gospels tell the stories of the disciples in the cornfield and the healing of the man with the withered hand, but Matthew puts his own slant on them. Just before we turn to them, it's worth noting this paradox. In many ways, Matthew's is the most conservative of the gospels, and certainly the gospel which is most warm to the place and significance of the Jewish Law to Jesus and in the life of the early church. Yet, throughout the gospel, there are many moments when it points to a new freedom beyond the old Law. The book from which I quoted Käsemann's story is called *Jesus Means Freedom* – a marvellously polemic short rampage through the New Testament. Lurking in Matthew's gospel is a real gospel of freedom, and it certainly surfaces here in these two linked Sabbath stories. The story begins with Jesus and his disciples on the way to the local synagogue on the Sabbath day. The hungry disciples pick some of the ears of corn, and Jesus is rounded on by the Pharisees, complaining that they are in breach of the holy Sabbath Law. Jesus offers two Old Testament passages in response. He reminds the opposition of the incident when David, who had been anointed King of Israel by the prophet Samuel, but at this point was fleeing for his life with some of his followers from the forces of King Saul, was given the holy bread from off the altar at Shiloh (1 Samuel 21:1–6), bread which only the priests were supposed to touch, far less eat. In quoting the example of David, there is the hint that in Jesus there is one who is greater than David – and the expected one greater than David was the Messiah.

Jesus also quotes the exception to the Sabbath rule which enjoins the Temple priests to offer sacrifice on the Sabbath. Then he adds: 'I tell you that there is something here greater than the Temple' (12:6). Greater than David, greater than the Temple, and, at the end of this section, 'Lord of the Sabbath'? Here we have a series of invitations in quick succession for us, the hearers, to recognise who Jesus is, as God's chosen one.

There's another scripture quotation. For the second time in Matthew's gospel, Jesus quotes the words of Hosea 6:6: 'What I want is mercy, and not sacrifice'. These words form an obvious link with and entry into the second of the two Sabbath stories, the story of the healing of the man with the paralysed hand before the synagogue congregation. One commentator writes: 'The rabbis speak of the Law, sacrifice and acts of love as the three pillars that together bear up the world' (Schweizer 1975 p. 278). In word and action, Jesus asserts that it is acts of love which undergird the other two. His loving restoration of the man's withered hand takes precedence over the Law's demands. 'Mercy, not sacrifice', acts of love before ritual observance, acts like a theme chorus outcropping again and again throughout the gospel.

So, we can see two things going on simultaneously in these passages about the Sabbath. We see Jesus reinforcing his claim to be God's chosen instrument. But that claim has nothing of self-aggrandisement about it; rather, it leads to a human freedom for all, through a profoundly kind and compassionate humanity elevated above all the fine points of the Law.

Servant Song

The bulk of Matthew 12:15–21 is made up of a quotation from Isaiah 42, one of the four Servant Songs in Isaiah. Another of the songs, the song of the Suffering Servant in Isaiah 53, is vital for our understanding of the cross in all of the first three gospels; but this is the only time and place that Isaiah 42 occurs. It is quoted by Matthew as a comment on Jesus' continued ministry in Galilee and particularly his ministry of healing. Here, says Matthew, you can see how and why Jesus fulfils God's purposes in his work of healing.

The Isaiah quotation begins with the warmest of language to describe and commend God's servant. The servant is described as the one whom God has chosen, loved and delights in. These are words of warmth, affirmation, love and beauty. But when we hear of chosenness, election, the warning lights come on. All too often, these words have been used in the history of the church to create division, conflict, exclusion, strife. Here are some wise words from Daniel Berrigan:

> This choice of God is a delicate matter. Are others not also loved and singled out? One must believe so, lest matters of religion, race or colour take on a questionable form. In classic Jewish commentary, the Servant Song was understood as a celebration of God's choice of a community. The loving and summoning voice extended out and out. If Jews were chosen, it was in order to offer a sign of loving compassion in the world. The everlasting arms enfolded all. Let us then refuse to read the text from the point of view of the ego, whether personal or political. Simply in being chosen, one becomes a sign of God's choice of everyone. Indeed our creation, our existence, and the joy of walking in the world indicate a primal choice of humans on God's part. From the start we are blessed, summoned, and rejoiced in.
>
> Baptism and confirmation are occasions to accept once more that first choice, to choose to be chosen. Symbolically we follow through on the first act of God, echo the divine yes with our own. Thus we find our dignity and our vocation.

157

> Therefore we take joy in all the living, the unborn, the rejected and despised, those declared expendable, the aged (so often also unwanted). We welcome them all! We rejoice in each and every one! (Berrigan 1996 p. 116)

With these cautionary words in mind, we continue with the quotation from Isaiah. The servant will receive the gift of the Spirit; what the Servant achieves will be by the Spirit's aid. His work will be the work of bringing justice, but his way will be the way of gentleness and healing. He will tread the earth lightly; his footsteps will be light on the grass. He will not stride in with heavy boots. The faint flame will be delicately fanned into life, not carelessly snuffed out.

The task of the servant is to proclaim justice to the Gentiles, to be the Gentiles' hope. In Matthew's gospel, at the beginning, the middle and the end, in this most Jewish of gospels, we hear about the gospel for the Gentiles, for all people. It is after the cross that the gospel for the Gentiles is made plain, and in this passage the shadow of the cross looms. It is foreshadowed when Matthew announces that, after the Sabbath incidents, the Pharisees conspired how to destroy Jesus (12:14), and a second time in this quotation from Isaiah with its stress on the way of gentleness. For this is not the way the nations behave. The way of the nations is the way of self-interest and aggression. It is far from the way of the servant. But the way of the servant is the true way. The words of Isaiah, the prophet from the eighth century before the Christian era, have become through Jesus Christ our way, the way to which we are summoned. Listen to Daniel Berrigan again:

> How does one become teachable, attentive to the simple and lowly things – candle flame endangered in the winds, reeds more fragile than the bones of small birds? The vulnerability and mortality of the symbols urge us to pause and to grow mindful. The flame, the reed are more than simple phenomena, to be passed by, more or less contemptuously or thoughtlessly trodden upon.
>
> All things are to be cherished and protected, as a hand cupped over a flame, or a gentle footfall upon the earth. We too are fragile. Someone must not quench or crush us.
>
> We name this mindful One, Providence.

In so describing the Servant, God describes herself. The qualities praised in the Servant are literally godly, as the life and death of Jesus illustrate. (Berrigan 1996 pp. 120–1)

Sight and sound

The gospel continues with the story of yet another healing. It is the healing of a man possessed who can neither see nor speak. Jesus both opens his eyes and loosens his tongue. We can see Jesus' healing here as a metaphor for what he does in so many lives, including our own. He opens our eyes to see the world in an altogether new light, through his eyes of faith and compassion, and he loosens our tongues so that we can speak the truth in love to one another and indeed so that we can be witnesses in the world to his love and glory. Making the blind see and the dumb speak were two of the distinguishing marks of the hoped-for Messiah; we can also hear this healing story as yet another sign and pointer to the true identity of Jesus as God's chosen one. Presumably that is why the crowd gives voice to its question: 'Can this be the Son of David?' (12:23).

The opposition saw it otherwise. The Pharisees said that Jesus' work of healing was simply the work of the devil. Spin is not a modern invention. Jesus counters their bad-mouthing of him robustly. 'Don't be daft', he says. 'The work of the devil is to disable and defeat human beings; how can my ministry of healing, which is the opposite of all the devil stands for, be the devil's work? If it's the devil's work, then he's defeating himself. A kingdom divided cannot stand. And', he continues, 'what about your healers, your exorcists? Are they too agents of Satan?' He then adds punch to his argument by borrowing from low life and comparing himself to a housebreaker entering the house of a strong man. The strong man has first to be disabled and restrained, and the strong man is the devil. This may well be a reference back for us readers to the story of Jesus' temptations in 4:1–11.

Central to Jesus' reply to his opponents is his reference to the Spirit of God. If Jesus' work is not the devil's work, then it is the work of the Spirit; and, if the work of the Spirit, then the kingdom of God has come (12:28). In Matthew's gospel, Jesus most often speaks of the Kingdom of heaven, the heavenly Kingdom; here, he quite specifically speaks of God's Kingdom, God's reign, God's reality earthed among us. He goes on at the end of this passage to say that the one unforgivable sin is the sin against the Holy Spirit (12:32). But what is that sin? In the context in which Jesus is speaking, it is the refusal to recognise the activity of God's Spirit in the work of Jesus himself.

By refusing to recognise the Spirit at work in Jesus, people condemn themselves, shut themselves off from the healing stream which can renew their lives. Tom Wright says: 'Once you declare that the only remaining bottle of water is poisoned, you condemn yourself to dying of thirst' (Wright 2002 p. 148). But the evidence about Jesus is plain – of limbs renewed, eyes opened, speech restored. The Spirit is here, the hidden Kingdom is becoming a reality, plain to see; and the one greater than David, greater than the Temple, the Lord of the Sabbath, is at work in the world, in his works of compassion and hope, in our works of compassion and hope. What God wants, from us today, is kindness, compassion, mercy, the gentle way – not sacrifice, not more and more religion. What God wants, and what through Jesus God enables, is kindness.

Watch your language!

The confrontation with some Pharisees continues. They have been busy bad-mouthing Jesus, name-calling him as the agent of Beelzebul, the prince of demons. Jesus has countered robustly. His last point has been that the Holy Spirit of God is witness to the truth he is and utters. The Spirit is at work in bringing people to a recognition of who Jesus is: Jesus is enabled to conduct his work of teaching and healing only with the Spirit's aid. Jesus pursues the theme of recognition. 'You recognise a tree by its fruits', he says; 'if a tree brings good fruit it is known as a good tree, and the converse is also true.' There is a strong echo here of Jesus' words towards the close of the Sermon on the Mount in 7:16–20. His next words, when he roundly denounces the Pharisees who are miscalling him, also sound familiar. 'You brood of vipers' uses the same words that John the Baptist used to address the Pharisees and Sadducees who came to him for baptism (3:7–11). Jesus continues, expressing a frequent theme in Matthew, that it is the heart, our inner motivation, which is the driver of our words and actions. Here, the emphasis is on words: 'out of the abundance of the heart the mouth speaks'(12:34b NRSV). This short passage, characteristically Matthean in tone, ends with a solemn warning that on judgement day we will have to account for every careless word we've spoken.

Lest we think that might mean we would have an awful long time to spend in the queue at the Pearly Gates, the context here suggests that Jesus is thinking specifically of words spoken against him and denying the Kingdom which is coming. But it's worth noticing what one commentator has seen, that already by this stage in the gospel, before we're halfway through,

> Jesus has taught against angry words (5:22–6), oaths (5:33–7), empty prayers (6:7), unforgiving words (6:14–15), anxious words (6:31, 10:19), words of judgement (7:1), hypocritical words (7:4–5), words of false confession (7:21–2), presumptuous words (8:19), fearful words (8:26), and, more immediately, words that resist Jesus' mission and God's purposes (9:11, 34, 10:33, 12:2, 24, 31–2). (Carter 2000 p. 276)

Maybe it's Matthew's instincts as a teacher which lead him to this stress and emphasis. Watch your language! is a pretty consistent biblical theme. The Bible has a high view of words as vehicles for conveying truth. Of course, they can be false when they are used to fashion the deliberate lie, and they can be hypocritical when there is no marriage of word and action, when we say one thing and do another. But the word of integrity, where word and action are one, the authentic word, as Jesus' own words are authentic in the one who has married word and action – the word of truth is a word of power. And so we pray for God's Spirit to be within us, to enable our tongues to be truthful, for our words come from a heart that is spirit-led.

The sign of Jonah

'Teacher, we want to see a sign from you.' The controversy with Jesus continues. The Pharisees are now joined by some scribes, who have together just witnessed Jesus' healing of the man who was blind and dumb. He has opened the man's eyes and released him from his dumbness, yet they still want a 'sign'. By a sign they mean something more than a mere healing miracle, some sort of divine thunderclap which would validate Jesus' claim, something a bit like the temptation Jesus refused when he turned his back on the possibility of throwing himself down from the pinnacle of the Temple (4:5–8).

Jesus answers them in no uncertain terms: 'An evil and adulterous generation asks for a sign, but no sign will be given it except the sign of the prophet Jonah'. He goes on to remind them of the three days and nights which Jonah spent in the belly of the sea monster before he was cast ashore to start again on his task of calling the people of Nineveh to repentance, to a radical changing of their ways. And he compares Jonah's time in the monster's belly with the time between his own crucifixion and resurrection. Of course, the comparison is not quite accurate, as Jesus is only two nights in the grave before his rising.

The question arising over this incident is whether these are the words of Jesus or whether this story has been inserted by Matthew from words circulating in the early church. Did Jesus know as precisely as this story suggests what lay ahead of him at the end of his earthly life? We'll never know the definite answer, one way or another. If Jesus did know with complete certainty what lay ahead of him, it raises questions about his full humanity, which is so precious to us. One of the aspects of our humanity is that we don't know the future, our future, in precise detail.

What we can say with certainty is that this story of the sign of Jonah points to the key significance that Easter held for the early church. It was the whole Easter event which brought the church into being. It was the mystery of that event, the strange contradiction of the crucifixion, something which could be called the polar opposite of the kind of divine sign the scribes and Pharisees here were looking for which brought the young church into being. The cross is anything but the conventional demonstration of divine power; instead, it speaks of humiliation, abandonment, godlessness: it was out of the contradiction of the cross, coupled with the shock and surprise of the resurrection, that the church was born, with its members' identity stamped as followers of Jesus of Nazareth, the crucified and risen One. The sign of Jonah, as Matthew interprets it here, is the strangest of signs, almost an anti-sign we might say: the sign that confounds those who are looking for signs – and, for that very reason, it has become the most profound and provocative sign of all. For who but God could conceive of the mystery of the Easter journey?

Matthew also couples the story of Jonah and the Ninevites with the story of the arrival of the Queen of Sheba at the court of King Solomon (1 Kings 10:1–13, 2 Chronicles 9:1–12). What the Ninevites and the Queen of Sheba have in common is that they are Gentiles, outsiders. The queen comes to Solomon seeking wisdom from this Hebrew king; the Ninevites are spared destruction through the reluctant agency of the Hebrew prophet Jonah. If these outsiders could recognise God's Spirit at work in Jonah and Solomon, the implication is clear – why can't the insiders, the scribes and Pharisees with their presumptuous question, recognise God's Spirit at work in Jesus? Does the question still stand for us as insiders? Is the sign that we recognise as the one which validates Jesus and reveals his true identity the sign of Jonah, the whole Easter event, the anti-sign, the sign that changes forever our view of the face of God and reshapes our understanding of what it means to be human?

In the references to Jonah and Solomon, it is said explicitly: 'Here is one greater than Jonah, here is one greater than Solomon', greater than the prophet, greater than the king. And, at the start of the chapter, we saw Jesus described as Lord of the Sabbath, greater than David, greater than the Temple. This chapter, and the one which precedes it, are concerned with people discerning Jesus' true identity, as God's chosen one. His enemies may address him as 'Teacher'. His disciples call him 'Lord' … greater than Jonah, Solomon, David, the Temple, Lord of the Sabbath.

The expanding family

All the way through chapter 12 of Matthew's gospel, we've seen Jesus in conflict with the established religious authorities of his day. What would be the effect of the cumulative opposition to Jesus from the authorities of his people? In our familiarity with the gospel, we're maybe a bit prone to write off the scribes and Pharisees as simply the baddies in the story and not see how their opposition, as those to whom their community had given a certain status and authority, must have cast a big question mark over the whole of Jesus' ministry. We know that, at the end, they are involved in his death; but all the way through they cast a shadow. How would we react to the appearance of a new 'prophet' in our land who was roundly criticised by the leadership of our churches? We'd have our doubts.

Maybe, by this point in the narrative, the first readers of the gospel were beginning to have their doubts too. With all this opposition, does this mean that Jesus' way is going to founder and fail? This last small section of chapter 12 tells us: 'No'. There are those who will take the way, carry on the story. The chapter ends with the very familiar passage where Jesus' family come looking for him, wanting to speak to him, and he really doesn't treat them very well (12:46–50). We remember as we hear this story that the ties of kin and family and the whole network of mutual obligation which these ties involved were infinitely stronger in Jesus' time than in our increasingly loose-knit western world. Family was the key unit of society. John Barclay has pointed out how remarkably loosely Jesus and the early church sat to the historic and traditional obligations of family life. And certainly that's true here.

Jesus says to the one who has brought him the message from his mother and his brothers: 'Who is my mother, and who are my brothers?' In Mark's gospel, he points to the crowd; in Matthew's gospel, he points specifically to the disciples and says: 'Here are my mother and my brothers! For whoever does the will of my Father in heaven is my brother and sister and mother' (12:48–50). It is the new household of faith, which no longer recognises the barriers of kith and kin, which is not based on birth, ethnicity or gender, which will carry the message on. It is a different kind of society from the conventional patriarchal household of the time. It's interesting that this new household, no longer based on conventional human patriarchy, is rooted in the will of the one whom Jesus calls 'My Father in heaven'. The love of the Father is indiscriminate and all-embracing, and it's those who 'do' the will of the Father whom Jesus recognises as his new kith and kin. Through their actions, the doors of the Kingdom continue to open.

Study

By yourself

Throughout the gospel, there is a theme of recognition. From the arrival of the men from the east to see the infant Jesus at the beginning (2:1–11) to the final parable of the sheep and the goats (25:31–46), Matthew keeps asking the question: 'Do you see Jesus in places and people which are unlikely and unexpected?' Ask yourself that question: 'Where do I see Jesus? Have I been surprised in finding him in places and people which have challenged and stretched my understanding?'

Chapter 16

MORE THAN MEETS
THE EYE

Matthew 13:1–52

The Parable of the Sower

(Mark 4:1–9, Luke 8:4–8)

That same day Jesus left the house and went to the lakeside, where he sat down to teach. The crowd that gathered round him was so large that he got into a boat and sat in it, while the crowd stood on the shore. He used parables to tell them many things.

'Once there was a man who went out to sow corn. As he scattered the seed in the field, some of it fell along the path, and the birds came and ate it up. Some of it fell on rocky ground, where there was little soil. The seeds soon sprouted, because the soil wasn't deep. But when the sun came up, it burnt the young plants; and because the roots had not grown deep enough, the plants soon dried up. Some of the seed fell among thorn bushes, which grew up and choked the plants. But some seeds fell in good soil, and the plants produced corn; some produced a hundred grains, others sixty, and others thirty.'

And Jesus concluded, 'Listen, then, if you have ears!'

The Purpose of the Parables

(Mark 4:10–12, Luke 8:9–10)

Then the disciples came to Jesus and asked him, 'Why do you use parables when you talk to the people?'

Jesus answered, 'The knowledge about the secrets of the Kingdom of heaven has been given to you, but not to them. For the person who has something will be given more, so that he will have more than enough; but the person who has nothing will have taken away from him even the little he has. The reason I use parables in talking to them is that they look, but do not see, and they listen, but do not hear or understand. So the prophecy of Isaiah applies to them:

"This people will listen and listen, but not understand;
    they will look and look, but not see,
because their minds are dull,
    and they have stopped up their ears, and have closed
        their eyes.
Otherwise, their eyes would see,
    their ears would hear, their minds would understand,
and they would turn to me, says God,
    and I would heal them."

'As for you, how fortunate you are! Your eyes see and your ears hear. I assure you that many prophets and many of God's people wanted very much to see what you see, but they could not, and to hear what you hear, but they did not.'

Jesus Explains the Parable of the Sower

(Mark 4:13–20, Luke 8:11–15)

'Listen, then, and learn what the parable of the sower means. Those who hear the message about the Kingdom but do not understand it are like the seeds that fell along the path. The Evil One comes and snatches away what was sown in them. The seeds that fell on rocky ground stand for those who receive the message gladly as soon as they hear it. But it does not sink deep into them, and they don't last long. So when trouble or persecution comes because of the message, they give up at once. The seeds that fell among thorn bushes stand for those who hear the message; but the worries about this life and the love for riches choke the message, and they don't bear fruit. And the seeds sown in the good soil stand for those who hear the message and understand it: they bear fruit, some as much as a hundred, others sixty, and others thirty.'

The Parable of the Weeds

Jesus told them another parable: 'The Kingdom of heaven is like this. A man sowed good seed in his field. One night, when everyone was asleep, an enemy came and sowed weeds among the wheat and went away. When the plants grew and the ears of corn began to form, then the weeds showed up. The man's servants came to him and said, "Sir, it was good seed you sowed in your field; where did the weeds come from?" "It was some enemy who did this," he answered. "Do you want us to go and pull up the weeds?" they asked him. "No," he answered, "because as you gather the weeds you might pull up some of the wheat along with them. Let the wheat and the weeds both grow together until harvest. Then I will tell the harvest workers to pull up the weeds first, tie them in bundles and burn them, and then to gather in the wheat and put it in my barn."'

The Parable of the Mustard Seed

(Mark 4:30–2, Luke 13:18–19)

Jesus told them another parable: 'The Kingdom of heaven is like this. A man takes a mustard seed and sows it in his field. It is the smallest of all seeds, but when it grows up, it is the biggest of all plants. It becomes a tree, so that birds come and make their nests in its branches.'

The Parable of the Yeast

(Luke 13:20–1)

Jesus told them another parable: 'The Kingdom of heaven is like this. A woman takes some yeast and mixes it with forty litres of flour until the whole batch of dough rises.'

Jesus' Use of Parables

(Mark 4:33–4)

Jesus used parables to tell all these things to the crowds; he would not say a thing to them without using a parable. He did this to make what the prophet had said come true:

'I will use parables when I speak to them;
I will tell them things unknown since the creation of the world.'

Jesus Explains the Parable of the Weeds

When Jesus had left the crowd and gone indoors, his disciples came to him and said, 'Tell us what the parable about the weeds in the field means.'

Jesus answered, 'The man who sowed the good seed is the Son of Man; the field is the world; the good seed is the people who belong to the Kingdom; the weeds are the people who belong to the Evil One; and the enemy who sowed the weeds is the Devil. The harvest is the end of the age, and the harvest workers are angels. Just as the weeds are gathered up and burnt in the fire, so the same thing will happen at the end of the age; the Son of Man will send out his angels to gather up out of his Kingdom all those who cause people to sin and all others who do evil things, and they will throw them into the fiery furnace, where they will cry and grind their teeth. Then God's people will shine like the sun in their Father's Kingdom. Listen, then, if you have ears!'

The Parable of the Hidden Treasure

'The Kingdom of heaven is like this. A man happens to find a treasure hidden in a field. He covers it up again, and is so happy that he goes and sells everything he has, and then goes back and buys that field.'

The Parable of the Pearl

'Also, the Kingdom of heaven is like this. A man is looking for fine pearls, and when he finds one that is unusually fine, he goes and sells everything he has, and buys that pearl.'

The Parable of the Net

'Also, the Kingdom of heaven is like this. Some fishermen throw their net out in the lake and catch all kinds of fish. When the net is full, they pull it to shore and sit down to divide the fish; the good ones go into their buckets, the worthless ones are thrown away. It will be like this at the end of the age; the angels will go out and gather up the evil people from among the good and will throw them into the fiery furnace, where they will cry and grind their teeth.'

New Truths and Old

'Do you understand these things?' Jesus asked them.

'Yes', they answered.

So he replied, 'This means, then, that every teacher of the Law who becomes a disciple in the Kingdom of heaven is like the owner of a house who takes new and old things out of his storeroom.'

'The reign of God, like a farmer's field'

In Matthew 13, we come to the third of the teaching blocks in the gospel. The great bulk of this chapter consists of parables, largely drawn from the life of a peasant agricultural community. They speak of the Kingdom of heaven, the reign of God: cumulatively they have two main messages; first, that the Kingdom Jesus has come to announce does bring division and judgement, but also, second, that to those who perceive it, the Kingdom is rich with promise and welcome. Warren Carter summarises what has already been made known to gospel readers about the Kingdom in the preceding twelve chapters.

- It is manifested in Jesus' words and deeds.
- It is God's gracious gift, initiative, and action.
- It resists, rather than endorses, Rome's empire.
- It is divisive; some welcome it, while others, especially the elite, resist God's claim.
- It is disruptive and disturbing, reversing previous commitments, imperial structures, practices and priorities, while creating a new way of life which counters dominant societal values.
- It conflicts and competes with the devil's reign.
- It is present in part, but for many life remains unchanged.

- Its present manifestation will be completed when God's reign is established over all including Rome's empire. (Carter 2000 p. 280)

The midpoint of the gospel is near. In a sense, this third teaching block draws together what has already been disclosed of the purpose of Jesus and the meaning of the Kingdom. Matthew, borrowing from Mark, sets the scene vividly. He describes the large crowds, so great that, to find a vantage point from which to teach, Jesus has to commandeer a boat and set off from the shore in order to be seen and heard. He sits to teach, assuming the usual posture of the authoritative teacher. Then he begins ...

Sowing seeds

'Listen! A sower went to sow.' Parables are provocations. They are the opposite of open-and-shut cases in which we get 'told' the answers, neatly packaged. They raise questions, invite us into the use of thought and imagination, summon us to explore. They say to us: 'Here's a wee story. Let it work in you, work on you. Think about it, brood over it, talk about it. Maybe the story itself will be like the good seed in the sower story, giving a return out of all proportion to its size.'

'Listen! A sower went to sow.' Ask the question: 'Who is the sower? Who is the one who throws about with hopeful purpose and prodigal abandon the seeds which have cost him dear and on which his future depends ... throws these tiny, minuscule, seeming dead husks with hope for the harvest ... throws to left and right, here and there, knowing some of the ground is too hard, some of the ground is too rocky, in some of the ground there lurks already the other seed of thorns and thistles ... but who knows too that there is good soil there, soil which will yield an increase and give a harvest?'

'Who is the sower?' Is it God, the Creator, Maker, Father? We could say 'Yes'. We could say that God is forever sowing seed, for God is the source of all life; the seed of God is all around us, in the myriad and pluriform works of creation, in the mystery of the gift of life to each of us, in the events of history and the life of nature, in the words of scripture, the song of the church, the quiet place of conscience and the still place of prayer, in the love of our friends, the welcome of the stranger, the words of our neighbour. Yes, we could say that God is forever sowing seed, and that the prodigality of God is truly amazing, when we stop to think about it.

Start again. 'Who is the sower?' Is it Jesus himself, the story-teller? We could say 'Yes'. We could say that Jesus is forever sowing seed, in the words of his teaching, in the actions of his healing, in his life with the disciples, in his life among the crowds. We could say that Jesus is so busy sowing seed in his ministry for, with and to others that, if he was a farmer, his arms each night must have been continually aching, so much does he spend himself. We remember the most costly seed-sowing of all, in his own words in John's gospel: 'In very truth I tell you, unless a grain of wheat falls into the ground and dies, it remains but a single grain; but if it dies it bears much fruit' (John 12:34). Christ the sower, Christ the seed, Christ sower and seed, bearer, bringer of costly grace, prodigal producer of faith's abundance.

Start a third time. 'Who is the sower?' It might be you ... or me, or you and me. And it might be about our calling as the followers of Jesus to sow the seed of faith in our world, through our words and our lives, through our witness and our service. It might be too about the way that faith can grow in us, in each one of us, in our own personal lives, and about the way faith can grow in us as a community of faith ... in both ways faith growing, hidden, mysterious, not without its setbacks and disappointments, but with a promise of fullness, maturity, abundance.

'Who is the sower?' It might be ... God the Creator, Christ the worker, you and me. It's not an either–or, it's a both–and. Remember how John's gospel weaves together the Father and Jesus and all who follow Jesus. One of the most remarkable, amazing verses in the Bible is: 'As you, Father, are in me and I am in you, may they also be in us, so that the world may believe that you have sent me' (John 17:21). What a wonderful, multiple interweaving. So, give thanks for God who is forever sowing the seeds of life, who gives us the seed that is Christ, and makes us living seeds, tiny yet fruitful, the scattering of his hand. Give thanks for Christ the seed and Christ the sower, who sows the seeds of faith in us, and calls and commissions us to be sowers of the seed in places both barren and fertile, and promises harvest, though the measure of the harvest is always his, not ours. Give thanks for our continuing part in the work of God in his world.

Why?

The next section, where the disciples come to Jesus out of the crowd and ask him about the purposes of the parables, has always been difficult to interpret. Matthew takes and amplifies the shorter comments of Jesus in Mark 4:10–12. The 'knowledge' and 'secrets' of 13:11 probably refer to ideas current in Matthew's community about the last things – in particular the final judgement, a key concept for Matthew. A first reading could suggest that Jesus told parables deliberately to conceal; but such a meaning runs contrary to the whole thrust of the gospel. A simple, more believable general explanation can run as follows. As this gospel progresses, it becomes increasingly sceptical about the ability of the 'crowd' to comprehend and accept Jesus and his Kingdom message. Remember that it is written out of the context of the rejection of Jesus and his disciples by the synagogue and the serious pain and disruption which this caused to the community of post-Easter disciples. This passage occurs well into the gospel, when the crowd has had many opportunities (like the disciples of John at the start of chapter 11) to 'see' and 'hear' Jesus, witness the works he performs and listen to the wise words he speaks. Many will choose to reject him, in spite of the evidence of their eyes and ears; speaking in parables will make little difference. Jesus is simply telling the disciples the way things are.

The point is reinforced by the quotation from Isaiah 6:9–10 from the Septuagint version, underlining the hard lot of a prophet of speaking to the apparently deaf. In the context of Isaiah, the prophet's first task after his call is to speak to King Ahaz; the ruler refuses to 'hear' him. Jesus continues in the prophetic role of speaking a word to unresponsive powers-that-be.

In contrast to the rejection of the seed of the Word by the multitude of the blind and deaf, the small band of disciples are 'blessed' by having seen and heard (13:16–17). What they have seen and heard is the truth and reality of Jesus himself and who he is. In their 'vision', they have been granted to 'see' what many in past generations longed for; they see it in Jesus himself.

Here's why

After the difficulties of interpreting 13:10–17, Jesus' explanation of the meaning of the sower parable is surprisingly simple. 'Field', 'seed' and 'harvest' were metaphors long associated with describing God's relationship to Israel his people. The reception of the seed is fourfold; three negatives and an overwhelming positive. The seed which falls on the path is easy meat for the waiting birds, which quickly devour it. The birds stand for the Evil One, and the seeds' reception is likened to those who hear the Word with no understanding. The seed falling on rocky ground has no room for real roots; it springs up one day but doesn't last long, as it shrivels in the sun. It represents those who hear the Word with initial enthusiasm but, when troubles come, and particularly persecution, they can't stand the heat – a situation very real within the context of Matthew's community. The seed sown among thorns and soon choked describes those who allow their receiving the Word to be smothered by their anxieties and love of material things. They remain fruitless. The seed which lands on good soil, however, yields at least a good and often an abundant harvest, out of all proportion to the smallness of the initial outlay. While faith will often encounter difficulties and opposition, it will also mature and produce real fruitfulness.

Judgement

The next parable of the weeds is found only in Matthew. Like the sower parable, it comes in two halves; first the parable (14:24–30), subsequently Jesus' explanation to the disciples alone within the enclosed context of a house (14:36–43). What does the parable of the weeds among the wheat say? Its message is twofold. It begins by being bluntly uncompromising in recognising the reality that there is good and evil in the world. It makes it quite clear that this world is a battleground between the forces of light and the forces of darkness. It also asserts unequivocally that we will all be called to account for our own deeds and misdeeds. Once again, we are brought face to face with the reality of judgement. In the end, the justice of God will prevail. The future belongs to God, and his way will out. Will we have furthered his way, or will we have hindered it?

The sting in the tail of this parable, however, lies in the second half, where Jesus makes very plain that, while judgement is sure, it always belongs to God and not to us mere mortals, even those who belong within the community of faith. Our quick and partial judgements are a hindrance rather than a help to God's harvest; they are just as likely to damage and kill off the good grain as to put an end to the weeds, a truth most gardeners and farmers have learned from their own bitter experience. 'Leave to God what belongs to God and keep labouring in the field' is the word of Jesus in this parable. In his own time, it would have a polemical reference to groups such as the Pharisees and the Qumran group. Both these communities excluded those who could not reach their own demanding standards, whereas the community which gathers around Jesus is a community open to all. The reference is not simply historical; the temptation to exclusivity is far from dead in the contemporary church.

The explanation of the parable (13:36–41) is thought by many scholars to be an editorial addition by Matthew on to Jesus' original words. The main thrust of the parable itself is to counsel disciples to refrain from judgement; the explanation comes down pretty heavily on the note of judgement and the fate of the wicked. In so doing, it blunts the message of the original parable. Is there a tension here which surfaces from time to time throughout this gospel? Is the gospel writer himself wrestling in his own mind with the tension between the wide-open door of the liberating gospel of grace, forgiveness, love of enemies, 'mercy, not sacrifice', and the heritage of a faith with a heavy emphasis on our being judged according to our works and deeds? Although there is a historical particularity here in Matthew's painful and costly struggle with his own faith roots, this issue is far from a dead one. Learning the far-reaching implications of Jesus' radical gospel of grace remains a continuing gift and task for contemporary disciples and the church of today. (The parable of the net, 13:47–50, reinforces the message of the explanation; some scholars think the original parable contained only the first sentence and that Matthew has added his heavy note of judgement.)

Growth ... and faith

Between the parable of the weeds and its explanation, there are the two short and important parables of hidden growth, of the mustard seed and the work of yeast (13:31–3). These very positive parables can refer to either the growth of the Kingdom on earth or the growth of faith in the believer. Since faith is such a key category both in our lives and in the gospel, it is worth lingering to explore it further. In 1867, Matthew Arnold wrote his famous poem 'On Dover Beach' in which he spoke of the 'melancholy, long, withdrawing roar' of the sea of faith. Arnold was beginning to sense, along with many of his contemporaries, a faith increasingly under threat. We often think of the Victorian era as a high point of faith. In reality, it was a time when many of the seeds of our present secularism were sown – the loss of the urban masses from the church, the time of the arrival of Marx's *Communist Manifesto* and Darwin's *Origin of the Species*.

Let's think for a moment about that metaphor of the retreating sea of faith. Arnold captures poetically the reality we all know in our own experience. In times past, faith, to a greater or lesser extent, could simply be assumed to be a reality in the lives of most people in the western world. Church was part of their lives, and people, as it were, were washed into it by the prevailing culture, the dominant social milieu ... washed in, largely unthinkingly and uncritically. What has changed in our times is that faith is no longer simply assumed as a given, to be generally taken for granted. It has to be consciously decided for, largely against the prevailing tides of received opinion. No longer are we, the faithful, seen as representatives of the natural order of things in our society. Increasingly, we are seen as a minority, doing our own rather quaint thing, practising faith, whatever that is.

And about what faith is, those around us have their own opinions or misconceptions. One of my professors said that some people think of faith as some kind of special talent or special taste, like a liking for caviar or appreciation of the music of Stravinsky, while others see it as a kind of irrationalist trick, an illegitimate attempt to find a short-cut through a jungle impenetrable to honest reason. He went on:

> But perhaps the commonest complication which you find among the most cultivated of the despisers of religion, or the enquirers about its credentials, is that faith is regarded as just one, perhaps the chief, of the burdens which you are required to carry if you want to be a Christian. They understand that you are required to love everybody; that you are to be amiable and optimistic – in general, more and more of a paragon; and then, on top of all this, you are required to have faith.... No wonder that it often becomes the last straw that breaks the camel's back! (Smith 1970 p. 11)

Now for something completely different. In today's gospel, Jesus says: 'The kingdom of heaven is like a mustard seed that someone took and sowed in his field; it is the smallest of all the seeds, but when it has grown it is the greatest of shrubs and becomes a tree, so that the birds of the air come and make nests in its branches'. Jesus is talking about faith. He is certainly not talking about the 'melancholy, long, withdrawing roar of the retreating sea of faith'; he is talking about the hidden mystery of its multiplying increase. He promises that faith will grow. Ah, but some will object, 'Jesus lived in times when faith was taken for granted. He knew nothing about the corrosive acids of modernity which eat away at faith in our times.' Well, yes, and no.

Yes, Jesus lived in a time when everybody had some kind of belief. But one of the marks of his ministry is to redraw for his own contemporaries, and for us, what faith is. Jesus lived in a time when his own people had faith but not much hope. They believed that their people's best days were yesterday, and that God had largely gone into eclipse for them. The message of Jesus, in word and action, is that God is not distant and indifferent, God is near. Look and listen and you will find God, in the world around you, in the way of prayer, in the people you meet, and in the taking of the way. And that faith you thought was tiny, insignificant, of no account, you will discover is a real and living thing, something that will become fruitful, something which will grow and multiply in your own life.

In a real sense for us, faith begins with Jesus. Yes, Jesus' own faith was forged and shaped by the faith of his people Israel, and we can't neglect or devalue the faith he inherited. We can't understand much of what he says without taking Israel's faith seriously. But Christian faith begins by saying 'yes' to Jesus, by taking him seriously, listening to his words, attending to his actions, recognising his truth, belonging to his continuing community today. And faith grows out of the continuing conversation, dialogue, between the reality of his life in the world 2,000 years ago and the reality of our lives in our world today. His world was very different from ours, and 2,000 years is a huge gap to span, but the continuing witness of faith is that, if we take Jesus seriously, if we are prepared to struggle with the gospel, he becomes for us amazingly and vividly relevant and contemporary, like the mystery of the mustard seed. So, faith begins and grows by saying 'yes' to him.

If we say 'Yes', he will reveal to us the reality of the Kingdom of heaven, the reality of God. There is a beyond working in our lives and the life of the world. We are not our own makers and keepers; all along the road of life we keep encountering the other, if we have eyes to see and ears to hear. Listening to the waves beating on the shores of his beloved Welsh coast, the modern poet R. S. Thomas hears a very different message from Arnold's bleak vision. In a short poem simply called 'The Other', he writes:

> There are nights that are so still
> that I can hear the small owl calling
> far off and a fox barking
> miles away. It is then that I lie
> in the lean hours awake listening
> to the swell born somewhere in the Atlantic
> rising and falling,
> wave on wave on the long shore
> by the village, that is without light
> and companionless. And the thought comes
> of that other being who is awake, too,

letting our prayers break on him,
not like this for a few hours,
but for days, years, for eternity.

(1993 p. 457)

As we come to trust that 'other being who is awake, too', so our faith, even in these times of a barren secularism, will grow, increase, wonderfully. Jesus has come to open up for us a window onto 'the living other'. We decide, we trust, we follow ...

Joy!

... which brings us naturally to the second pair of parables, short, yet gleaming like gems: the parables of great joy, of the hidden treasure and the pearl of great price (13:44–6). They point to the sheer joy of discovering the Kingdom. In the 'Yes' of that discovery, those who find the hidden treasure, the precious pearl, will divest themselves of all that they have in order to claim their prize. There's an obvious echo in the story of Jesus and the rich young man (19:16–22). Once again, Jesus shines a bright ray of sunlight on the discipleship way. 'Following me on the Kingdom way will be costly', he has been saying; 'it will mean hardship, struggle, division. But that's not all; it's the way to life, to the full life in all its costly glory. Come on.'

New and old

The teaching block of seven parables ends with Jesus asking the disciples if they have understood and their affirmative reply. With his comment (13:52) about the teacher of the Law becoming a disciple in the Kingdom, he stresses the continuity of his call and his teaching with the traditions of Israel and his radical new interpretation of it. The section ends (13:53) with the formal ending to each of the five blocks of teaching.

Study

By yourself

'O Lord, increase our faith.' Simply use this prayer and reflect on it daily for the coming month.

For group work

Using and adding to Carter's list of attributes of the Kingdom of God which Jesus has come to announce (see p. 170–1), discuss how you see the Kingdom at work in your life, and in the life of the world.

Chapter 17

NO AND YES

Matthew 13:53–8
Jesus is Rejected at Nazareth
(Mark 6:1–6, Luke 4:16–30)

When Jesus finished telling these parables, he left that place and went back to his home town. He taught in the synagogue, and those who heard him were amazed. 'Where did he get such wisdom?' they asked. 'And what about his miracles? Isn't he the carpenter's son? Isn't Mary his mother, and aren't James, Joseph, Simon and Judas his brothers? Aren't all his sisters living here? Where did he get all this?' And so they rejected him.

Jesus said to them, 'A prophet is respected everywhere except in his home town and by his own family.' Because they did not have much faith, he did not perform many miracles there.

Matthew 14
The Death of John the Baptist
(Mark 6:14–29, Luke 9:7–9)

At that time Herod, the ruler of Galilee, heard about Jesus. 'He is really John the Baptist, who has come back to life', he told his officials. 'That is why he has this power to perform miracles.'

For Herod had earlier ordered John's arrest, and he had him chained and put in prison. He had done this because of Herodias, his brother Philip's wife. For some time John the Baptist had told Herod, 'It isn't right for you to be married to Herodias!' Herod wanted to kill him, but he was afraid of the Jewish people, because they considered John to be a prophet.

On Herod's birthday the daughter of Herodias danced in front of the whole group. Herod was so pleased that he promised her, 'I swear that I will give you anything you ask for!'

At her mother's suggestion she asked him, 'Give me here and now the head of John the Baptist on a dish!'

The king was sad, but because of the promise he had made in front of all his guests he gave orders that her wish be granted. So he had John beheaded in prison. The head was brought in on a dish and given to the girl, who took it to her mother. John's disciples came, carried away his body, and buried it; then they went and told Jesus.

Jesus Feeds a Great Crowd

(Mark 6:30–44, Luke 9:10–17, John 6:1–14)

When Jesus heard the news about John, he left there in a boat and went to a lonely place by himself. The people heard about it, so they left their towns and followed him by land. Jesus got out of the boat, and when he saw the large crowd, his heart was filled with pity for them, and he healed those who were ill.

That evening his disciples came to him and said, 'It is already very late, and this is a lonely place. Send the people away and let them go to the villages to buy food for themselves.'

'They don't have to leave', answered Jesus. 'You yourselves give them something to eat!'

'All we have here are five loaves and two fish', they replied.

'Then bring them here to me', Jesus said. He ordered the people to sit down on the grass; then he took the five loaves and the two fish, looked up to heaven, and gave thanks to God. He broke the loaves and gave them to the disciples, and the disciples gave them to the people. Everyone ate and had enough. Then the disciples took up twelve baskets full of what was left over. The number of men who ate was about 5,000, not counting the women and children.

Jesus Walks on the Water

(Mark 6:45–52, John 6:15–21)

Then Jesus made the disciples get into the boat and go on ahead to the other side of the lake, while he sent the people away. After sending the people away, he went up a hill by himself to pray. When evening came, Jesus was there alone; and by this time the boat was far out in the lake, tossed about by the waves, because the wind was blowing against it.

Between three and six o'clock in the morning Jesus came to the disciples, walking on the water. When they saw him walking on the water, they were terrified. 'It's a ghost!' they said, and screamed with fear.

Jesus spoke to them at once. 'Courage!' he said. 'It is I. Don't be afraid!'

Then Peter spoke up. 'Lord, if it is really you, order me to come out on the water to you.'

'Come!' answered Jesus. So Peter got out of the boat and started walking on the water to Jesus. But when he noticed the strong wind, he was afraid and started to sink down in the water. 'Save me, Lord!' he cried.

At once Jesus reached out and grabbed hold of him and said, 'How little faith you have! Why did you doubt?'

They both got into the boat, and the wind died down. Then the disciples in the boat worshipped Jesus. 'Truly you are the Son of God!' they exclaimed.

Jesus Heals the Sick in Gennesaret

(Mark 6:53–6)

They crossed the lake and came to land at Gennesaret, where the people recognised Jesus. So they sent for the sick people in all the surrounding country and brought them to Jesus. They begged him to let those who were ill at least touch the edge of his cloak; and all who touched it were made well.

No place like home!

The locus of the action moves, and this section begins with Jesus back in his home town of Nazareth. In this chapter, the links between the different stories are telling. Looking at them in pairs can be enlightening as they either reinforce or contrast with each other. We begin with two stories of rejection: the rejection of Jesus among his own people, and the killing of John the Baptist at the court of Herod. Matthew shows the opposition to the prophetic movement of Jesus and John operating across very different levels of society. It begins at home. The story of the reaction of the townsfolk of Nazareth to Jesus is told by Matthew, Mark (6:1–6) and Luke (4:16–30). In Luke, it is a key story at the gospel's beginning. Matthew largely borrows the story from Mark, with slight but significant differences. He omits reference to Jesus' disciples; and, more importantly, he softens Mark's final sentence: 'He was not able to perform a single miracle there'. Matthew's high view of Jesus' authority has him gloss Mark's reference to Jesus' inability.

Both accounts report the 'offence' the townspeople of Nazareth take to Jesus. We are reminded of his words to the disciples of John in 11:6 after he has pointed them in the direction of the signs of his powerful ministry. 'His own' simply cannot believe in the grace and authority of one of 'their own'. To them, he's just 'the carpenter's son', though from the beginning of the gospel (1:18–25) we have been told differently. The story of the rejection of Jesus by 'his own', shown in a small scale here at Nazareth, is of course one of the underlying themes throughout Matthew. This incident comes hard after the encounter with Jesus' own family (12:46–50). Taken together, both point to the gospel's ambiguous attitude to 'kith and kin'. In a society where the ties of both immediate and wider family networks were of crucial and virtually sacrosanct importance, Jesus sits remarkably loosely to them as he creates a new community which is open to all where the dynamic ties of love and mutual acceptance and forgiveness are the ones that bind rather than mere genetic inheritance.

A deadly feast

The scene darkens significantly with Matthew's account of the death of John the Baptist, the second story of rejection. The Herod in the frame here is Herod Antipas, ruler of Galilee, one of the sons of the Herod of Matthew 2. This incident highlights the cruelty and bankruptcy of mere power and the deadly earnestness of the opposition to the prophetic movement of John and Jesus, even if John's execution rests on a mere drunken whim rather than serious political calculation. Matthew stresses the similarity of the fates of John and Jesus.

> Matthew is concerned to draw a close parallel between the fate of John and that of Jesus. Verse 5 explicitly labels the execution of John the murder of a prophet, whereas Mark 6:20 speaks only of 'a good and holy man'. In Matthew 23:29–39, Jesus will condemn Israel for killing the prophets and identify himself with the company of these prophets. And in 17:12 Jesus states openly that he must go the way of the Baptist. What can be dimly sensed in Mark is here depicted in much bolder lines: the way of the Baptist leading to martyrdom will also be taken by Jesus, and his disciples will fare no differently, as already stated in 5:12, 10:17ff., 34ff. (Schweizer 1975 p. 318)

A feast of life

After the description of the decadent feast of death at the table of Herod comes the contrast of the feast of life in the meal in the desert. The contrasts are so obvious ... between the death-dealing arrogance of power and the power of compassionate sharing, between the stink of corrupt luxury reeking from Herod's table and the forces of life as Jesus nurtures folk even in the simple stark barrenness of the desert; between Herod, the apparently powerful, unable to do the right thing, and Jesus, with no power in social and political terms, who can make bread multiply and leave people satisfied. Jesus has withdrawn into the desert but, rather than finding solitude, he has been found by a hungry crowd of over 5,000 people. Such is the importance of the desert meal that it appears in all four gospels. It's a meal which points backwards to the primal experience of Israel in their forty years of wilderness wandering, daily fed from God's hand on the manna bread of life. And it's a meal which points forward to the Last Supper on 'the night he was betrayed', and to the Communion which lies at the heart of his community called 'church'.

The story begins with Jesus in the desert (another link with John), confronted by a crowd of people in need of bread and healing. In this marginal place he is met by marginal people, and his heart goes out to them (14:14). After ministering among them, when evening comes, the necessity of the crowd's feeding arises and is brought to Jesus by his disciples. They want to send the people away to buy food. Jesus says: 'They don't have to leave; you feed them'. 'All we've got are five loaves and two fish.' 'Bring them, get everyone to sit down, and watch.' The crowd is hungry. The crowd needs to be fed. Jesus is concerned with and involved in the basic physical needs of people. How, we don't know – but from the unpromising beginning of the five loaves and two fish, and the simple action of taking, blessing, breaking and giving – a sequence we recognise as at the heart of every service of Communion – the crowd is fed, every member, men, women and children.

He takes, blesses, breaks and gives – such a suggestive paradigm for our life in the world. He takes what is there, however humble, simple; indeed, it may seem mean and inadequate. He takes our offering, of the fruits of the earth, of our labour, our resources, our faith. He blesses and gives thanks. He gives thanks for what is there, for what he has. It may not seem much; it is what's provided, and any food, any offering, any faith is miraculous in its way, not simply to be taken for granted. He breaks. What is there is to be shared. As it is shared, it is multiplied. Sharing doesn't mean less, it means more. And so does giving. He doesn't keep what's there for the top table, for himself and his disciples. There's no top table at this desert meal; what is here is for all, to be given away. Thus, even in the desert place, all are fed.

It's a paradigm for our life and the world's life. Take what's offered. Treasure it as gift, give the blessing of thankfulness. Share the gift out, give away ... and watch with wonder. This is not just a paradigm, it's a promise that, in God's economy, all will be fed. There will be enough. God forgive the decadence and tightfistedness of our present western world in which we are all complicit. God give us grace to begin to see that the economy of the desert meal and the Lord's Supper, so simple, so profound and so life-giving, so realistic, is there for us to embrace, if we have eyes to see, and the will to do, in our world now.

There's one final comment to make on the desert feeding. In Year A of the *Common Lectionary*, this story is linked with Genesis 32:22–31, the story of Jacob's wrestling with the unknown one at the brook Peniel on the night before he meets again his estranged and wronged brother Esau. It's a profound story of guilt, confession, identity and prayer. The form of the story is very ancient, but the truths it contains are subtle and far from primitive. In the encounter with the mystery, the guilt-wracked, fear-ridden Jacob has to reveal who he is, and his very name means 'heel-twister', 'over-reacher', 'supplanter', 'grabber'. Out of his dark desert solitary encounter, he receives a new and honourable name and a permanent wound. He is 'grabber' no longer, but he will always walk with a limp. How suggestive it is to 'pair' the two desert stories. If we truly 'see' into the meaning of the desert feeding, we receive the grace of the wound of compassion, and we, even in our rampantly acquisitive times, become 'grabbers' no longer but sharers in the grace by which all may be fed.

Against the wind

The next scene is striking and dramatic. The action occurs just after Jesus has fed the crowd in the wilderness. He has sent the disciples on ahead of him in a boat to cross the lake while he dismissed the crowds and went up the mountain to be alone in prayer. Out on the lake, throughout the night, the disciples make little headway in a rough sea. We can well imagine them, tired, cold, apprehensive, even if many of them were fishermen, probably exhausted and a bit deflated after the stirring events of the day before.

Just before the dawn, Jesus comes walking towards them across the water. The disciples are terrified. Jesus calms them down ... and then Peter, Peter, never backward about coming forward, decides to get in on the act. He says: 'Lord, if it is you, tell me to come to you on the water'. 'Come on', says Jesus, 'Come on.' And the story says that

Peter got out of the boat and he too started to walk toward Jesus on the water. Then he realised where he was and what he was doing, with the wind in his face and the waves splashing around him in the inky blackness, and his nerve failed and he began to sink. 'Lord, save me', he shouts. Jesus takes him by the hand and catches him. 'How little faith you have', he says, 'why do you doubt?' They got to the boat and calm descended. Those in the boat worshipped him. They said: 'Truly you are the Son of God'.

How do we read this story today? Very often, people read it in one of two ways. The sceptics among us say: 'It is a dramatic story, but people walking on water, that's way outside my experience. My experience is that nobody can walk on water. This is just a wonder story, common enough in its time, put into the gospel to have us marvel at Jesus' so-called supernatural powers. But I don't see what it has to do with me now.' On the other hand, those who hold a high view of the Bible's inspiration say: 'I know it's true that ordinary mortals don't walk on water, but that's just the point, Jesus is no ordinary mortal. This story is literally true, it is here to increase our faith, so just believe it, and worship as the disciples did in the story itself.'

Both these views are problematic. Neither of them reads this story closely and carefully enough. All the attention gets concentrated on the walking on the water – and the rest of the significant detail in Matthew's telling of this tale, rich in symbolism, gets missed or ignored.

So, let's start at the beginning again. Immediately after the feeding, which must have been a huge and a draining event for both Jesus and the disciples, Jesus first sends the disciples away and then dismisses the crowd. He goes up the hill to pray. Notice the disciples being sent away first. It tells us that a significant time elapsed before Jesus next appeared to them. They were on their own, separate from their Lord, for quite a period. We're meant to notice this time of separation. It's when the disciple is separate from his Lord that things start to go wrong. In the boat in a stormy sea with the wind against them, they make no headway. The metaphorical lesson is clear: stick close to Jesus, don't get separated, attend to him.

The disciples are in the boat. Jesus is at prayer. In the gospels, Jesus is pictured at prayer before times of struggle and engagement.

At its beginning, there are the forty days and nights of prayer in the wilderness. At its end, there is the crucial, unforgettable time of prayer in the dark of the night and the darkness of forthcoming events when Jesus sweats blood in the garden of Gethsemane. We see Jesus engaged in prayer as preparation, seeking, both in the temptations and at Gethsemane, to align his will to the will of God, to attune himself to God's spirit and God's purposes. Here, we see Jesus at prayer after an event which must have thoroughly drained him, teaching and feeding the crowd in the wilderness. He goes apart to give thanks, to seek new strength. It's before and after times of struggle and engagement that we find Jesus at prayer. Lesson two: make a time to go apart, take time to prepare, take time to give thanks, take time to seek new guidance and new strength.

Back to the disciples. We're now at the moment just before Jesus comes to them. They're all at sea: remember, in the Bible, the sea is often used as a symbol of the forces of evil and chaos which threaten our lives. They're tired, flat, apprehensive, in the dark, going nowhere, battling against the elements, forces seeming too big for them. Recognise the scene. I do. It's the way not a few of my colleagues describe their ministry and their church today. But let's not stick with them. It's the way I feel from time to time, in the face of my own failures, my inability to get done what needs done, to move things on. It's the way I feel in the face of many of the prevailing currents of our time, the drift from faith, the inequities and cruelties in our own society, the world ill-divided when it need not be so. Where the disciples are, I've been there, and, I suspect, maybe you have also. It's into this scene Jesus enters in a way that is uncanny, surprising. So unexpected is his entrance that the disciples' first reaction is not one of thankful welcome but of deepened fear and terror. Jesus does not let the mood persist. He says three vital things in one short sentence. 'Take heart', he says. 'Courage, get out of your downer, for ... It is I.'

'It is I'. Three words, and three meanings. 'It is I' ... it's me. You're not seeing things, you're not being haunted, it's me, recognise *me*. That first. 'It is I' ... I'm here, I am with you. I haven't left you, you're not out in the middle of the darkness and the storm alone any longer; know my presence, I am with you. That second. 'It is I' ... '*I am*'. 'I am' is the great name for God given to Moses at the burning bush (Exodus 3). 'I am with you, and in my being with you, God is with you.' Hear these words spoken now to each one of us, and know there is every reason to take heart, to find new courage.

The final word amplifies this. 'Do not be afraid.' In the dark of the night, in that time of loneliness and separation, what a monster is fear, which transfixes, paralyses, disables us. To all of us, both as persons and as a community, Jesus is saying: 'Look, you're not on your own in your struggles in this present time. I am with you, I will stay with you; courage, take heart, don't give in to your fears.'

Come on!

Enter Peter. Just before we meet him, a word from Søren Kierkegaard, the great and tortured Danish thinker of the nineteenth century. He said: 'Faith is to walk out over 50,000 fathoms of water'. This whole section of the gospel is much about faith, faith as trust, risk, daring, doing. Enter Peter, often fallible, and often failing, but never afraid to try, to venture; Peter on whose faith the church is built.

'If it is you, tell me to come to you on the water.' 'Come on', says Jesus, 'come on.' Now, what is fascinating about this scene is that Peter gets out of the boat and starts to walk on the water, heading for Jesus. He doesn't get out of the boat and sink like a stone. To begin with, he's doing well. But then what happens? The gospel is quite specific: he realises where he is, and starts to flounder. At that moment, I have infinite sympathy with Peter, for I am presently the world's second worst swimmer. And the reason I know I am the world's second worst swimmer is that I used to be the world's worst. Swimming's about confidence, about relaxing, about not getting uptight about where you are, about trusting the water underneath you. Swimming's about confidence, trust, and I used not to have any in the face of the water. I got overwhelmed by my own negativity before I ever got overwhelmed by the water around me.

I like the theory that what happened to Peter here is that he took his eye off Jesus, got transfixed by the difficulties around him, turned in on himself and panicked. As he flounders, as he cries out for help, so he discovers again the presence that will save him, bear him up. Jesus stretches out a hand to him, catches him and says:

'How little faith you have, why do you doubt?' That's a bit hard, Peter has shown more faith than the rest of the disciples, including ourselves. 'How little faith you have, why do you doubt?' Maybe 'doubt' is not the best word here. We use 'doubt' very often to mean honest questioning, which is certainly legitimate. We see a positive aspect to doubt. Often, however, doubt is used much more negatively, frequently coupled with fear – 'the night of doubt and fear', as the prayer says. 'How little faith you have, why are you frightened?' probably catches the sense of Jesus' words here better. The message to Peter is the same as the one to the disciples as a whole. 'Don't be frightened, I am with you.' The third lesson is: don't be afraid, Jesus is with you, Jesus is with us. Keep your eye fixed on him, from first to last.

'When they got into the boat, the wind ceased.' There came calm, there was an end to opposition, there was a time of peace. The picture reinforces the theme from various parts of the gospel of Jesus at one with God's creation, come to bring healing, harmony and restoration to a bruised, rebellious and wounded world in all its aspects. Cherish this moment of peace.

The story ends in a moment of praise. 'Those in the boat worshipped Jesus, saying, "Truly you are the Son of God"' (14:33). The ending is interesting. This is the second storm scene in the gospel. At the end of the first storm scene, the disciples are shown wondering who Jesus is (8:23–7). Now they have been with him a little longer. Like the mustard seed, their faith has grown. Here is an encouraging truth of the discipleship way: to be with Jesus is to see faith grow, to know of faith's growing in the disciple's life, even in and through life's storms. In John Wesley's translation of Paul Gerhardt's hymn:

> Through waves, and clouds, and storms
> he gently clears your way;
> await his time; so shall this night
> soon end in joyful day.
> Leave to his sovereign sway
> to choose and to command;
> then you shall marvel at his way
> how wise, how strong his hand.

> (*Ch 4* (Hymn 270) 2005)

191

The edge of his garment

The chapter concludes with the landing of Jesus and the disciples at Gennesaret and a short summary of the resumption of his demanding healing ministry (14:35–6). It serves as another reminder of the continuing work of Jesus throughout his ministry in Galilee and its environs of healing the sick, bringing release and liberation to those bowed low or bound either by physical illness, societal taboos, the oppression of the powerful, or demonic forces.

Study

By yourself

In some ways in Matthew's gospel, Peter stands as an exemplar of discipleship, a model of what following Jesus means. Picture yourself as Peter in the scene on the waters of the lake; write an account of what the whole experience felt like and what it meant to you.

Chapter 18

OLD AND NEW

Matthew 15
The Teaching of the Ancestors
(Mark 7:1–13)

Then some Pharisees and teachers of the Law came from Jerusalem to Jesus and asked him, 'Why is it that your disciples disobey the teaching handed down by our ancestors? They don't wash their hands in the proper way before they eat!'

Jesus answered, 'And why do you disobey God's commands and follow your own teaching? For God said, "Respect your father and your mother," and "Whoever curses his father or his mother is to be put to death." But you teach that if a person has something he could use to help his father or mother, but says, "This belongs to God," he does not need to honour his father. In this way you disregard God's command, in order to follow your own teaching. You hypocrites! How right Isaiah was when he prophesied about you!

"These people, says God, honour me with their words,
but their heart is really far away from me.
It is no use for them to worship me,
because they teach human rules as though they were my laws!"'

The Things that Make a Person Unclean

(Mark 7:14–23)

Then Jesus called the crowd to him and said to them, 'Listen and understand! It is not what goes into a person's mouth that makes

193

him ritually unclean; rather, what comes out of it makes him unclean.'

Then the disciples came to him and said, 'Do you know that the Pharisees had their feelings hurt by what you said?'

'Every plant which my Father in heaven did not plant will be pulled up', answered Jesus. 'Don't worry about them! They are blind leaders of the blind; and when one blind man leads another, both fall into a ditch.'

Peter spoke up, 'Explain this saying to us.'

Jesus said to them, 'You are still no more intelligent than the others. Don't you understand? Anything that goes into a person's mouth goes into his stomach and then on out of his body. But the things that come out of the mouth come from the heart; and these are the things that make a person ritually unclean. For from his heart come the evil ideas which lead him to kill, commit adultery, and do other immoral things; to rob, lie and slander others. These are the things that make a person unclean. But to eat without washing your hands as they say you should – this doesn't make a person unclean.'

A Woman's Faith

(Mark 7:24–30)

Jesus left that place and went off to the territory near the cities of Tyre and Sidon. A Canaanite woman who lived in that region came to him. 'Son of David!' she cried out. 'Have mercy on me, sir! My daughter has a demon and is in a terrible condition.'

But Jesus did not say a word to her. His disciples came to him and begged him, 'Send her away! She is following us and making all this noise!'

Then Jesus replied, 'I have been sent only to the lost sheep of the people of Israel.'

At this the woman came and fell at his feet. 'Help me, sir!' she said.

Jesus answered, 'It isn't right to take the children's food and throw it to the dogs.'

'That's true, sir', she answered; 'but even the dogs eat the leftovers that fall from their masters' table.'

So Jesus answered her, 'You are a woman of great faith! What you want will be done for you.' And at that very moment her daughter was healed.

Jesus Heals Many People

Jesus left there and went along by Lake Galilee. He climbed a hill and sat down. Large crowds came to him, bringing with them the lame, the blind, the crippled, the dumb, and many other sick people, whom they placed at Jesus' feet; and he healed them. The people were amazed as they saw the dumb speaking, the crippled made whole, the lame walking, and the blind seeing; and they praised the God of Israel.

Jesus Feeds Another Great Crowd

(Mark 8:1–10)

Jesus called his disciples to him and said, 'I feel sorry for these people, because they have been with me for three days and now have nothing to eat. I don't want to send them away without feeding them, for they might faint on their way home.'

The disciples asked him, 'Where will we find enough food in this desert to feed this crowd?'

'How much bread have you?' Jesus asked.

'Seven loaves', they answered, 'and a few small fish.'

So Jesus ordered the crowd to sit down on the ground. Then he took the seven loaves and the fish, gave thanks to God, broke them, and gave them to the disciples; and the disciples gave them to the people. They all ate and had enough. Then the disciples took up seven baskets full of pieces left over. The number of men who ate was 4,000, not counting the women and children.

Then Jesus sent the people away, got into a boat, and went to the territory of Magadan.

Tradition!

Enter the opposition. It is gathering weight; here are introduced to a group of Pharisees and scribes who have come from the heartland of Jerusalem. They have an argument to pick with Jesus. 'Why do your disciples not wash their hands properly before they eat?' The issue is not hygiene but the so-called proper observance of ritual. The Pharisees in particular were fond of ritual. Around the original Commandments they had built up a mass of oral regulations which were simply impossible for the ordinary poor of the land to keep in full. The effect was to build a wall of exclusiveness around them. In this particular case, the Jewish scriptures did contain regulations for ritual cleansing, but there are none about washing before eating.

Here is a particular instance of the general tendency within religions for a multitude of practices and regulations to spring up around the original kernel of belief and practice. So often, they can end up producing a stout and off-putting thicket, impenetrable to the outsider and masking or obscuring the primal thrust of the basic insight. A lively and aware faith will always be on the lookout for taken-for-granted assumptions on the one hand and the elevation of mere customs and practices to the status of holy writ on the other. At this time of rapid change, we need to be especially open to questioning both our ideas and practices lest we fall into the pit opened by a speaker at a renewal conference who suggested that the seven last words of our churches might be: 'We Never Did It That Way Before'.

Relations to the Law

In this passage, in reply to the question of the men from Jerusalem, Jesus goes on the attack. He changes the subject by responding to their question by posing another. 'Why do *you* disobey the Law by substituting your own tradition?' He goes on to give an example of how accrued religious practice can nullify the basic humanitarian thrust of an original Commandment. It was possible to make a binding vow, called 'Corban' (see Mark 7:11), by which a person could pledge money to the Temple or their local synagogue. One result of this vow could be to prevent that person from having sufficient resources to support their parents in their old age, and so to negate the primary obligation of the Commandment to 'honour your father and your mother'. By any humane reckoning, support of the aged, particularly within the family (so says this recently retired pensioner), must come before a purely religious obligation. So says Jesus.

Jesus here is in the role of reformer, and he does what reformers so often do: he goes back to the source. He returns to the Commandments and makes it clear that the original Commandments have precedence over mere tradition. The Commandments are given to help people's relations with one another; traditions can further enable this, but, when raised to absolute commands, they can also hinder and indeed have precisely the opposite of their intended effect.

After the specific instance, Jesus launches into a more general public attack on the Pharisees' ways. The epithet of 'hypocrite', so common in Matthew with his stress on congruence between heart and action, is hurled against them and immediately followed and reinforced by a quotation from the Septuagint version of Isaiah 29:13. Jesus then returns to the original question of what does or does not make a person unclean – not what goes in but what comes out of the mouth is the answer. Having addressed his initial reply to the original question to the scribes and Pharisees from Jerusalem, he is now speaking to the crowd in general. In quick succession, there's a further change of audience. Now Jesus will answer his disciples who come to tell him that he's hurt the Pharisees' feelings (15:12)! His response would do nothing to mollify them. First, he talks of the uprooting of every plant not planted by the Father. He's employing the commonly used and understood metaphor of Israel as a vineyard, e.g. Isaiah 5:1–7; the 'plants not planted by my Father' is clearly a reference to the Pharisees. Jesus goes on to talk of the fate of those who entrust themselves to the leadership of the blind. In Jewish teaching, it was the Gentile world which was considered blind; to compare the Pharisees with their exclusive claim to insight with Gentile blindness was a put-down indeed.

The request of Peter, representative of the disciples, for an explanation of Jesus' 'parable' (NRSV 15:15) allows Jesus to expand and intensify his words in 15:10–11. Now he stresses that it is not just the words from a person's mouth which make them unclean; the heart, our inner being, drives the mouth. He then lists the forbidden and formidable sins from the second half of the Commandments beside which handwashing is small beer indeed.

That closes the matter, conclusively. From this passage, we can infer that the Commandments were treated with reverence within Matthew's community but were also to be interpreted in the light of Jesus' own teaching.

Outsiders

Jesus now moves into Gentile territory (near the cities of Tyre and Sidon (15:21) – not Israel's favourite places). Across the barriers of gender, ethnicity and faith, Jesus is accosted by a woman whose daughter is in crying need of healing. She is described by Matthew, in contrast to Mark, who also tells this story (Mark 7:24–30), as 'Canaanite' – a term very familiar to readers with a Hebrew background.

Jesus' behaviour throughout this encounter often raises modern eyebrows; it appears at best dismissive of the woman, if not positively rude. It's therefore worth looking at the exchange closely. The woman's initial cry is 'Son of David! Have mercy on me, Lord!' 'Son of David' implies that this foreign woman has already some insight into who Jesus is. 'Have mercy' would be recognised by Matthew's readers from the practice of their liturgy as a cry for forgiving acceptance. 'Lord', a stronger word than the GNB translation 'Sir', occurs thrice in this short incident; its use suggests that the woman accepted and trusted Jesus' authority. Despite the insight that the woman shows in her opening cry, Jesus' first response is simply to ignore her. His disciples are more blunt in their rejection. 'Send this noisy nuisance packing!' is their plea to Jesus. He then speaks for the first time and verbalises his dismissal of the woman by saying that his mission is solely to the wayward and lost people of Israel. The woman will not be put off. She falls at his feet, indicative of both her desperation on her daughter's behalf and her acknowledgement of Jesus' power, and pleads again for help. Jesus' reply that it is wrong to give the children's food to the dogs is downright offensive. 'Dogs' was the derogatory term used by Jesus' people to refer to the Gentiles. The woman persists. Quick as a flash, she retorts to Jesus: 'Yes, but even the dogs get the scraps which are left at their masters' table'. Something happens ... to Jesus' perception of the woman. He sees her in a new light. Jesus acknowledges that the woman's sheer persistence across the barriers of convention, distrust and racial enmity, her selfless concern for her daughter and her refusal to be put down, indicate a doughty humanity and a trusting faith to which he warms. He commends her faith and tells her that the daughter is healed.

All's well that ends well? Not quite. The initial treatment of the woman by both Jesus and the disciples still grates on our modern sensibilities. We need to remember where Matthew was coming from. He is clear that Jesus' initial mission was 'to the lost sheep of Israel'. For him, Jesus had come to bring the elected nation, the chosen people, back to God; that was the first step. As a godly nation once more, they could then exercise their true vocation of being a light to all the nations. It is only with the failure of his mission to 'his own' that, after the resurrection, Jesus commissions the disciples to go 'to all nations' (28:19). Israel first, then the Gentiles, is the plot for Matthew. This story of the healing of the Canaanite woman's daughter, together with the other Gentile healing of the centurion's servant (8:5–13), act as anticipations of the coming Gentile mission after the regrettable and painful failure of Israel. Carter summarises (2000 pp. 324–5):

> Her witty response opens up new possibilities for Jesus and her daughter. Jesus now responds positively to her continued recognition of his ability to help her and her persistent requests. ... Her persistence in the face of Jesus' obstructions, her challenge to the ethnic, gender, religious, political, and economic barriers, her reliance on his power, and her recognition of his authority over demons comprise her *faith* (see 8:10, 9:2, 22, 29). In contrast to its lack among the religious leaders, and the 'little faith' of the disciples (6:30, 8:26, 14:31, 16:8), she is like the Gentile centurion (8:10) in showing *great ... faith*, the only time this adjective is used to describe faith in the gospel. Like the centurion, this despised woman calls Jesus Lord (cf. 8:6), engages him in dialogue (cf. 8:8–10), surprises him with her faith (8:10) and elicits a (long-distance?) miracle from him (8:13).

Summary

Matthew 15 throughout follows the sequence of events in Mark 7, with two exceptions: he omits the graphic story of the healing of the deaf mute (Mark 7:31–7) – perhaps because it does not describe an instant cure but a rather slower recovery of sight – and instead inserts another of his summary passages describing Jesus' healing ministry. Jesus has returned to Galilee, climbed a hill (indicative of the holy) and sat down (the posture of the authoritative teacher). The crowds gather with all manner of poor folk in need of healing and freedom from their bonds. They are brought to Jesus' feet; there he heals them, to the people's amazement, which evokes from them the praise of 'the God of Israel' (15:31).

The second feeding

Matthew 15 ends with the second feeding story of a great crowd, this time of more than 4,000. We have already been told the setting, by Lake Galilee, on a hill. The hillside setting conjures echoes of the wonderful description of the great feast for all people in Isaiah 25:6–9. Once again, Jesus' compassion for the members of the hungry crowd is drawn to our attention (15:32). He cares that those who have come to meet him will have exhausted any rations they have brought with them. It's three days the crowd has been with Jesus; the mention of 'three days' will gather significance as the gospel moves to its dénouement. Once again, the disciples are stumped; where will they find the resources to feed this crowd (15:33)? The locus of the first feeding was described as 'a lonely place' (14:15); the second feeding occurs in a 'desert'. The Exodus echo of 'manna' in the wilderness during Israel's forty years' journey to the land of promise is clear. This whole narrative bristles with symbolism, but we must not ignore the primary reality of Jesus' feeding of a crowd which is hungry; he is the attentive provider of food to meet a basic human need.

Again, after the pattern of the Eucharist, Jesus takes, blesses, breaks and gives the bread and fish. There is more than enough for all, making an implicit contrast between the abundance which Jesus' way provides and the scarcity which was so often the lot of the poor and marginal folk of the crowd sweating under the oppressions of empire. After the feeding, Jesus sends the crowd away and takes ship for Magadan, a location which has not been satisfactorily identified.

Study

By yourself

Using the method described at the end of Chapter 12 above, be present at the encounter between Jesus and his disciples and the Canaanite woman. In particular, what are the questions you would want to ask the woman, the disciples and Jesus? What do you hear them saying to you?

For group work

Take a searching look at the life of your faith community.

Can you make a list of 'traditions' which might be off-putting to any stranger who comes into your midst?

Are there elements in today's church which are inhumane and unwelcoming? What should we do about them?

Chapter 19

THE CHRIST

Matthew 16

The Demand for a Miracle

(Mark 8:11–13, Luke 12:54–56)

Some Pharisees and Sadducees who came to Jesus wanted to trap him, so they asked him to perform a miracle for them, to show that God approved of him. But Jesus answered, 'When the sun is setting, you say, "We are going to have fine weather, because the sky is red." And early in the morning you say, "It is going to rain, because the sky is red and dark." You can predict the weather by looking at the sky, but you cannot interpret the signs concerning these times! How evil and godless are the people of this day! You ask me for a miracle? No! The only miracle you will be given is the miracle of Jonah.'

So he left them and went away.

The Yeast of the Pharisees and Sadducees

(Mark 8:14–21)

When the disciples crossed over to the other side of the lake, they forgot to take any bread. Jesus said to them, 'Take care; be on your guard against the yeast of the Pharisees and the Sadducees.'

They started discussing among themselves, 'He says this because we didn't bring any bread.'

Jesus knew what they were saying, so he asked them, 'Why are you discussing among yourselves about not having any bread? How little faith you have! Don't you understand yet? Don't you remember when I broke the five loaves for the five thousand men?

How many baskets did you fill? And what about the seven loaves for the four thousand men? How many baskets did you fill? How is it that you don't understand that I was not talking to you about bread? Guard yourselves from the yeast of the Pharisees and the Sadducees!'

Then the disciples understood that he was not warning them to guard themselves from the yeast used in bread but from the teaching of the Pharisees and the Sadducees.

Peter's Declaration about Jesus

(Mark 8:27–30, Luke 9:18–21)

Jesus went to the territory near the town of Caesarea Philippi, where he asked his disciples, 'Who do people say the Son of Man is?'

'Some say John the Baptist', they answered. 'Others say Elijah, while others say Jeremiah or some other prophet.'

'What about you?' he asked them. 'Who do you say I am?'

Simon Peter answered, 'You are the Messiah, the Son of the living God.'

'Good for you, Simon son of John!' answered Jesus. 'For this truth did not come to you from any human being, but it was given to you directly from my Father in heaven. And so I tell you, Peter: you are a rock, and on this rock foundation I will build my church, and not even death will ever be able to overcome it. I will give you the keys of the Kingdom of heaven; what you prohibit on earth will be prohibited in heaven, and what you permit on earth will be permitted in heaven.'

Then Jesus ordered his disciples not to tell anyone that he was the Messiah.

Jesus Speaks about His Suffering and Death

(Mark 8:31–9:1, Luke 9:22–7)

From that time on Jesus began to say plainly to his disciples, 'I must go to Jerusalem and suffer much from the elders, the chief priests, and the teachers of the Law. I will be put to death, but three days later I will be raised to life.'

Peter took him aside and began to rebuke him. 'God forbid it, Lord!' he said. 'That must never happen to you!'

Jesus turned around and said to Peter, 'Get away from me, Satan! You are an obstacle in my way, because these thoughts of yours don't come from God, but from human nature.'

Then Jesus said to his disciples, 'If anyone wants to come with me, he must forget self, carry his cross, and follow me. For whoever wants to save his own life will lose it; but whoever loses his life for my sake will find it. Will people gain anything if they win the whole world but lose their life? Of course not! There is nothing they can give to regain their life. For the Son of Man is about to come in the glory of his Father with his angels, and then he will reward each one according to his deeds. I assure you that there are some here who will not die until they have seen the Son of Man come as King.'

Proof

We come to a short but crucial chapter in Matthew's story of Jesus. The question of Jesus' identity has been raised frequently in the preceding chapters: at the climax to this chapter, Peter will make his momentous faith declaration of who Jesus is in a statement full of significance. But Peter's faith statement is immediately followed by an announcement by Jesus which rocks Peter and the disciples to the core as it turns their expectations upside down. Perhaps our reception of this story is a bit dulled by familiarity: look out for surprises, shocks galore.

The chapter begins familiarly enough. Jesus is pictured having another encounter with the opposition – this time, says Matthew (*contra* Mark), some Pharisees and Sadducees. This unlikely combination of religious and secular power represents official Judaism as seen by Matthew. The question they put to Jesus is also familiar: we've heard it before in 12:38. They demand a sign, a miracle. One of Matthew's narrative devices to reinforce and carry along his story is the use of doublets and repetitions. Here is one; can you spot any more? Jesus' reply is that, while his questioners are probably quite skilled in weather forecasting, they are unable to read the action of God in the events before their eyes. He reiterates the gospel's ambiguity about 'signs' and quotes again the unlikely 'sign of Jonah'. This time, there is no immediate reference to his death and resurrection as in 12:40; it will come soon enough.

Beware!

In Matthew's account, Jesus is alone when he has this encounter with the Pharisees and Sadducees; he is now joined by his disciples, who have however forgotten the provisions, and specifically bread. 'Bread' recalls us to the recent desert feeding, the food given to the dogs in the encounter with the Canaanite woman, and the controversy about handwashing before food with scribe and Pharisee. Jesus bids the newly rejoined disciples to watch out for the yeast of Pharisees and Sadducees. They think he's referring to their failure to bring the loaf. Jesus is somewhat exasperated by their literalism. 'It's a metaphor, silly! Remember where you've come from, and the two great feedings. They demonstrate that I have come to meet people's real needs. The "yeast" of our opponents is their teaching, it serves their own interests rather than hungry people: it simply does not satisfy. It looks predictably backward; it will not prepare you to be open to what God is about to do.'

Who am I?

The scene changes again. Jesus now takes the disciples away to the territory near Caesarea Philippi. The name is redolent of Roman rule and influence, yet it is in this place that the identity of one greater than Caesar will be revealed. The identity question reaches its moment of truth. Jesus quizzes the disciples: 'Who are people saying that I am?' They give four possibilities: John the Baptist and Elijah, both seen as forerunner figures, preparers of the way; and also Jeremiah or one of the prophets. All the answers locate Jesus firmly in the tradition of the radical prophet seeking to bend unlikely and unprofitable times and people to the will of God.

Now the question becomes sharper, more pointed. Jesus says to the disciples very directly: 'But you, what about you? Who do you say I am?' It is Peter who answers: 'You are the Messiah, the Son of the living God'. Some scholars argue that 'Son of the living God' is a post-Easter addition. It is, however, apt and appropriate in terms of Matthew's narrative, confirming what we readers have already heard, at Jesus' baptism (3:17), during his temptations (4:3, 6) and in the dark night on the lake (14:33). In the gospel to this point, 'Son of God' points to Jesus' authority and the authentic source of his authority, God the Father himself. 'Son of God' will recur in the next episode of the gospel story at Jesus' transfiguration (17:5) and then significantly at the cross. The meaning will subtly change. For now, the question of Jesus' identity is answered as, for the first time, 'Messiah', 'Christ' appears on the lips of a disciple.

The rock

The disciple is Simon Peter – and the words which Jesus addresses to him, uniquely in Matthew's gospel, give to Peter a place of leadership and authority in the young church. There is dispute among scholarly circles as to whether Jesus did say these words here. There is, however, a convincing argument that the words are not Matthew's own invention; there is much evidence of their originating in an Aramaic-speaking community. In particular, 'you are Peter and upon this rock' is a pure pun only in Aramaic. The evidence points to a strong tradition of the leadership of Peter within the church from an early date; whether that tradition is sufficiently strong to support the structures of hierarchy and authority which later generations have built upon it is, of course, a matter of continuing ecumenical debate.

The references to 'the keys of the kingdom' (16:19) and 'binding and loosing' (16:19) need to be seen against their Jewish background. The keepers of the keys were the teachers of the Law on whom Jesus pronounces 'Woe' in 23:13 for shutting up the doors of heaven from the people. Against the Law's contemporary keepers, the scribes and Pharisees, Jesus here sets Peter as steward of the Kingdom on earth. 'Binding and loosing' mainly refers to Peter's authority as teacher, obviously in a post-Resurrection setting. Jesus does not confer on Peter any absolute authority; his is an authority under God to interpret for the young church. Together with this authority to interpret teaching also goes the secondary authority to approve or condemn those who teach; always in the light of Jesus' strong words to the same Peter on forgiveness in 18:21–2. As we shall see, Matthew 18 is much concerned with practice and discipline within his church. There is a danger that the words of Jesus here to Peter can be used to paint a picture of church as an exclusive citadel community, after the models of the Pharasaic community or the community of Qumran. Such a picture is quite at odds with the rest of the gospel, which shows the community being formed around Jesus as open to all. It should also be remembered that, while Matthew is a strong advocate of the authority of Peter in the early church, the evidence of the New Testament as a whole is that leadership in the church was corporate and fluctuating: James the brother of Jesus is mentioned as leader in Acts and Galatians, and the debate between Peter and Paul about the status of the Gentiles takes up many of the pages of Acts. Nevertheless, Peter is a major figure in the story of Jesus and the formation of the early church, and the tracing of his own faith journey with its highs and lows, achievements and failures in the gospels and Acts remains salutary and instructive to us latter-day disciples.

The announcement of the cross

Discussion of Peter's place and authority must not be allowed to obscure the next key and crucial moment in this passage. 'From that time on' (16:21) is the same phrase Matthew used to introduce Jesus' ministry of proclamation in Galilee (4:17). As soon as Peter has made his confession, the shadow of the cross, which will loom over the rest of the story, falls. Jesus now begins to tell his disciples about the cross which lies ahead of him. The news bursts on the discipleship band like a bombshell. The notion of a suffering Messiah was contrary to almost all contemporary expectations of a strong national deliverer. Peter now tries to take Jesus quietly aside and ask him, not so quietly, if he's taken leave of his senses: 'God forbid. This must never happen to you' (16:22). Jesus' reply is equally robust, metaphorically addressing him as 'Satan' and using the same strong verb as in the temptation scene of 3:10. We remember Satan's original role as the tempter of God's people; Jesus sees Peter as all too tied to our human shrinking from pain and all too conformed to the standards of this world. Peter, who has so recently been called 'the foundational rock', is now 'the stone as obstacle, the cause of stumbling'. There is an interesting interplay throughout this passage between foundation stones and stumbling blocks, both of which are recurrent New Testament themes. Jesus, however, will not be deflected, while Peter needs to be 'reconverted', this time to the way of the cross.

> The double nature of the community of Jesus can already be observed in Peter. It is chosen by God, endowed with the gift of new knowledge, and under way toward the Kingdom of heaven; at the same time it continues to live in peril of temptation and even under threat of judgement. It has not been taught about the 'deep secrets of Satan' (Revelation 2:24); these it experiences in its own disobedience, above all in its resistance to a theology – or, better, a practice – of the cross. Just as Peter is called back to discipleship, where he must learn to think God's thoughts, so too is the community. Once more Peter represents every disciple. The way is paved for a theology of the cross arising from experience, like Paul's theology of suffering and defeat. (Schweizer 1975 p. 346)

... and ours

Schweizer's quotation forms a good link into Jesus' next words, which speak not of his cross but ours. We rightly interpret these words as a call to surrender, self-denial and sacrifice, a summons to the task of conforming our minds, hearts and actions to the discipline of Jesus' crossway. The words that Jesus addresses to his disciples in 16:24–6 are a provocation to leave behind a life of cosseted self-concern and the delusive search for security and to look, see, feel, move and act outwards.

It is also to be remembered that crucifixion in the time of Jesus had a huge socio-political dimension. To speak of 'taking up the cross' is above all a summons to faith in the midst of the power struggles and contradictions of life in this world, as Bonhoeffer has shown us most clearly in his later writings. 'The cross' is always about more than our inner discipline of self-denial, however significant that discipline is. It calls for the way of courage, to stand firm against the powers of this world, the real tangible social and political powers which stifle dissent, legitimate oppression and build and use monstrous arsenals of destruction. It summons us to an imaginative identification with the marginalised, the voiceless, the powerless of our world, those who today may well suffer in the words of Auden's poem 'a death reserved for slaves' (from the poem 'Friday's Child: In memory of Dietrich Bonhoeffer, martyred at Flossenburg, April 9th, 1945', in Auden 1968 p. 86). It also invites us to make common cause with all who resist these malign powers of today's 'imperiums', often at real personal cost.

> To do so is not to endorse the symbol but to counter and reframe its violence. As the end of the gospel shows, it is to identify with a sign which ironically indicates the empire's limits. The empire does its worst in crucifying Jesus. But God raises Jesus from death to thwart the empire's efforts and to reveal the limits of its power. (Carter 2000 p. 344)

Even in the darkness of the announcement of the cross for Jesus and disciple alike, a light shines: 'On the third day he will be raised' (16:21) ... 'For the Son of Man is to come with his angels in the glory of his Father ...' (16:27).

Study

By yourself

What does 'take up your cross' mean for you? How does your answer compare with what you wrote at the end of Chapter 13 in response to the invitation to write a simple account of what following Jesus means to you?

Chapter 20

HIGH AND LOW

Matthew 17:1–23

The Transfiguration

(*Mark 9:2–13, Luke 9:28–36*)

Six days later Jesus took with him Peter and the brothers James and John and led them up a high mountain where they were alone. As they looked on, a change came over Jesus: his face was shining like the sun, and his clothes were dazzling white. Then the three disciples saw Moses and Elijah talking with Jesus. So Peter spoke up and said to Jesus, 'Lord, how good it is that we are here! If you wish, I will make three tents here, one for you, one for Moses, and one for Elijah.'

While he was talking, a shining cloud came over them, and a voice from the cloud said, 'This is my own dear Son, with whom I am pleased – listen to him!'

When the disciples heard the voice, they were so terrified that they threw themselves face downwards on the ground. Jesus came up to them and touched them. 'Get up', he said. 'Don't be afraid!' So they looked up and saw no one there but Jesus.

As they came down the mountain, Jesus ordered them, 'Don't tell anyone about this vision you have seen until the Son of Man has been raised from death.'

Then the disciples asked Jesus, 'Why do the teachers of the Law say that Elijah has to come first?'

'Elijah is indeed coming first', answered Jesus, 'and he will get everything ready. But I tell you that Elijah has already come and people did not recognize him, but treated him just as they pleased. In the same way they will also ill-treat the Son of Man.'

Then the disciples understood that he was talking to them about John the Baptist.

Jesus Heals a Boy with a Demon
(*Mark 9:14–29, Luke 9:37–43a*)

When they returned to the crowd, a man came to Jesus, knelt before him, and said, 'Sir, have mercy on my son! He is an epileptic and has such terrible fits that he often falls in the fire or into water. I brought him to your disciples, but they could not heal him.'

Jesus answered, 'How unbelieving and wrong you people are! How long must I stay with you? How long do I have to put up with you? Bring the boy here to me!' Jesus gave a command to the demon, and it went out of the boy, and at that very moment he was healed.

Then the disciples came to Jesus in private and asked him, 'Why couldn't we drive the demon out?'

'It was because you haven't enough faith', answered Jesus. 'I assure you that if you have faith as big as a mustard seed, you can say to this hill, "Go from here to there!" and it will go. You could do anything!'

Jesus Speaks Again about His Death
(*Mark 9:30–32, Luke 9:43b –45*)

When the disciples all came together in Galilee, Jesus said to them, 'The Son of Man is about to be handed over to people who will kill him; but three days later he will be raised to life.'

The disciples became very sad.

A moment of epiphany

From the low point of the announcement of the cross, Matthew's story now moves to high ground, literally and metaphorically as Jesus takes Peter, James and John to climb a mountain. We have already noticed the association between high places and holiness and events of revelation. The particular incident of Jesus' transfiguration is heavy with echoes of Moses' encounter with God on Mount Sinai in Exodus 24 and 34. Matthew inserts

211

'his face shone like the sun' to the description in Mark 9, both echoing Moses, alluding to the belief developed during the inter-Testamental period that the resurrection faces of the righteous would shine like the sun, and anticipating the description of Jesus in Revelation 1:16: 'his face was like the sun, shining with full force'.

We can identify with the words of Peter, again the spokesperson: 'Lord, it is good for us to be here', witnessing to this moment of truth, glory and promise. It is a moment which points to an end beyond the pain and travail of the recently announced crossway. Peter's speech is interrupted by the voice of God from the shining cloud which both conceals and reveals the Godhead. The voice reiterates precisely the words of blessing and favour spoken to Jesus at the moment of his baptism (3:17) but adds the command: 'listen to him'. 'Listening' can be interpreted either as an injunction to hear and obey Jesus' ethical teaching, or to be particularly attentive to the events about to unfold on the way to the cross. The importance of the divine voice from the cloud at this stage of the gospel, with its shattering announcement of the turn towards the cross, is to legitimate and reinforce this turning. It is in and through the taking of the crossway that the fullness of the meaning of Jesus' 'sonship' with the Father will be revealed.

The reaction of the disciples to the divine epiphany is to end up on the ground, prone and fearful. Notice the way Jesus deals with them. He goes to them and touches them. How important touch is; how many meanings it can convey. We see Jesus' action here as simply one of reassurance to frightened men; we are also aware of how central the gift of his touch has been in Jesus' healing ministry. The connection with healing is reinforced by the words with which Jesus addresses them: 'Get up' also belongs to the ministry of healing and to the raising of the dead. 'Don't be afraid' recalls the divine presence in the midst of the storm (8:26, 14:27). Cumulatively, these hints reinforce the importance of this incident as a healing moment and an anticipation of resurrection given to help the disciples' understanding in the days of trial ahead.

The event of the Transfiguration takes place on a quiet hill before three amazed disciples far from the corridors of power. It occurs at the margins, far from the metropolitan heartland, yet we should have no doubts that this is a story about power. It's a story which raises the question of where real power lies in the world. I find it impossible to comment on this story in our time without bringing to mind the coincidence that the first atomic bomb was dropped on the Japanese city of Hiroshima on 6 August 1945, a day kept as the Feast of the Transfiguration by many parts of the Christian church. People argue still about the rights and wrongs of dropping the bomb; it remains an act of brute and horrific violence and destruction against a civilian population. It serves as a constant reminder of the awesome powers of force and destruction which lie at the fingertips of the powerful in our world. Yet, as the Iraq war and its aftermath clearly testifies, it remains much easier to win a war than to build a peace. The resurrection of a nation is a slow and painstaking business, as is the healing and mending of bodies and souls, the nurturing of new life and the care of the vulnerable and the frail. Such is the cross way and, as the Transfiguration affirms, the God way. The power to nurture and mend, to bring new life often out of the deadest of ends by the slow way of love, eschewing the frequently disastrous quick fixes of naked power, is the power of which the gospel speaks and makes manifest in Jesus, shining with the light of God on the hillside, sweating in his healing work among the crowd, suffering on the cross of humiliation. It is the power of creation and a redemptive power. It is the power of God entrusted into our human hands.

Elijah and John

The descent of the mountain begins. Despite Peter's desire to linger, the moment passes, and down the hill there is much work to be done and a hard road to travel. On the descent, Jesus bids his companions to remain silent about what they have just witnessed. Uniquely, Matthew has Jesus describe the Transfiguration as a 'vision'. Again, Jesus speaks of the raising of the Son of Man from the dead, and the disciples ask a question about the tradition that Elijah would appear before the coming of the Messiah. Jesus answers by saying that Elijah will come at the future eschaton;

then he adds that Elijah has already come and suffered the same fate as lies in store for himself, death at the hands of a corrupt power. Unlike Mark's gospel, where one of the main themes of the journey to the cross is the growing incomprehension of the disciples, here the disciples do understand that Jesus is referring to John the Baptist. This positive identification of John with the great prophet Elijah points to a mutual rapprochement between the disciples of Jesus and John. Generally, Matthew is much less 'hard' on the disciples' lack of understanding and faith than the Markan source from which he so often borrows.

Moving mountains

As the little band meets up with the rest of the disciples surrounded by a crowd, they are confronted with a minor crisis. A man with an epileptic, literally 'moonstruck', boy rushes to fall at the feet of Jesus, pouring out the story of the boy's proneness to self-harm during his fits. He beseeches Jesus in the familiar words: 'Lord, have mercy on my son', and continues by telling Jesus he has brought the boy to the disciples, who were unable to cure him. Jesus is clearly exasperated and exclaims: 'You faithless and perverse generation ...' (17:17). It is less clear who is the object of the exasperation; is it the crowd or is it the disciples? A case can be made out for both. The minor crisis is resolved as Jesus casts out the demon which is destroying the boy, but the aftermath gives us the real reason for the inclusion of this story.

The disciples come to Jesus privately to ask why they were unable to effect a cure; Jesus had earlier given them authority to cast out demons (see 10:8). Presumably that authority had enabled them to effect cures previously, but not this time. Why? Jesus replies: 'Because of your little faith'. Had their faith been shaken and diminished through the shock of learning of the cross? Jesus reassures them: little faith can be enough. It can work like the grain of mustard seed (13:31–2) which, small as it is, can grow into a great plant. It can be strong enough to move mountains, moving mountains being a familiar image in Jewish thought. Nothing is impossible for faith, for nothing is impossible for God. The whole incident is an encouragement for fresh faith: only believe.

The cross ... again

In two short verses, Jesus for a second time announces the cross path which lies before him and the disciples. Following Mark, Matthew stresses the seriousness of the impending cross by showing Jesus three times foretelling his future destiny. He speaks of it curtly and briefly, but we are left in no doubt about the importance and significance of the announcement which will shape the future of this story. The disciples are also summarily described as 'greatly distressed'. How often significant events can be described with an economy of words.

Study

By yourself

A moment of insight and truth, a time of failure, an announcement full of foreboding: this chapter tells of the highs and lows of faith, coming quickly one after the other. Make two lists for yourself, one of the moments of insight, epiphany, glory when your faith has been affirmed and confirmed, and a second list of the dark times of doubt, disappointment, failure. Pray through them both in the coming week.

For group work

Use the 'By yourself' exercise as the raw material for sharing within the group. Make sure that people are not pressured into revealing any more than they wish of their own 'By yourself' material. All must be given permission to keep silent about what they wish to keep to themselves.

Chapter 21

TAXATION ... AND FREEDOM

Matthew 17:24–7

Payment of the Temple Tax

When Jesus and his disciples came to Capernaum, the collectors of the temple tax came to Peter and asked, 'Does your teacher pay the temple tax?'

'Of course', Peter answered.

When Peter went into the house, Jesus spoke up first, 'Simon, what is your opinion? Who pays duties or taxes to the kings of this world? The citizens of the country or the foreigners?'

'The foreigners', answered Peter.

'Well, then', replied Jesus, 'that means that the citizens don't have to pay. But we don't want to offend these people. So go to the lake and drop in a line. Pull up the first fish you hook, and in its mouth you will find a coin worth enough for my temple tax and yours. Take it and pay them our taxes.'

A local legend

After the heaviness of the announcements of the cross, we come to a bit of an interlude which I would introduce in this way. I would claim to be an adopted citizen of Glasgow, where I have spent most of my adult life. Legend tells us that the city's founding saint was Mungo, or Kentigern, who lived from the second half of the sixth century through to the beginning of the seventh and who founded a monastic community on the banks of the Molendinar burn, not far from the site of the present Glasgow Cathedral. Stories about Mungo are legion, but one of the best known concerns an incident about a ring. The queen of these parts had foolishly got herself involved in a liaison with a soldier, and, even more foolishly, had given the soldier a ring which had been a present from her husband, the king. To get quickly to the punchline, the story goes that the king discovered that the soldier had the ring, and removed it, and flung it into the river. He then bade the queen to come to dinner with him, wearing the ring, which, of course, she no longer possessed. Stricken with fear and remorse, the queen sought out the saint and told Mungo the whole story. When the saint was satisfied that the queen was suitably repentant, he promised to help her. He went down to the River Clyde and started fishing. He soon landed a fine salmon, and lodged in its mouth was ... the missing ring, which the queen was able to wear to dinner, to the king's bafflement or relief. And they all lived happily ever after.

The story sounds familiar after the equally strange and unlikely story of how Peter, under the instructions of Jesus, found, in the mouth of a fish, exactly the right coin to pay the tax which was due, and about which Peter had been agonising. The legends of the Celtic saints are famous for containing incidents which sound fantastic and far-fetched to our modern sceptical ears. Many of them seem to have their origin in some of the miracle stories in the New Testament, but some saints collect a record of working miracles which leave Jesus of Nazareth very much as an also-ran. It's not difficult to see the Mungo story as a borrowing of part of today's gospel reading, given in part to enhance the saint's standing as a wonder-worker.

But what about the gospel story itself? It's told to us by Matthew as a realistic narrative of an actual historical incident – but be careful. Stories very like this were part of the stock-in-trade of the teaching of the rabbis before Jesus' time, in Jesus' time and for long afterwards. This story has about as much historical probability as the story of Jonah. One of the problems we have in interpreting both the gospels in particular and the Bible as a whole is that we are dealing with a world which had very different notions of fact and fiction from ours, and where folk tales get all mingled in with genuine historical narration as we today would understand it. Having said that, let me say again that one of the most striking aspects of the four gospels we have in the New Testament, compared to the many other so-called gospels written about Jesus, is how little of the fantastic and the miraculous they contain.

A matter of taxation

Taking this story at the level of a folk tale, a piece of imaginative truth, means that we're not so much concerned with what happened as with what this story means. When we come to the question of meaning, this story is bang up to date, for it deals with a perennial question in the history of human civilisation and contemporary society, the question of taxation. So, back to earth with a bump. This is about grubby money and paying taxes. Maybe I should say here that, in our modern affluent democratic society, I don't share the jaundiced view that all taxation is of the devil. I'm glad I'm well enough off to be paying taxes in the first place, and I also think that, while the state among others may waste our money from time to time, there are many things which we should do collectively, like our National Health Service, and be quite willing to pay for them.

But enough of the personal asides; to the gospel story itself. This is a very interesting story, and the small print is well worth studying. It begins with the collectors of the temple tax asking Peter whether Jesus pays the temple tax or not. This is more than a question of principle, it's clearly also a request for payment. Peter replies that Jesus does pay the tax. When he comes back to Jesus, Jesus divines what's on his mind. The question is raised tangentially. 'Tell me, Peter', says Jesus, 'who do the kings of this world exact taxation from? From their children or others?' (This is the NRSV translation, closer to the Greek than the GNB's 'citizens and foreigners'.) 'Others', says Peter. 'Then the children are free', says Jesus. 'However, so that we do not give offence to them, go, catch a fish, take the first fish that comes up. You'll find a coin in its mouth; take it and pay the tax with it.'

That phrase, 'the kings of the earth', has a bit of a history. It's not a neutral term; its connotations are negative. Already in Matthew's gospel there have been four instances cited of earthly rulers exercising capricious and destructive power. Matthew has a pretty bleak view of this world's powerful. In this exchange with Peter, Jesus is saying that the powerful of this world are well known for being pretty good to their own. Their children go free while the rest are taxed. 'Then the children are free', says Jesus. But, using these words to refer to the community of the disciples, they are not the children of any earthly ruler, they are the sons and daughters of God, they are citizens of the heavenly kingdom. And they are free. So, ultimately the obligation does not fall on them, for it is to God they are primarily obliged; but, as Jesus says, 'So that we do not give offence ... go and find this fish in which God will provide, and pay up, anyway'.

One other little piece of background information: the Greek word for the temple tax is actually two drachma, which was the amount payable by one person. The word for the coin in the fish's mouth is *stater*, which was a coin worth four drachma. So, the coin in the fish's mouth was enough to pay the tax for both Jesus and Peter.

Relevance

What's interesting about this story is that, although it's set in Jesus' own life, Matthew tells it to give guidance to the people of his own community, living round about the year AD 70. If he is writing before the year 70, then the background is that the temple tax was payable for the upkeep of the Jerusalem temple. The question in the minds of the young community of Christians with Jewish roots is whether they should continue to pay the tax for the temple, which implies that they are still living under the obligations of the Jewish Law. The answer is that in, an ultimate sense, they are free of that law; in and through Jesus they, and we, are brought to a fundamental and unshakeable liberty. However, in the conditions of everyday life, they do not go around flaunting their freedom and finding situations of unnecessary confrontation all over the place. They conform to the prevailing social norm, knowing that they are not bound to it.

It is also possible that the gospel is written after AD 70, the year when the Temple at Jerusalem was destroyed. After the Temple's destruction, the Romans continued to levy the temple tax, but the Emperor Vespasian co-opted it to help rebuild the temple to Jupiter in Rome. Such an action was, of course, deeply insulting to both Jews and the young Christian community alike, paying to support a temple to a pagan god. 'Pay it', remains the answer, 'pay the tax.' This is not the issue to die for. There's the reminder of a famous incident in the life of Bonhoeffer when he was standing with a friend at some public place and seemingly enthusiastically joined in with the company in giving the salute, 'Heil Hitler'. When his friend questioned and upbraided him afterwards, Bonhoeffer's answer was: 'Not now, this is not the right time, place or issue to make our protest'.

'Pay it' is the answer, or part of the answer. Christians have no easy escape from the pains of living, the sufferings, ambiguities and vicissitudes of life. We are, rather, given a new perspective to deal with them. We live in the same world as everybody else, and are subject to the same conditions, but ... in Matthew's gospel, there have been three previous references to fish. Two of them are in the two stories of the feedings of the hungry crowd, where, in a situation of need and apparent hopelessness, God provides. The third is the words of the Sermon on the Mount, also about God's good provision. 'Would any of you offer your child a stone when they ask for bread, or a snake when they ask for fish? If you, bad as you are, know how to give good gifts to your children, how much more will your heavenly Father give good gifts to those who ask him' (7:9–11). 'How much more ...'

'Pay it' is the answer, but only part of the answer. The other part is in the fish, wonderfully provided. 'How much more.' In the time of Jesus and the early church, the Roman emperor, the supreme 'king of the earth' was often credited with godlike powers, so godlike that not only people, but also the creatures of the animal kingdom, like fish, recognised and paid homage to him. The fish in our story doesn't. His homage is paid to the living God. And Jesus and Peter are wonderfully provided. They only pay what God provides. If this is homage to the 'king of the earth', it is a deeply subversive homage.

This light-hearted story is about our Christian freedom in face of the constraints of daily life. It speaks also about our hope in Christ, that the conditions and pains under which we live, often inflicted by others, are not the last word. It occurs immediately after the second cross announcement and the description of the disciples as 'distressed'. It offers hope. We can read these words today, from the other side of Easter. We know, trust, believe, Jesus has been raised, he is risen, he lives among us now, on the other side of death. The narrow way to the cross is not the last word. God indeed does strangely and wonderfully provide ... sometimes in our lives, too, in ways as incredible and unexpected as Peter's finding the coin in the fish's mouth. 'Who would ever have believed it?' Thanks be to God.

Study

By yourself

'Then the children are free.' What does the freedom of the children of God mean to you? When do you need to think of others in exercising that freedom?

Chapter 22

CHURCH RELATIONSHIPS

Matthew 18

Who is the Greatest?

(Mark 9:33–7, Luke 9:46–8)

At that time the disciples came to Jesus, asking, 'Who is the greatest in the Kingdom of heaven?'

So Jesus called a child, made him stand in front of them, and said, 'I assure you that unless you change and become like children, you will never enter the Kingdom of heaven. The greatest in the Kingdom of heaven is the one who humbles himself and becomes like this child. And whoever welcomes in my name one such child as this, welcomes me.'

Temptations to Sin

(Mark 9:42–8, Luke 17:1–2)

'If anyone should cause one of these little ones to lose his faith in me, it would be better for that person to have a large millstone tied round his neck and be drowned in the deep sea. How terrible for the world that there are things that make people lose their faith! Such things will always happen – but how terrible for the one who causes them!

'If your hand or your foot makes you lose your faith, cut it off and throw it away! It is better for you to enter life without a hand or a foot than to keep both hands and both feet and be thrown into the eternal fire. And if your eye makes you lose your faith, take it out and throw it away! It is better for you to enter life with only one eye than to keep both eyes and be thrown into the fire of hell.'

The Parable of the Lost Sheep

(Luke 15:3–7)

'See that you don't despise any of these little ones. Their angels in heaven, I tell you, are always in the presence of my Father in heaven.

'What do you think a man does who has a hundred sheep and one of them gets lost? He will leave the other ninety-nine grazing on the hillside and go and look for the lost sheep. When he finds it, I tell you, he feels far happier over this one sheep than over the ninety-nine that did not get lost. In just the same way your Father in heaven does not want any of these little ones to be lost.'

A Brother or Sister who Sins

'If your brother sins against you, go to him and show him his fault. But do it privately, just between yourselves. If he listens to you, you have won your brother back. But if he will not listen to you, take one or two other persons with you, so that "every accusation may be upheld by the testimony of two or more witnesses", as the scripture says. And if he will not listen to them, then tell the whole thing to the church. Finally, if he will not listen to the church, treat him as though he were a pagan or a tax collector.'

Prohibiting and Permitting

'And so I tell all of you: what you prohibit on earth will be prohibited in heaven, and what you permit on earth will be permitted in heaven.

'And I tell you more: whenever two of you on earth agree about anything you pray for, it will be done for you by my Father in heaven. For where two or three come together in my name, I am there with them.'

The Parable of the Unforgiving Servant

Then Peter came to Jesus and asked, 'Lord, if my brother keeps sinning against me, how many times do I have to forgive him? Seven times?'

'No, not seven times', answered Jesus, 'but seventy times seven, because the Kingdom of heaven is like this. Once there was a king who decided to check on his servants' accounts. He had just begun to do so when one of them was brought in who owed him millions of pounds. The servant did not have enough to pay his debt, so the king ordered him to be sold as a slave, with his wife and his children and all that he had, in order to pay the debt. The servant fell on his knees before the king. "Be patient with me," he begged, "and I will pay you everything!" The king felt sorry for him, so he forgave him the debt and let him go.

'Then the man went out and met one of his fellow-servants who owed him a few pounds. He grabbed him and started choking him. "Pay back what you owe me!" he said. His fellow-servant fell down and begged him, "Be patient with me, and I will pay you back!" But he refused; instead, he had him thrown into jail until he should pay the debt. When the other servants saw what had happened, they were very upset and went to the king and told him everything. So he called the servant in. "You worthless slave!" he said. "I forgave you the whole amount you owed me, just because you asked me to. You should have had mercy on your fellow-servant, just as I had mercy on you." The king was very angry, and he sent the servant to jail to be punished until he should pay back the whole amount.'

And Jesus concluded, 'That is how my Father in heaven will treat every one of you unless you forgive your brother from your heart.'

The lesson of the child

The playful incident of Jesus, Peter and the coin in the fish's mouth with its profound and liberating note of Christian freedom, coupled with an injunction to be careful about how that freedom is exercised in the day-to-day life in the world, serve as an introduction to the important themes of Matthew 18 which deal with issues of daily life within Matthew's church. Its words are addressed to all disciples, then and now. The chapter begins with the incident of the child in the midst which Matthew borrows from Mark 9:33–7 but places his own stamp upon. The story starts with the disciples coming to Jesus to ask an open question about greatness within the Kingdom, unlike in Mark where Jesus places the child in the midst as a riposte and admonition to the disciples' squabbling about their own pecking order. Not for the first time, Matthew shows the disciples in a more favourable light than Mark.

Here, as in Mark, Jesus uses a real child as a living parable. Remember the status of children in the world of Jesus' time: they had none, and were therefore living embodiments of powerlessness and marginalisation, lowly outsiders in the power game. Jesus places the child in front of the disciples and bids them 'change and become like children'; only with such change will they enter the Kingdom of God. Schweizer makes the interesting point that Jesus' mother tongue of Aramaic had no words for 'back' or 'again': he couldn't literally say 'become a child again', so he has to use the circumlocution 'change (repent) and become like children'. This may well be an original saying of Jesus which Matthew adds to Mark's account here. The message is straightforward: life in the community of Jesus is to be characterised by a profound humility, before God and towards one another. It is a humility which is certainly not to be confused with obsequiousness towards the powerful; verse 5, which takes us back to Mark's version, makes it crystal clear that the expected humility is to be manifest as much to the children, 'the little ones', who are the object lessons of Jesus' teaching here. This humility gives us the grace and openness to welcome those whom the world sees of no account.

Founded under the inspiration of Jean Vanier, across the contemporary world the communities of L'Arche, in which people with learning difficulties live with those who care for them and journey with them in an atmosphere of mutual respect and an awareness that all in the community are 'gifted', provide profound and joyful examples of the liberating effects of the humility that Jesus taught and embodied. Jean Vanier himself has written (1988 pp. 110–11) of living life with 'the broken ones', 'the little ones':

> It means going down the ladder
> and washing their feet
> as Jesus did,
> discovering the beatitude of littleness:

> to be hidden servants,
> taking the last place;
> it is there we find Jesus.
> John the Baptist said that he must decrease
> that Jesus might increase.
> The power of God's glory grew only as Jesus disappeared,
> descending to the lowest place.
> Jesus said: 'It is good that I go,
> so that I can send you my Spirit;
> that you may grow
> and bear much fruit.'
> And so, Jesus died on the cross,
> and then hid himself in the bread of the Eucharist.
> In the same way, those of us who are the strongest
> or the elders in a community,
> must learn to disappear,
> to take the last place,
> to become like bread,
> so that others may be nourished and grow.

(Excerpt from *The Broken Body*,
copyright © 1988 by Darton, Longman & Todd, Ltd.)

The phrase 'the beatitude of littleness' is one to ponder and cherish. It is a gift to be nourished; it gives us the inner springs to extend an indiscriminate welcome and acceptance to all, particularly 'the little ones'.

Take care!

The text moves naturally from the picture of the child as a model (of humility) to the child in his or her vulnerability as the recipient of care within the community. Here, the child should be understood not only as referring to children but as a metaphor for all the 'little ones', those within the faith community whose faith is new, young or vulnerable. Matthew has Jesus issue a stern warning to any who would undermine, threaten or abuse such faith. As Tom Wright says, Jesus is using the device of hyperbole once more:

226

So Jesus issues a stark warning, with typical exaggeration. There must be easier ways of drowning someone than making them carry an enormous millstone around their neck and taking them in a boat far out to sea so that they can sink into the deepest part; but that's what the picture suggests, like a vivid and overdramatized cartoon. Large circular stones, with a central hole for the mechanism, were used to grind corn; the biggest were so large it took a donkey to work them. That's the type Jesus is talking about, the type he says you should imagine having round your neck as a collar. (Wright 2002 p. 29)

The vivid, indeed brutal exaggeration continues as the focus changes from threatening the faith of others to losing one's own faith. Amputation and blindness are thoroughly drastic measures to take (18:8–9). Together, these verses contain a realistic acknowledgement of the realities of sin and temptation which threaten every believer and all communities of faith: realities which have to be fought with a costly vigour. They also point to the particular situation of Matthew's young Christian community, emerging after its painful struggle with the Judaism in which it had been born. For the coming-to-birth church, apostasy, losing or renouncing faith, was always seen as one of the gravest of threats and dangers.

A glimpse of heaven

The theme of God's care for the little ones, delegated to the faith community, returns in the parable of the Lost Sheep. Luke also uses this parable (Luke 15:3–7), but Matthew makes it his own with a different introduction and conclusion. The parable is introduced with Jesus' command not to despise or ignore 'one of these little ones' because 'in heaven their angels continually see the face of my Father ...' (18:10 NRSV – a fuller and more accurate translation than the GNB). The 'angels' of the little ones seeing the face of God is of real significance. In Judaism, while the throne of God was surrounded by the attendance of the angelic host, members of the host did not see God. Remember the classic description of Isaiah 6 with the angels covering their faces before God's awesome holiness. While the Old Testament teaches that God sends his angels to protect the righteous, at the time of Jesus the notion of a personal guardian angel was still in its infancy. These angels were seen as present protectors on earth rather than intercessors at the court of heaven. So, to site the angels of the little ones at the court of heaven and have them look without reserve upon the face of God is startlingly bold.

> We are not dealing with the pretty little cherubs of popular art; angels are cosmic powers through which God rules the universe or intercessors who bring before God all the evil that befalls men (Tobit 12:15, Ethiopian Enoch 104:1). The little ones are so important that God's universal sovereignty is for their benefit: their plight is seen, their prayer is heard. (Schweizer 1975 p. 368)

The point is obvious: it is the very ones whom we are tempted to despise or ignore who see and are seen before the face of God. The old who are allowed to become invisible, shut away at home or in an institution, the young who are so easily demonised, the handicapped who are ignored, the strangers in colour, language, sexual orientation or religion who are shunned make up the beginnings of a list of the invisible and discounted ones in our society. There is no such discounting and denigrating in the community called church if we are seeking to be faithful to this teaching of Jesus.

The teaching continues in the parable of the Lost Sheep itself. Perhaps we have a picture of shepherding being a cooperative operation from the picture of the shepherds on Bethlehem's hillside on the night of Jesus' birth in Luke 2; a much more common practice would have been of an individual shepherd caring for his own small flock as in the parable. To leave the vast majority of the flock unprotected and go and search for the one wanderer was an unusual and risky business, yet the shepherd does just that. Great is his joy when the lost sheep is found and restored. Now Matthew changes the punchline. Where Luke stresses the joy in heaven over one sinner who repents, the outsider returned to the fold (Luke 15:7), Matthew has: 'So it is not the will of your Father in heaven that one of these little ones should be lost' (18:14). Both Matthew and Luke are familiar with the theme that, in Jesus, God is exercising a ministry of caring shepherding over his people. While Luke's emphasis is on Jesus as the welcomer of the sinner, Matthew's main concern in this passage is the care of the 'little ones'. That care is not exercised by Jesus alone; rather, he delegates it to the community of disciples. By changing the context of the parable, Matthew brings us up short and throws out a challenge. In his parable, the good shepherd is not only Jesus, it is every disciple. We all share the calling of care for the little ones and the challenge of bringing those who have strayed back home.

Dealing with deviance

For us, living in a society which is increasingly litigious, quick to blame and condemn and determined to conduct so much of the business of personal relationships in the public eye, the words of Matthew 18:15–20 offer a refreshingly sane and restrained corrective. The issue being addressed is how the community's members should deal with those who they perceive have wronged them. In the first instance, they are simply to go on their own, without witnesses, to the one who has 'sinned against them' and put to the 'sinner' the perceived fault. If this action achieves reconciliation, well and good: the bonds of community are restored and the brother or sister is received quietly back into fellowship. If the 'sinner' will not 'listen' to the complaint against them, i.e. will neither hear nor acknowledge their fault, the one who has been wronged is enjoined to take one or two witnesses with him and try again. The function of the witnesses is twofold. It both allows the accusation, if valid, to be upheld by more than simply the accuser; it also allows for the correction of the accuser if the witness deems the charge they are making either unfounded or too severe. If this second remedy fails, then, and only then, is the matter to be brought before the whole congregation. If the 'sinner' will not heed the correction of the congregation, then, for the peace of the whole, they are deemed to be no longer part of it.

> Towards one another, the disciples lead lives that comport themselves with a community presided over by Jesus: in recognition of their total dependence on God, they deal with one another in the spirit of loving concern, of circumspection, of mutuality, and of forgiveness.
> (Kingsbury 1986 p. 115)

229

There follows the fascinating verse 18, fascinating because it gives
to the whole congregation the authority to permit and prohibit, or,
in more traditional language, 'loose and bind'. It appears that the
authority given to Peter in 16:19 is only given to him as exemplar for
the whole community: here, it is quite clear that, without hierarchy,
authority is delegated by heaven to the community on earth. Is there
a congregational authority here which has been too long delegated
– or relegated – to a hierarchical model of church life? This teaching
is placed just before some vital words of Jesus about forgiveness
and reconciliation. Ian Fraser, whose life work has been all about
empowering ordinary Christians and Christian communities in all
sorts of places, gives an example of a congregation's mature work of
reconciliation and welcome in his little book, *The Way Ahead: Grown-
Up Christians*. It's from much earlier in his life, when he was a parish
minister in Rosyth in Fife:

> An elder of our church was jailed for embezzlement. When he got out
> he found it very difficult to rejoin the congregation, some of whom
> had suffered financial loss at his hands. He would try – and then duck
> out at the last minute. At last he made himself share in the morning
> worship. I saw him afterwards and asked how it had been. Tears came
> into his eyes: 'They didn't either look down on me or fuss over me.
> It was, "Jim, we're glad you're back".' These were the words of a
> body which had become theologically mature. If people had used the
> traditional words, 'Jim, we forgive you,' that would have left them
> on the judgement seat, him on the sinner's stool. Their bringing him
> alongside made real the welcome back into their company. (Fraser
> 2006 pp. 30–1)

Two or three gathered ...

Just before the teaching about forgiveness, there is the precious
verse of 18:20: 'Where two or three come together in my name, I
am there with them'. There is a twofold background. In Judaism,
ten males were required to be present for corporate worship; here,
the number is foreshortened to two or three. Such is enough to
make the prayer of the community valid. There was also a familiar
Jewish statement which said: 'When two sit together and engage
themselves with the words of the Torah, the Shekinah (a paraphrase

for God's presence) is in their midst'. Jesus' words here are formed against that background. They are clearly post-Easter words, the words of Christ, risen and exalted, promising to be present wherever and whenever they call on his name, however few in number they may be.

490?

The chapter ends with a short seminal exchange between Jesus and Peter, followed by the parable of the unforgiving servant. The exchange encapsulates Matthew's teaching about his key theme of forgiveness, which is central to all life together in community. In the dialogue, Peter is the fall guy. He asks, in search of innocent approval: 'Lord, how often am I to forgive my brother if he goes on wronging me? As many as seven times?' Peter thinks he's being generous – until he hears the reply: 'I do not say seven times, but seventy times seven', which of course means not 490 times, but times without number.

Our human consciousness is an amazing gift, with the ability it gives us to stand back from ourselves and reflect on our lives and live not just in the present, but through the gift of memory, in the past, and through the gifts of hope and fear, in the future also. It doesn't take us more than a second's reflection, however, to be aware that the gift of our consciousness doesn't come without its burdens from both the past and the future, which can weigh very heavy on our present lives.

The problem about the future is relatively simple to describe. No one knows. We do not know what awaits us, and the weight of that insecurity can bring us low. One way, one very important way, we can share that burden with one another and ease each other's load, is in the making and keeping of promises, so that we don't face tomorrow alone.

The past is more complex. For, in the bruising business of life, the reality we all know is that we wound and we are wounded. We get hurt and we hurt other people, and both affect us profoundly. The hurts we receive can and do mark us deeply; we get angry, resentful, discouraged, bitter, defeated; the list could go on and on. We have to deal with them for ourselves, and we have to deal with the one who has hurt us. The hurts we know we have inflicted – these too cause their own psychic pain which can linger long.

If our promises are a way to share the facing of the burden of the future, then our acceptance of one another, our forgiveness of hurts inflicted, wrongs done, is a vital way to the healing of the burden of the past. It's not at all easy in face of the pains mentioned a moment ago. Probably the least helpful thing to be said here is: 'You must forgive'. Forgiveness is not a direct 'ought' like that. It comes, as the parable in the gospel hints, from seeing something else, something we can call 'the grace of forgiveness'.

This might help. Richard Holloway wrote a little book on forgiveness. In it, he says what is very obvious, but what we sometimes miss. He says: 'We forgive people, not sins. We forgive and accept people, in spite of their acts against us.' In other words, in forgiving people, we are not condoning actions, we are accepting people, in spite of. Jesus says: when you begin to understand that, you can do it again and again and again. Grace grows. And, far from being something supine, as the action of the father in the parable of the Prodigal Son shows, forgiveness is about taking the initiative in a relationship, though it may never be put into words at all.

In both the human story and the Christian story, I believe it is very difficult to overestimate the importance of forgiveness and its twin, acceptance. It is forgiveness which overcomes estrangements, brings reconciliation, breaks the iron bands of revenge and recrimination, delivers from bitterness and resentment, frees from guilt and fear. It is something that we do practise in the daily round of our lives; it's a balm for the bumps and bruises we keep inflicting on one another; it's an oil which keeps the engine of community running within family life, community life, church life. It's something we should always be praying for the grace to practise better. Forgiveness is indeed a great grace and for us springs from our understanding of the grace of our gracious God, made known in Jesus Christ.

We have all experienced the grace of forgiveness and acceptance shedding their oil and light on our day-to-day living. Are there, however, some things which are simply, by any measure at all, unforgiveable? By all human standards that is so; but, every so often, human beings arise who somehow transcend the ill done to them and their people. Richard Holloway again, telling this time of standing at Nelson Mandela's cell:

> I once stood outside the cell he had occupied on Robben Island and saw the thin mat on the cold floor on which he had slept for 18 years and was choked by the enormity of his graciousness. Those are the conditions that normally produce enraged avengers, whose actions we deplore, yet whose embittered logic we can understand. The enormity of forgiveness flowing from such conditions is impossible to understand. It is the insanity of grace. We hear it in the voice of the crucified forgiving those who are hammering in the nails. (Holloway 2002 p. 88)

'The insanity of grace.' Jacques Derrida, the philosopher, speaks of moments of forgiveness in the human story in face of monstrous wrong, and calls them instances of 'the madness of the impossible', moments which defy all human logic, yet have their own meaning, and bring the indescribable light of grace into the deepest darkness. The insanity of grace, the madness of the impossible. What wonderful descriptions these are of the events at the very heart of our Christian story, of the passion of our Lord, of the cross and resurrection of Jesus Christ. That's where forgiveness starts for us. Forgiveness flows from the cross. It is there we learn that we are accepted, in spite of everything, that we are forgiven, in spite of all our irresponsible actions for which we're responsible; there we learn we are accepted with our part in the collective guilt of humankind. It is there we are enrolled in the school of grace, freely to give as we have freely received. How do we witness to the Easter faith? In things big and small, keep remembering, 'Seventy times seven'.

The unforgiving steward

Matthew has Jesus illustrate his reply to Peter with the parable of the unforgiving servant at the end of chapter 18 (vv. 22–35). The gross comparison between the 'millions of pounds' (GNB; 'ten thousand talents' NRSV) of the first servant's debt, which the king forgives, and the debt of 'few pounds' (GNB; 'one hundred denarii' NRSV), which the first servant refuses to forgive his fellow servant, illustrates the vast gulf between God's forgiveness of us and our forgiveness of one another. The parable, with its ending; 'And Jesus concluded, "That is how my Father in heaven will treat every one of you unless you forgive your brother from your heart"' offers a doctrine of conditional forgiveness – you will be forgiven only if you forgive. This chimes in with the teaching in Matthew 6:14–15, but seems strangely at odds with the unconditional forgiveness offered by the father in the parable of the prodigal son in Luke 15:11–24. Holloway believes that another reading of the 'unforgiving servant' parable is possible:

> The offence of the ungrateful slave was his refusal to connect his own situation to that of a fellow victim's. This seems to fit one aspect of Jesus' doctrine of conditional forgiveness – only if we forgive others can we ourselves be forgiven – but a deeper reading may be possible. Is there some kind of universal awareness emerging here that by any calculus of revenge we all deserve punishment for something, because we are all enmeshed in the web of collective guilt that history has spun round humanity? In real life, some are never punished, because they are never found out or because they are too powerful to be challenged; some are punished not for offences they did commit, but for those they did not commit; and some seem to be punished for no reason at all. The human situation, it is being suggested here, is so complex that it is impossible to apply a rational system of moral accountancy to it with any accuracy, so we should not even bother to try. Instead of laboriously working out the exact and proportionate revenge that is someone's due, we should refuse to get involved in the punishment process at all. (Holloway 2002 p. 73)

We come to the end of this crucial chapter for the life of the church. It is good always to remember that the whole teaching of the chapter is set within the granite-like foundations at the beginning and end of humility and forgiveness. It is these attitudes and the practices which follow from them which are to be the rocks on which the life of our faith communities are built.

> It is clear that Matthew 18 has been constructed as the 'Rule for the Congregation' under the strong influence of the basic principles of Jesus' teaching: his preaching about those standards which are

valid before God – his call to repentance and humility (1–5), his love commandment (6–14), and his demand for the unlimited readiness to forgive (21–35) – while being assured of the presence of the *Kurios* (Lord) in their midst and the expectation of the coming kingdom ... living as disciples and followers implies living by the mercy of God which in turn must be realized in the relation to the brother (21–35). (Bornkamm 1995 p. 109)

Study

By yourself

Take and ponder this short hymn in the week ahead.

'Forgiveness is your gift,
both cleansing and renewing,
to catch us when we drift,
our base desires pursuing;
and hug us back to life
and bring us to a feast
where all will celebrate
the life your love released.

Your grace goes out to meet
the sinful and the doubting,
your arms and dancing feet
speak louder than all shouting:
O God, how great your love
which takes us empty in,
and, with our love unproved,
lets better life begin.'

(Ian M. Fraser in *CH4* (Hymn 361) 2005,
words copyright Stainer & Bell)

For group work

Matthew 18 offers a picture of the dynamics of the life of a community of faith. Share how you would interpret Jesus' words about the place of children, the search for the lost, the implementation of discipline and the practice of forgiveness within your faith community today.

Chapter 23

FAMILY VALUES?

Matthew 19

Jesus Teaches about Divorce

(*Mark 10:1–12*)

When Jesus finished saying these things, he left Galilee and went to the territory of Judea on the other side of the river Jordan. Large crowds followed him, and he healed them there.

Some Pharisees came to him and tried to trap him by asking, 'Does our Law allow a man to divorce his wife for whatever reason he wishes?'

Jesus answered, 'Haven't you read the scripture that says that in the beginning the Creator made people male and female? And God said, "For this reason a man will leave his father and mother and unite with his wife, and the two will become one." So they are no longer two, but one. No human being must separate, then, what God has joined together.'

The Pharisees asked him, 'Why, then, did Moses give the law for a man to hand his wife a divorce notice and send her away?'

Jesus answered, 'Moses gave you permission to divorce your wives because you are so hard to teach. But it was not like that at the time of creation. I tell you, then, that any man who divorces his wife for any cause other than her unfaithfulness, commits adultery if he marries some other woman.'

His disciples said to him, 'If this is how it is between a man and his wife, it is better not to marry.'

Jesus answered, 'This teaching does not apply to everyone, but only to those to whom God has given it. For there are different reasons why men cannot marry: some, because they were born that way; others, because men made them that way; and others do not marry for the sake of the Kingdom of heaven. Let him who can accept this teaching do so.'

Jesus Blesses Little Children

(Mark 10:13–16, Luke 18:15–17)

Some people brought children to Jesus for him to place his hands on them and to pray for them, but the disciples scolded the people. Jesus said, 'Let the children come to me and do not stop them, because the Kingdom of heaven belongs to such as these.'

He placed his hands on them and then went away.

The Rich Young Man

(Mark 10:17–31, Luke 18:18–30)

Once a man came to Jesus. 'Teacher', he asked, 'what good thing must I do to receive eternal life?'

'Why do you ask me concerning what is good?' answered Jesus. 'There is only One who is good. Keep the commandments if you want to enter life.'

'What commandments?' he asked.

Jesus answered, 'Do not commit murder; do not commit adultery; do not steal; do not accuse anyone falsely; respect your father and your mother; and love your neighbour as you love yourself.'

'I have obeyed all these commandments', the young man replied. 'What else do I need to do?'

Jesus said to him, 'If you want to be perfect, go and sell all you have and give the money to the poor, and you will have riches in heaven; then come and follow me.'

When the young man heard this, he went away sad, because he was very rich.

Jesus then said to his disciples, 'I assure you: it will be very hard for rich people to enter the Kingdom of heaven. I repeat: it is much harder for a rich person to enter the Kingdom of God than for a camel to go through the eye of a needle.'

When the disciples heard this, they were completely amazed. 'Who, then, can be saved?' they asked.

Jesus looked straight at them and answered, 'This is impossible for human beings, but for God everything is possible.'

Then Peter spoke up, 'Look', he said, 'we have left everything and followed you. What will we have?'

Jesus said to them, 'You can be sure that when the Son of Man sits on his glorious throne in the New Age, then you twelve followers of mine will also sit on thrones, to rule the twelve tribes of Israel. And everyone who has left houses or brothers or sisters or father or mother or children or fields for my sake, will receive a hundred times more and will be given eternal life. But many who now are first will be last, and many who now are last will be first.'

Leaving Galilee, heading for Jerusalem

Chapter 19 begins with Matthew's usual way of announcing the end of a block of Jesus' teaching, this time the fourth. Matthew then continues by giving another hugely significant announcement. He tells us that Jesus left Galilee and crossed the Jordan into Judea. We can see the Jordan as Jesus' Rubicon. Matthew is telling us that the journey to the cross is beginning in earnest. Jesus leaves the home territory of Galilee, the scene of so much of his active ministry, and enters the heartlands of Judea, the centre of the forces of opposition as well as the geographical centre of his people's faith. As he goes, large crowds follow him and the work of healing continues.

The new household of faith

As Jesus journeys, he continues to teach. There is much teaching contained in the six scenes which make up chapters 19 and 20, which end by bringing us to Jesus' entry into Jerusalem itself. The scenes are as follows:

19:3–12	Marriage and divorce
19:13–15	Children
19:16–30	Wealth
20:1–16	Parable of the householder

| 20:17–28 | Being slaves |
| 20:29–34 | Healing two blind men. |

It's helpful to see the teaching as centred round the theme of the new household of faith which Jesus has come to bring. The household was seen as the basic unit of any society. Warren Carter offers a very useful analysis of the traditional views of household relationships which held sway in the world contemporary with Jesus:

> The household was understood to consist of four basic dimensions, namely, three relationships (husband–wife, father–children, master–slave) and the male's task of earning wealth. A power dynamic controlled the relationships in which the husband/father/master *ruled over* the wife/children/slaves. The household was hierarchical and patriarchal in that the male held power over women and children. It was marked by strict gender differentiation. The woman was to attend to household tasks while the man represented the household in society. Under the pressures of daily life, many households, especially at the lower societal levels, may well have functioned in ways that differed significantly from this pattern. Yet this structure continued to be advocated aggressively. ...
>
> While chapters 19 and 20 utilize this household structure, they do not endorse this cultural norm. Rather, siding with some other minority cultural views, the two chapters subvert this hierarchical and patriarchal structure by instructing disciples in a more egalitarian pattern (cf. 20:12). (Carter 2004 pp. 376–7)

In the course of exploring these two chapters, we shall see how true these comments of Carter's are.

Marriage and divorce

After the description of Jesus' movement from Galilee into Jordan, the first incident of chapter 19 tells of an encounter and a disputation between Jesus and some Pharisees. Matthew states that the purpose of their questioning is not neutral or in the search for enlightenment; they are seeking to lure Jesus into a statement of indiscretion which they can then use against him. The question they ask concerns divorce: 'Does our Law allow a man to divorce his wife for whatever reason he wishes?' The question was a live one among the rabbinic schools at the time of Jesus, where the two main schools of Hillel and Shammai held opposing views; Hillel taught that divorce was allowed for almost anything, Shammai held a much more rigorous and restrictive view. It is significant that the question asked concerns itself only with male rights in the question of divorce. There were circumstances, albeit limited, which allowed for the female to seek divorce; here, they are not mentioned. The Pharisees mirror the patriarchal view of society with its emphasis on male power and rights.

Jesus' answer is both clever and radical. 'Haven't you read....?' he begins. The clear implication is that, if the Pharisees knew their scripture as well as they claimed to, they would not need to come to Jesus with their question. The reading to which Jesus draws their attention takes them back behind the Law of Moses to the time of creation itself and the foundational description of humanity as 'made male and female' – a statement which more than hints at an equality of the sexes which must have sounded radical indeed. He amplifies and strengthens his statement by quoting from Genesis 2:24 about a man leaving his father and mother to become bonded to his wife as 'one flesh'. Here, the picture is of the new husband leaving the patriarchal nest to create in the union together with his wife this new unit based on a mutual giving and receiving. They become 'one' according to the will of God – and what God has joined together, no one should separate.

The answer is not good enough for the disputatious Pharisees. In reply, they revert to the understanding and rules contained in the Mosaic Law, in particular Deuteronomy 24:1–4, where it is permitted for a man to write out a bill of divorce against his wife if he finds her 'objectionable'. Jesus gives their reply short shrift. He interprets the Mosaic teaching as a concession to the people's 'hardheartedness', i.e. stubborn refusal to walk fully in the ways of justice in their keeping of the Law and dealings with one another. He returns to emphasise again the 'back to basics' of the creation account with its weight on the male/female relationship as a partnership of mutuality. He ends with the hard saying that any man who divorces his wife for any reason other than unfaithfulness commits adultery if he marries another. Presumably the exception of unfaithfulness is given because, in such a case, the woman has already broken the one-flesh bond. Jesus uncompromisingly asserts the values of commitment to the male/female relationship within the bonds of marriage as fulfilling both the purposes of the Creator and fulfilling to those who have entered into this commitment. (All this teaching occurs within the context of very early and arranged marriage!)

But ...

The disputation with the Pharisees is over, but Jesus' disciples, hearers of the conversation, have a question. They find this attack on male patriarchy and the accompanying demand for lifelong commitment difficult. Might it not be better not to marry at all? John the Baptist was unmarried, as was Jesus himself. Celibacy was frowned upon in Jewish society and in the world of Jesus' time generally. With life expectancy so low and the complete lack of a state social-security system, the emphasis on the duty of each generation to provide offspring for the sake both of the family and the society was heavy indeed. There were, however, marginal groups which did not frown on celibacy.

Jesus' reply is fascinating. He states that his teaching here does not apply to everyone but only to those able to accept it, though he is also clearly setting it out as a norm for disciples. In very few places does Jesus make any concessions because what he asks entails a difficult practice. He then continues by talking about eunuchs, in other words males who were impotent. He states that some were born that way, which implies that, in their orientation and condition, such was the way God made them; some had suffered castration, presumably either voluntarily or more frequently as slaves under duress; and some would remain voluntarily celibate, like himself, for the sake of the Kingdom of heaven.

In general terms, eunuchs occupied a highly marginal and ambiguous place in society. They were outsiders, despised and dishonoured figures, frequently slaves, not infrequently the spoils of war, yet they could also achieve situations of trust and responsibility within a household or a state. In Jewish society they were forbidden from taking part in worship, yet in Isaiah 56:3–5 they are included in God's future promise of inclusion. It is a

241

strikingly bold stroke to compare the life of a disciple with those of this despised and marginal group. Jesus invites all who hear to think again, about both the reality of discipleship and the place of those whom others despise.

Today ... a thought

Those of us who live in western society at the beginning of the twenty-first century inhabit a very different world and world view from that of the first-century world. Indeed, within the last fifty years, our societies have experienced huge changes in the patterns of family and community life. In April 2007, the United Kingdom Office of National Statistics (ONS) published a survey which showed just how much our patterns of life have changed. Through all the changes recently experienced, what remains constant is the importance of our human relationships across and within the sexes. Our capacity within relationships to affirm and upbuild one another, or to hurt or harm, is ever one of the privileges and perils of being human. Blair Robertson, a Glasgow hospital chaplain, reflected on what is changed and what is constant in our life together in a Thought for the Day on BBC Radio Scotland the day after the ONS report was published. Here are his wise and hopeful words:

'I used to live in a flat in a traditional Glasgow tenement stair. But the households weren't that traditional. In the stair there was a single parent, a same-sex couple, a cohabiting couple, a single person – and a traditional family. We were a slice of society.

But what is a traditional family now? According to the Office of National Statistics everything's changing, and perhaps the changes over the last 35 years or so are greater than suspected. For example, a quarter of all children now live in a single-parent household. Seven million people live on their own today compared to three million in 1971. Divorces are down – but fewer people are getting married. At the same time, more Civil Partnerships have been registered than was envisaged.

It's fascinating stuff – but what does it prove – apart from the fact that 'the times they are a-changing?' Some people will argue that the changes prove that society is going to the dogs. But it's surely not as simple as that. Do people give up on relationships quicker than they used to? Is commitment taken lightly?

It's easy to pass judgement. As a Christian I hear the command of Jesus not to judge people – and rather than judge I see more point in supporting people in their relationships whatever they are, knowing that most of us don't choose every circumstance of our lives.

Jesus himself was born out of wedlock to a teenager and never got married. He taught that our human relationships ought to be secondary to serving God. That's a difficult teaching.

My new home's not a traditional Glasgow tenement but a house in a suburban area. There are more traditional families around. I now have Chinese and Asian neighbours. It's different to that tenement stair and it's a different slice of our diverse society. We have to live as neighbours. The greenhouse of communities and neighbourhoods and the incubator of intimate relationships are places where love, honesty and commitment can grow no matter where we live'. (Blair Robertson, Thought for the Day, BBC Radio Scotland, April 2007)

Children

The second incident in chapter 19 gives Matthew's version of Jesus' blessing of the little children. This is the second occasion within two chapters (see 18:1–5) where children have featured prominently. In Matthew 18, the child is held up by Jesus as a model of discipleship; here, along with their blessing and welcome, Jesus asserts that the Kingdom of heaven belongs to them. As background, we note that the bringing of children to rabbis for blessing is common; common also was the belief in the world of Jesus generally that children were persons of no status and rights. Once again, Matthew has pared down in his version the account given in Mark 10:13–16; he does not mention Jesus' indignation at the disciples for blocking the children's access to Jesus (the only occasion in the gospel when Jesus is described as 'indignant'). Omitting mention of Jesus' indignation is another example of Matthew being less 'hard' on the disciples than Mark. He also does not show Jesus taking the children into his arms by way of blessing; he merely lays his hands upon them.

It remains a crucial and vivid incident. There is the strong contrast between the disciples' perverse and off-putting barring of the way to Jesus, their officious discouragement of the mothers and children and Jesus' immediate and ready welcome. There is the intimacy and assurance of the moment of blessing itself, both of which have been taken up into Christian liturgy in the Sacrament of Infant Baptism. The incident affirms the place of children and other outsiders and nobodies within the loving purposes of God in Christ; it also confirms Jesus' teaching about children and discipleship in Matthew 18. As Carter says, 'All disciples are children, there are no parents' (19:13–15; see Carter 2000 p. 386); in other words, we are all humble learners together in the school of Christ. There is one other vivid contrast to note: this story is followed immediately by the encounter of Jesus with the rich young man (19:16–30). The young man possesses everything in worldly terms, but it is precisely the burden of what he has which prevents him from accepting Jesus' invitation to follow him. The contrast between the young man who has so much and the children who have nothing in worldly terms is obvious. In our society, where so much of its life is driven by the pursuit of wealth, have we the ears to hear that it is to the 'little ones', the 'have nots' that the very Kingdom of heaven belongs, not in the sense of 'pie in the sky' but in terms of finding and sharing the life abundant, the Kingdom life, here and now?

Wealth

Karl Barth famously remarked that, for their devotional life, Christians should have the Bible in one hand and the daily newspaper in the other, for it is in the clash and dialogue between the claims of the gospel and the life of the world that true discipleship is hewn out and formed. Some cynics have said that today the daily newspaper has been particularised down to its financial pages and that, for most western Christians, their discipleship represents an uneasy compromise between following Jesus and following the stock market; seldom, if ever, have Christians had to work out their obedience in a society so obsessed with wealth creation, individual and collective. All of this goes to make the story of the encounter of Jesus with the rich young man an 'Ouch' story. It does and should profoundly disturb our comfort levels.

The following background is helpful. Judaism is not an ascetic, world-denying faith. On the contrary: more than most of the world's major religions, it affirms materiality, sees the material and the spiritual as one whole, rejoices in God's good creation and is happy for people to enjoy its fruits. What makes Judaism unhappy, both in the Mosaic Law itself and in the later development of the prophetic tradition, is the unequal division of the fruits of God's goodness. In a world where its resources were seen as finite, riches were often seen as suspect. Those who pursued riches above all else were equated with the oppressors, the wicked. To have so much meant that the poor had too little. The original hearers of this story would be immediately suspicious on learning of this young man's wealth.

The meeting

In describing Jesus' encounter with the young man, Matthew once again follows Mark but with some significant differences. At the beginning of the story, the young man does not address Jesus as 'Good teacher', but simply as 'Teacher', a word often used by the opponents of Jesus to greet him. Presumably, Matthew, with his high view of Jesus' authority, wants to avoid the statement in Mark where Jesus appears to deny his goodness. 'Good teacher, what must I do to inherit eternal life?' 'Why do you call me good? No one is good but God alone' (Mark 10:17–18). Jesus' reply continues by exhorting his questioner to keep the commandments. 'Which ones?' comes the retort.

Matthew has Jesus quote the same commandments as Mark, with one subtraction and one addition. Significantly, it is the second half of the Ten Commandments which are quoted – and these all, without exception, have to do with our just dealings with one another as human beings. Matthew omits Mark's addition of 'you shall not cheat' but adds at the end the words from Leviticus 19:18, 'you shall love your neighbour as yourself' – words which sum up both the other commandments and also so much of Jesus' social teaching. The young man wants more. 'What do I still lack?' he asks. Jesus, perhaps sensing that this young man loved other than God and neighbour, throws out the challenge and the invitation: 'If you want to be perfect' (19:21). 'Perfect' is a synonym for the 'eternal life' with which the story began. Beware the dangers of its misuse to suggest that there are Christians whose vocation is to strive for perfection while the rest of us are just 'ordinary' Christians. Now comes the moment of truth. The young man's deepest attachment is neither to the commandments nor to the way of Jesus, but to his wealth. That's what defines him and where he finds his ultimate security. He, uniquely in the gospel, refuses Jesus' call to follow; 'he went away grieving, for he had many possessions'. Herzog comments:

> The four commandments, go, sell (dispossess), give (distribute), and follow me, summarize Jesus' reading of the Decalogue as seen through its debt codes. His four commandments are neither a transcending of the Torah nor a replacing of the Torah with a 'Christian' ethic, as many have wrongly suggested ... Just as Jesus is bold enough to interpret the creation intent of God in the argument over divorce (Mark 10:2–9, culminating in the citation of Genesis 2:24), so here Jesus is audacious enough to interpret the intent of Yahweh in giving the Decalogue. The Torah is about the distributive justice of God, who gave the land as a gift to be received and shared, not hoarded at the expense of ruining others. So Jesus challenges the rich man to practise the principle of extension by dispossessing and redistributing his wealth to the utterly destitute. It is a challenge steeped in the tradition of the jubilee but not a challenge likely to be well received. The man turns away, stunned. (Herzog 2000 pp. 166–7)

Getting stuck

Jesus and his disciples reflect together over this intense encounter. In the vivid hyperbolic metaphor of the struggling laden camel seeking to get through the needle's eye, Jesus strongly brings the disciples up short with his warning of how difficult it is for a rich person to enter the Kingdom. The metaphor is clear in suggesting that the rich are carrying too much baggage; their wealth is an encumbrance to both seeing and seeking Kingdom realities. It gives them an inflated sense of their own power and importance, lulls them into a false sense of security, tempts them into seeking the wrong priorities and blinds them to the real plight of the poor who are all about them. The disciples despair, recognising that the pursuit of wealth is ingrained deep in the human psyche. Jesus looks them straight in the eye (19:26) and says: 'Make God your priority; with God all things are possible'. We can hear these words as a renewed call to discipleship. Carter comments on this story: 'Following Jesus, not procuring wealth and status, defines discipleship' (19:16–30).

The promise

The conversation ends with Peter pointing out how much the disciples have already given in their following of Jesus. Jesus replies by promising them a special place 'at the renewal of all things' (19:28). Only in Matthew is there mention of the disciples sitting on twelve thrones judging the twelve tribes of Israel – a typical example of the Jewish cast of the gospel. Jesus goes on to say how much the new company of Jesus will receive compared to what they have left behind. The new community formed by the gospel will be a place of abundant fellowship and sharing; disciples will receive 'a hundredfold and will inherit eternal life' – back to the rich young man's question (19:16). Significantly, Matthew omits from Jesus' list of promises the promise of persecution; see Mark 10:28. Was that too near the bone?

The chapter ends with yet another variation of the discipleship litany which runs all the way through the gospel from the time of the announcement of the cross. 'Many who are first will be last, and the last will be first.' These words also lead into the parable at the start of Matthew 20.

Study

By yourself

A friend of mine is fond of reminding me of the connection between 'worship' and 'worth'. True worship is giving God his due honour, and true worship is measured by what we make the priorities of our lives. Two of these priorities are how we get and how we spend our money. Both are deeply spiritual questions. Reflect on them; it may help for you to keep a close check for a period of perhaps three months on exactly what you do spend your money on. Better still, after the exercise, share your findings with a group of those whom you trust.

Chapter 24

KINGDOM ECONOMICS

Matthew 20:1–16

The Workers in the Vineyard

'The Kingdom of heaven is like this. Once there was a man who went out early in the morning to hire some men to work in his vineyard. He agreed to pay them the regular wage, a silver coin a day, and sent them to work in his vineyard. He went out again to the market place at nine o'clock and saw some men standing there doing nothing, so he told them, "You also go and work in the vineyard, and I will pay you a fair wage." So they went. Then at twelve o'clock and again at three o'clock he did the same thing. It was nearly five o'clock when he went to the market place and saw some other men still standing there. "Why are you wasting the whole day here doing nothing?" he asked them. "No one hired us," they answered. "Well, then, you also go and work in the vineyard," he told them.

'When evening came, the owner told his foreman, "Call the workers and pay them their wages, starting with those who were hired last and ending with those who were hired first." The men who had begun work at five o'clock were paid a silver coin each. So when the men who were the first to be hired came to be paid, they thought they would get more; but they too were given a silver coin each. They took their money and started grumbling against the employer. "These men who were hired last worked only one hour," they said, "while we put up with a whole day's work in the hot sun – yet you paid them the same as you paid us!"

'"Listen, friend," the owner answered one of them, "I have not cheated you. After all, you agreed to do a day's work for one silver coin. Now take your pay and go home. I want to give this man who was hired last as much as I have given you. Don't I have the right to do as I wish with my own money? Or are you jealous because I am generous?"'

And Jesus concluded, 'So those who are last will be first, and those who are first will be last.'

Wealth continued: a day in the life

The last chapter ended with the story of the rich young man and Jesus' concluding words: 'But many who are first will be last, and the last will be first' (19:30). This chapter begins with a parable which ends with Jesus saying: 'So the last will be first, and the first will be last' (20:16). The connection is intimate and obvious: both illuminate the discipleship journey and anticipate the cross. The immediate subject remains essentially the same; Matthew is talking in both the story and the parable about wealth and wealth distribution. The perspective, however, is from opposite ends of the economic ladder; while the rich young man stood at the top, the principal characters in the parable, the day labourers, were firmly at the bottom. As the unemployed in the marketplace looking daily for work and pay their existence was marginal indeed. The parable has long been known as 'the parable of the labourers in the vineyard'; in recent times, it has acquired an alternative title as 'the parable of the householder' with reference to the other principal character, the man who hires out the labourers.

After the introduction, 'The Kingdom of heaven is like ...', Jesus introduces us to the householder or landowner. With surprise, we notice that it is this rich and powerful man himself who goes down to the town marketplace looking for day labourers to hire to work in his vineyard; he doesn't merely send his steward or retainer. His first visit is early in the morning when he selects some workers and agrees with them their wage for the day, which is fair but not generous. Several times in the course of the day, he returns and selects more workers, his final visit being just an hour before the day's work ends.

Then follow the big surprises. At the end of the day, when the workers assemble to get paid for their work – the rules said that a day labourer had to be paid on the day of his work lest he have no bread – the owner this time sends his steward with the instruction that those who were hired last and have worked least are to be paid first. To everyone's complete astonishment, they are paid the same as the amount agreed with those hired at sun-up and who have toiled and sweated throughout the heat of the day. There's more than astonishment; the first workers are furious. We can feel their anger; they say that they feel their work has been demeaned and they have been slighted. The owner appears on the scene once more and hears their complaint. It sounds as if they have a spokesman, for the owner replies to one of them: 'I haven't cheated you. I've paid you the agreed rate. Can't I do what I choose with my own money?' ... and the punchline: 'Why be jealous, because I am kind?'

Justice and grace

This is a very fertile parable which produces a number of rich and powerful fruits. There is the significance of the 'grumbling' of the day labourers over the equal payment made to all, regardless of their hours of labour. We are reminded of the repeated 'grumbling' against God of the Israelites in the desert after their deliverance from Egypt. How easy it is and how soon to forget God's gifts and God's goodness. If, as has usually been understood, the owner in the parable equates to God the message is clear: all have equally received of God's bounty. The warning is also clear. In the community of faith, comparisons are odious, as the proverb says. The original Greek text of the verse (20:15) which the GNB translates as 'Are you jealous because I am generous?' is 'Is your eye evil because I am good?' Looking around with the evil eye is to be motivated by jealousy and a spirit of judgementalism, both of which are death to fellowship.

Is there also a sub-text which relates particularly to Matthew's situation as a Jewish Christian in a church which is increasingly filling with Gentiles? In that case, Matthew is forcibly making the point to his fellow Jewish Christians that Gentile Christians are a reality, brought into the church by the same grace which has led them, and, though they have come lately, now in a position of complete equality with their elder Jewish Christian brothers and sisters. 'There is neither Jew nor Greek', as St Paul would say, more than once.

This parable is also about money and equality. It follows fairly hard on the heels of the parable of the unforgiving steward which (18:21–35) has also taken a side-swipe at inequality. In considering that parable, we noted Richard Holloway's assertion that we live lives of such moral complexity that any simple schema of right and wrong, blame and retribution is clearly inadequate. Is there a similar question being raised here about the rationality and fairness of our economic systems? I remember a Roman Catholic Latin American Bishop from the slums of Brazil who visited the United Kingdom on a speaking tour and told his Scottish audience in the 1990s with his tongue in his cheek: 'I'm a very devout man. Every night I pray for three things. I pray that the Pope will ordain women to the priesthood. I pray that the Pope will ordain married priests, and ... I pray for the overthrow of the present world economic system.' He was making the point that the way money and power work in the world can appear very rational and right, but, as soon as we probe deeper, we know things are not right. There is a huge irrationality about the poverty of so many of the people and nations in Africa in our world so rich in resources of all kinds. There is a huge irrationality that, closer to home, the rich get richer and the poor poorer. It doesn't make sense; in the end, it doesn't make sense for any of us. It certainly doesn't make Kingdom sense, this parable tells us; it is a denial of God's justice where each is given enough from day to day.

Most frequently, this parable has been seen as a powerful and evocative assertion of God's free grace, what Schweizer calls 'the surprising righteousness of God'. It picks up and fills out the words of Jesus in the Sermon on the Mount when he speaks of God 'making his sun rise on the evil and the good, and sends his rain on the righteous and the unrighteous' (5:45). Here is a God who shows no partiality, who provides for each according to their needs, not by the reckoning of a scale of their good works, who deals in gifts, not wages. The parable opens a window into the mystery of God's grace, the wonder of a God who is kind to each and all, so that in turn, those who understand the kindness they have received may be a people of 'mercy, not sacrifice' as the gospel so often enjoins.

Carter says: 'The parable of the householder in 20:1–16 exemplifies God's distinctive and different ways of ordering life'. Welcome to the upside-down Kingdom. 'So the last will be first, and the first will be last', says Jesus.

Study

By yourself
Most of us will have experience of suffering a perceived slight or injustice like the labourers who had worked all day. Recall any such experiences and pray through them to find the ability to offer forgiveness and find peace.

For group work
Take your findings from the 'By yourself' exercise at the end of Chapter 23 which invited to you to look at the way you get and spend your money and share it with the group (if the group trusts each other enough). In light of Jesus' teaching, what could and should we learn as Christians from the credit crunch and global economic crisis of 2008–9?

Chapter 25

APPROACH TO JERUSALEM

Matthew 20:17–34

Jesus Speaks a Third Time about his Death

(Mark 10:32–4, Luke 18:31–4)

As Jesus was going up to Jerusalem, he took the twelve disciples aside and spoke to them privately, as they walked along. 'Listen', he told them, 'we are going up to Jerusalem, where the Son of Man will be handed over to the chief priests and the teachers of the Law. They will condemn him to death and then hand him over to the Gentiles, who will mock him, whip him, and crucify him; but three days later he will be raised to life.'

A Mother's Request

(Mark 10:35–45)

Then the wife of Zebedee came to Jesus with her two sons, bowed before him, and asked him a favour.

'What do you want?' Jesus asked her.

She answered, 'Promise me that these two sons of mine will sit at your right and your left when you are King.'

'You don't know what you are asking for', Jesus answered the sons. 'Can you drink the cup of suffering that I am about to drink?'

'We can', they answered.

'You will indeed drink from my cup', Jesus told them, 'but I do not have the right to choose who will sit at my right and my left. These places belong to those for whom my Father has prepared them.'

When the other ten disciples heard about this, they became angry with the two brothers. So Jesus called them all together and said, 'You know that the rulers of the heathen have power over them, and the leaders have complete authority. This, however, is not the way it shall be among you. If one of you wants to be great, he must be the servant of the rest; and if one of you wants to be first, he must be your slave – like the Son of Man, who did not come to be served, but to serve and give his life to redeem many people.'

Jesus Heals Two Blind Men

(Mark 10:46–52, Luke 18:35–43)

As Jesus and his disciples were leaving Jericho, a large crowd was following. Two blind men who were sitting by the road heard that Jesus was passing by, so they began to shout, 'Son of David! Take pity on us, sir!'

The crowd scolded them and told them to be quiet. But they shouted even more loudly, 'Son of David! Take pity on us, sir!'

Jesus stopped and called them. 'What do you want me to do for you?' he asked them.

'Sir', they answered, 'we want you to give us our sight!'

Jesus had pity on them and touched their eyes; at once they were able to see, and they followed him.

The cross, once again

'So the last will be first, and the first will be last' is the final comment of Jesus on the parable of the labourers. It links in and is immediately followed by a third prediction of the event which will overturn the world's order of things, Jesus' being handed over to his enemies, his humiliation and crucifixion, and on the third day, his being raised. Matthew describes Jesus taking the disciples aside to hammer home to them the ordeal before them all. We notice the unholy combination of the powers-that-be massing to destroy Jesus: chief priests, scribes and Gentiles. Matthew omits Mark's description of the disciples being 'filled with fear and alarm' (Mark 10:32); once again Matthew's view of the disciples is more positive than that of Mark.

... followed by the crass

At this point in Matthew's story, the links between its separate incidents are very clear. One incident informs another whether by reinforcement or by contrast. Strong contrast is at work in what comes next. Immediately after Jesus has made his third prediction of the looming cross, he is approached by the mother of James and John with the totally inappropriate request that they should sit in the places of honour, on the right and left-hand sides of Jesus when he comes into his Kingdom. Sometimes fond mothers have a lot to answer for! But wait a minute. When Mark tells this same story (Mark 10:32–45), it is the brothers themselves who ask for the best seats. They seem well able to speak for themselves!

The appearance of the mother of James and John here has been a justifiable target for the feminist's ire. It looks very much as if she has been put up by Matthew to divert criticism away from the male disciples. On the positive side, her presence here is a timely reminder of the presence of a significant group of women in the discipleship band, a group who will come much more to the fore as the story reaches its climax.

Being slaves

Jesus responds to the mother by speaking not only to her but to the brothers also, or perhaps the brothers alone. He makes it clear to them that, while they can share the 'honour' of his suffering, it is not within his gift to offer them the seats of privilege in the request; that gift belongs to the Father alone. Word soon percolates to the other ten disciples of what's going on. They are angry, but their very human anger at the request of James and John for a place of privilege suggests that they too have not fully understood the new ways of the Kingdom community where equality, service and mutuality are the core values at its very heart. They have yet to know the fullness of that 'heart' conversion.

This passage ends the sequence of passages from the beginning of chapter 18 which have largely been dealing with life in the new community of Jesus. It provides a powerful summary. Jesus deals with the anger and dissension in the discipleship community by calling them all together, an action which both stresses his authority and has James and John's 'crime' dealt with in a community context. He doesn't rush in immediately to blame the brothers; on the contrary, he puts a distance between his teaching here and the original cause of the dispute. He appeals to the disciples' knowledge of the ways of the world, 'You know', he says; but he then asserts that this will not be the way in their new community. This is a striking difference from Mark's account. In Mark 10:43, Jesus says: 'This *is* not the way among you', present tense, appealing to their living experience of life with Jesus. Here, Matthew says (20:26): 'It *will* not be so among you', future tense, expressing a command and a hope. Each reading has much to offer.

With the final variation of the discipleship litany of the crossway, the passage ends. We have already heard the two versions of 'the first shall be last, the last first'. Now Jesus offers his last version as the discipleship band comes to the edge of the city of Jerusalem and the time of testing. 'Whoever wants to be great among you' (plenty room for the right kind of ambition) 'must be your servant, and whoever wishes to be first among you must be your slave' (no best seats but plenty scope for footwashing); why? ... 'just as the Son of Man came not to be served but to serve, and to give his life a ransom for many' (20:26–8). At the beginning of the gospel, in the Sermon on the Mount, Jesus has invited all with ears to hear to 'love your enemies, and pray for those who persecute you, *so that you may be children of your Father in heaven*' (5:44). Now, with his passion looming, he bids disciples to take upon themselves the way of humble service, for it is thus that they will show that they are the followers of the Son of Man. These are strong words which Jesus uses here; the invitation to be a 'slave' carries an 'ouch' punch with a force not much less than the call to take up your cross. Carter sums up the attitude which is to determine both the inner life of the disciples and the outer shape of the believing community. He says: 'All disciples are slaves like Jesus, there are no masters' (20:17–28).

A caution

The important word in Carter's quotation is 'all', without exception. As the year of 2007, with its anniversary of the abolition of the slave trade, reminded us, slavery was a vile condition of subjection and oppression. It took a very long time for the Christian and the national consciousness to become aware of its iniquities and its incompatibility with a gospel of liberation. Down through history, there are many examples where it has been all too easy for the rich and powerful to co-opt the gospel call for submission and servanthood to aid their own oppressive ends. Iain Whyte, in *Scotland and the Abolition of Black Slavery, 1756–1838* (2006), has unearthed this comment from James Boswell, man about town and biographer of Samuel Johnson. Boswell observed on the natural state of slavery: 'slavery, subjection, what you will,/have ever been and will be still', and in an extraordinary biblical interpretation continued: 'each bear the yoke, th' Apostle spoke/And chiefly they who bear the yoke/From wise subordination's plan/Springs the chief happiness of man' (James Boswell, quoted in *Thomas Crawford, Boswell, Burns and the French Revolution* (Edinburgh 1990) p. 37). A century later, the Irish hymnwriter Mrs Alexander was still able to pen a verse in the continuing favourite, 'All things bright and beautiful', which said:

> The rich man in his castle
> The poor man at his gate
> God made them high and lowly
> And ordered their estate.

With my own eyes, I have seen these words printed in wedding orders of service; we didn't sing them! There are no favourites, no elite, no hierarchy in the new community of grace. Each serves the other, so that the world, with its other ways, may see a new reality, cross-born.

Healing two blind men

There is one last incident before Jesus enters Jerusalem. Matthew tells of the healing of two blind men as Jesus and the disciples, followed by a large crowd, leave Jericho on the final lap of their journey. There are significant differences from the account of the healing of blind Bartimaeus in Mark 10:46–52, the story which occupies a similar position for Mark. Matthew omits any reference to entering Jericho. He also tells the story of the healing much more tersely, without the moment when the blind beggar throws away his cloak – symbol of his livelihood and identity as well as provider of warmth – and without Jesus saying to the blind: 'Your faith has healed you'. Characteristically, Matthew is concerned to demonstrate Jesus' power to heal, even in these unpropitious and threatening circumstances. He also stresses Jesus' compassion for the men, a compassion which has shone throughout his healing ministry; disciples are enjoined to practise 'mercy, not sacrifice', for this is the constant way of their Lord. The authority of the merciful one is not neglected; the shouts of the blind men, 'Have mercy on us, Lord, Son of David!' attest to who he is. In conclusion, we note that the result of the blind men's receiving back their sight is that they move to follow Jesus. Even at this last hour, maybe particularly at this last hour, people are enabled to 'see' Jesus as the one in whom to put their trust and give their allegiance. Carter's comment is:

> The story of Jesus healing the blind men who beg for mercy offers disciples hope that they too will be enabled by Jesus' power to live this alternative and against-the-grain existence (20:29–34). That is, as Jesus journeys to Jerusalem to die, the chapters provide disciples with instruction on an alternative household that befits the empire or reign of God. In countering social norms, this household embodies the way of the cross … Disciples live a marginal existence, as societal participants yet as outsiders, over against dominant societal values.
> (Carter 2000 p. 377)

How critical is that word, 'hope'. The framework of the way of discipleship and the outlines of the new community of faith have been drawn in these last chapters on the way to Jerusalem. Now comes the time of the disciples' and the community's greatest testing. They walk into the darkness, and the darkness will be very dark indeed. In and through the darkness a light glimmers, a light of hope, light enough to see and to follow until a new reality is born in the Easter faith which is not only a once-and-for-all wonder, but an event in the life of faith which comes again and again and again.

Study

By yourself

For the next month, keep a note of any examples you come across of the way of humble service.

Chapter 26

THE KINGDOM CLAIMED

Matthew 21:1–22

The Triumphant Entry into Jerusalem

(*Mark 11:1–11, Luke 19:28–40, John 12:12–19*)

As Jesus and his disciples approached Jerusalem, they came to Bethphage at the Mount of Olives. There Jesus sent two of the disciples on ahead with these instructions: 'Go to the village there ahead of you, and at once you will find a donkey tied up with her colt beside her. Untie them and bring them to me. And if anyone says anything, tell him, "The Master needs them"; and then he will let them go at once.'

This happened in order to make what the prophet had said come true:

'Tell the city of Zion,
Look, your king is coming to you!
He is humble and rides on a donkey and on a colt, the foal of
   a donkey.'

So the disciples went and did what Jesus had told them to do: they brought the donkey and the colt, threw their cloaks over them, and Jesus got on. A large crowd of people spread their cloaks on the road while others cut branches from the trees and spread them on the road. The crowds walking in front of Jesus and those walking behind began to shout, 'Praise to David's Son! God bless him who comes in the name of the Lord! Praise God!'

When Jesus entered Jerusalem, the whole city was thrown into an uproar. 'Who is he?' the people asked.

'This is the prophet Jesus, from Nazareth in Galilee', the crowds answered.

Jesus Goes to the Temple

(Mark 11:15–19, Luke 19:45–8, John 2:13–22)

Jesus went into the Temple and drove out all those who were buying and selling there. He overturned the tables of the moneychangers and the stools of those who sold pigeons, and said to them, 'It is written in the Scriptures that God said, "My Temple will be called a house of prayer." But you are making it a hideout for thieves!'

The blind and the crippled came to him in the Temple, and he healed them. The chief priests and the teachers of the Law became angry when they saw the wonderful things he was doing and the children shouting in the Temple, 'Praise to David's Son!' So they asked Jesus, 'Do you hear what they are saying?'

'Indeed I do', answered Jesus. 'Haven't you ever read this scripture? "You have trained children and babies to offer perfect praise."'

Jesus left them and went out of the city to Bethany, where he spent the night.

Jesus Curses the Fig Tree

(Mark 11:12–14, 20–4)

On his way back to the city early next morning, Jesus was hungry. He saw a fig tree by the side of the road and went to it, but found nothing on it except leaves. So he said to the tree, 'You will never again bear fruit!' At once the fig tree dried up.

The disciples saw this and were astounded. 'How did the fig tree dry up so quickly?' they asked.

Jesus answered, 'I assure you that if you believe and do not doubt, you will be able to do what I have done to this fig tree. And not only this, but you will even be able to say to this hill, "Get up and throw yourself in the sea," and it will. If you believe, you will receive whatever you ask for in prayer.'

Jerusalem

The discipleship band with Jesus draws near to Jerusalem. The final, ultimate act in the drama of the life of Jesus of Nazareth begins. 'Act' is a most appropriate word to use to describe Jesus' entry into the city which was both the seat of his most dangerous enemies and the focus of his people's faith. The procession from the Mount of Olives into the heart of the city shows every sign of being carefully stage-managed by Jesus. How else can we explain the ready provision of ass and colt for the short journey heavy with symbolism? It is clear that, after often seeking to divert people's attention away from him in his ministry up to this point, now he invites all eyes to be focused on him. Only through the imminent forthcoming events will we come to understand the fullness of who he is. Into the lions' den, into the holy place goes Jesus. We watch and wait.

Procession: is it triumphal?

The set-up entry into Jerusalem mimics a species of procession well known to Jew and Roman alike. The ancient world was thoroughly familiar with victory processions or cavalcades to announce the entry of a king or governor to a city. Carter (2000 p. 414) lists a number of common features of these processions: appearance of the ruler/general with troops supporting, procession into the city, welcoming and celebrating crowds, hymnic acclamation, fulsome speeches from the local elite, a cultic act (often sacrifice) in a temple symbolic of the ruler taking possession of the city. All of these features appear in Matthew's story with two striking exceptions. There are no welcoming words from the local elite. They are ironically replaced by the question from Jerusalem's citizens about the unknown arrival from Galilee. 'Who is this?' There is certainly no culminating cultic act in the temple; instead, Jesus embarks on an action of disruptive mayhem targeted at those who exploit and profit from the sacrifices of the poor (21:12–13). These differences are crucial. What seems familiar suddenly becomes shocking and arresting: 'pay attention!' is once more the narrative's underlying note.

Also vital in the entry story are the biblical quotations in verses 5 and 9. The references are in verse 5 to Isaiah 62:11 and Zechariah 9:9; in verse 9 to Psalm 118:26, a psalm of victory. The acclamation 'Praise to the son of David!' has appeared in the two stories of the healing of two blind men in Matthew 9:27 and more recently in 20:30–1. It will recur later in chapter 21 at verse 15. The quotation from Zechariah 9:9 is yet another Matthean 'twin'; Matthew quotes the Septuagint version which speaks of 'an ass and the foal of an ass'. Don't get stuck with the question about how Jesus could ride two horses at once; what is significant in these words is the intimation of the coming of a peaceful Messiah, humble and gentle. This is no warlord's 'triumph'; it is its antithesis. 'Jesus, who promised salvation to the wretched and humble in his Beatitudes, now stands at the beginning of his own humiliation (Passion) story' (Schweizer 1975 p. 404). The challenge to the accepted way of thinking is heightened when we ponder the acclamation, 'Son of David'. In Jewish thought, the Messiah, David's 'son', was often portrayed as warrior victor, triumphant deliverer; in Matthew, 'Son of David' is intimately linked to Jesus' ministry of mercy and healing.

There is another twosome in the story; it is the tale of two distinct crowds. The crowd which greets Jesus enthusiastically, laying cloaks and spreading festal palm branches before him, is composed of the pilgrim peasants who have journeyed in gathering numbers from the suspect region of Galilee. The Jerusalem crowd, with metropolitan world-weariness, is interested but far from convinced by the man at the centre of this disturbance. We have already noted their question. 'Who is he?' they ask. The lesson will soon be provided if they have eyes to see and ears to hear. The answer of the accompanying crowd from Galilee summons to attention. 'This is the prophet Jesus, from Nazareth in Galilee.' To the people of urban Jerusalem, he may not be quite as outlandish as John the Baptist from the wilderness; but Jesus is still an unfashionable figure from the country, the margins, the edge.

The clatter of tables and the song of children

The traditional welcome procession would have climaxed around a series of fulsome and syrupy speeches from the local dignitaries to the visiting VIP. In Matthew's story, the VIP arriving at the holy place, the Temple, is distinctly unimpressed. Amid the noise of the clatter of upturned tables, the tinkling of scattered coins and the cooing of liberated pigeons – no doubt also the loud protests of the moneychangers and the sacrifice-sellers – Jesus embarks on the action known as the cleansing of the Temple. It is another story of such significance that it appears in all four gospels, though John places it early in Jesus' ministry rather than in the time just before the Passion (John 2:15–22).

Matthew's telling of the cleansing is brief and terse. In his account, it appears that Jesus goes directly to the Temple on the same day as his arrival into the city. Providing services for worshippers and pilgrims was a lucrative business which was under the control of the privileged caste of the high priest's family. The business was monopolistic and exploitative, particularly of the poor. The Temple, most holy symbol of the people's faith, focus of their hopes and dreams which should have been a place of freedom and liberation, had become a burden on the people's back and a vehicle for the making of tawdry profit. Jesus' action is swift, violent and decisive, although it is important to notice that Matthew does not report Jesus displaying any violence against any person.

In the uproar, it is important to catch the words of Jesus which accompany the action: 'My house shall be called a house of prayer; but you are making it a den of robbers' (21:13). The second half is from Jeremiah 7:11, words of tough judgement on Israel. The first part is a quotation from Isaiah 56:7, without however Isaiah's reference 'to all nations'. While this omission may well reflect Matthew's preoccupation with the people of Israel, it is also to be noted that Isaiah 56 is a great chapter of inclusion, speaking of foreigners and eunuchs, those previously excluded, being welcomed into the household of faith.

The theme of inclusion continues with the final scene at the Temple (21:14–17), a scene only found in Matthew. He describes Jesus' work of healing continuing even at this fraught time and right within the Temple courts. The reference to the coming of the blind and lame for healing is pointed, in 2 Samuel 5:8 they are excluded: not now. There's also the children. This little incident of Jesus accepting and rejoicing in the praise of children must be

For group work

Concentrate again on the place of children in your faith community.

How do you welcome and value them?

How do you encourage them to 'offer perfect praise'?

Chapter 27

'WHAT RIGHT HAVE YOU?'

Matthew 21:23—22:14

The Question about Jesus' Authority

(Mark 11:27–33, Luke 20:1–8)

Jesus came back to the Temple; and as he taught, the chief priests and the elders came to him and asked, 'What right have you to do these things? Who gave you this right?'

Jesus answered them, 'I will ask you just one question, and if you give me an answer, I will tell you what right I have to do these things. Where did John's right to baptize come from; was it from God or from human beings?'

They started to argue among themselves, 'What shall we say? If we answer, "From God," he will say to us, "Why, then, did you not believe John?" But if we say, "From human beings," we are afraid of what the people might do, because they are all convinced that John was a prophet.' So they answered Jesus, 'We don't know.'

And he said to them, 'Neither will I tell you, then, by what right I do these things.'

The Parable of the Two Sons

'Now, what do you think? There was once a man who had two sons. He went to the elder one and said, "Son, go and work in the vineyard today." "I don't want to," he answered, but later he changed his mind and went. Then the father went to the other son and said the same thing. "Yes, sir," he answered, but he did not go. Which one of the two did what his father wanted?'

'The elder one', they answered.

So Jesus said to them, 'I tell you: the tax collectors and the prostitutes are going into the Kingdom of God ahead of you. For John the Baptist came to you showing you the right path to take, and you would not believe him; but the tax collectors and prostitutes believed him. Even when you saw this, you did not later change your minds and believe him.'

The Parable of the Tenants in the Vineyard
(Mark 12:1–12, Luke 20:9–19)

'Listen to another parable', Jesus said. 'There was once a landowner who planted a vineyard, put a fence around it, dug a hole for the winepress, and built a watchtower. Then he let out the vineyard to tenants and went on a journey. When the time came to gather the grapes, he sent his slaves to the tenants to receive his share of the harvest. The tenants seized the slaves, beat one, killed another, and stoned another. Again the man sent other slaves, more than the first time, and the tenants treated them the same way. Last of all he sent his son to them. "Surely they will respect my son," he said. But when the tenants saw the son, they said to themselves, "This is the owner's son. Come on, let's kill him, and we will get his property!" So they seized him, threw him out of the vineyard, and killed him.

'Now, when the owner of the vineyard comes, what will he do to those tenants?' Jesus asked.

'He will certainly kill those evil men', they answered, 'and let the vineyard out to other tenants, who will give him his share of the harvest at the right time.'

Jesus said to them, 'Haven't you ever read what the Scriptures say?

> "The stone which the builders rejected as worthless
> turned out to be the most important of all.
> This was done by the Lord; what a wonderful sight it is!"

'And so I tell you', added Jesus, 'the Kingdom of God will be taken away from you and given to a people who will produce the proper fruits.'

The chief priests and the Pharisees heard Jesus' parables and knew that he was talking about them, so they tried to arrest him. But they were afraid of the crowds, who considered Jesus to be a prophet.

22 The Parable of the Wedding Feast

(*Luke 14:15–24*)

Jesus again used parables in talking to the people. 'The Kingdom of heaven is like this. Once there was a king who prepared a wedding feast for his son. He sent his servants to tell the invited guests to come to the feast, but they did not want to come. So he sent other servants with this message for the guests: "My feast is ready now; my bullocks and prize calves have been butchered, and everything is ready. Come to the wedding feast!" But the invited guests paid no attention and went about their business: one went to his farm, another to his shop, while others grabbed the servants, beat them, and killed them. The king was very angry; so he sent his soldiers, who killed these murderers and burnt down their city. Then he called his servants and said to them, "My wedding feast is ready, but the people I invited did not deserve it. Now go to the main streets and invite to the feast as many people as you find." So the servants went out into the streets and gathered all the people they could find, good and bad alike; and the wedding hall was filled with people.

'The king went in to look at the guests and saw a man who was not wearing wedding clothes. "Friend, how did you get in here without wedding clothes?" the king asked him. But the man said nothing. Then the king told his servants, "Tie him up hand and foot, and throw him outside in the dark. There he will cry and grind his teeth."'

And Jesus concluded, 'Many are invited, but few are chosen.'

The arguments begin

We have seen how the arrival of Jesus in Jerusalem and at the Temple has already been the cause of both rejoicing and disturbance. After the initial uproar has subsided, Matthew, following Mark, takes his readers into a series of verbal confrontations between Jesus and his various opponents; in some they will take the initiative, in some he will. In the first of these, Jesus has to respond to a question from the establishment of the Jerusalem Temple, the chief priests and elders. Jesus has returned to the Temple and calmly sat down to teach; the powers-that-be, presumably still shaken and enraged by the previous events, have what on the one hand seems a perfectly reasonable question to ask him, yet which, on the other, is also a bit of a trap. The question is: 'By what authority do you do these things? What or who gives you legitimation?' The trap is that, if Jesus claims to be operating under his own authority, he stands accused of an impertinent claim to an authority which is not his; if he claims God's authority, he can then be accused of blasphemy.

In these dangerous times, Jesus neatly sidesteps the question by asking one of his own. 'Before you ask about me, let me ask you about John the Baptist. Where did John the Baptist's authority come from? God? Or human beings?' (21:25). The opposition are flummoxed, thrown into disarray. If they answer: 'From God', then Jesus as recipient of John's blessing and baptism and seen as his successor is validated. If they say: 'Just from human hands', they risk the wrath of the crowd, who revered John as a prophet for the people. They are forced to say: 'We don't know'. This is not an answer of genuine ignorance or indecision; in their own minds, they do not believe in the claim of Jesus to legitimacy. They temporise and are condemned out of their own mouths. Jesus summarily ends the argument. 'If you don't know about John after the completion of his work, I'm not going to tell you about myself. Conversation closed.'

The two sons

Jesus now goes on to attack the opposition in a series of three parables, of the two sons (21:28–32), of the tenants in the vineyard (21:33–46) and of the wedding feast (22:1–14). First comes the parable of the two sons, where Jesus sketches out a scenario which will be familiar to many households. Significantly it's about 'doing the will of the father'. We remember also that the vineyard is often a symbol for the people of Israel. The father asks the elder son to go to work; after an initial refusal, he changes his mind and goes. When the other son is asked, he says 'Yes, I'll go', but, hours later, he's still to be found idle at home. 'Who does the will of the father?' asks Jesus. 'The elder son', appears to be the unanimous answer.

Jesus goes on to comment that the tax collectors and prostitutes will enter the Kingdom of God ahead of the establishment figures. This is the only instance in Matthew where he uses 'Kingdom of God', rather than 'Kingdom of heaven' which argues for Matthew's using here a pre-existing saying in the community (21:31). The parable has a double application: in the context of Jesus' own ministry, the younger son who says 'Yes' but fails to deliver refers to the religious leaders of his community, who appear to assent to God's teaching with their lips but are consistently condemned as 'hypocrites' by their failure to practise what they preach. The initial refuseniks, personified in the elder son, are the scorned 'sinners' who later turn their lives round and find life. In the context of Matthew's community, we can see that it refers to Jew and Gentile. We also note Jesus' continued recognition and affirmation of the ministry of John the Baptist.

Underlying the parable is a characteristic theme of Matthew's which emphasises that faith is never merely a matter of intellectual understanding or verbal assent; in the end, it must always issue in doing. Faith is only good faith, faith that is fruitful, when it results in a person's doing the will of the Father, quietly, faithfully, day in, day out.

A bloody harvest

The second parable, of the tenants in the vineyard, is common to Matthew (21:33–46), Mark (12:1–12) and Luke (20:9–19). Matthew largely follows Mark's version; two significant differences occur. In verse 39, Matthew reverses the sequence in Mark, describing the murder of the son as him being seized, thrown out, and then killed, rather than killed and his body cast out, as in Mark. Matthew's version is truer to the events of Jesus' crucifixion, where he is taken 'outside the city gates' to be then crucified. In verse 45, Matthew specifically adds 'the Pharisees' to those who heard the parable as a polemic against them. Mark simply speaks of the 'Jewish leaders' (12:12). The likely explanation is that, at the time of Matthew's writing of the gospel, the Pharisees were the chief Jewish opponents of Matthew's emerging church.

The above leads to the surmise that, once again, the gospel writer has taken an original parable of Jesus and put it in a fresh context relating to the writer's own situation. As the parable stands in Matthew, it clearly has a post-Easter reference to Jesus the son and heir who is killed but subsequently vindicated. The other tenants (21:41), who are given stewardship of the vineyard when the owner returns to re-establish his possession, signify the opening up of the Jesus community to the Gentiles.

In its present form in the gospels, the gospel writers have given the parable pointed reference to the events of the Passion and the subsequent history of their own early church. The key reference is in Jesus' interpretation of the parable, where he quotes from Psalm 118:22–3. From this psalm of vindication, he repeats the psalmist's words about 'the stone which the builders rejected becoming the head of the corner' – undoubtedly a reference to his own Easter. Jesus as stumbling block and cornerstone is a frequent New Testament theme (see 1 Peter 2:6–10; Romans 9:25–6, 32–3; 1 Corinthians 1:18–25). Some manuscripts include a verse 44 which refers back to Daniel 2:34–5 and 44–5; and there is also here a double reference to Isaiah 8:14–15 and 28:16. We can note also at the end of this passage, where Matthew describes the reaction of chief priests and Pharisees, a typical piece of Matthean duplication. Matthew tells how the authorities were afraid to arrest Jesus for fear of the crowds who considered Jesus to be a prophet (21:46), which was just what the crowd thought of John the Baptist (21:26). Again, Matthew makes a link between Jesus and John.

The amount of blood spilt and the growing pile of corpses in this story make it sound like a modern TV detective drama. Underneath the blood and gore, greed and anger which seethe through this parable, there is a clear message of hope. As the cross grows nearer and the darkness deepens around Jesus and the disciple band, remember the rejected stone which will yet be raised up and vindicated. All is not lost; what seems to be will be overturned, dramatically.

The wedding feast from Hell

Blood and gore continue to drip in the last of the three parables considered here. I should confess that I've always compared it unfavourably to the very similar parable in Luke 14:15–24. Luke tells of an invitation not specifically to a wedding feast, just to a big dinner party. After the invited guests have made their excuses – 'I've just bought a field, I've just bought some new oxen, I've married a wife and therefore I cannot come' – the host sends out his servants, not once, but twice, to bring in the poor, the crippled, the blind, the lame, the homeless. Luke's picture of the ragged men's banquet speaks eloquently and directly about the expansiveness of the gospel, the prodigality of grace.

There are two jarring notes in Matthew's version. One is the note of violence early on, where some of the invited guests, rather than just refusing the invitation, kill the slaves who have brought the invitation; and, in retribution, the king sends in his troops to slay the murderers and burn down their city. (Only Matthew elevates the person of the host to kingship; in Luke's account, the host is merely a rich man.) The second is the fate of the guest who turns up at the party with the wrong clothes on (22:11–14), the guest at the wedding feast without his wedding robe, who gets bound hand and foot and is summarily slung out into outer darkness. The action of the king's first-century bouncers seems both extreme and unfair. It appears pretty harsh to get booted out of the feast simply for wearing the wrong clothes, as in one of these so-called superior golf clubs where no one is allowed into the dining room unless they're wearing a tie.

Sympathy for the guest with his old clothes on is, however, misplaced. The parable, as Matthew tells it, is worth a close look. It's different from most of the gospel parables in that most parables make one fairly direct point, whereas this one is much more like an allegory, where each part of the parable has its own significance. It begins with the king giving a wedding feast for his son. The king is God, the wedding feast points to the banquet of the Messiah (see Isaiah 25:6–9), the time of fulfilment of God's purposes, and the son is Jesus. The guests are the elite of Jesus' own people of Israel who have refused his invitation to see God's purpose in him, just as in the past they have ignored and maltreated God's previous servants, the prophets (21:33–46). The destroying of the murderers and the sacking of the city is a clear contemporary reference to the fall of Jerusalem around the year AD 70.

When the elite guests refuse the invitation, there's then a general invitation for everybody – and, typically of Matthew, those who are brought in consist of 'good and bad alike' (22:10). It's an invitation which encompasses the non-elite of Jesus' society and may well include the Gentiles also. And so the wedding hall is full. But what about the man with the wrong clothes on? He's very interesting. For he's the one who can stand for you or me. He's the insider, he's there at the feast, he's heard Jesus' invitation to come to the feast of the Messiah, to enter the ways of the Kingdom of heaven; but the fact that he's made no special preparations to come, that he's failed to put on the garments of rejoicing, shows that he hasn't taken the invitation seriously, he hasn't truly seen that Jesus' presence is about transformation, and so he hasn't begun to embrace the change Jesus has come to offer. John Barclay comments that he's a bit like the elder brother in Luke's story of the Prodigal Son (Luke 15:25–32); both have come within the structure of grace, but, in their failure to see and be glad in that grace, they exclude themselves. Tom Wright says this about this parable:

> The point of the story is that Jesus is telling the truth, the truth that political and religious leaders often like to hide: the truth that God's kingdom is a kingdom in which love and justice and mercy and holiness reign unhindered. They are the clothes you need to wear for the wedding. And if you refuse to put them on, you are saying you don't want to stay at the party. That is the reality. (Wright 2002 vol. 2 p. 85)

Elsewhere in the gospel, Jesus has been quite clear: 'Why do you call me, Lord, Lord, and do not the things which I say?' The gospel challenge is always addressed just as much to us, the insiders, as it is to those outside. The image of the man who hadn't bothered to put on the wedding garments evokes an image of which George MacLeod was particularly fond. He often spoke of Christ's disciples as those who put on the wedding garments; for him, faith always had a festive element, a note of rejoicing, in spite of everything.

One of his favourite New Testament passages was Colossians 3:12–17, which begins: 'As God's chosen ones, holy and beloved' ... *clothe* yourselves in the wedding garments of Christ, 'compassion, kindness, humility, meekness and patience'. How our faith would soar if we were more aware, day and daily, that we are fresh happed in the garments of Christ, the wedding garments, which speak peace to our souls, harmony to our faith communities, and life to the world. There's much that's positive, inclusive, challenging, inspiring in Matthew's telling of this parable. There's also a 'but' which is worthy of the short following pause to reflect.

Study

By yourself
Read Colossians 3:12–17 daily through the next week; brood over and savour its invitation.

Pause

Grace or rigour, mercy or judgement?
The final words of Matthew's parable of the wedding feast see the man without the wedding garments of rejoicing cast out into outer darkness, where, in a characteristic Matthean phrase, 'there will be wailing and gnashing of teeth' (22:14). Just a few verses earlier (22:10), Matthew has also described the feast as a great occasion of inclusive grace where good and bad alike – again typically Matthean – are welcomed together into the banquet of the end time. It appears to me, as an amateur exegete, that Matthew has taken Luke's perfectly good parable and complicated it by introducing the killing of the king's servants and the subsequent vengeance on the murderers and the strange little incident at the end of the man who came to the wedding with the wrong clothes on. In so doing, he introduces a tension which runs all the way through this gospel. It is the tension between the announcement of an inclusive grace and a call to a lifestyle of forgiving gentleness on the one hand and, on the other, a harsh demand for obedience with the penalty for refusal a merciless judgement. Certainly, the life of a disciple is always lived out of the tension between the glorious freedom of grace and the demand

for a costly and sacrificial obedience. Yet, the harsh note of judgement which outcrops from time to time in Matthew sounds very discordant. We have to ask whether there is an unresolved tension in the mind of Matthew between the legalism of his past and the freedom of the gospel. Is what we find in this parable an example of this tension? The story in its present form is off-putting. We need to dig deep to find the gold among the dross.

I think we find here, in the New Testament itself, what was originally a story of grace on the lips of Jesus, getting mauled up with Matthew's best intentions, to become a source of unnecessary confusion. I don't see here the generous God who is the Father of our Lord Jesus Christ. Rather, I'm reminded of the story that Gerard Hughes, one-time Roman Catholic chaplain at Glasgow University, used to tell about Uncle George. 'Uncle George' is the picture of God he frequently got from listening to students who were questioning or had deserted their faith:

> It was as if as little children our parents had taken us to meet 'good old Uncle George', the family favourite, enormously wealthy, highly influential, and loved by all. He had a white beard, gruff voice, and lived in a large, gloomy mansion. At the end of the visit he turns to us and says, 'I want to see you here regularly every Sunday, dears, and if you fail to come, let me show you what will happen to you'. He then leads them downstairs to the mansion's cellars. The heat becomes intense, the smell noxious, and we hear hideous screams. Uncle George opens a steel door revealing blazing furnaces into which little demons are hurling innumerable members of the people of God – men, women and children. He assures us that the furnace is our ultimate destination if we do not visit him regularly, and leads us back to our parents. We clutch at both in terror and are taken back home. On the way, mummy leans over and says, 'Don't you love Uncle George with all your heart and soul, mind and strength?' Remembering the furnaces, we say, 'Yes, I do'. We obey Uncle George's orders: in our hearts we consider him a monster, but dare not admit this even to ourselves. (Excerpt from *God Where Are You?*, copyright © 1997 by Darton, Longman & Todd, Ltd, pp.125–6.)

Gerard Hughes goes on to comment that of course this is a caricature, but that it illustrates one form of the many deformed pictures of God which have nothing to do with the God of grace. He goes on:

> We become what we worship. If we worship a God who is primarily a God of judgement, whose main interest lies in our failings and inflicting suitable punishments, we become like that to ourselves and to others. We become people of the law, hardliners, intolerant, self-righteous, condemnatory, practising a Christless Christianity and calling it orthodoxy.

The result is that, instead of being witnesses to the God of grace, the God of unconditional welcome, the God of unconditional regard, for us, and for all, we end up sending out the same mixed messages which come from today's gospel, where Matthew gets a great story of grace mixed up with the angers of his own agenda.

It is pertinent to raise this issue as we move to the gospel's climax and the moment of unconditional grace which is the cross. It is also pertinent to raise it at this point in the gospel as the controversy between Jesus and his enemies is heightened. There are two related issues here. The global issue is about the relationship between grace and judgement, where the question is whether Matthew's inherited view of judgement from time to time in the gospel dulls the sheen of the light of Jesus' gospel of grace which, in so many ways, Matthew has caught and faithfully reflected to us, his readers. The particular issue at this point in the story is whether the controversy between Matthew's emergent Christian community and the leadership of the Jewish community after the fall of Jerusalem has so scarred Matthew that his treatment and portrayal of his Jewish enemies is much less than fair and gracious. Richard Hays raises that particular question. The question of how we love the enemy who has hurt and wounded us is still highly relevant amid the wars and conflicts great and small of our own times:

> According to Matthew, the leaders of the Jewish people have imposed upon them intolerable burdens and have led them astray from the true obedience of God. The battle between Matthew's community and emergent rabbinic Judaism has left indelible scars on Matthew's Gospel, in the form of scathing prophetic denunciations of the scribes

and Pharisees. Matthew's text provides no clues about how this implacable hostility toward the traditional representatives of Israel is to be integrated with Jesus' teaching concerning the love of enemies. (Hays 1996 p. 109)

Chapter 28

QUESTIONS AND MORE QUESTIONS

Matthew 22:15–46
The Question about Paying Taxes
(Mark 12:13–17, Luke 20:20–6)
The Pharisees went off and made a plan to trap Jesus with questions. Then they sent to him some of their disciples and some members of Herod's party. 'Teacher', they said, ' we know that you tell the truth. You teach the truth about God's will for people, without worrying about what others think, because you pay no attention to anyone's status. Tell us, then, what do you think? Is it against our Law to pay taxes to the Roman Emperor, or not?'

Jesus, however, was aware of their evil plan, and so he said, 'You hypocrites! Why are you trying to trap me? Show me the coin for paying the tax!' They brought him the coin, and he asked them, 'Whose face and name are these?'

'The Emperor's,' they answered.

So Jesus said to them, 'Well, then, pay the Emperor what belongs to the Emperor, and pay God what belongs to God.'

When they heard this, they were amazed; and they left him and went away.

The Question about Rising from Death
(Mark 12:18–27, Luke 20:27–40)
That same day some Sadducees came to Jesus and claimed that people will not rise from death. 'Teacher', they said, 'Moses said that if a man who has no children dies, his brother must marry the widow so that they can have children who will be considered

the dead man's children. Now, there were seven brothers who used to live here. The eldest got married and died without having children, so he left his widow to his brother. The same thing happened to the second brother, to the third, and finally to all seven. Last of all, the woman died. Now, on the day when the dead rise to life, whose wife will she be? All of them had married her.'

Jesus answered them, 'How wrong you are! It is because you don't know the Scriptures or God's power. For when the dead rise to life, they will be like the angels in heaven and will not marry. Now, as for the dead rising to life, haven't you read what God has told you? He said, "I am the God of Abraham, the God of Isaac, and the God of Jacob." He is the God of the living, not of the dead.'

When the crowds heard this, they were amazed at his teaching.

The Great Commandment

(Mark 12:28–34, Luke 10:25–8)

When the Pharisees heard that Jesus had silenced the Sadducees, they came together, and one of them, a teacher of the Law, tried to trap him with a question. 'Teacher', he asked, 'which is the greatest commandment in the Law?'

Jesus answered, '"Love the Lord your God with all your heart, with all your soul, and with all your mind." This is the greatest and most important commandment. The second most important commandment is like it: "Love your neighbour as you love yourself." The whole Law of Moses and the teachings of the prophets depend on these two commandments.'

The Question about the Messiah

(Mark 12:35–7, Luke 20:41–4)

When some Pharisees gathered together, Jesus asked them, 'What do you think about the Messiah? Whose descendant is he?'

'He is David's descendant', they answered.

'Why, then,' Jesus asked, 'did the Spirit inspire David to call him "Lord"? David said,

> "The Lord said to my Lord:
> Sit here on my right
> Until I put your enemies under your feet."

If, then, David called him "Lord", how can the Messiah be David's descendant?'

No one was able to give Jesus any answer, and from that day on no one dared to ask him any more questions.

A 'wow!' word about God

A few years ago at our church weekly study group, one of our members, a professional astronomer, spoke to us with obvious excitement about a radio programme on how larger and larger mirrors are enabling astronomers to see more and more distant objects, to look farther and deeper into space. A recent project, using one of the biggest reflector telescopes yet built, swept a patch of sky to count galaxies. If you imagine one grain of sand, held at arm's length, that's about the size of the piece of sky involved. In that tiny area, researchers counted about 1,500 galaxies. Very recent work suggests now that this figure should be doubled – 3,000 galaxies in a piece of sky that looks no larger than a grain of sand to our naked eye. Multiplying up, researchers now estimate that we are surrounded by around 100 billion galaxies, that is, 100,000,000,000 – 100 with nine nothings after it.

Wow! Hearing that sounds like a Wow! moment, though the figures are so vast we can't really get our heads round them at all. The question someone immediately asked was: what does this knowledge do to our picture of God? ... with the implication that perhaps it threatened faith. It certainly does make nonsense of any cosy, domesticated, cut-down-to-size, picture of 'my God'. We are always being tempted to reduce God to a picture we can touch and handle, to a being we can feel comfortable and at home with, always trying to contain God within the limits of our concepts of God. The book which pours the biggest bucket of cold water over these efforts of ours is the Bible itself, with its consistent battle against all images and its continuing insistence on the unnameability, unknowability of God, the God whose thoughts are not our thoughts nor his ways our ways. The picture of the galaxies in the grain of sand might make us ask: 'Is our picture of God too small? Have we forgotten that God always breaks out of the efforts of our minds to contain God, even the efforts of the minds of the world's greatest theologians?'

On the other hand, if we hold to the view that God is the Creator of all that is, ever at work in creation, then contemplating the galaxies in the grain of sand becomes an aid rather than a barrier to faith. It blows our mind to think of God as the maker of all that is. We then recognise the mystery of God as more immense than the immense and mysterious creation he has made, of which we only apprehend a fraction. And, before our discussion ended, someone else said: 'Yes, but it's not just telescopes looking at the stars which fill us with wonder, it's also microscopes, helping us to see the micro-levels of life, which also show us dimensions of life which are simply amazing'.

Anybody got a penny?

What has all the immensity of creation to do with the question of taxation in the first incident in this chapter? The story is of an attempted entrapment of Jesus by an unholy and unlikely combination of two usually opposing parties within Jesus' faith community, some Pharisees and some Herodians. They ask Jesus the trick question: 'Should we be paying the poll tax to the Roman authorities?' If Jesus says 'Yes', then he's a backslider, compromising the purity of his people's faith. If he says 'No', then he's encouraging civil disobedience to the lawful authority. Jesus says neither 'Yes' nor 'No'. He asks his opponents to produce a coin; rather, not any coin, but the kind of coin needed to pay the tax. The clear implication is that he, himself, doesn't have one. His opponents do produce the coin, which had on it the head of Caesar, and the claim of Caesar's divinity which, to all across the Jewish faith community, was blasphemous. Jesus is already halfway out the trap set by having his opponents produce the hateful coin; he springs it completely by his enigmatic reply: 'Render to Caesar the things which are Caesar's and to God the things which are God's'. Sadly, this is a text with a long and baneful history of misinterpretation based on the false assumption that somehow Jesus and his hearers considered Caesar and God as equals. The galaxies in a grain of sand kill such a notion stone dead. Caesar and God are not equals, they are opposites. Caesar is a puny human being like us; God is God.

'Give to Caesar the things which are Caesar's and to God the things which are God's.' What does Caesar represent? The authority of the state, power and obviously money. Caesar is entitled to his due. Christians owe obligations to the state, any state, to live peaceably with their neighbours, to act as responsible citizens and to obey the state's laws, just as long as they do not come into conflict with a higher law, the law of God. Different people will have different ideas as to when these laws clash and the claims of the higher obedience clash with civil obedience.

Caesar has a place in the economy of God, Caesar in this instance meaning any earthly ruler. The Old Testament lesson speaks in glowing terms of the Persian emperor Cyrus, calls him 'God's anointed', the 'Messiah' – for, though he was far from sharing the faith of Israel, he was the instrument through which Israel was freed from its exile in Babylon. It's not only in the natural world that the ways of God are too big for our comprehension; in the world of history, of people and events, the Bible tells us God's hidden hand is at work – and, in and for such work, God will choose whom God will choose, and God may well choose the most unlikely of instruments. The working out of his purposes, for weal or woe, certainly do not depend solely on us, as the community of faith. Again the question is raised for us is: 'Is our God too small?'

Getting loose of Caesar

Always there is the call to the higher obedience. The coin may well have been stamped with the image of the emperor; our calling is as those who bear the image of God, made in the very likeness of the awesome creator. The old idols of money and power are just as alluring and seductively attractive in our time as in biblical times. Indeed, we could well say more so, for a strong argument could be made that it is on the powers of money and power that our present society rests. So, how are we to give to God what is due to God, which is what in essence Jesus asks here? An ever-present danger and temptation to our church life is to allow that life to be invaded and colonised by current worldly fashions of thought. The following comment is pertinent.

> Judgement falls heavily upon the Christian churches today. For Christian formation to be authentic, it must dilute our appetite for what modern society offers as a lure. But to restore the Church's capacity for evoking change this deep, even our analogies require conversion. The present fad is to model the church in terms of business processes and language. The Church is pictured as being a business, with a bureaucracy intent on fulfilling efficiently the desires of their 'customers'. But that imagery is all wrong. Not only is the Church not a business; at its heart it is not even an institution. Our urgent need is to rediscover images capable of reclaiming the nature of the Church as organic. The Church is deeply alive, an organism, with each of us vital participants in every part, from heart to fingernails. Renewal requires nothing less than discovering in a deeply mysterious way that the Church is the very 'Body of Christ', with Christ organically the head.
>
> Unfortunately, we are engulfed by the efficient machines and fabricated products of our ever more rapid technology, and we become impatient with the slow organic processes of growth. Yet, against modern society, the Church must stand straight and true in her calling. She is no less than 'Holy Mother Church', alive with the rich mysteries that intersect spacious time and timeless space. The transcendent dimension of the Church is Jesus Christ in ongoing Incarnation. (Jones 2000 pp. 80–1)

'Give to Caesar the things that are Caesar's and to God the things that are God's.' Keep in mind the context of this incident. It occurs only days away from the day we call Good Friday. Good Friday is the day when Caesar demands his due. Good Friday is the day when the barrenness and futility of the ways of Caesar are totally exposed. The way of God seems to have come to a pointless, futile, bloody end. Not so fast, mortal. Easter is one key moment when we learn that we are far from knowing it all about the God who made heaven and earth and whose hidden hand is ever at work in the world. Calvary is but one step from the empty tomb.

Up comes the sun. Caesar does not win. 'All in his strength and beauty our risen Lord stands fair'. Death does not contain God's Christ, his anointed. His way is vindicated. Give God his due. His due begins in thanksgiving and gratitude, in overflowing praise: it continues in taking the way of God's faithful servant, in a life of generosity, forgiveness and making peace. In our dark world, made dark by the darkness of the use of power wantonly to destroy human light and life, we bear witness to another power, the power of the love that made all things.

One bride for seven brothers

After the failure of the unholy and unlikely combination of Pharisees and Herodians to entrap Jesus into making a false move over the question of paying taxes to the emperor, enter the next set of disingenuous questioners, a group of Sadducees. They were part of the Jerusalem inner circle of power; not only did they comprise the rich families in the chief priest's circle, they also were sceptical and conservative in their thinking. For the purpose of understanding this incident, it is important to know that Sadducees didn't believe in any general resurrection of the dead, which shows up their question as both opportunistic and cynical. The example which the Sadducees offer to Jesus was from the common practice of levirate marriage in which a man's widow would marry his brother for the continuance of 'a man's line, property, inheritance, and name, and which affirmed the woman's (widow's) childbearing place in her husband's family' (Carter 2000 p. 441). The particular and unlikely instance that they quote is of a wife who is six times widowed and marries seven husbands in succession; their question: 'at the resurrection, whose wife would she be?' (22:28).

In response, Jesus gives their phony question short shrift. He has already been critical of patriarchal views of marriage which view the wife as largely male property. Here, he simply states that they are wrong, both in their reading of the scriptures and in their knowledge of God's power – presumably a reference to their disbelief in the transforming power of God to bring life out of death (i.e. resurrection). He asserts that present earthly patterns of human

286

relationships and societal structures are superseded in heaven and then continues by quoting from the seminal passage of Exodus 3 where Moses encounters the living God before the burning bush. 'I am the God of Abraham, the God of Isaac, the God of Jacob.' The inference Jesus draws is that because God *is* (present tense) the God of these patriarchs long passed from this earth, they are somehow (not specified) alive now in God, i.e. God has resurrected them. The argument is over and the crowd is amazed.

'Love your neighbour'

After the convoluted question of the Sadducees, the third encounter/ confrontation has a ring of elemental simplicity. The question is: 'What is the greatest commandment?' (22:36). This story, like the others in our chapter, Matthew shares with Mark (12:28–34); it is also the one which he most significantly alters. The story also appears in Luke but in a different context; Luke uses it as the introduction to the parable of the Good Samaritan (10:25–8). It may well be that the command to love God and neighbour was such an important piece of teaching that it circulated in varied and various forms in the hands of catechists before being written into the gospels.

Here in Matthew, it begins with the picture of a group of Pharisees entering into a conspiring huddle in an attempt to manufacture a question to trap Jesus; Mark has a teacher of the Law ask Jesus a genuine question after noting with approval Jesus' rebuttal of the Sadducees (Mark 12:28). The conversation between Jesus and his questioner is significantly longer in Mark; by its end, Jesus has commended the lawyer with the words: 'You are not far from the Kingdom of God' (Mark 12:34). The impression comes over strongly in Mark of two opponents coming to warm to one another; Matthew, on the other hand, is at pains to stress once again the opposition of the Pharisees to Jesus, reflecting his own situation.

Matthew's editing has two results: the first is to portray the Pharisees in a bad light, once again; the second is to allow the question and answer here to stand out in stark relief. The answer to the question 'What is the greatest commandment?' is foundational – 'Love the Lord your God with all your heart, with all your soul, and with all your mind'. The second is like it: 'Love your neighbour as you love yourself'. The first quotation concerning the love of God comes from Deuteronomy 6:5. It expresses a call to love God with our whole being. The second occurs in Leviticus 19:18. This chapter in Leviticus draws a picture of the acts of love necessary for the creation of a fair, just, harmonious and caring society, showing how personal obligation goes to create the relationships necessary for good community. The thrust of the conjoining of the two commandments is to enjoin disciples not only to love God *and* our neighbour but also to love God *through* our neighbour. This short exchange, set amid the tensions and controversies of Jesus' last days, is a timely reminder of the essentials of discipleship.

One last question

The final question which closes both this chapter and the confrontations and disputations which have been raging since Jesus entered Jerusalem is asked by Jesus. Once again, the controversy is with a gathering of Pharisees. Although Matthew introduces the exchange with the words: 'Jesus asked them this question', there are two questions. 'What do you think of the Messiah? Whose descendant (son) is he?' Behind the theoretical questions lies the real question of Jesus' own identity and whether it will be acknowledged by his opponents. They answer correctly the theoretical question about the Messiah's 'line': he is indeed 'the Son of David', a title which we remember has been used not infrequently to refer to Jesus (e.g. 20:29–31), usually in connection with his ministry of healing and compassion.

Jesus continues with a second rhetorical question. 'Why did the Spirit inspire David to call him [the son] Lord?' As backing for his question, Jesus quotes from the royal Psalm 110, verse 1 of which is cited or referred to more frequently in the New Testament than any other verse from the Psalter (see R. Davidson, *The Vitality of Worship*, 1998, p. 363). 'The Lord [David] said to my Lord [son, Messiah]: Sit here until I put your enemies under your feet.' If David calls his heir 'My Lord', then the heir is elevated to a position far higher than mere son. The Messiah is greater than his father David. The opposition can find no way to refute the argument. They are silenced.

Study

By yourself

Make for yourself two lists:

- of those you consider exemplars of giving to God his worth, rather than Caesar
- of those you consider exemplars of true love of our neighbours.

For group work

Putting God's claims before those of Caesar involves putting a distance between ourselves and the values and attitudes of our contemporary world; loving God through our neighbour thrusts us straight back into the world of everyday. Discuss with one another how we can and do hold these tensions together.

Chapter 29

WOES AND MORE WOES

Matthew 23:1–36

Jesus Warns against the Teachers of the Law and the Pharisees

(*Mark 12:38–9, Luke 11:43, 11:46, 20:45–6*)

Then Jesus spoke to the crowds and to his disciples. 'The teachers of the Law and the Pharisees are the authorized interpreters of Moses' Law. So you must obey and follow everything they tell you to do; do not, however, imitate their actions, because they don't practise what they preach. They tie on to people's backs loads that are heavy and hard to carry, yet they aren't willing even to lift a finger to help them carry those loads. They do everything so that people will see them. Look at the straps with scripture verses on them which they wear on their foreheads and arms, and notice how large they are! Notice also how long are the tassels on their cloaks! They love the best places at feasts and the reserved seats in the synagogues; they love to be greeted with respect in the market places and to be called, "Teacher". You must not be called, "Teacher", because you are all members of one family and have only one Teacher. And you must not call anyone here on earth "Father", because you have only one Father in heaven. Nor should you be called "Leader", because your one and only leader is the Messiah. The greatest one among you must be your servant. Whoever makes himself great will be humbled, and whoever humbles himself will be made great.'

Jesus Condemns their Hypocrisy

(Mark 12:40, Luke 11:39–42, 44, 52, 20:47)

'How terrible for you, teachers of the Law and Pharisees! You hypocrites! You lock the door to the Kingdom of heaven in people's faces, and you yourselves don't go in, nor do you allow in those who are trying to enter!

'How terrible for you, teachers of the Law and Pharisees! You hypocrites! You sail the seas and cross whole countries to win one convert; and when you succeed, you make him twice as deserving of going to hell as you yourselves are!

'How terrible for you, blind guides! You teach, "If someone swears by the Temple, he isn't bound by his vow; but if he swears by the gold in the Temple, he is bound." Blind fools! Which is more important, the gold or the Temple which makes the gold holy? You also teach, "If someone swears by the altar, he isn't bound by his vow; but if he swears by the gift on the altar, he is bound." How blind you are! Which is more important, the gift or the altar which makes the gift holy? So then, when a person swears by the altar, he is swearing by it and by all the gifts on it; and when he swears by the Temple, he is swearing by it and by God, who lives there; and when someone swears by heaven, he is swearing by God's throne and by him who sits on it.

'How terrible for you, teachers of the Law and Pharisees! You hypocrites! You give to God a tenth even of the seasoning herbs, such as mint, dill, and cumin, but you neglect to obey the really important teachings of the Law, such as justice and mercy and honesty. These you should practise, without neglecting the others. Blind guides! You strain a fly out of your drink, but swallow a camel!

'How terrible for you, teachers of the Law and Pharisees! You hypocrites! You clean the outside of your cup and plate, while the inside is full of what you have obtained by violence and selfishness. Blind Pharisee! Clean what is inside the cup first, and then the outside will be clean too!

'How terrible for you, teachers of the Law and Pharisees! You hypocrites! You are like whitewashed tombs, which look fine on the outside but are full of bones and decaying corpses on the inside. In the same way, on the outside you appear good to everybody, but inside you are full of hypocrisy and sins.'

Jesus Predicts their Punishment

(*Luke 11:47–51*)

'How terrible for you, teachers of the Law and Pharisees! You hypocrites! You make fine tombs for the prophets and decorate the monuments of those who lived good lives; and you claim that if you had lived during the time of your ancestors, you would not have done what they did and killed the prophets. So you actually admit that you are the descendants of those who murdered the prophets! Go on, then, and finish what your ancestors started! You snakes and children of snakes! How do you expect to escape from being condemned to hell? And so I tell you that I will send you prophets and wise men and teachers, you will kill some of them, crucify others, and whip others in the synagogues and chase them from town to town. As a result, the punishment for the murder of all innocent people will fall on you, from the murder of the innocent Abel to the murder of Zachariah son of Berachiah, whom you murdered between the Temple and the altar. I tell you indeed: the punishment for all these murders will fall on the people of this day!'

A health warning!

The sum and substance of this chapter comprises a concentrated and bitter attack on the leadership of Jesus' people, the scribes and Pharisees. Matthew has gathered from a number of different sources a variety of raw materials which he stirs together into a pot of toxic vitriol. For those who wish to study the pot in more detail, an extensive examination and exegesis of this chapter is to be found in Schweizer, *The Good News According to Matthew*, pp. 427–47; this commentary will limit itself to the broad outlines. This chapter should rightly begin with what I've called a 'health warning'. We noted earlier Richard Hays' comment concerning Matthew's failure to reconcile his savage attacks on both the leadership of Jesus' people and the people themselves with the injunction in the Sermon on the Mount to love our enemies. We cannot ignore the baneful use to which these words of Matthew have been put in the history of Jewish persecution and Christian anti-semitism. In our post-Holocaust times, we must live by the maxim: 'Never again'.

Two further words can be said at the outset, not of mitigation but of explanation. First, Matthew's writing here belongs to a genre with which his readers would probably be familiar. A list of this kind of polemic against one's enemies or opponents was a common device in the contemporary literature of the time. Second, we, as Gentiles, need always to remember that we here are intruding into a family fight, and family fights are often the most bitter and divisive. Matthew writes in the aftermath of the fall of Jerusalem, when the symbolic centre of the people's faith disappeared almost overnight. Judaism survived thanks to the efforts of the Pharisees, who substituted for the no longer possible Temple worship adherence to a strict moral and religious code, resulting in an inner closing of the ranks. On the other hand, the young church, inspired by the Holy Spirit but not without its own real struggles described in the book of Acts, was in outward-looking and outward-moving mode, prepared to accept the challenge of the assimilation of Gentile converts and to question its relationship with the old Law of Moses. The historical forces at work made a clash between these two opposing movements virtually inevitable, heading as they were in different directions. The division was deeply tragic, and its pain is expressed not only in Matthew's bitter words but also frequently in the writings of St Paul. The bottom line remains: the cumulative effects of the criticisms levelled here at the scribes and Pharisees are excessive and profoundly unfair. They are a gross caricature. 'Pharisaism' as a pejorative term for an inward-looking judgementalism is far from being confined to Judaism, however; it rears its head in the Christian church and remains a temptation to every believer. If these over-the-top words give us cause to look within ourselves and our faith communities, there is at least one small gain.

Contrasting communities

The introduction begins by showing Jesus speaking both to his disciples and the crowds. Jesus' opening words invite attention to be paid to the teaching of scribe and Pharisee as the custodians of the Law of Moses. Matthew, on more than one occasion, shows a great respect for the scribal calling: it is not the office but the way the officers fail to live up to the demands of the office which evoke his condemnation. It is so here; the consistent complaint is that the practice fails to measure up to the words. Having said that, the first criticism here is that the demands which they lay upon the people, mostly poor, are far heavier than the people can bear. A measure of wealth and leisure was necessary to keep the Law in full accord with the Pharisees' multitudinous strictures; such a keeping was well beyond the resources of the mass of the people, who suffered under the 'blame the victim' syndrome.

The remaining criticisms in this first section (23:1–7) condemn the love of outward show, in ostentatiously religious dress (tassels and phylacteries), love of the best seats at feasts and synagogue, and obvious pleasure in being greeted with the honorific title of 'Teacher'. In contrast to this elitist community, Jesus then (23:8–11) stresses the way things are to be in the new community he has come to create. No one has the title of 'Teacher'; there is only one Teacher: everyone else belongs closely together as equals. No one is to be called 'Father'; all are children of the one Father in heaven. Finally, no one is to be addressed as 'Leader'; Jesus, the Messiah, is the only Leader. The community is communal, mutual, egalitarian. The section climaxes with yet another variant of the discipleship litany, calling for servanthood and humility to be the driving forces behind the life of the community. How does your faith community measure up to this quick thumbnail sketch?

Woe to ...

Now follow the denunciations of seven 'woes' against the scribes and Pharisees. In six of them, they are called by that favourite word of Matthew's, 'hypocrites' – those whose actions do not measure up to their words and are therefore lacking in the integrity and sincerity which Matthew regards as key virtues for the faithful disciple. Prepare for the full blast of Matthew's assault!

1. The first charge (23:13–14) is that the scribes and Pharisees lock people out of the Kingdom of heaven. It was the generally held belief that the key of David was in the hands of the teachers of the Law; they were the ones entrusted with the book and the interpretation of the book. Matthew's charge is that, by the multitude of their regulations, they had made the Law's keeping impossible for the people, and further, that the burdens which they laid on others they often failed to keep themselves. There is an obvious correspondence with the charge of laying heavy burdens in 23:4.

2. The second charge (23:15) relates to converts to Judaism. It serves as a reminder that Judaism was also a proselytising faith. Many 'God-seekers' found their way to the Temple and the synagogue, and some did embrace the full rigours of the keeping of the Law. The charge that the new convert, full of zeal, was more fanatical about their new faith than its long-established adherents is hardly unique to Judaism. T. S. Eliot's cautionary words bear repeating:

> in the piety of the convert
> Which may be tainted with a self-conceit
> Displeasing to God and disrespectful to the children

> (from 'The Cultivation of Christmas Trees',
> Eliot 1969b, p. 111)

3. The third charge (23:16–22) concerns the swearing of oaths. This is the one 'woe' where Jesus' opponents are not called 'hypocrites'; here, they are addressed as 'blind guides', and blindness is the charge laid against them throughout this 'woe'. The attack is levelled against their lack of discrimination and their failure to discern what is truly important. How can the gold in the sanctuary be more important than the sanctuary itself? ... or the gift on the altar than the altar which gives meaning to the gift? 'Distinctions of binding and non-binding oaths (23:16–19), miss the point of doing God's will. They are a means of evading God's will ...' (Carter 2000 p. 457). Already in the gospel Jesus has displayed scepticism about the swearing of oaths and asserted that they are not necessary (5:33–7). A person's word should be a sufficient bond – again

the emphasis is on integrity and sincerity. This third charge (23:22) demonstrates how the swearer of oaths can come perilously close to breaking the third commandment (Exodus 20:7) about not taking the name of the Lord God in vain.

4. The fourth charge (23:23–4) again attacks a lack of discernment. It pours scorn on a fusspot religion which is immersed in trifles to the neglect of the big picture. Concern for the tithing of herbs is contrasted with lack of vigour in the practice of what the Law is truly about; justice, mercy and faith – Matthew's consistent themes. If that picture isn't ridiculous enough, it is capped by the saying about straining out a gnat and swallowing a camel. The contrast is deliberately gross. Eating camels wasn't simply an enormous task, evoking echoes of today's riddle about how to eat an elephant; eating camels was forbidden (Leviticus 11:4, Deuteronomy 14:7).

5. Following the little-and-large 'woe', the fifth charge (23:25–6) echoes the complaints of 23:5–7 and contrasts the difference between having a show of cleanliness and rectitude on the outside while the inside remains tainted with 'greed and self-indulgence'. The image is of a cup, clean on the outside, filthy within.

6. The cup image is reinforced by an even stronger metaphor in the sixth charge (23:27–8), which likens the scribes and Pharisees to 'whitened sepulchres', fine and polished, while lurking beneath or within lies a putrefying mass of bones. Death and uncleanness were closely linked in the society of the time of Jesus.

7. The final woe (23:27–36) continues the image of the tomb-stone. Its complaint is that, while the tombs of the prophets of old are tended and honoured, and those who honour such past heroes of the faith exclaim sentimentally and with the benefit of hindsight: 'Dear me, we would never have done such a thing as to shed the blood of such heroes', even now these same grave-tenders are involved in the persecution and murder of contemporary living prophets. The reference both to the coming cross and to the persecution of Matthew's own

faith community is unmistakeable. The verdict is that, by their present actions against today's witnesses to the truth, opponents of Jesus and the young church are linked in blood guilt with all those who have brought death to the righteous, back to the killing of Abel (Genesis 4:1–16). (The reference to Zechariah, son of Barachiah, is obscure.) These final words of this passage have a clear reference to the fall of Jerusalem and its aftermath of Jewish/Christian division. It should be noted that the condemnation in this passage is not of the people as a whole, but of their religious leadership.

Contemporary Pharisaism

What can be salvaged as edifying from the bitter words above, which could be characterised as a Pharisaic condemnation of Pharisaism? Many commentators consider the gospel writers' depiction of the Pharisees as often a less than fair caricature and that, in some ways, the Pharisees as a reform movement within Judaism shared many similarities with the Jesus discipleship movement and the young church. Again, the image of the bitterness of a family fight comes to mind. The net result of the gospel writers' depiction has been to make Pharisee and Pharisaism pejorative terms. The temptation to Pharisaism in these terms is one which is certainly not the exclusive preserve of Judaism; it is there in all faiths.

What aspects of the Pharisee do you detect in your own faith and faith community? In ascending order of importance, the 'woes' highlight three perennial temptations to any believer and all faith communities. They are the tendencies to nit-picking, legalism and hypocrisy. Nit-picking first. 'Isn't it terrible, the preacher is wearing the wrong liturgical colours for the season?' 'No, it's not. It's an unfortunate mistake, but far from terrible.' Beware the danger of stirring up storms in ecclesiastical teacups. Remember the big picture which the gospel makes plain: being grasped by the wonder of the good grace of a generous God and responding to the call of discipleship. Legalism comes next, the danger of dogmas and rules. Of course they matter; but, if they become all that matters, our *raison d'être*, they kill rather than give life. We need something more, the breath of the spirit and a firm grasp on the fundamental importance of relationships which only endure with the aid of the oils of love and forgiveness. Finally, there is hypocrisy – again, Matthew's key theme. It would be better to say that Matthew continues to pose the opposites of hypocrisy versus integrity. The person of humble and merciful integrity is his model of the ideal person of faith. Yet, in a sense, when we have the courage and the honesty to look deep within, the seeds of hypocrisy are buried deep in all of us. We too confess that 'all our righteousnesses are as filthy rags' (Isaiah 64:6). One alone is righteous: Jesus Christ. We are about to see him demonstrate an integrity of word and action beyond our understanding. We speak of our integrity always and only in and through him.

Study

By yourself
Reflect on how you deal with the angers and resentments against those whom you see as opponents or enemies in the light of the words of Jesus, 'Love your enemies'.

Chapter 30

TROUBLE AHEAD

Matthew 23:37—25:13
Jesus' Love for Jerusalem
(*Luke 13:34–5*)

Jerusalem, Jerusalem! You kill the prophets and stone the messengers God has sent you! How many times have I wanted to put my arms round all your people, just as a hen gathers her chicks under her wings, but you would not let me! And so your Temple will be abandoned and empty. From now on, I tell you, you will never see me again until you say, "God bless him who comes in the name of the Lord."'

24   Jesus Speaks of the Destruction of the Temple

(*Mark 13:1–2, Luke 21:5–6*)

Jesus left and was going away from the Temple when his disciples came to him to call his attention to its buildings. 'Yes', he said, 'you may well look at all these. I tell you this: not a single stone here will be left in its place; every one of them will be thrown down.'

Troubles and Persecutions

(*Mark 13:3–13, Luke 21:7–19*)

As Jesus sat on the Mount of Olives, the disciples came to him in private. 'Tell us when all this will be', they asked, 'and what will happen to show that it is the time for your coming and the end of the age.'

Jesus answered, 'Be on your guard, and do not let anyone deceive you. Many men, claiming to speak for me, will come and say, "I am the Messiah!" and they will deceive many people. You are going to hear the noise of battles close by and the news of battles far away; but do not be troubled. Such things must happen, but they do not mean that the end has come. Countries will fight each other, kingdoms will attack one another. There will be famines and earthquakes everywhere. All these things are like the first pains of childbirth.

'Then you will be arrested and handed over to be punished and be put to death. All nations will hate you because of me. Many will give up their faith at that time; they will betray one another and hate one another. Then many false prophets will appear and deceive many people. Such will be the spread of evil that many people's love will grow cold. But whoever holds out to the end will be saved. And this Good News about the Kingdom will be preached through all the world for a witness to all nations; and then the end will come.'

The Awful Horror

(Mark 13:14–23, Luke 21:20–4)

'You will see "The Awful Horror" of which the prophet Daniel spoke. It will be standing in the holy place. (Note to the reader: be sure to understand what this means!) Then those who are in Judea must run away to the hills. Someone who is on the roof of his house must not take time to go down and get his belongings from the house. Someone who is in the field must not go back to get his cloak. How terrible it will be in those days for women who are pregnant and for mothers with little babies! Pray to God that you will not have to run away during the winter or on a Sabbath! For the trouble at that time will be far more terrible than any there has ever been, from the beginning of the world to this very day. Nor will there ever be anything like it again. But God has already reduced the number of days; had he not done so, nobody would survive. For the sake of his chosen people, however, God will reduce the days.

'Then, if anyone says to you, "Look, here is the Messiah!" or "There he is!" do not believe it. For false Messiahs and false prophets will appear; they will perform great miracles and wonders in order to deceive even God's chosen people, if possible. Listen! I have told you this before the time comes.

'Or, if people should tell you, "Look, he is out in the desert" – don't go there; or if they say, "Look, he is hiding here!" – don't believe it. For the Son of Man will come like the lightning which flashes across the whole sky from the east to the west.

'Wherever there is a dead body, the vultures will gather.'

The Coming of the Son of Man

(Mark 13:24–7, Luke 21:25–8)

'Soon after the trouble of those days, the sun will grow dark, the moon will no longer shine, the stars will fall from heaven, and the powers in space will be driven from their courses. Then the sign of the Son of Man will appear in the sky; and all the peoples of earth will weep as they see the Son of Man coming on the clouds of heaven with power and great glory. The great trumpet will sound, and he will send out his angels to the four corners of the earth, and they will gather his chosen people from one end of the world to the other.'

The Lesson of the Fig Tree

(Mark 13:28–31, Luke 21:29–33)

'Let the fig tree teach you a lesson. When its branches become green and tender and it starts putting out leaves, you know that summer is near. In the same way, when you see all these things, you will know that the time is near, ready to begin. Remember that all these things will happen before the people now living have all died. Heaven and earth will pass away, but my words will never pass away.'

No One Knows the Day and Hour

(Mark 13:32–7, Luke 17:26–30, 34–6)

'No one knows, however, when that day and hour will come – neither the angels in heaven nor the Son; the Father alone knows.

The coming of the Son of Man will be like what happened in the time of Noah. In the days before the flood people ate and drank, men and women married, up to the very day Noah went into the boat; yet they did not realize what was happening until the flood came and swept them all away. That is how it will be when the Son of Man comes. At that time two men will be working in a field: one will be taken away, the other will be left behind. Two women will be at a mill grinding meal: one will be taken away, the other will be left behind.

'Be on your guard, then, because you do not know what day your Lord will come. If the owner of a house knew the time when the thief would come, you can be sure that he would stay awake and not let the thief break into his house. So then, you must always be ready, because the Son of Man will come at an hour when you are not expecting him.'

The Faithful or the Unfaithful Servant

(*Luke 12:41–8*)

'Who, then, is a faithful and wise servant? It is the one that his master has placed in charge of the other servants to give them their food at the proper time. How happy that servant is if his master finds him doing this when he comes home! Indeed, I tell you, the master will put that servant in charge of all his property. But if he is a bad servant, he will tell himself that his master will not come back for a long time, and he will begin to beat his fellow-servants and to eat and drink with drunkards. Then that servant's master will come back one day when the servant does not expect him and at a time he does not know. The master will cut him in pieces and make him share the fate of the hypocrites. There he will cry and grind his teeth.'

The Parable of the Ten Young Women

'At that time the Kingdom of heaven will be like this. Once there were ten young women who took their oil lamps and went out to meet the bridegroom. Five of them were foolish, and the other five were wise. The foolish ones took their lamps but did not take any extra oil with them, while the wise ones took containers full of oil for their lamps. The bridegroom was late in coming, so the women began to nod and fall asleep.

'It was already midnight when the cry rang out, "Here is the bridegroom! Come and meet him!" The ten women woke up and trimmed their lamps. Then the foolish ones said to the wise ones, "Let us have some of your oil, because our lamps are going out." "No, indeed," the wise ones answered, "there is not enough for you and for us. Go to the shop and buy some for yourselves." So the foolish women went off to buy some oil; and while they were gone, the bridegroom arrived. The five who were ready went in with him to the wedding feast, and the door was closed.

'Later, the other women arrived. "Sir, sir! Let us in!" they cried out. "Certainly not! I don't know you," the bridegroom answered.'

And Jesus concluded, 'Be on your guard, then, because you do not know the day or the hour.'

Jerusalem, Jerusalem!

The tone changes from bitter denunciation to sad, regretful and tender lament. Jesus' lament over Jerusalem is the agonised cry of a frustrated lover. His ambivalence towards the city is understandable. He has found its holiest place held captive to the powers-that-be, who use it for the purposes of maintaining their own power, wealth and esteem. Yet he still reveres it as the symbolic mother of his people, and he wishes its fate would be otherwise than its destruction. What a strong, tender, feminine image of loving care he evokes with the picture of gathering the people under his protection like a mother hen her chicks – yet the reality is that she will be left desolate, as indeed the city was at the time of its fall in AD 70. Prior to the physical destruction of the Temple when the might of Rome put down the Jewish revolt, the Temple has already been abandoned: God is no longer at home in this building no longer fit for his purposes. None of our holy buildings or other artefacts can ever capture or contain God.

The Temple's fate

The future fate of the Temple is then spelled out in the short conversation between Jesus and some disciples at the start of

Matthew 24. Unlike Mark 13:1 and Luke 21:5, Matthew does not picture the disciples as standing in misplaced awe before the Temple building. Jesus simply bids his friends take a good look at Jerusalem's supreme piece of architectural splendour before he says with emphasis that it will all too soon be a mere heap of stones. It is clear that both Jesus' lament over the city and the prediction of the Temple's destruction have at least as much relevance to Matthew's readers soon after the fall of the city as to Jesus' disciples immediately before the cross.

The end

The previous two short passages on the fate of Jerusalem and its Temple form a bridge into the fifth and final teaching section of Matthew (24–5), which is followed immediately by the narrative of the Passion itself. This section takes the form of words of preparation for the disciples concerning what they are to expect in the future. They certainly predict that the disciples' post-Easter life will hardly be a bed of roses. There are major trials ahead. These trials of course reflect not only Jesus' predictions; they represent the experience of Matthew's own church. Jesus' words here are aimed at a double audience: in literary form the disciples' pre-Easter, in historical reality Matthew's church.

Matthew 24 and 25, however, contain more than mere historical predictions. There is also much apocalyptic writing pointing to the expected but unpredictable and uncontainable end of all things when the Son of Man would return and, after judgement, re-establish in its fullness on earth the heavenly Kingdom, the reign of God. The debate continues about the extent to which Jesus himself thought that his second coming was imminent. Certainly belief in that coming in the near future was strong in the church's early days, and the gospels all express in different ways the reality of the young church coming to terms with the coming's delay and having to prepare for the long road through history. There is much here about the importance of discernment and the discipline of faithful waiting. Taken together, these two chapters contain a mixture of practical experiential advice and vivid parable, beginning with the advice.

Life between the times

Throughout this final teaching section, Jesus is pictured sitting on the Mount of Olives giving instruction to the disciples alone. 'Sitting on the Mount of Olives' emphasises Jesus' authority; the Mount had associations with the power and presence of God (Ezekiel 11:22–4), and also with the coming judgement and salvation (Zechariah 14:4). The scene is of a crisis moment, with the Jesus community receiving its farewell and final instruction. It begins with a question; thereafter, Jesus speaks uninterrupted untill the end of chapter 25. The question is in two parts: 'When will all this be?' 'What will be the sign of your coming and of the end of the age?'

> Matthew clearly distinguishes between the judgement upon Israel for rejecting Jesus (first question), which can be seen in the destruction of the Temple in AD 70, and the second coming of the Son of Man, which will inaugurate the Last Judgement. It is between these two events that the community of Jesus lives, here represented by the disciples. (Schweizer 1975 pp. 448–9)

Jesus begins with a plea for discernment and a warning to avoid hasty judgements or actions. Many will appear claiming to be the instruments of Israel's salvation: this was the experience of Israel during the turbulent times between AD 66 and 70. These false Messiahs, with their seductive but soon destructive call to rise up in violent overthrow of Rome's occupying power, are to be ignored and shunned. Likewise, the noise of battles near and far, wars and rumours of wars, are not to be taken as signs that the end is near. Famine and earthquake were also common apocalyptic signs; once more, the warning is to avoid any hasty jumping to conclusions. The threat of persecution and death was an experiential reality for the people of Matthew's church, as was the experience of hatred for being aligned to Jesus' people. In that dangerous and pressured situation, naturally the temptation to deny faith was real, and the pressure to betray friends likewise. It is noteworthy that there is as much threat from within the discipleship community as from without. There is a second warning against being deceived by false prophets. In this fiery furnace of menace and evil, it will be all too easy for love to grow cold, perhaps the greatest betrayal of all in this gospel of 'mercy, not sacrifice'. However, 'Whoever holds out to the end will be saved'. Again the picture is of Matthew's hero, the disciple who simply, humbly, courageously endures through thick and thin, and who neither wavers nor strays from the Christ way. It is a picture for every place and time, a picture to which we can put names and faces from our own experience. Finally (24:14), the good news of the Kingdom will be made known throughout the world to all nations – a verse which anticipates the gospel's penultimate verse, Matthew 28:19.

The next section (24:15–22) deals specifically with what will happen in Judea. The 'Awful Horror' was first used to describe the desecration of the Jerusalem Temple by Antiochus Epiphanes IV in 168 BC (see Daniel 11:31, 12:11; 1 Maccabees 1:54). Here, it becomes a contemporary reference to the behaviour of the Roman troops in the Temple in AD 70 when they committed acts of desecration. 'It is the way of tyrants to desecrate the temple and to flaunt their imperial authority in the face of God. It will happen again. The events of AD 70 are not the end, though they are part of the tribulation leading to the end' (Carter 2000 p. 473). Disciples are encouraged to flee from the city; the burden of defence of Jerusalem and its Temple is not theirs. The reference to the Sabbath in 24:20 is worthy of note. Matthew adds it to the text of Mark (13:18). Schweizer posits that Matthew would not have such a strict view of Sabbath observance by the time of his gospel's writing; he may well have borrowed this older strict tradition because of sensibilities within his community where the Sabbath was still kept with rigour.

This section ends with yet another warning to beware of false prophets (24:23–8). Matthew inserts more detail than is found in Mark 13:21–3. He may have had in mind a prophet from Egypt mentioned in Josephus who led 30,000 into the desert to repeat the journey from Egypt to the Promised Land. They appeared finally at the Mount of Olives, where the 'prophet' deserted them and they were largely butchered by the Roman army.

The coming of the Son of Man

After the lengthy list of warnings to beware of false dawns, from verse 29 the real thing appears, i.e. the coming of the Son of

Man. The portents will be cosmic, with darkened skies and falling stars, familiar signs of the coming of the Day of the Lord in the Old Testament, a day pregnant with the themes of judgement and restoration. There are numerous references; key is the passage in Daniel 7:9–18 from which Matthew quotes in 24:30. Once again, secular literature often associated such heavenly manifestations with the power of emperors. Carter writes (2000 p. 478): 'It is "lights out" time for all tyrants, Jesus' coming returns the whole created cosmos to God's sovereignty'.

The reference to 'all the tribes of the earth shall mourn' is significant. The quotation is from Zechariah 12:10–14, which speaks of the day of God's coming to Jerusalem. It was early picked up by the young church and taken to refer to the events of Jesus' Passion. Some commentators believe that the 'sign of the Son of Man' which will appear in the heavens is the sign of the cross; it may simply be a banner in the sky which accompanies the sound of trumpets indicating both judgement and victory. The moment of the awesome epiphany of the returning Son ends with the gathering of the faithful from 'the four winds', i.e. an inclusive gathering of Jew and Gentile from the ends of the earth.

Nature lesson

Once again, Jesus offers a lesson from observing the fig tree, this time clearly a metaphorical tree. Nature gives signs of the passing seasons, and specifically the fig tree gives intimations of a coming time of full summer. Likewise the events previously described from 24:3–29 are given as signs of the coming end time. Here, Matthew appears to expect an imminent parousia rather than a coming delayed. What is vital is that, whether the coming be late or soon, the words of Jesus will never pass away. They remain to be fed upon and obeyed.

Be ready

'But' is the key opening word in 24:36. It opens a series of three pieces of teaching, one general, two parables, all of which call the disciples to an attitude of alert, continual watchfulness. Jesus has just announced his coming again soon, yet he immediately goes on to repeat his assertion that the precise time of his coming cannot be given. The lesson is repeated for emphasis three times, though its import seems lost on all those millenarians down through the Christian centuries who reckon they have managed to calculate the exact time of Jesus' return and travel far and climb high to await the moment – which inevitably disappoints by the Lord's non-appearance. Watchfulness, vigilance is of course a central theme of the season of Advent, and Matthew 24:36–44 and its variant in Mark 13:32–7 with the relatively close variant in Luke 21:25–36 are the gospel readings for the First Sunday in Advent in the three-year cycle of the Common Lectionary.

The example given of a failure to be attentive is taken from the story of Noah. Jesus describes the people of that time carrying on their lives as normal, in blissful unawareness of the flood about to engulf them. They are not berated for their sinfulness, they are doomed through their lack of alertness. The suddenness of the coming and its accompanying judgement is highlighted in the parallel examples of the two men working in the field; one taken, one left, and the two women grinding their meal at the mill who suffer the same fate. The final picture of the returning Jesus as a thief in the night (24:43) is provocative. It's not the only time in the gospels Jesus compares himself to a thief (see Mark 3:27). Hopefully, it shocks Matthew's readers into wakefulness.

Be prepared

The two parables of preparedness end this chapter. First comes the comparison between the faithful or unfaithful slave/servant. In Matthew 23, Jesus has fiercely berated the 'hypocritical' Pharisees. In this passage (24:45–51), he turns his attention on possibly backsliding disciples. He describes the diligence of the faithful servant who takes charge of the household in his master's absence and well serves his fellow servants and co-workers at the right and proper time. The master will return to find his household well in order and reward him with more responsibility. By contrast, the unfaithful servant abuses his position in the master's absence, being violent to his fellow-workers, indulging his own appetites by falling in with the local hard-drinking set. The master will return, unexpectedly of course, to find his household a shambles. The fate of the unfaithful servant is typically Matthean; banishment to the place of weeping and gnashing of teeth. The behaviour of the two servants as stewards of the master's house is starkly contrasted, but in the story there aren't two servants at all; there's only one servant who must choose to behave either wisely or foolishly, well or wickedly. It's the choice which lies continually before every disciple, to remain faithful to the way and so upbuild the household of faith, or to follow their own selfish agenda and wreak havoc among the flock.

Finally, we come to another wedding scene in the parable which belongs only to Matthew (25:1–13). In biblical times, as now, weddings and banquets went hand in hand as occasions of great human and familial celebration. So, it's hardly surprising that Jesus should use the symbol of the wedding feast and the arrival of the bridegroom to denote the end time when 'all will be well'. Ten young women bridesmaids await the arrival of the bridegroom, who, however, is seriously delayed. Five are 'wise' (meaning 'seeing', 'with eyes open', in Hebrew), and five are foolish. The purpose of the bridesmaids is to shed light on the festivities with the bridegroom's arrival (see 5:14 'You are the light of the world'). The wise five have brought with them extra oil in case their lamp's fuel runs out, while the foolish have made no preparations to carry extra resources. When, at midnight, well through the night, the word goes out that the groom is arriving, the foolish discover that their lamps are going out. They have to go to the village store – 'Open all hours' – to replenish their oil. While they are away, the groom arrives and goes into the feast, closing the doors fast behind him and refusing entry to the foolish when they return too late, having missed the 'kairos' moment.

In contrast to some of these other parables of waiting which stress the imminent arrival of the Son of Man, this parable is concerned, like the one immediately previous (24:45–51), with the right response of disciples if the Son's arrival is delayed much longer than the community's expectations – obviously a dilemma that Matthew's community would be wrestling with. The returning Jesus is the bridegroom and the community of faith the bridesmaids. The message is clear: whether he arrive late or soon, the community through its alert, careful, wakeful vigilance is to be prepared and ready for Jesus' return. To it is committed the task of faithful waiting though the bridegroom tarry. The message for disciples of every age, soon to be reinforced in the final parable of the gospel at 25:31–46, is to be constantly alert, ready and able to 'see' the presence of Jesus in their midst.

Study

By yourself

Reflect through the week with the help of the short song:

> 'Wait for the Lord, his day is near, wait for the Lord, be strong, take heart'.

For group work:

Talk together about your experience of waiting in everyday life. Make a list of times of waiting.

From your reading of this chapter, share together how you can best participate in the active, faithful, expectant waiting for which the gospel calls.

Chapter 31

'WHEN DID WE SEE YOU?'

Matthew 25:14–46

The Parable of the Three Servants

(*Luke 19:11–27*)

'At that time the Kingdom of heaven will be like this. Once there was a man who was about to go on a journey; he called his servants and put them in charge of his property. He gave to each one according to his ability; to one he gave five thousand gold coins, to another he gave two thousand, and to another he gave one thousand. Then he left on his journey. The servant who had received five thousand coins went at once and invested his money and earned another five thousand. In the same way the servant who had received two thousand coins earned another two thousand. But the servant who had received one thousand coins went off, dug a hole in the ground, and hid his master's money.

'After a long time the master of those servants came back and settled accounts with them. The servant who had received five thousand coins came in and handed over the other five thousand. "You gave me five thousand coins, sir," he said. "Look! Here are another five thousand that I have earned." "Well done, you good and faithful servant!" said his master. "You have been faithful in managing small amounts, so I will put you in charge of large amounts. Come on in and share my happiness!"

'Then the servant who had been given two thousand coins came in and said, "You gave me two thousand coins, sir. Look! Here are another two thousand that I have earned." "Well done, you good and faithful servant!" said his master. "You have been faithful in managing small amounts, so I will put you in charge of large amounts. Come on in and share my happiness!"

'Then the servant who had received one thousand coins came in and said, "Sir, I know you are a hard man; you reap harvests where you did not sow, and you gather crops where you did not scatter seed. I was afraid, so I went off and hid your money in the ground. Look! Here is what belongs to you."

' "You bad and lazy servant!" his master said. "You knew, did you, that I reap harvests where I did not sow, and gather crops where I did not scatter seed? Well, then, you should have deposited my money in the bank, and I would have received it all back with interest when I returned. Now, take the money away from him and give it to the one who has ten thousand coins. For to every person who has something, even more will be given, and he will have more than enough; but the person who has nothing, even the little that he has will be taken away from him. As for this useless servant – throw him outside in the darkness; there he will cry and grind his teeth." ' '

The Final Judgement

'When the Son of Man comes as King and all the angels with him, he will sit on his royal throne, and the people of all the nations will be gathered before him. Then he will divide them into two groups, just as a shepherd separates the sheep from the goats. He will put the righteous people on his right and the others on his left. Then the King will say to the people on his right, "Come, you that are blessed by my Father! Come and possess the kingdom which has been prepared for you ever since the creation of the world. I was hungry and you fed me, thirsty and you gave me a drink; I was a stranger and you received me in your homes, naked and you clothed me; I was sick and you took care of me, in prison and you visited me."

'The righteous will then answer him, "When, Lord, did we ever see you hungry and feed you, or thirsty and give you a drink? When did we ever see you a stranger and welcome you in our homes, or naked and clothe you? When did we ever see you sick or in prison, and visit you?" The King will reply, "I tell you, whenever you did this for one of the least important of these members of my family, you did it for me!"

'Then he will say to those on his left, "Away from me, you that are under God's curse! Away to the eternal fire which has been prepared for the Devil and his angels! I was hungry but you would not feed me, thirsty but you would not give me a drink; I was a stranger but you would not welcome me in your homes, naked but you would not clothe me; I was sick and in prison but you would not take care of me."

'Then they will answer him, "When, Lord, did we ever see you hungry or thirsty or a stranger or naked or sick or in prison, and would not help you?" The King will reply, "I tell you, whenever you refused to help one of these least important ones, you refused to help me." These, then, will be sent off to eternal punishment, but the righteous will go to eternal life.'

The parable of the talents

Matthew reinforces the message of the parable of the ten young women with the following parable of the talents. He makes the link with the new parable's opening words, 'For' (NRSV), 'At that time' (GNB). The further link in the text itself is that both deal with the delay of the coming one: 'After a long time' (25:19). In the words of commendation to the first two slaves, 'Well done, good and trustworthy slave, ... enter into the joy of your master' (25:21 NRSV), there is an echo of the invitation to the Messianic banquet at the end time. Matthew therefore uses this parable as another instruction to disciples about how to conduct themselves as they wait, possibly for a long time, for their master's return.

The sums the slaves/servants are entrusted with – ten, five and one talents – are not inconsiderable. Real responsibilities and opportunities are given to them. The parable commends the diligence of the first two servants, who have doubled the sum given to them during their master's absence, and vilifies the third servant even although he has made careful plans to safeguard his master's money against his return. The message to be active and industrious and make good use of the gifts entrusted to our stewardship is clear enough. The third servant is castigated for his timidity and lack of enterprise. Some commentators see the third servant as standing for the previously attacked scribes and Pharisees; the charge against them is that they take God's Law and bury it away for their own ends, refusing to allow it to be a living word for the people of their own day.

Alternatively?

The parable, as Matthew contextualises it, is an injunction to faithful waiting and hard work. 'Use well the gifts you have been given.' It stretches the point more than a little to use it, as it has been, to justify the present world economic system! On the contrary, commentators have been puzzled by Matthew's interpretation both on account of too easy an identification of the aristocratic master with God and the behaviour of the slaves/servants in earning their reward. They look suspiciously like moneylenders. Using recent research, and in particular the work of William R. Herzog II in seeking to uncover the original parable that Jesus told from its appropriation by the gospel writer, in this case Matthew, an alternative reading could look as follows (see Herzog 1994).

Matthew has grafted an original parable of Jesus as a didactic tool for his own narrative purposes. The first hearers of the parable from the lips of Jesus would not see the master in this story as a neutral figure; they would see him as one who profited from the iniquitous economic system responsible for their poverty and insecurity. The slaves/servants would be regarded as the hirelings, possibly corrupt, whom he had co-opted to further his purposes. Landlords frequently went missing to enjoy the fruits of their lavish lifestyle. Such a lifestyle was built on lending money to peasant farmers and then, when in times of hardship the peasants were unable to repay the debt, taking their land in return for payment and thereby reducing the farmers to the highly marginal and precarious status of day labourers. The landlord represented the top 2 per cent of the population in economic terms.

The story is therefore not a shining example of good business practice, but of thoroughly dodgy exploitation, masked, as it so often is, by the rhetoric of fine words.

The praise offered by the oppressive aristocrat mystifies the ugly realities suppressed beneath the profit margin: 'Well done, good and trustworthy slave'. Both retainers are good in terms of the aristocrat's values because they have proven to be effective exploiters of the peasants, and they have been trustworthy because they have produced a level of increased wealth in line with the aristocrat's expectations. (Herzog 1994 p. 163)

On the other hand, the third servant/slave, the one who buries the money, both keeps safe what has been entrusted to him and tells the truth. The truth is that his master is a harsh man, and so on (25:24 ff.). He is the real hero of the story through his truth-telling, which will for him have serious consequences as he is fired from his master's employ and banished from the household. He will know, in Matthew's pet phrase, 'weeping and gnashing of teeth' (25:30), but it will not be on the occasion of final judgement; rather in face of the hard realities of hunger and poverty which await him as a result of his honest and courageous speaking. Far from being 'afraid' (25:25), he is a person of some considerable courage in being prepared to name the iniquitous system and face the consequences. In a curious way, the parable acquires a pointed and telling relevance which it is doubtful if Matthew intended. It is placed almost immediately before the start of the Passion, which at one level can be read as the story of Jesus naming and unmasking the powers that threaten and disable our humanity, at such extreme personal cost.

If this is a fair reading of this parable's original intent, one of its purposes must be to make us aware of the use and abuse of language. This reading highlights the way the smooth speech of praise by the aristocrat of his two so-called 'faithful' slaves/servants hides the ugly reality of their collusive economic exploitation of poor farmers. On the other side, the speech of the third servant, castigated by his lord as 'wicked and lazy', simply and honestly tells it like it is. He is the one who reveals reality. Our world is far from short of the use of neologisms and euphemistic speech to cloak unpalatable reality both in the world of warfare and in the politico-economic sphere. 'Collateral damage' springs to mind as an obvious military example of hiding the reality of civilian casualties behind bland phraseology; the name 'supply-side economics' of the 1980s gave a spurious legitimacy to the calculated tactic of the transfer of wealth from the poor to the rich. The need for vigilance and, in Herzog's terms, 'whistleblowers' who will demythologise the pretensions of language is a necessary and prophetic task for our times.

Last but not least

The fifth and final block of Jesus' teaching concludes and climaxes with the magnificent parable, unique to Matthew, of the sheep and the goats (25:31–46). After the preceding sections instructing disciples in the disciplines of waiting, watchfulness and hard work in the period before the Lord's coming, the section ends with Matthew's portrayal of the final judgement when the Son of Man arrives as judge and king. He comes in power and glory with an angelic host in attendance and takes his seat on the throne of judgement. Before him are gathered 'all the nations'. The judgement concerns seeing the face of Christ in the poor and the marginalised: can it be read both as a call for individual sensitivity, compassion and action and also as a challenge to those national 'blind spots' where international structures prevent the doing of justice to the poor – a huge issue in our ill-divided world?

The sheep and the goats

After the initial imagery of the arrival of the king in splendour, the parable turns to the image of the shepherd, well familiar as a metaphor for divinity in Jewish tradition. It draws on the common practice of shepherds being in charge of mixed flocks of sheep and goats. Sheep and goats are separated, the sheep to the favoured position on the right hand, with the goats relegated to the left. The sheep on the right hand are warmly invited into the Kingdom 'prepared for you before the foundation of the world' (25:34), stressing the sureness and security of God's Kingdom. The sheep on the right hand, by verse 37 called 'the righteous', express their surprise at finding themselves in this place of blessing and honour. They have just heard from the mouth of the king, shepherd, judge of six traditional categories of the marginalised – the hungry, thirsty, stranger, naked, sick, prisoner – in whom Christ dwells and to whom they have ministered, albeit unwittingly. There has long been a question as to whether this discerning of the face of Christ applies to the marginalised in general or to oppressed and needy disciples in particular. Although exegesis of the passage in its original context may favour the latter, i.e. confining those in need of succour to the discipleship community, in today's shrunken and pluriform world there is much to be said for giving it the first and universal application.

This final scene can be understood as the ultimate summation of Matthew's recurrent theme of 'mercy, not sacrifice'. Yet, in a strange way, we find here mercy, understood as acts of care, and sacrifice, understood as acts of worship, interwoven. In this picture, the mystical meets the practical. It is well expressed and articulated in the following words from Archbishop Oscar Romero of El Salvador, delivered a mere ten days before he was assassinated while saying mass. He was killed for his commitment to the poor of his land, for becoming a voice for the voiceless. He has not been silenced:

God in Christ dwells near at hand to us.
    Christ has given us a guideline:
        'I was hungry and you gave me to eat'.
When someone is hungry, there is Christ near at hand.
        'I was thirsty and you gave me to drink'.
When someone comes to your house to ask for water,
        it is Christ if you look with faith.
In the sick person longing for a visit Christ tells you,
        'I was sick and you came to visit me'.
Or in prison. How many today are ashamed to testify for the
    innocent!
What terror has been sown among our people
        that friends betray friends whom they see in trouble.
If we could see that Christ is in the needy one, the torture victim,
        the prisoner, the murder victim,
and in each human figure so shamefully thrown by our roadsides
        would see Christ himself cast aside,
we would pick him up like a medal of gold to be kissed lovingly.
        We would never be ashamed of him.
How far people are today,
        especially those who torture and kill
and value their investments more than human beings,

> from realizing that all the earth's millions are good for
>   nothing,
> are worthless compared to a human being.
> The person is Christ,
>   and in the person viewed and treated with faith
> we look on Christ the Lord.

(Comment on Matthew 25:35–6, 16 March 1980,
ten days before his assassination: Romero 1988 pp. 202–3)

Christians see the gift and task of compassion for those on the margins, powerless and without a voice, often superficially unattractive, as stemming from the understanding that in them we can discern the face of Christ. Spiritual and practical giants like Oscar Romero, Mother Teresa of Calcutta and Jean Vanier, the founder of the L'Arche communities, stand as luminaries, pointing the way in our time. Yet the categories of the needy whom Matthew quotes have a long history within the Jewish tradition. An outstanding voice from that tradition today is Jonathan Sacks, the Chief Rabbi of Great Britain and Ireland. He offers these wise words on the conjunction of mercy and sacrifice:

> The link between monotheism and the moral life is that a universe seen as the home of many gods or none is an arena of conflicting forces in which the strong prevail, the weak suffer, the manipulative exploit the vulnerable, and might is sovereign over right. A world without a Judge is one in which there is no reason to expect justice. The human condition becomes a tragic script in which ideals prove to be illusions, revolution a mere change of places in the seats of power, and the ship of hope destined to be wrecked by the cold iceberg of reality.
>
> The holy and the good are not the same but they are linked in a cyclical process of engagement and withdrawal. Our prayers, texts and rituals hold before us a vision of how the world might be. Our work, service to the community and social life take us into the world as it is, where we make a difference by mending some of its imperfections, righting wrongs, curing ills, healing wounds. The juxtaposition of the two creates moral energy, and when they are disconnected, the energy fails. The holy is where we enter the ideal: the good is how we make it real. Long ago, alone at night, Jacob dreamed a dream of a ladder connecting heaven and earth, and of angels ascending and

318

descending. Life is that ladder, for earth cannot be mended without a glimpse of heaven, nor heaven live for humankind without a home on earth. (Sacks 2005 p. 173)

John Barclay of Durham University says that 'Matthew's hero is the unnoticed Christian who just gets on with it in a committed and disciplined way – it's not till the end that the sheep and the goats know who they are and what they've been doing or not doing'. The sheep in this story certainly represent just such people. There is an echo of the African American spiritual quoted by Rowan Williams in his book, *On Christian Theology*: 'No One Knows Who I Am till the Judgement Morning' (2000 p. 276).

On the left-hand side, represented by the goats, are those who merit condemnation through their failure to see and serve the presence of Jesus in the poor. 'When did we fail to take care of you?' is their question. 'Take care' means 'serve' and 'to serve'; 'be a servant' has been a key theme throughout the gospel. The way of humble service is the way of discipleship, and those on the left hand have failed both to see and to act like disciples. They have neither been close enough to Jesus nor close enough to the ground. They are summarily condemned, which perhaps raises the previously stated uneasiness about the severe alacrity of Matthew's condemnations, particularly in this story which has as its main theme an invitation to full-blooded compassion.

Straying into the opening words of Matthew 26, this final block ends with the now familiar formula, 'When Jesus had finished saying all these things …'. These words now acquire a deep poignancy: the time for words is almost over; we are about to be launched into the ultimate acts beyond words, the Passion of Christ itself.

Study

By yourself

Through the next week, use the following song to meditate upon.

> The King will sit upon the judgement seat
> with angels round in glory in the height.
> 'Bring sheep and goats before me', he will say,

'and separate them into left and right.'
Then fondly to the right-hand sheep he says,
'Come to my joy, enter my kingdom free,
for in the poor, the prisoner, the despised,
you each have truly ministered to me'.

Jesus, we come before you, servant king,
and pray that we your way might deeply learn.
May we in humbly serving broken folk
your features in the poor and least discern.

As one example of the categories of those in whom Jesus bids us recognise his features, think on this quotation about Scotland's prison population:

Compared with the population as a whole, prisoners are fourteen times more likely to have been taken into care as a child, six times more likely to be single teenage parents, five times more likely to have no educational qualification, twelve times more likely to have experienced long-term unemployment, fifty times more likely to suffer from three or more mental disorders, thirty times more likely to be homeless. (Andrew McLellan, Chief Inspector for Scottish Prisons)

Chapter 32

ENEMIES AND FRIENDS

Matthew 26:1–16
The Plot against Jesus

(Mark 14:1–2, Luke 22:1–2, John 11:45–53)

When Jesus had finished teaching all these things, he said to his disciples, 'In two days, as you know, it will be the Passover Festival, and the Son of Man will be handed over to be crucified.'

Then the chief priests and the elders met together in the palace of Caiaphas, the High Priest, and made plans to arrest Jesus secretly and put him to death. 'We must not do it during the festival', they said, 'or the people will riot.'

Jesus is Anointed at Bethany

(Mark 14:3–9, John 12:1–8)

Jesus was in Bethany at the house of Simon, a man who had suffered from a dreaded skin disease. While Jesus was eating, a woman came to him with an alabaster jar filled with an expensive perfume, which she poured over his head. The disciples saw this and became angry. 'Why all this waste?' they asked. 'This perfume could have been sold for a large amount and the money given to the poor!'

Jesus knew what they were saying, so he said to them, 'Why are you bothering this woman? It is a fine and beautiful thing she has done for me. You will always have poor people with you, but you will not always have me. What she did was to pour perfume on my body to get me ready for burial. Now, I assure you that wherever the gospel is preached all over the world, what she has done will be told in memory of her.'

Judas Agrees to Betray Jesus

(Mark 14:10–11, Luke 22:3–6)

Then one of the twelve disciples – the one named Judas Iscariot – went to the chief priests and asked, 'What will you give me if I betray Jesus to you?' They counted out 30 silver coins and gave them to him. From then on Judas was looking for a good chance to hand Jesus over to them.

Getting ready

'You know that after two days the Passover is coming, and the Son of Man will be handed over to be crucified' (26:2). With these stark words of Jesus to his disciples, we are plunged into the dark night of the Passion narrative. The down-to-earth announcement comes just after the picture of the arrival of the Son of Man at the throne of glory for the great judgement scene of 25:31–46. The blaze of light from the glorious throne quickly dims as grim earthly realities take centre stage. The opening verses of Matthew 26 offer four different perspectives of preparation for what is to come. First, in the announcement quoted above, Jesus seeks yet again, for a fourth time, to prepare his disciples. Second, the enemies of Jesus conspire together to make their plans. Third, an unnamed woman disciple performs an act of lavish outpouring, great tenderness and prophetic insight: her action is immediately followed by the last act of preparation, as Judas goes to the chief priests to ask the price for his betraying Jesus.

In the chapter's opening verses, most of the main actors in the succeeding drama are named: the disciples, the crowd/people, the chief priests and elders, Caiaphas the High Priest, and Jesus himself. Only Pilate and the Roman soldiery are missing. On the one hand are ranged unfaithful disciples, a fickle crowd and the might of the religious and political establishment; on the other, just Jesus. It is a just Jesus – Matthew throughout will portray Jesus' sufferings as those of an innocent victim. We should prepare for the Passion by acquainting ourselves again with two psalms which are pleas from the depths for justice in face of suffering and persecution, Psalms 22 and 69, and also with

Isaiah's song of the suffering servant from Isaiah 52:13—53:12. They outcrop from time to time in the narrative and are always in the background.

Friends

The story begins with the fourth and final announcement of Jesus' forthcoming sufferings and death (see 16:23, 17:22–3, 20:17–19). Matthew has Jesus give the now familiar news quite baldly to his friends, the discipleship band. He has Jesus link it to the imminent Passover, the annual remembrance of the historical liberation of his people. The familiar announcement acquires an altogether new urgency in the light of the fast-approaching crisis. At this stage, Matthew makes no reference to the disciples' incomprehension or failure to last the pace. That will come later. What is significant in Matthew's account of the Passion, although it largely follows the narrative pattern of Mark, is that, throughout, Jesus is portrayed, even when he is handed over into the malevolent hands of others, as in charge of his own destiny. He is the willing victim, one who not only knows but is also complicit in the outcome, his own sufferings and death.

> Amazing love! how can it be
> that thou, my God, shouldst die for me?
>
> (Charles Wesley in *CH 4* 2005 no. 396)

Enemies

Immediately after Jesus speaks of his looming trials to his friends, the opposition is brought on stage. Matthew reminds us of the powerful forces within Jesus' own people who are lined up against him: the establishment from the religious power centre of the Jerusalem Temple, the chief priests and elders, and the High Priest, Caiaphas. They plot together how best to do away with Jesus, but are shown as fearful of the crowd, who are still portrayed as friendly to Jesus. It is interesting that these establishment figures' rationale for not arresting Jesus during the festival has nothing to do with the sacred meaning of the festival and everything to do with avoiding crowd trouble – a pretty cynical motivation, not unknown in today's world.

These first four stories of preparation work by a significant pair of contrasts. Initially, there is the contrast between the friends of Jesus, his disciples, and his enemies, the Jerusalem religious establishment. This is followed by the striking difference between a woman's act of love and Judas' act of betrayal.

Devotion

There are moments when the dark night of the Passion story is lit up by flashes of light. We come to the first of these in the incident of Jesus' anointing at Bethany (26:6–13). In a variety of forms, the kernel of this story is told in all four gospels (see Mark 14:3–9, Luke 7:36–50, John 12:1–8). Its fourfold appearance speaks of its significance for the gospel writers. It is an extraordinary story, full of sensuousness, with more than a hint of the erotic. Matthew tells the story very simply, largely following the account in Mark; but, even in Matthew's staid account, the power and intimacy of this moment break through. The action takes place in the home of Simon the leper, yet another signal of the presence of Jesus in the midst of the shunned and marginalised. The sweet scent of the perfume fills the room as the unnamed woman pours it over the head of Jesus in her act of love, but the costliness of the ointment and the bold and loving act of the woman scandalise the accompanying disciples. 'What a waste!' they say – the predictable response of rational man. Jesus chides them: 'Why do you put this woman down? She has done a good thing ... by pouring this ointment on my body she has prepared me for burial' (26:10–12).

There is a profound merging of body and spirit in this moment. Jesus interprets the action of the woman as at one and the same time an act of love, an act of tenderness and a moment of prophecy about what lies ahead for him. Her 'wastefulness' prefigures the holy waste which is the cross in circumstances of the utmost profanity. It is a story which has been treasured because of the woman's prophetic insight into the sacrificial abandon of the cross; it deserves equally to be treasured for its portrayal of a moment of loving humanity in the midst of the dark night of hate and fear. The touching love of this woman stands in stark contrast to the various men around Jesus who will betray him with a false kiss, abandon him altogether or lay violent hands upon him. From this moment shines the light of the prodigality of love. Let her story live as her Lord commanded (26:13)!

Betrayal

Immediately, we are plunged back into darkness. Once again, with spare narrative, Matthew chronicles Judas' action in going to the chief priests to ask the price for his betrayal of Jesus. It is thirty pieces of silver, and it is not high. The money is handed over, and Judas begins to look for an 'opportune time' to perform his act of perfidy. For the first time, we see from within the discipleship community the appearance of the seeds of Jesus' destruction. The Greek word for 'opportune time' is significant. It is connected with the word, *kairos*, which means 'the right time', 'the significant moment', 'God's time'. Here is a first intimation of the depths of the mystery of the Passion, that the 'right time' for Judas is also, in the mystery of things, the right time for God. It is through the very destructive actions of the enemies of Jesus that there comes our salvation.

Study

By yourself
Meditate on the 'wastefulness, prodigality of love'.

For group work
Divide into three groups and enact a role-play of the story of the anointing of Jesus, some taking the part of the woman, some of the disciples, some of Jesus.

Discuss with each other what your thoughts are before the action, during and afterwards.

What does this story tell us about love?

Chapter 33

'THIS IS MY BODY'

Matthew 26:17–30

Jesus Eats the Passover Meal with his Disciples

(*Mark 14:12–21, Luke 22:7–13, 21–3, John 13:21–30*)

On the first day of the Festival of Unleavened Bread the disciples came to Jesus and asked him, 'Where do you want us to get the Passover meal ready for you?'

'Go to a certain man in the city', he said to them, and tell him, '"The Teacher says, My hour has come; my disciples and I will celebrate the Passover at your house."'

The disciples did as Jesus had told them and prepared the Passover meal.

When it was evening, Jesus and the twelve disciples sat down to eat. During the meal Jesus said, 'I tell you, one of you will betray me.'

The disciples were very upset and began to ask him, one after the other, 'Surely, Lord, you don't mean me?'

Jesus answered, 'One who dips his bread in the dish with me will betray me. The Son of Man will die as the Scriptures say he will, but how terrible for that man who betrays the Son of Man! It would have been better for that man if he had never been born!'

Judas, the traitor, spoke up. 'Surely, Teacher, you don't mean me?' he asked.

Jesus answered, 'So you say.'

The Lord's Supper

(Mark 14:22–6, Luke 22:14–20, 1 Corinthians 11:23–5)

While they were eating, Jesus took a piece of bread, gave a prayer of thanks, broke it, and gave it to his disciples. 'Take and eat it', he said; 'this is my body.'

Then he took a cup, gave thanks to God, and gave it to them. 'Drink it, all of you', he said; 'this is my blood, which seals God's covenant, my blood poured out for many for the forgiveness of sins. I tell you, I will never again drink this wine until the day I drink the new wine with you in my Father's Kingdom.'

Then they sang a hymn and went out to the Mount of Olives.

More preparation

'My hour has come' (26:18). The Greek word for 'hour', 'time' is *kairos*, the same word which has been used immediately previously to describe the action of Judas in waiting for 'the right time' to betray Jesus (26:16). *Kairos* is a word of profound meaning; it now announces Jesus' moment of destiny as into the ancient feast of liberation, the Passover, Jesus brings the blood of the new covenant through his cross. Before the cross and the impending night and day of darkness, the feast must be celebrated. More preparations are made. Once more, Matthew tells the story in bare terms; he does not mention any of the cloak-and-dagger details like Mark (14:13–15), where the disciples are sent to find a man who will be recognised by the unlikely detail of carrying a water jug on his head. The impression is still conveyed of careful preparation for the twelve to share this final meal together, a meal which will become so full of meaning for all subsequent disciples. The disciples find both the man and the room, and all is made ready.

A step further into darkness

The meal itself is set within the context of the gathering crisis. At its end, Jesus will leave to go to the garden of Gethsemane for the time of deep agony in his final preparations for his cross-bearing. Before the breaking of the bread, Jesus tells the disciples what we, the readers, already know – that one of them will betray him. He calls down a 'woe' on the one who will shatter the circle of trust in the discipleship community. The disciples both display their dismay and protest their loyalty. The narrative focuses in on words between Judas and Jesus. While the disciples call Jesus 'Lord', Judas addresses him as 'Rabbi', i.e. 'teacher', which is both a term used by Jesus' opponents and a title whose use was forbidden by Jesus in 23:7–8. Judas' deceit is obvious to us; it appears also that Jesus had already discerned who his betrayer would be. He lets Judas know that his cover is blown without, however, 'outing' him before the rest of the disciples. It is therefore in an atmosphere of suspicion and sadness, fear and apprehension that the community sits to eat.

'He took the bread' ... at the crossroads of time

The last corporate act of the discipleship community is to sit and share a meal together. The narrative of the meal we have come to know as the Lord's Supper is once more spare and terse. Matthew's account has, however, been influenced by the growing importance of the meal as a set part of the life of the young Christian community. The words of Jesus, 'Take, eat: this is my body ... Drink from it all of you, for this is my blood of the covenant, which is poured out for many for the forgiveness of sins' (26:27–8), suggest a more definite and uniform liturgical use across the expanding church.

'Covenant' is a key biblical term from the time of the patriarchs through Moses to the later prophets such as Jeremiah. It means a binding agreement, biblically between God and his people. 'I will be your God, you will be my people' (Leviticus 26:12, Jeremiah 11:4, 30:22). While any covenant is between two parties, there is no implication that the parties are equal; always God is the greater and God is the initiator. The key covenant for the people of Israel was the covenant sealed at Sinai, where, in response to their liberation from Egypt, the people committed themselves to the keeping of the Law as their part of the agreement. Much of the rest of the Old Testament tells with commendable honesty of the people's failure to live up to their promise. The new covenant which Jesus brings, sealed by his own sacrifice, is the renewed invitation to find faith in

God through him and to enter into the new community of faith and freedom, forgiveness and love, which he creates through his actions and his sufferings. In this community, the new 'law' is formed for disciples out of the obligations of love to God and neighbour. The Lord's Supper is a continuing reminder of God's new initiative as Jesus takes bread and breaks it.

Sharing a meal, eating and drinking together, are fundamental human activities. Their importance is highlighted in the gospels, where Jesus is frequently to be found sharing with others, often the despised and the disreputable. Meal-sharing is a key place of conviviality and welcome. Food itself satisfies a basic need. The hungry need to be fed; and, in the desert meals (14:13–21, 15:32–9), Jesus has demonstrated his ability and concern for the feeding of the hungry. Jesus' commitment to feeding the hungry and welcoming the outsider also finds expression in some of the parables of the Kingdom. It is against this human and material background that the Lord's Supper takes place, as a culmination and example of all our earthly human meals and fellowships. This means, on the one hand, that we should be careful not to separate the Lord's Supper from the context of the rest of Jesus' meal-sharings and concerns for justice; on the other, the Lord's Supper stands as a model for the everyday sharing of our bread with friend and stranger.

> The centrality of food in the Kingdom and in the achievement on earth of God's will is brought out in the close association between these realities in the Lord's Prayer, where the hallowing of God's name, the coming of the Kingdom, and the provision of daily bread are placed together (6:11, Luke 11:3). (Leach 1985 p. 269)

The notion of a meal with ultimate significance has a wider biblical pedigree than the meal-sharings of Jesus. The Passover itself was foundational as the feast of liberation from the slavery of Egypt. A tradition grew up during the time of the major prophets of the future hope of a Messianic banquet when, in a feast of plenty, present woes would be replaced by festivity and rejoicing (see Isaiah 25:6–9). Already in the Passover celebration, there was a looking backwards and a looking forwards, a remembrance and a hope, a return and an anticipation.

These elements are all taken up in the words and actions of the Lord's Supper, provision of the necessity of daily bread for all, welcoming and including, remembering and hoping. There are other elements also. The feast is a moment of glory unveiled, which is both rooted in the present moment and an anticipation of future peace. It is a moment of sacrifice; we remember that blood biblically stands for life rather than death. In the sacrificial act, the broken is restored, the relationship with God we have lost is remade through the initiative of Jesus' giving of himself. Above all, the breaking of the bread and the sharing of the wine is a moment of presence, both holy and wholly worldly.

> In Holy Communion, the liturgical action reaches its peak: here human beings share in the life of the social God, the eucharistic God, the God of the common life. Here God becomes as small as a piece of bread, and little people taste the wonder of eternity. In this essentially social act, the mystical quest becomes one with the quest for community and equality among people. (Leach 1985 p. 293)

Paradigm

'While they were eating, Jesus took a loaf of bread, and after blessing it he broke it, gave it to his disciples and said, "Take, eat; this is my body"' (26:26). In the breaking of the bread, Jesus enacts a sign of his own willingness to allow the breaking of his body to make us whole, to restore our broken relationships with God and with one another. Taking, blessing, breaking, giving – the four central acts of the Communion action are far more than mere liturgy; they are given as a paradigm for the life of discipleship in the world. When in 1 Corinthians 11:24 Paul quotes Jesus saying: 'Do this to remember me', the 'doing' is not confined to the action within the Communion liturgy; 'doing' flows out of the new life of discipleship in the new covenant created by Jesus' life and death, recalled at every Lord's Table, enacted in daily living.

Like all good liturgy, the celebration of the Eucharist sends us out and moves us on to live with a new faith and energy in the midst of the world. Duncan Forrester strikes the right note:

330

But the Lord's Supper must be, and is, far more than exemplary and challenging to the lovelessness and injustices of the world. It nourishes holiness and right action. In it we find the presence of God and our neighbour, forgiveness, grace, solidarity and peace. The lifestyle of the disciples that flows from the Lord's Supper is not a matter of anxious ethical striving, or the earning of merit. It is rather to do with the nourishing of disciples, and setting them free to allow grace to flow through them to the world. The Supper frees us from obsession with ourselves to give our loving, unselfconscious attention to God, our neighbours and the needs of the world. For holiness is a matter of delight rather than effort. (Forrester 2005 pp. 120–1)

Bread for the world

Allow me one final story concerning Communion. Not long after the death of George MacLeod, Iain Mackenzie, late of the BBC, paid tribute to George in a Glasgow lecture. In it, he spoke of how, for more than one generation of Presbyterians, George, particularly on Iona, had brought the Communion alive with an unforgettable sense of pulsating power and presence. More than anyone else in the Church of Scotland, George had revivified the Communion tradition. Yet, towards the end of his life, in his increasingly frail nineties, George told Iain of this experience (Iain was trying to persuade George to do an interview for television):

He had been walking up the Mound to the General Assembly Service of Holy Communion, and was suddenly stopped in his tracks by a devastating thought. 'Why am I going to this so-called Communion? Am I really saying that Christ's presence is more real in bread and wine than in the whole of life? We don't touch God in dedicated bread. We touch reality everywhere. We should just get on with it.'

I said, 'Do you want to say that on film tomorrow, you who have made Holy Communion central again in Presbyterianism?'

'If I have made Communion central,' he said, 'then I have failed. I only wanted to make love central.'

(Ian Mackenzie, in lecture delivered to Institute of Contemporary Scotland (ICS), 7 June 2001, printed in the *Scottish Review*, January–June 2007 p. 69)

I'm not sure why Iain Mackenzie calls George MacLeod's thought 'devastating'. It seems to me that all George was doing was giving articulation to what his life was about, that the distinction between the material and the spiritual, the holy and the worldly is spurious, and God is found in the whole of life, and the liturgical act of Communion is there to make us aware of the communion of the Holy Spirit which is all around us. And love is central. Let these words ring in our ears as we go from the warmth of the common table into the cold darkness of Gethsemane. 'Love is central.'

Study

By yourself

Use this hymn verse as a prayer.

> Round your table, through your giving,
> show us how to live and pray
> till your kingdom's way of living
> is the bread we share each day:
> bread for us and for our neighbour,
> bread for body, mind and soul,
> bread of heaven and human labour –
> broken bread that makes us whole.

> (from *CH4* 2005 no. 655 verse 3)

Chapter 34

THE DARK NIGHT

Matthew 26:31–75
Jesus Predicts Peter's Denial
(Mark 14:27–31, Luke 22:31–4, John 13:36–8)

Then Jesus said to them, 'This very night all of you will run away and leave me, for the scripture says, "God will kill the shepherd, and the sheep of the flock will be scattered." But after I am raised to life, I will go to Galilee ahead of you.'

Peter spoke up and said to Jesus, 'I will never leave you, even though all the rest do!'

Jesus said to Peter, 'I tell you that before the cock crows tonight, you will say three times that you do not know me.'

Peter answered, 'I will never say that, even if I have to die with you!'

And all the other disciples said the same thing.

Jesus Prays in Gethesemane
(Mark 14:32–42, Luke 22:39–46)

Then Jesus went with his disciples to a place called Gethsemane, and he said to them, 'Sit here while I go over there and pray.' He took with him Peter and the two sons of Zebedee. Grief and anguish came over him, and he said to them, 'The sorrow in my heart is so great that it almost crushes me. Stay here and keep watch with me.'

He went a little farther on, threw himself face downwards on the ground, and prayed, 'My Father, if it is possible, take this cup of suffering from me! Yet not what I want, but what you want.'

Then he returned to the three disciples and found them asleep; and he said to Peter, 'How is it that you three were not able to keep watch with me even for one hour? Keep watch and pray that you will not fall into temptation. The spirit is willing, but the flesh is weak.'

Once more Jesus went away and prayed, 'My Father, if this cup of suffering cannot be taken away unless I drink it, your will be done.' He returned once more and found the disciples asleep; they could not keep their eyes open.

Again Jesus left them, went away, and prayed the third time, saying the same words. Then he returned to the disciples and said, 'Are you still sleeping and resting? Look! The hour has come for the Son of Man to be handed over to the power of sinners. Get up, let us go. Look, here is the man who is betraying me!'

The Arrest of Jesus

(Mark 14:43–50, Luke 22:47–53, John 18:3–12)

Jesus was still speaking when Judas, one of the twelve disciples, arrived. With him was a large crowd armed with swords and clubs and sent by the chief priests and the elders. The traitor had given the crowd a signal: 'The man I kiss is the one you want. Arrest him!'

Judas went straight to Jesus and said, 'Peace be with you, Teacher', and kissed him.

Jesus answered, 'Be quick about it, friend!'

Then they came up, arrested Jesus and held him tight. One of those who were with Jesus drew his sword and struck at the High Priest's slave, cutting off his ear. 'Put your sword back in its place', Jesus said to him. 'All who take the sword will die by the sword. Don't you know that I could call on my Father for help, and at once he would send me more than twelve armies of angels? But in that case, how would the Scriptures come true which say that this is what must happen?'

Then Jesus spoke to the crowd, 'Did you have to come with swords and clubs to capture me, as though I were an outlaw? Every day I sat down and taught in the Temple, and you did not arrest me. But all this has happened in order to make what the prophets wrote in the Scriptures come true.'

Then all the disciples left him and ran away.

Jesus Before the Council

(Mark 14:53–65, Luke 22:54–5, 63–71, John 18:13–14, 19–24)

Those who had arrested Jesus took him to the house of Caiaphas, the High Priest, where the teachers of the Law and the elders had gathered together. Peter followed from a distance, as far as the courtyard of the High Priest's house. He went into the courtyard and sat down with the guards to see how it would all come out. The chief priests and the whole Council tried to find some false evidence against Jesus to put him to death; but they could not find any, even though many people came forward and told lies about him. Finally two men stepped up and said, 'This man said, "I am able to tear down God's Temple and three days later build it up again."'

The High Priest stood up and said to Jesus, 'Have you no answer to give to this accusation against you?' But Jesus kept quiet. Again the High Priest spoke to him, 'In the name of the living God I now put you on oath: tell us if you are the Messiah, the Son of God.'

Jesus answered, 'So you say. But I tell all of you: from this time on you will see the Son of Man sitting on the right of the Almighty and coming on the clouds of heaven!'

At this the High Priest tore his clothes and said, 'Blasphemy! We don't need any more witnesses! You have just heard his blasphemy! What do you think?'

They all answered, 'He is guilty and must die.'

Then they spat in his face and beat him; and those who slapped him said, 'Prophesy for us, Messiah! Guess who hit you!'

Peter Denies Jesus

(Mark 14:66–72, Luke 22:56–62, John 18:15–18, 25–7)

Peter was sitting outside in the courtyard when one of the High Priest's servant women came to him and said, 'You, too, were with Jesus of Galilee.'

But he denied it in front of them all. 'I don't know what you are talking about', he answered, and went on out to the entrance of the courtyard. Another servant woman saw him and said to the men there, 'He was with Jesus of Nazareth.'

Again Peter denied it and answered, 'I swear that I don't know that man!'

After a little while the men standing there came to Peter. 'Of course you are one of them', they said. 'After all, the way you speak gives you away!'

Then Peter said, 'I swear that I am telling the truth! May God punish me if I am not! I do not know that man!'

Just then a cock crowed, and Peter remembered what Jesus had told him: 'Before the cock crows, you will say three times that you do not know me.' He went out and wept bitterly.

Disintegration

From the safety and solidarity of the upper room, Jesus leads the disciples out into the exposure of the dark and threatening night. The darkness deepens with Jesus' forthright prediction to the disciple band that they will all desert him at the moment of his greatest trial. If they have ears to hear, however, they will find comfort in his promise that he will go before them back into Galilee. Matthew seeks to give weight to this incident by quoting scripture. The reference to Zechariah 13:7 uses the familiar image of sheep and shepherd. As confrontation ahead beckons, we are reminded of the distinction between Jesus as the true shepherd, following in the line of the prophets, and the false shepherds of the people who will so soon condemn him.

Peter strenuously refutes Jesus' foreboding: 'Not me, I will never desert you' (26:14). Jesus replies by predicting Peter's threefold denial before cockcrow. 'Deny' is of course the word which Jesus used at the key moment of Caesarea Philippi (16:13–28) when Peter first called him 'the Christ' and Jesus made plain the coming crossway for both himself and disciples: 'let them deny themselves and take up their cross and follow me' (16:24). Peter and the disciples together promise faithfulness even to death. Events will prove otherwise.

'Gethsemane can I forget?'

The little band has arrived at the garden of Gethsemane. Jesus bids the majority of the disciples to sit and wait for him while he goes to pray. He takes with him Peter, James and John. We think of them as forming an inner core to the twelve; perhaps there is another reason for their being chosen to accompany Jesus into this moment of struggle and agony. These three have all given evidence of not understanding the nature of Jesus' mission and purpose. Peter earned rebuke at Caesarea Philippi by calling into question Jesus' embrace of the crossway (16:22–3), and James and John have shown profound misunderstanding of the dynamics of the new community born from under the cross in accompanying their mother's request for them to have the seats of honour in the coming kingdom (20:20–1). At this place, they will learn that the Kingdom will only come through the deepest suffering, struggle and self-denial.

They begin their watch over Jesus' agony. Jesus shows visible signs of distress and gives voice to his pain. It is one of very few moments in the gospel when we are given any entrance into Jesus' inner feelings; here the pain is palpable. Jesus' words echo the cry of Psalms 42 and 43: 'Why are you cast down, O my soul, and why are you disquieted within me?' (NRSV). Psalm 42 quotes the adversaries of the Psalmist asking the mocking question: 'Where is your God?' (Psalm 42:10). A sense of absence, silence, aloneness falls on the scene. That sense of absence and silence from heaven pervades the Passion narrative. It raises the question acutely: 'Where is God in all of this?' Jesus has come into the world to bring heaven near; now, alone, Jesus goes apart to wrestle with heaven's silence.

He falls to the ground in an attitude of struggle and surrender. The weight of the world's sin and pain lies heavy upon him. He first prays: 'Father, let this cup pass from me, if it is possible; yet not what I want, but what you want' (26:39). The disciples, fearful and exhausted, sleep. They are not there for him. Jesus prays a second time: 'My father, if this cup cannot pass unless I drink it, your will be done' (26:42). The use of the petition from the Lord's Prayer, 'your will be done', is striking. It gets to the heart of the matter of Jesus' surrender to the will of the Father, in spite of everything; it is also a reminder of the link between the prayer of Jesus and the prayers of his disciples. This is our prayer also, if we dare to make it. Once again, the disciples are found sleeping. Once more, Jesus goes apart for his third time of prayer, praying the same words.

Now the struggle before the struggle, the act before the act, is over; Jesus has lived through his time of prayerful waiting. He is ready. He returns to the sleeping disciples. 'Get up, the time has come, it's time to move on.' They are going nowhere; it is the action which moves on. Judas, the betrayer, is seen approaching.

Gethsemane is a place where we can only watch and wait. It is a place which calls us to be still and to suspend our ordinary rationality before a situation too deep for our everyday thoughts and words. If not prostrate, we fall to our knees. Only the prayer-filled cry from the heart will suffice. Yet, out of the struggle in the darkness and the surrender to the silent absence comes a renewed will, an ability to face what lies before. Henri Nouwen, looking forward to the cross, plumbs well the mystery of this deep prayer when he writes:

> In prayer, God's presence is never separated from God's absence and God's absence is never separated from God's presence. The presence of God is so much beyond the human experience of being together that it quite easily is perceived as absence. The absence of God, on the other hand, is often so deeply felt that it leads to a new sense of God's presence. This is powerfully expressed in Psalm 22:1–5:
>
> > My God, my God, why have you deserted me?
> > How far from saving me, the words I groan!
> > I call all day, my God, but you never answer,
> > all night long I call and cannot rest.
> >
> > Yet, Holy One you
> > who make your home in the praises of Israel,
> > in you our fathers put their trust,
> > they trusted and you rescued them,
> > they called to you for help and they were saved,
> > they never trusted you in vain.
>
> The prayer not only is the expression of the people of Israel, but also the culmination of the Christian experience. When Jesus spoke these words on the cross, total aloneness and full acceptance touched each other. In that moment of complete emptiness all was fulfilled. In that

hour of darkness new light was seen. While death was witnessed, life was affirmed. Where God's absence was most loudly expressed, God's presence was most profoundly revealed ... It is into this mystery that we enter when we pray. (Nouwen from 'Reaching Out', quoted in 2000 p. 173)

The fatal kiss

With a kiss. It is with the kiss of Judas Iscariot that Jesus is given over into the hands of his enemies. Is this history's most fateful kiss? Why the kiss? The question could mean: why did Judas do it? What lay behind his terrible act of betrayal? Was it disillusionment with Jesus, or with the whole discipleship movement; was it an arrogant and mistaken attempt to force Jesus to show the power of his hand; was it born out of the sense of an imagined slight; was it for a reason completely different? 'For the money' is one of the less likely answers; thirty pieces of silver was a fairly meagre sum. We could, and people do, speculate endlessly about the motivation which drove Judas to this act. There has grown up quite an industry of books about Judas.

The question 'Why the kiss?' could also be asking: 'Was the kiss necessary?' It is argued that the authorities would know Jesus well enough to make their own recognition without the help of a mole from within the camp. On the other hand, Jesus was a relative outsider in Jerusalem; at his entry into the city, the people of Jerusalem had to ask: 'Who is he?' (21:10). The authorities may have had good cause to be grateful for the recruiting of an insider to ensure that they got the right man. And it was night. However the 'Why the kiss?' question is answered, the kiss remains as a moment of a cruel betrayal of faith. To kiss implies intimacy, defencelessness, welcome. These are all scorned and devalued by Judas' action. Yet Jesus, at the very least, offers no resistance to the traitor's advance. He invites recognition. There is this strange sense of Jesus using the malign motivations and actions of his enemies to fit his own purposes, bending history by his surrender.

As shameful as the kiss are the words of Judas' greeting of Jesus: 'Peace be with you' (26:49). 'Peace be with you' was a familiar and conventional greeting. In this context, it is charged with heavy irony; what Judas is doing is to cause Jesus the greatest of dis-peace. Remember the greeting, we will meet it again as the first words that the risen Jesus will speak to his disciples (28:9). There, they become the words of a glorious benediction. Judas also greets Jesus not as 'Lord', as he is usually called by his disciples, but as 'teacher', a term of address used frequently by his enemies.

The useless sword

This section begins with the description of Jesus, still speaking to his disciples in the garden, being interrupted by a considerable crowd of heavily armed men sent by the authorities to arrest Jesus. The numbers and force employed suggest overkill on the part of fearful authority – or is it an attempt at intimidation of Jesus' followers? Their rough seizure of Jesus provokes a reaction on the part of one of the disciples (only named as Peter in John 18:10). The disciple draws his sword and cuts off the ear of the High Priest's slave. Jesus tells the disciple to put his sword away, quoting: 'All who take the sword will die by the sword' (26:33). Armed resistance is futile; it is also quite at odds with who Jesus is and what his movement is about. At this moment, it is peculiarly counter-productive, understandable but quite wrong-headed; Jesus is on his way to making the ultimate act of non-violent resistance in the face of his enemies and the enemies of humanity, human and demonic.

An over-zealous author?

Matthew continues by putting on the lips of Jesus a piece of rhetoric in which he says that, if he wished, he could call down the hosts of heaven to intervene on his behalf at this moment. He won't, as to do so would prevent the fulfilment of the scriptures. This provokes the interesting comment from Gabriel Josipovici:

> In his anxiety to drive home the reasons for Jesus' life and actions Matthew throws away his strongest card. By making fulfilment appear to be purely mechanical, he seems to deny Jesus his power of choice and so, ultimately, his humanity. This comes out clearly in the great scene which Matthew describes so graphically, when, in the garden of Gethsemane, one of Jesus' followers takes out a sword to defend him:

> Then said Jesus unto him, Put up again thy sword into his place: for all they that take the sword shall perish with the sword. Thinkest thou that I cannot now pray to my Father, and he shall presently give me more than twelve legions of angels? But how then shall the scriptures be fulfilled, that this must be? (Matthew 26:52-4 KJV)

Matthew subverts Jesus' real message here by his manner of telling. For if Jesus' weakness, his humanity, is only a front, only there to bring about the fulfilment of prophecy, then it is no different, in essence, from the deployment of twelve legions of angels. We can no more identify with Jesus, respond to his plight, in the one case than in the other. (Josipivici 1988 pp. 214–15)

It is precisely the willing powerlessness of Jesus, his handing over of himself defenceless into the hands of his enemies throughout the Passion, at which we marvel. This is new truth, revelation indeed.

The arrest sequence has a twofold ending. Jesus upbraids his captors over the amount of power assembled to take him captive, and over the manner of his arrest by force and under cover of darkness. He stresses that he has not been hiding; on the contrary, he has been highly visible, teaching in the Temple in the previous days. Why not arrest him then? We know the answer: the authorities' fear of the people (26:4). Finally, we are told of the flight of his disciples. Jesus is faced not only with the strength of his enemies but also by the betrayal and desertion of his friends. Now he stands alone.

Before Caiaphas: kangaroo court

It stinks! This first trial of Jesus before the religious authorities of his own people gives off a very unpleasant odour of malpractice and corruption. The whole scene is heavy with irony and contradiction. One irony pervades it throughout. This trial is convened by those charged with upholding the faith laws of their people – the Temple establishment, the scribes as guardians of the Law and the elders – but the trial which they convene is illegal. It was not lawful to have such a trial during the hours of darkness. From the outset, Matthew states that the authorities had no interest in mounting a fair trial; they simply wanted to find a plausible excuse, with the help of false witnesses, to do away with Jesus. Unfortunately, they couldn't get their witnesses' testimonies to agree with one another, so there was no corroboration until, at last, a pair of witnesses both testified that Jesus had threatened to destroy the Temple and raise it in three days. Irony again: in their terms, their witness was false, as Jesus had not threatened physically to destroy the Jerusalem Temple and raise it again; but, in Jesus' own Passion, these words are fulfilled.

Jesus refuses to answer the charges brought against him. When the trial reaches its peak and Caiaphas asks Jesus under oath (remember Jesus' words on oaths in 5:33–7) if he is the Messiah, Jesus' reply is cryptic: 'You say so'. However, he then goes on to elaborate his answer using his own name for himself, 'the Son of Man'. He speaks of his enthronement in heaven and his role as judge (see again Daniel 7:13–14). The accused turns accuser. It is more than enough for Caiaphas and his coterie. With a show of dismay, the high priest tears at his clothes and shouts: 'Blasphemy'. The verdict is the unanimous one of 'Guilty, deserving death'. How ironic that the religious establishment, with the presence of the holy standing before them, should call the holy one 'blasphemer'. This scene is indeed one of a clash of powers. On the surface, it seems as if Caiaphas and his henchmen are in control: Jesus is bound and reduced to silence. Yet it is he who, in the few words he utters, speaks truth to power, as Eduard Schweizer writes:

> Matthew emphasises the divine authority of Jesus: he could destroy the Temple and rebuild it, and his Passion is the way to enthronement, so that those who condemn him will know him as Lord of the universe and coming judge. Veiled beneath impotence, in the outcast of Nazareth there is taking place God's saving judgement of the world; the one who renounces all violence and willingly accepts execution is appointed Lord of all the world. (1976 p. 501)

The trial ends with a disgraceful but still all-too-common scene. Having condemned Jesus, his judges descend to degrading him, offering physical and verbal abuse to this bound and powerless human being. They are the ones who are degraded. Would that such scenes were not so prevalent in our world. Thank God for Amnesty International and all those who work to expose such abuses and end them.

Peter's dark night

There is one final scene completing this night's desolation. The show of force at Jesus' arrest and the flight of his disciples is paralleled by the court's sentence of death and Peter's denial (26:69–75). Two distinct forces combine to create Jesus' dereliction: the power of his enemies and the failure of his friends. Now the failure of even the rock, Peter, is exposed honestly and in full view. Peter has come into the courtyard of the high priest, where he waits at a distance to see how things turn out for Jesus. One of the serving girls says to him: 'You were with Jesus, the Galilean'. He denies it. A second serving girl says, not directly to him but to those who are standing around: 'This man was with Jesus of Nazareth'. With a forbidden oath, i.e. more vehemently, he denies it once more. The reference to Galilee and Nazareth is pointed; Galileans were regarded with a mixture of scorn and suspicion by their metropolitan counterparts, just like 'outsiders' in today's world.

The third 'accuser', one of the bystanders, says to Peter: 'You were with him; your accent gives you away'. Again Peter swears an oath, curses and states: 'I do not know the man!' The cock crows. Dawn will come up as usual, but not this day for Peter. Even the rock has crumbled. He remembers Jesus' all-too-accurate prediction. He breaks down and weeps bitter tears of remorse.

Study

By yourself

Read again the story of Jesus in Gethsemane (26:34–46). Visualise the scene ... be present and awake with Jesus. What do you notice, feel, think? What do these moments say to you about Jesus and about prayer?

The trial of Jesus before the high priest is a story of injustice and torture. Find out more about the victims of injustice and torture in the contemporary world (Amnesty International and the Medical Campaign for the Victims of Torture are good sources). Reflect on what part you can play in the struggle against such dehumanisation.

For group work

Read Matthew 26:31–75 together. The passage naturally splits into two halves and tells of two quite different trials, the first half around Jesus' wrestling with God the Father in the garden and the second around the trial before the high priest. Divide your study time in half. Read the whole passage aloud with either one or a number of voices, then read the first half (26:31–46) again and share your reflections upon it. Repeat the process for the second half (26:47–75).

Chapter 35

TRIALS

Matthew 27:1–26
Jesus is Taken to Pilate
(Mark 15:1, Luke 23:1–2, John 18:28–32)

Early in the morning all the chief priests and the elders made their plans against Jesus to put him to death. They put him in chains, led him off, and handed him over to Pilate, the Roman governor.

The Death of Judas
(Acts 1:18–19)

When Judas, the traitor, learnt that Jesus had been condemned, he repented and took back the 30 silver coins to the chief priests and the elders. 'I have sinned by betraying an innocent man to death!' he said.

'What do we care about that?' they answered. 'That is your business!'

Judas threw the coins down in the Temple and left; then he went off and hanged himself.

The chief priests picked up the coins and said, 'This is blood money, and it is against our Law to put it in the temple treasury.' After reaching an agreement about it, they used the money to buy Potter's Field, as a cemetery for foreigners. That is why that field is called 'Field of Blood' to this very day.

Then what the prophet Jeremiah has said came true, 'They took the thirty silver coins, the amount the people of Israel had agreed to pay for him, and used the money to buy the potter's field, as the Lord had commanded me.'

Pilate Questions Jesus

(Mark 15:2–5, Luke 23:3–5, John 18:33–8)

Jesus stood before the Roman governor, who questioned him. 'Are you the king of the Jews?' he asked.

'So you say', answered Jesus. But he said nothing in response to the accusations of the chief priests and elders.

So Pilate said to him, 'Don't you hear all these things they accuse you of?'

But Jesus refused to answer a single word, with the result that the Governor was greatly surprised.

Jesus is Sentenced to Death

(Mark 15:6–15, Luke 23:13–25, John 18:39—19:6)

At every Passover Festival the Roman governor was in the habit of setting free any one prisoner the crowd asked for. At that time there was a well-known prisoner named Jesus Barabbas. So when the crowd gathered, Pilate asked them, 'Which one do you want me to set free for you? Jesus Barabbas or Jesus called the Messiah?' He knew very well that the Jewish authorities had handed Jesus over to him because they were jealous.

While Pilate was sitting in the judgement hall, his wife sent him a message: 'Have nothing to do with that innocent man, because in a dream last night I suffered much on account of him.'

The chief priests and the elders persuaded the crowd to ask Pilate to set Barabbas free and have Jesus put to death. But Pilate asked the crowd, 'Which one of these two do you want me to set free for you?'

'Barabbas!' they answered.

'What, then, shall I do with Jesus called the Messiah?' Pilate asked them.

'Crucify him!' they all answered.

But Pilate asked, 'What crime has he committed?'

Then they started shouting at the top of their voices, 'Crucify him!'

When Pilate saw that it was no use to go on, but that a riot might break out, he took some water, washed his hands in front of the crowd, and said, 'I am not responsible for the death of this man! This is your doing!'

The whole crowd answered, 'Let the responsibility for his death fall on us and our children!'

Then Pilate set Barabbas free for them, and after he had Jesus whipped, he handed him over to be crucified.

'The Field of Blood'

'There was evening and there was morning, the first day' (Genesis 1:5 NRSV). For Jesus' people, the new day began at sundown. The final day of Jesus' earthly life started with the sharing of the meal together in the upper room; it has already run much of its tumultuous course with the agony in the garden, betrayal, arrest, the trial before Caiaphas, the desertion of the disciples and the denial of Peter. Now, at daybreak, the religious opposition make their preparations to ensure Jesus' death. He is bound, led off and handed over to Pilate, the Roman governor, the one who has the power of life and death over him. The contrast between Jesus' present powerlessness and the authority which he displayed throughout his ministry of healing and welcome in Galilee, where the power he wrought for good was evident to people's amazement, is stark. Yet he is no less the holy one of God in his present state; here indeed is the culminating fulfilment of his vocation.

Before Matthew takes his readers to the confrontation between Jesus and Pilate, there is a diversion to make known the fate of Judas, the betrayer. Matthew may well be drawing on legend which sprang up early about Judas' end. Schweizer forensically dissects how the legend grew in pages 502–5 of his commentary, *The Good News according to Matthew*. The picture Matthew gives us is of Judas being stricken with remorse on learning of Jesus' condemnation by the authorities. He recognises himself as guilty, guilty of betraying the blood of an innocent man. He goes to the authorities, who give him short shrift; they will accept no responsibility. Throwing down the blood money in the Temple court, he goes off and hangs himself. Is his death the suicide of a despairing man, or his own attempt at justice for being implicated in the death of the innocent Jesus?

The authorities now do display some scruples. They refuse to return what is now 'blood money' to the Temple treasury; instead, they use it to buy 'the potter's field' as a cemetery for foreigners. Matthew says this was done to fulfil a prophecy of Jeremiah. In fact, the quotation cited (27:9–10) is from Zechariah 11:12–13. While the quotation is wrongly attributed, the buying of the potter's field reflects the content of Jeremiah 18–19 and 32:6–15. There is an irony here, that the money which has been used to betray Jesus, whose mission at the end will expand to include welcome to all people (28:16–20), is finally put to use to provide a resting place in death for outsiders and strangers.

In a Glasgow cemetery, there is an area, largely unmarked, which is used as a burial place for those in the city who have no known relatives or friends able to be responsible for their funeral arrangements. Many of those who find a last resting place there are homeless men. Campbell Robertson was a Church of Scotland minister who had an outstanding ministry among Glasgow's homeless in the 1970s and 80s. When he died too young of cancer in his fifties, it was his wish that he should be buried in that same plot as the homeless among whom he had lived and worked. He had become an outsider to be with outsiders in the name of Jesus, who, in Matthew's story, is now about to be crucified, 'outside the gate' (Hebrews 13:12). So, the work and witness continues.

Before Pilate

The narrative returns to focus on Jesus, now standing before the Roman governor, Pilate. The governor's initial question is the one we would expect him to ask: 'Are you the king of the Jews?' (27:11). Pilate's concern is with order and power – any threat to order within his jurisdiction, any rising opposing power, must be dealt with firmly and ruthlessly. The only answer Jesus makes before Pilate is to respond to this first question with the enigmatic 'You say so', the same response he has made to Caiaphas (26:64). To the accusations of the chief priests and elders, Jesus says nothing, even after the prompting of Pilate. The silence is eerie. By Jesus' silence, Pilate is described as 'greatly amazed', the same word as has been used earlier in the gospel to show the reaction of the people to Jesus' teaching and healing (e.g. 7:28–9, 9:33). This silence in the face of accusation and suffering recalls the reader to the song of the suffering servant in Isaiah 53, here in particular Isaiah 53:7.

'With the elite's accusations, Jesus' silence, and Pilate's amazement, the questioning is now finished! No witnesses; no clarification of the charges; no oaths; no verdict; not even a convinced judge' (Carter 2000 p. 525). Under the façade of imperial justice, the proceedings are murky indeed. Pilate now raises the possibility of releasing Jesus under the custom of releasing a prisoner to the people on the occasion of Passover. He gives them a choice, Jesus Son of Man or Jesus Barabbas, a 'notorious' criminal whose name ironically means, 'son of the father'. Pilate strays on dangerous ground, given the ability of the Temple authorities to whip up the local crowd; before a decision is reached there is an interruption.

Pilate's wife

The interruption, only found in Matthew, comes in the form of a message to the governor from his wife. It comes to Pilate, sitting on the seat of judgement. Irony again: throughout the story of the crucifixion, the question of who is being judged lurks under the surface. Pilate's wife has had a dream on the previous night which has caused her much pain. Its import is to refuse to condemn the innocent man Jesus. This interruption by a Gentile woman who has received a communication via a dream (26:19) reminds us of the Gentile magi, at the start of the gospel, who were also warned in a dream to avoid Herod on their way home after finding the young child Jesus at Bethlehem (2:12). At both the beginning and end of the gospel, we find Gentiles in receipt of revelation.

Clean hands and blood guilt

The warning is in vain, as Pilate is intent on avoiding trouble rather than administering justice; he provides a classic example of the powerlessness of power. The chief priests and elders have primed the crowd to shout for Barabbas and to clamour for Jesus' crucifixion.

Sensing the start of a riot, at an incendiary time when keeping the peace was paramount, Pilate feels trapped. He asks for a basin of water and symbolically washes his hands before the people, seeking to deny his complicity in the death of Jesus. 'I am innocent of this man's blood' (26:28). The crowd makes its notorious response: 'His blood be on us and our children!' While the crowd has been pictured as ambivalent, this is the first instance in the gospel of their depiction as totally hostile to Jesus. Who are the crowd? They are largely the local Jerusalem population, duped by their cynical and self-serving leaders. Christian history has too frequently demonised them to include the whole Jewish people with shameful and catastrophic results. The truth is that we are witnessing the last stages of a bitter family fight within Judaism, since the destruction of the Temple, between the Jewish followers of Jesus and the newly emerging Jewish leadership. The Jesus group are seeking to open up their fellowship; post-Temple Judaism seeks to ensure its future by advocating the keeping of the Law with a new rigour. The lesson is to avoid the poison of family fights, wherever they occur.

Without due process of law, Jesus is condemned by Pilate. Once again, his condemnation becomes an excuse for abuse and humiliation. Handwashing or not, Pilate orders the prisoner to be flogged. Jesus is handed over to be crucified.

Study

By yourself
What happened when Pilate got home after his day's work in the seat of judgement? Write an imaginary conversation between Pilate and his wife as Pilate seeks to justify his actions and his wife pleads the cause of the innocent Jesus.

Chapter 36

THE COSMIC CROSS

Matthew 27:27–56

The Soldiers Mock Jesus

(Mark 15:16–20, John 19:2–3)

Then Pilate's soldiers took Jesus into the governor's palace, and the whole company gathered round him. They stripped off his clothes and put a scarlet robe on him. Then they made a crown out of thorny branches and placed it on his head, and put a stick in his right hand; then they knelt before him and mocked him. 'Long live the King of the Jews!' they said. They spat on him, and took the stick and hit him over the head. When they had finished mocking him, they took the robe off and put his own clothes back on him. Then they led him out to crucify him.

Jesus is Crucified

(Mark 15:21–32, Luke 23:26–43, John 19:17–27)

As they were going out, they met a man from Cyrene named Simon, and the soldiers forced him to carry Jesus' cross. They came to a place called Golgotha, which means, 'The Place of the Skull'. There they offered Jesus wine mixed with a bitter substance; but after tasting it, he would not drink it.

They crucified him and then divided his clothes among them by throwing dice. After that they sat there and watched him. Above his head they put the written notice of the accusation against him, 'This is Jesus, the King of the Jews'. Then they crucified two bandits with Jesus, one on his right and the other on his left.

People passing by shook their heads and hurled insults at Jesus: 'You were going to tear down the Temple and build it up again in three days! Save yourself if you are God's Son! Come on down from the cross!'

In the same way the chief priests and the teachers of the Law and the elders jeered at him: 'He saved others, but he cannot save himself! Isn't he the king of Israel? If he comes down off the cross now, we will believe in him! He trusts in God and claims to be God's Son. Well, then, let us see if God wants to save him now!'

Even the bandits who had been crucified with him insulted him in the same way.

The Death of Jesus

(Mark 15:33–41, Luke 23:44–9, John 19:28–30)

At noon the whole country was covered with darkness, which lasted for three hours. At about three o'clock Jesus cried out with a loud shout, '*Eli, Eli, lema sabachthani?*' which means, 'My God, my God, why did you abandon me?'

Some of the people standing there heard him and said, 'He is calling for Elijah!' One of them ran up at once, took a sponge, soaked it in cheap wine, put it on the end of a stick, and tried to make him drink it.

But the others said, 'Wait, let us see if Elijah is coming to save him!'

Jesus again gave a loud cry and breathed his last.

Then the curtain hanging in the Temple was torn in two from top to bottom. The earth shook, the rocks split apart, the graves broke open, and many of God's people who had died were raised to life. They left the graves, and after Jesus rose from death, they went into the Holy City, where many people saw them.

When the army officer and the soldiers with him who were watching Jesus saw the earthquake and everything else that happened, they were terrified and said, 'He really was the Son of God!'

There were many women there, looking on from a distance, who had followed Jesus from Galilee and helped him. Among them were Mary Magdalene, Mary the mother of James and Joseph, and the wife of Zebedee.

More torture

The journey of which we had intimation as early as Matthew 16 inches its way to Golgotha. Before setting out on the final stage, Jesus has to endure one further episode of pain and indignity, so often the lot of political prisoners then and now. Pilate's soldiers assemble to abuse Jesus; Matthew reports that 'the whole company [cohort]' (27:27) gathers. A cohort was upwards of 600 men: here is both a display of imperial might and a claustrophobic sense of intimidation. They take and strip Jesus. Mockingly for them, ironically for the reader, they put on him a scarlet robe and twist a crown of thorns around his head, fake symbols of kingship. The red robe of suffering and the jagged thorns of pain are all too real. They signify the road Jesus has willed to take rather than the world's way of oppressive domination. They simulate obeisance by kneeling before him and calling out, 'Hail, King of the Jews!' 'Some king', they cry in mockery; 'some king', we cry in amazement.

The soldiers have also given him a false sceptre which they then use to beat him once more. Their spitting, like that of the Sanhedrin earlier (26:67), recalls two of Isaiah's servant songs, both Isaiah 50:6 and the whole of 53. Jesus endures both physical pain and verbal mockery. His silence is palpable; his lack of struggle in contrast to the soldiers' violent abuse of power is humbling. Having put his own clothes back on him, they lead him away to be crucified.

Crucifixion

The final stages of Jesus' walk to the cross begin (27:32). An African, Simon of Cyrene, is pressed into service to carry Jesus' cross, perhaps because successive beatings have left him too weak to carry it himself. The presence of another Simon reminds us of the absence of Simon Peter, the one who would be expected to be at Jesus' side in the time of his greatest need. The sad procession eventually reaches the designated place of crucifixion, called Golgotha, probably through the skull-like shape of the little hill outside the city wall. It may well also have been close by a busy thoroughfare; the Romans chose to crucify their victims where the example of the victims' death could be displayed to the best possible advantage. In mockery, a drink of vinegary wine mixed with gall is offered to Jesus; he does not drink it. Throughout the crucifixion scene, there are echoes of the psalms of lament; here, Psalm 69:21 is clearly in mind.

Matthew records the actual crucifixion in a subordinate clause (27:35) – a strange downplaying of a crucial moment. He records the soldiers casting lots for the condemned man's clothes; another echo, this time from Psalm 22:18. Jesus, naked, hangs on the cross while the soldiers keep watch. As we watch, we feel his painful vulnerability; we also see that, stripped bare, he has nothing to hide. This is his true self, the moment when he most clearly reveals who he is, not by his physical nakedness, but in his awesome act of giving. Ironically, the soldiers also attest to his identity with the charge sheet that they nail above his head: 'This is Jesus, the King of the Jews'.

Two bandits are crucified with him, one on his left and one on his right. The picture of Jesus hanging between the two criminals offers an ironic reversal of the usual trappings of the royal throne of kingship, yet the cross is indeed a judgement seat on us and our world. The presence of the criminals also recalls ironically the incident with James and John and their request to sit at the places of honour in the heavenly kingdom (20:20–8).

Bandits, bystanders, chief priests, scribes and elders combine to shower a hail of mockery on their helpless and silent victim (see Isaiah 53:7). It is worth noting the unholy combination from across society who come together to abuse Jesus, from the lawless criminals to the upholders of the Law who, however, have given clear evidence of their cynical disregard for justice in the trumped-up trial of Jesus. Each of the taunts invites Jesus to end his agony by stepping down from the cross to which he is bound. Much of their abuse comes from the accusations made against Jesus – destroying the Temple and raising it in three days, claiming to be 'King of Israel', 'Son of God'. In all the accusations, there is more than a grain of ironic truth. It will take three days for Jesus' vindication. 'He trusts in God; let God deliver him now.' One taunt stands out: 'He saved others; he cannot save himself' (27:42). Had the mockers said: 'He saved others; he *will* not save himself', they would surely have been right.

Jesus dies

As an untimely darkness falls upon the scene, the taunts subside. From noon until three in the afternoon, a thick gloom envelops Golgotha. It seems, the very elements grieve through the death throes of Jesus. Silence also reigns apart from one terrible word from the cross. Matthew, like Mark, records the cry of Jesus, so vital that it is rendered first in his own Hebrew tongue: 'Eli, Eli, lama sabachthani?' 'My God, my God, why have you forsaken me?' It is a moment of utter and complete aloneness and abandonment. The one who at the gospel's outset was called 'Emmanuel', 'God with us' (1:23), feels now without God, God-forsaken. Never is the sense of absence greater. Yet the paradox is that it is through this time of absence that we learn of the reality of an unbreakable presence. Jesus, in his humanity, knows this experience of God-less-ness, and it is with that knowledge he remains Emmanuel, God with us in our most dire moments of godforsakenness and abandonment.

The bystanders mishear Jesus' cry. They think he is calling for Elijah to come and save him; we remember Jesus has said that Elijah has already come in John the Baptist (11:13). Once more, they give him wine to drink. Soon, with a loud voice, Jesus cries out and 'breathes his last/gives up his spirit' (27:50). In the words of John's gospel: 'It is completed' (John 19:30). There is perhaps an echo of the cry of the righteous man to God for justice in Psalm 22 at verses 2, 5 and 24. The answer is not yet.

The cosmic cross

Matthew, however, gives four 'signs' which follow hard on Jesus' death. The first and last he shares with Mark, whose account of the Passion he has been following closely. The initial sign is that, at the very moment of Jesus' death, the Temple veil was torn in two from top to bottom (27:31). The tearing of the veil is indicative of the beginning of God's judgement on the Temple and its ways. It can also be read as a symbol of the end of the division between Jew and Gentile. Temples in the ancient world were the places of God's dwelling on earth; the tearing veil can also indicate the new reality that God is no longer to be found in this pile of wood and stone, however venerable. Jesus is the new locus of God's dwelling on earth; as 'God with us', he is the new Temple – now destroyed, on the third day raised. Through Jesus, as 1 Peter 2 makes plain, we together are called to be God's Temple, a place of his indwelling on earth.

The final sign is the declaration of the Gentile centurion and his companions, witnesses to all the happenings around Jesus' crucifixion, that 'Truly, this man was God's son' (27:54). The testimony of an outsider and opponent carries its own weight.

In between these first and last signs, Matthew gives two more which are unique to his gospel. He describes an earthquake, in which tombs were open and 'many bodies of the saints who had fallen asleep were raised. After his resurrection they came out of their tombs and entered the holy city and appeared to many.' We find that difficult. There are a number of difficulties. The first is that this part of the account of the crucifixion appears in none of the other gospel accounts. There is no corroboration. The second is that it is an account of such an extraordinary event. We could expect an earthquake to produce such disturbance as to spill some dead bodies from their resting places, particularly when we remember that the usual practice of the times was not to bury bodies in the ground but to lay them in caves and vaults. But for these dead bodies to be raised to life and walk into the city – that's stretching things. It's also stretching things insofar as it diminishes the central thrust of the resurrection of Jesus, which is its uniqueness. It is the very fact that what happens to Jesus after Good Friday does not happen to anyone else which gives it its significance. What's Matthew doing here? It may be that he's simply taking over a tradition which was current in some sections of the early church and repeating it. From the non-canonical gospels, we can see that there were many fantastic traditions about Jesus which did not find their way into our four gospels. What's most striking about them in comparison with some of these more exotic gospels is their restraint and lack of accounts which are bizarrely miraculous. It seems unlikely that Matthew would take over a more outré tradition and repeat it without a good deal of thought. Matthew is a careful editor.

Perhaps this is more likely. Matthew's gospel is strongly eschatological. He sees Jesus, the Messiah, as the one who would bring in the 'Day of the Lord' – that final day of judgement and hope well summed up in the hymn verse:

The day in whose clear-shining light
All wrong shall stand revealed
When justice shall be throned with might
And every hurt be healed;
When knowledge, hand in hand with peace
Shall walk the earth abroad,
The day of perfect righteousness,
The promised Day of God.

(F. L. Hosmer in *CH4* 2005 no. 473)

One of the things hoped for on the great day of judgement, at least by some groups at the time of Jesus, was a general resurrection. Matthew may have inserted this passage because of the general expectation of such a day, and he saw the Easter event being of such significance that the resurrection of these saints was given as a foretaste of what was to come. The earthquake, one of the signs predicted for the Day of the Lord, would certainly fit this interpretation.

Matthew is saying that the death of Jesus has a cosmic significance. It marks the beginning of a process towards the redeeming of all things, the rebirth of hope and the healing of the earth itself. In the fallen world and the groaning creation in which we live, we know that these things are not yet, but we also know that, with the coming of Jesus, and the redeeming significance of his death, the way of the world's healing has been inaugurated and continues. The wonder is that we are called to be part of the process of its continuance. We are called to be part of the way of healing after the example of our Lord. This hope for between the times is well caught in one of George MacLeod's prayers. Taking up the language of Romans 8, he says:

Holy Spirit, Enlivener:
breathe on us, fill us with life anew.

In Your new creation, already upon us, breaking through,
   groaning and travailing,
but already breaking through, breathe on us.
Till that day when night and autumn vanish:
and lambs grown sheep are no more slaughtered:
and even the thorn shall fade
and the whole earth shall cry Glory at the marriage feast of the
   Lamb.
In this new creation, already upon us,
fill us with life anew.

(MacLeod 1985 pp. 9–10)

Matthew's imagery of the earthquake and the empty graves may
jar on our modern sensibilities – I doubt if they were ever meant to
be understood as other than metaphors – but the import of what he
is saying remains central. He says, the cross changes everything, as
this verse of an ancient hymn well expresses that:

> His the nails, the spear, the spitting,
> reed and vinegar and gall;
> from his patient body pierced
> blood and water streaming fall:
> earth and sea and stars and mankind
> by that stream are cleansed all'.

(Venantius Honorius Clementianus Fortunatus
(sixth century), CH4 no. 398 verse 3)

'Is it nothing to you, all you who pass by?'

The above question from Lamentations 1:12 is often used during
Holy Week as an invitation to pause before the mystery of Christ's
cross and passion and reflect on its meaning. It is no exaggeration
to say that the church was born out of the experience of Easter and
shaped by what Paul called in 1 Corinthians 1:23 'the scandal of the
cross'. Richard Rohr, speaking in Glasgow in June 2007, reminded
his audience of the saying that 'Jesus died not in order that God
might change his mind about humanity, but that humanity might
change its mind about God'. From the cross, Jesus gives us a new,
unexpected and wonderful picture of God as one who comes and

enters into our human condition and our world in a way that is costly and complete. In Matthew's picture of the crucifixion, the bystanders at the cross are notable for their hardened cynicism and supreme unawareness of the significance of the event they are witnessing. We are bidden to watch and wonder and let the depth of the significance of this Passion possess us, reshape our understanding and shake the comfort of our lives. We ask, after the cosmic cross: how can we let ourselves be addressed and shaken by the sublime mystery of the cross? Learning afresh who we are and who God is, how can we once again speak the word of the cross with power? Victor Westhelle writes:

> The theology of the cross is neither a discourse nor a doctrine. It is a way of life that we live out. It is a practice that involves a risk. It is a story that, if truly told, courts danger but moves also into hopeful solidarity, the solidarity of those who are moved by the pain of God in the midst of this world, or by the pain of this world in the midst of God. (2006 pp. ix–x)

In his book *Christ on Trial: How the Gospel Unsettles Our Judgement*, Rowan Williams in a chapter on Matthew's witness to the Passion speaks of the task of doctrine and tradition being to focus our attention before Jesus himself. He quotes Dietrich Bonhoeffer's famous letter to his godson (Bonhoeffer 1967 p. 172), where Bonhoeffer laments that the church's words have lost their power largely because Christians have become too timorous and inward-looking. He continues:

> It is not that the words are mistaken, or that they are – in the modern sense – irrelevant, so that we need clearer and simpler ideas. Far from it. The problem lies in the speakers. There is not enough depth in us for the words to emerge as credible; they have become external to us, tokens we use while forgetting what profound and frightening differences in the human world they actually refer to. If the point of traditional doctrinal forms is to hold us still, it is also, we could say, to create a depth in us, a space for radical change in how we think of ourselves and how we act. (Williams 2000a p. 38)

More than mere words are needed for the making of credible witnesses. Behind the words, there needs to be commitment and action. Bonhoeffer spoke in that same letter of 'prayer and doing the right' as the two essentials of discipleship in a dark time. Matthew would certainly approve of prayer and righteous action constituting the basic lineaments of being a disciple. As the cross stands at the crossroads, so the locus of the faithful life is in the midst of the world. The invitation is well expressed in Kathy Galloway's hymn/ poem:

> Do not retreat into your private world,
> that place of safety, sheltered from the storm
> where you may tend your garden, seek your soul,
> and rest with loved ones where the fire burns warm.
>
> To tend a garden is a precious thing,
> but dearer still the one where all may roam;
> the weeds of poison, poverty and war
> demand your care, who call the earth your home.
>
> To seek your soul it is a precious thing,
> but you will never find it on your own;
> only among the clamour, threat and pain
> of other people's need will love be known.
>
> To rest with loved ones is a precious thing,
> but peace of mind exacts a higher cost;
> your children will not rest and play in quiet
> while they still hear the crying of the lost.
>
> Do not retreat into your private world,
> there are more ways than firesides to keep warm;
> there is no shelter from the rage of life,
> so meet its eye, and dance within the storm.

Faithful witnesses

At the end of the story of Jesus' death, we are told of the presence of some of Jesus' women disciples (26:55–6), who have been with him in Galilee, have followed him from Galilee and are now found keeping vigil at his cross from a distance. They have provided for him and the discipleship band on the way from Galilee – and now, at the last, they keep their grieving, faithful watch. What a contrast they provide to cynical bystanders and hardened soldiers, and also the male disciples in their significant absence! The presence and naming of the women is important not only in the context of the cross, a presence which kindles a huge respect for their devotion, but also for what comes after. In the continuing story of Jesus, the women are central witnesses. We wait with them.

Study

By yourself

Here are two hymn verses, speaking of Jesus' invitation to discipleship, for reflection:

> Come now, and follow me,
> before us stands a cross.
> Don't run away and flee,
> learn of the happy loss
> where power is dumb and self is past,
> and last is first and first is last.

> Come now, and follow me,
> watch where I walk alone,
> climb on the awful tree,
> enter my bloody throne
> as I make war on hate and pain
> and bear all things and rise again.

For group work

Discuss the following two questions.

In what ways does the cross of Jesus challenge and change our picture of God?

What does following in the way of the cross mean for us?

Chapter 37

DEAD END?

Matthew 27:57–66
The Burial of Jesus
(Mark 15:42–7, Luke 23:50–6, John 19:38–42)

When it was evening, a rich man from Arimathea arrived; his name was Joseph, and he also was a disciple of Jesus. He went into the presence of Pilate and asked for the body of Jesus. Pilate gave orders for the body to be given to Joseph. So Joseph took it, wrapped it in a new linen sheet, and placed it in his own tomb, which he had just recently dug out of solid rock. Then he rolled a large stone across the entrance to the tomb, and went away. Mary Magdalene and the other Mary were sitting there, facing the tomb.

The Guard at the Tomb

The next day, which was a Sabbath, the chief priests and the Pharisees met with Pilate and said, 'Sir, we remember that while that liar was still alive he said, "I will be raised to life three days later." Give orders, then, for his tomb to be carefully guarded until the third day, so that his disciples will not be able to go and steal the body, and then tell the people that he was raised from death. This last lie would be even worse than the first one.'

'Take a guard', Pilate told them; 'go and make the tomb as secure as you can.'

So they left and made the tomb secure by putting a seal on the stone and leaving the guard on watch.

Dead and buried

Jesus died at three o'clock in the afternoon. Time has passed, and it is now evening; the Sabbath is imminent. Matthew tells how Joseph of Arimathea, a rich man and a disciple of Jesus, went to Pilate to ask for the release of Jesus' body for burial. Sometimes the corpses of the crucified were left hanging on their crosses, where they became fodder for scavenging animals. Perhaps Joseph's wealth and standing play a part in his ability to persuade Pilate to allow the release of the body of Jesus for burial. The presence of Joseph as a disciple at a key moment in the narrative serves as a reminder that the possession of wealth was no bar to discipleship; it was the degree of a person's attachment to it, and their willingness as good stewards to share it within the needs of the community. Joseph takes the body of Jesus and wraps it in a clean linen cloth, a sign of purity. He then lays it in a new tomb in the rock and seals the entrance with a 'great stone' (27:60). Both the fact that the tomb only contains the one body, that of Jesus, and the rolling-up of a heavy stone, will be mute witnesses to the coming resurrection. Once again the women are present, represented here by Mary Magdalene and 'the other Mary'. They sit in an attitude of mourning and watchfulness.

The long Saturday

With nightfall the Sabbath has come, the time when Jesus' body 'rests' in the tomb, as God 'rested' on the seventh day of Creation. There is a silence and an emptiness, a sense of absence, hanging over the long hours of this day. Often, it has been a day to pass quickly over in haste to get to resurrection morning. It is a day of deep significance; once more, we should not pass so hurriedly by. Theologically, it is important. The day when, after death and burial, the body of Jesus lies in the grave is an enduring sign and guarantee of his total humanity. It is a humanity which is joined to our human lot as suffering beings ultimately programmed for death. Our own times are littered with 'grave signs'. Alan Lewis, writing on the atom-bombing of Hiroshima on the Feast of the Transfiguration, 6 August 1945, asks: 'Was Easter Saturday and its "end of the world" ever more comprehensively and tragically enacted?' (2001 p. 277).

George Steiner ends his book *Real Presences* with these insightful words into the human significance of this Saturday called 'Holy':

> There is one particular day in Western history about which neither historical record nor myth nor Scripture make report. It is a Saturday. And it has become the longest of days. We know of that Good Friday which Christianity holds to have been that of the Cross. But the non-Christian, the atheist, knows of it as well. This is to say that he knows of the injustice, of the interminable suffering, of the waste, of the brute enigma of ending, which so largely make up not only the historical dimension of the human condition, but the everyday fabric of our personal lives. We know, ineluctably, of the pain, of the failure of love, of the solitude which are our history and our private fate. We know also about Sunday. To the Christian, that day signifies an intimation, both assured and precarious, both evident and beyond comprehension, of resurrection, of a justice and a love which have conquered death. If we are non-Christians or non-believers, we know of that Sunday in precisely analogous terms. We conceive of it as the day of liberation from inhumanity and servitude. We look to resolutions, be they therapeutic or political, be they social or messianic. The lineaments of that Sunday carry the name of hope (there is no word less deconstructible).
>
> But ours is the long day's journey of the Saturday. Between suffering, aloneness, unutterable waste on the one hand and the dream of liberation, of rebirth on the other. (Steiner 1989 pp. 231–2)

Steiner's prose tellingly evokes the place where we all, as human beings, live – between suffering and hope, death and rebirth, the dead ends of failure and loss and the possibilities of new life and beginnings. He sees that place as the locus for art and the artist, in the widest sense, giving articulation to both the pain and the hope, and pointing, often obliquely, to a 'beyond' in the midst of it all. For Christians, the 'beyond' has come; the clock will tick its way through this longest of days until the coming of the third day and the dawn of Easter morning, shedding a light which enables us to live through these long Saturdays which surely come. Alan Lewis writes:

> It is in the story about this man, first crucified, then raised, that we have heard the astounding news that love as self-surrender is the truth

for us, because it is first the truth of God's own life and being ... God's risky, self-surrendering Yes to the nullity of a godless grave is by the same token a resounding Yes of self-fulfilment in the cause of saving love. Nowhere more than in this self-negation is God's identity so powerfully asserted or more gloriously manifested as the resurrecting Lord of life, triumphant over death.

Once we have seen this happen, however much it puzzles us, we are compelled to ask how it could ever have been otherwise. How could the godless grave and the resurrecting God ever have been kept apart? Could the God we know conceivably refrain from identity with humanity at its lowest, hell-like depths? And could the consequences of such profound self-giving be anything less than the snapping of the deadly power of self-regard and sin? How could the God of *love* not take the path of self-surrender, giving selfhood up to death for the sake of the world the Creator made and loved? How could the *God* of love, going to the inconceivable extremes of life-creating grace, fail to surpass and overcome the demonic opposition when it had gone to unthinkable extremes of life-denying evil? Could the God of resurrection ... *not* first have been upon a cross and in a grave? Could the God of suffering, death, and burial ... *not* become at length the God of Easter glory?' (Lewis 2001 pp. 99–100)

The fog of suspicion

We look now at two passages which are unique to Matthew, one before and one after the resurrection but two halves of the one story. The references are to 27:62–6 and 28:11–15. 'He's a fake. It's all a con.' It obviously didn't take long before the disciples' announcement of Jesus' resurrection became thoroughly mired in controversy and suspicion. What the gospel tells us is that Jesus, the risen Jesus, only appeared to his disciples. It was on their words and witness and theirs alone that the spread of the infant faith depended. Then as now, the truth of the resurrection depended on faith. Out of the ambiguity, you choose. The cynics and the enemies were not slow to cast doubt. 'His disciples have stolen the body' was one of the first stories put about to discredit the disciples. Perhaps because he was closest to the continuing Jewish community, Matthew wants to put the record straight.

Look at the evidence, he says. First, Jesus was laid in a tomb which had never been used before. Therefore, there was no danger of getting his remains confused with those of anyone else. His body was the only one there. Second, there was the big stone. It could not be easily moved. Third, Pilate agreed to the request of Jesus' opponents, the chief priests and the Pharisees, to have a guard posted over the tomb until after the third day when Jesus had said he would rise again. Pilate agreed, as long as the guard was provided by the authorities' own soldiery.

It was all in vain, says Matthew. The stone was moved, though not by the disciples; the body was gone, though not removed by the disciples. When the guards went and told their superiors, they were bribed to keep their mouths shut, or rather to say that the disciples had stolen the body while they were asleep. Official cover-ups have a very ancient pedigree. For some people, the story stuck; and Matthew said you could still hear it being told among the Jewish people in his own day.

So, Matthew tells this story to try to set the record straight, to make it clear that, about the resurrection, there is no fakery. Any such practice on the part of the disciples would have been a complete denial of all that Jesus had taught and stood for. But of course, what Matthew inadvertently witnesses to is the reality that, right from the beginning, the resurrection was shrouded not just in mystery but also in ambiguity and controversy. And we're back where we were at the beginning of this short section. Of Jesus rising, there is no overwhelming proof. He does not appear to his enemies and bowl them over with a manifestation of his glory. There is nothing of coercive power here. He makes himself known through faith to faith. The choice remains. Do we listen to the cynics who say that the gospel resurrection accounts are basically a lie? Or do we admit that we stand before a miracle, a real miracle, that out of this one willing death comes a new life which shatters all that has gone before and brings new life to us and to our world? The risen Jesus makes himself known through faith to faith. We await Easter morning. Thanks be to God.

Study

By yourself
A Holy Saturday hymn for reflection:

Loving hands remove the Saviour
from the shame-filled, awful cross,
quick, before the hour of sunset,
sad, with shock and pain and loss,
take the body to the garden,
set it in the tomb, alone,
silent leave, and seal the entrance
with a heavy final stone.
Don't be quick upon your leaving,
wait a moment, kneel and pray.
In the void, be yet believing,
didn't Jesus recent say,
tell about a stone, rejected,
with another in its stead,
how that stone would be elected,
raised to be the living head?

Will the stone of our despairing
ever move before the tomb?
Will we, this world's burdens sharing,
ever find an end to gloom?
Soft, upon our pain-filled waiting,
as we in the darkness grope,
steals a light, beyond our making –
coming, kindling, birthing hope.

Chapter 38

RISEN!

Matthew 28:1–15

The Resurrection

(Mark 16:1–10, Luke 24:1–12, John 20:1–10)

After the Sabbath, as Sunday morning was dawning, Mary Magdalene and the other Mary went to look at the tomb. Suddenly there was a violent earthquake; an angel of the Lord came down from heaven, rolled the stone away, and sat on it. His appearance was like lightning, and his clothes were white as snow. The guards were so afraid that they trembled and became like dead men.

The angel spoke to the women. 'You must not be afraid', he said. 'I know you are looking for Jesus, who was crucified. He is not here; he has been raised, just as he said. Come here and see the place where he was lying. Go quickly now, and tell his disciples. "He has been raised from death, and now he is going to Galilee ahead of you; there you will see him!" Remember what I have told you.'

So they left the tomb in a hurry, afraid and yet filled with joy, and ran to tell his disciples.

Suddenly Jesus met them and said, 'Peace be with you.' They came up to him, took hold of his feet, and worshipped him. 'Do not be afraid', Jesus said to them. 'Go and tell my brothers to go to Galilee, and there they will see me.'

The Report of the Guard

While the women went on their way, some of the soldiers guarding the tomb went back to the city and told the chief priests everything that had happened. The chief priests met with the elders and made their plan; they gave a large sum of money to the soldiers and said, 'You are to say that his disciples came during the night and stole his body while you were asleep. And if the Governor should hear of this, we will convince him that you are innocent, and you will have nothing to worry about.'

The guards took the money and did what they were told to do. And so that is the report spread round by the Jews to this very day.

A new dawn

The day after the Sabbath had come, the third day since Jesus was crucified. It was the first day of the week, the first day of the original creation, therefore symbolically full of the possibilities of a new beginning, a new creation. Around the tomb of Jesus, a disparate collection of beings, human and heavenly, gather, just as dawn is breaking ...

The women

First to be mentioned are, once again, Mary Magdalene and the other Mary, who have been noted twice: with a group of other women at the cross (27:56), and with Joseph of Arimathea at the tomb at the time of Jesus' burial, where they subsequently keep watch (27:61). Unlike Mark's account (Mark 16:1ff.), where three women go to anoint the body of Jesus, having been interrupted in their task by the onset of the Sabbath, the two Marys are given no such task by Matthew. Why are they there? They are keeping watch. Is theirs simply a watch of grief, a time to sit at the last resting place and remember, share and weep? Or have they, of all the disciples, kept in mind Jesus' own words about the third day (16:21, 17:22, 20:19)? Is their waiting tinged with expectancy?

The angel

Their vigil is 'suddenly' interrupted by the arrival of a heavenly messenger, appropriately dressed with 'clothing white as snow and appearance like lightning' and accompanied by an earthquake, frequently the portent of divine presence and activity. The angel moves the stone and sits upon it. The guards faint in terror, 'become like dead men' (28:4). Matthew's account of the resurrection is very different from that of Mark, where the main witness is the enigmatic figure of 'a young man, dressed in a white robe' (Mark 16:5). Writing later than Mark, Matthew is evidence of a tendency which will increase through the years, of surrounding the resurrection with more and more fantastic details. But, in contrast to the later non-canonical resurrection accounts, the resurrection stories in the four gospels are characterised by their restraint and sense of mystery.

The guards

The story of the guards has already been told in the previous chapter. We can notice here their paralysis in the face of divine intervention. The message is clear: the powers of the Sanhedrin and even Caesar's empire are rendered powerless before the presence of God's emissary. It is also clear that the story of the guarding of the tomb introduces a note of uncertainty and ambiguity into the resurrection accounts. Not all believed; there is still the need for faith.

The message

The accompaniments to Matthew's resurrection account create linkage at the gospel's end with its beginning. The story of Jesus' birth is full of accounts of angels as agents of divine revelation (e.g. 1:20, 2:13); we also recall how the visitors from the east were 'overwhelmed with joy' (2:10) as they approached the house where the young child lay. As well as fear, the women leave the tomb of Jesus 'with great joy' (28:8). There is a symmetry between the beginning and end of the gospel.

These distinctive features of Matthew's account should not distract us from noting that the message of the angel is largely the same as that of the young man in Mark. What matters is the message, not the medium, the 'Word' from God announcing of Jesus: 'he is not here; he has been raised'.

'He is not here.' We have noticed the importance of absence in the story of the Passion; the desertion of the disciples, Peter's failure, the cry of dereliction from Jesus on the cross. Here, we meet a totally different kind of absence. Jesus is no longer to be found in the place of death. From death's clutches he has gone. 'He has been raised.' The passive voice reminds us of the primacy of God's agency. God has raised him from the dead. The cynics are silenced. The taunts that Jesus endured on the cross have proved prophetic; God has delivered him from all that bound him.

'Come and see for yourself.' Have a look; see the absence. He is alive, and gone.

'He is going ahead of you into Galilee.' He is going ahead, he will always be ahead – for, as he was the one to follow in the flesh, now he goes ahead as the risen Lord. It's into Galilee he is going, to the place where it all started, the place of the ministry of teaching, healing and welcome, the place where the disciples learned to follow; yet also the place on the margins, the unlikely, unfashionable place.

'There you will see him.' See, discern, recognise ... the gift of the eye of faith, to know the presence – that is the promise.

Jesus

The angel's message ended, the women leave the tomb in fear and great joy, dashing to pass on the news to the disciples. They have become the first unlikely witnesses of the resurrection, although even they have not been witness to the moment of Jesus' being raised. None of the gospels gives account of the moment of raising; all preserve a reticent and reverent silence before the mystery. The women are suddenly stopped on their hurried way as they meet the living presence of Jesus himself. He greets them. They take hold of his feet in worship – an action very different from the rough hands which have so recently been laid on Jesus. Jesus confirms the message of the angel. 'Go and tell my brothers [and sisters] to go to Galilee, and there they will see me' (28:10). 'Brothers' speaks of a relationship, a fellowship restored after the breaking moment of the disciples' desertion. It may well be a final echo of the verse from the Passion Psalm 22 which speaks of deliverance at last. 'I will tell of your name to my brothers and sisters, in the midst of the congregation I will praise you' (Psalm 22:22). We join in the praise, for we know that the Easter deliverance of Jesus is not for himself alone but for all, as the final verses of the gospel will make very plain.

Study

By yourself

An Easter prayer for reflection:

Commitment

To you, O God,
who has led us out of captivity
through the wilderness,
into the garden of Gethsemane
and to the cross,
we cling.

To you, O God,
who has led us out of captivity
through the wilderness,
into the garden of burial
and to an empty tomb,
we cling.

O Risen Christ,
unclasp our clinging hands.
Turn us from death to life,
and as we commit ourselves
anew to you,
send us out
to tell others
the good news
of your Easter.

(McIlhagga 2004 p. 135)

For group work

The resurrection is both a great joy and a profound mystery. Surprise, new life which is different, old life which is reborn, love come again are some of the aspects of the story, then and now, since Easter is not just about what happened to Jesus but also about what happens in our own lives and communities. Share together your experiences of the elements of resurrection listed here.

Chapter 39

INTO ALL THE WORLD

Matthew 28:16–20
Jesus Appears to His Disciples
(Mark 16:14–18, Luke 24:36–49, John 20:19–23, Acts 1:6–8)

The eleven disciples went to the hill in Galilee where Jesus had told them to go. When they saw him, they worshipped him, even though some of them doubted. Jesus drew near and said to them, 'I have given you all authority in heaven and on earth. Go, then, to all peoples everywhere and make them my disciples; baptise them in the name of the Father, the Son, and the Holy Spirit, and teach them to obey everything I have commanded you. And I will be with you always, to the end of the age.'

The final mountain

We've arrived at the end of Matthew's gospel. We pause before his last words where Jesus gives a continuing task to his disciples. Matthew takes us back to Galilee of the margins, where it all began. He leads us to a mountain which Jesus has arranged as a meeting place with his disciples. We remember the great significance of mountains for Matthew; they are the scene of the Sermon on the Mount (5–7) and the locus of the epiphany of the Transfiguration (17:1–13). When the disciples gather, Matthew reports that 'they worshipped, but some doubted' (28:17). Why does Matthew make mention of the doubt/hesitation? He doesn't need to put this in. It's not altogether clear, but perhaps it is to draw attention to the doubters' Hebrew scruples about worshipping any human being.

Indirectly, Matthew is saying: 'this is the Messiah, God's chosen one; now that all has been made plain, it is very right to give him due honour'. Jesus' authority is now revealed, an authority which comes through the crucible of suffering, the authority of one who has revealed a new and different face of God.

Into all the world

Now Jesus' Easter spreads out to embrace first the disciples and then the world. Jesus has a commission to give to his disciples. They are to 'go', 'make disciples', 'baptise' and 'teach'. Each of the verbs has a weight of meaning. 'Going.' The task of the disciples is active, outward and universal. It is to all the nations. After the events of Easter, the gospel is all-embracing and for all. The mission is to the Gentile world, though a continuing mission to the Jews is not excluded. 'Making disciples' initiates people into Jesus' way. Naturally, such an initiation implies telling the Jesus story. 'Baptism' is the mark of the beginning of the discipleship journey, and 'teaching' is a key element of both Matthew himself and the Jesus he presents to us, who is both the teacher and the message. There is therefore something very characteristic of Matthew in this great commission with its stress on teaching and discipleship. It eschews triumphalist evangelism or aggressive proselytism; rather, it invites disciples to commend and instruct in the way of the gentle Christ. In the face of the current modern distrust of universals, the great commission to disciples stands; indeed, it carries greater weight through making no distinctions between 'the nations'. In our world riven with divisions of wealth and poverty, class, religion, sex, power – a world where so many are thrust to the margins of powerlessness by gender, poverty, homelessness, persecution, war and terror – the gospel's blind disregard of these human divisions has a new and urgent relevance.

'In the name of the Father and of the Son and of the Holy Spirit'

Baptism is in the threefold name of the Father, Son and Holy Spirit. There is a danger that we read into these words in Matthew's gospel the complex doctrines of the Trinity worked out in the controversies of the fourth and fifth centuries. Matthew is inspired here in linking together the three names of the Godhead and thus invoking the communion of love out of which all life flows. It is interesting that he does so, as, while Father and Son have featured prominently in the gospel, references to the Holy Spirit are notable by their absence. Jesus is seen, however, as the bearer of God's wisdom; and, in the Old Testament, Wisdom is closely related to the Spirit. 'Naming' was very significant in the Hebrew world; it denoted both power and presence. Baptism, therefore, was no mere empty rite; it was a sign of entrance into the living community of God and God's people.

'I am with you, always'

Matthew's gospel ends with the commission/command of Jesus to his disciples, plus a promise. There is no story in Matthew of Jesus' ascension to the Father; instead, there is something else of great worth. At the beginning of the gospel, the angel spoke to Joseph to tell him that the name of Mary's child would be 'Emmanuel', meaning: 'God is with us' (1:23). At the gospel's end, Jesus' final word is the promise to his disciples: 'Remember, I am with you, always, to the end of the age' (28:20). Jesus promises to his disciples, now let loose on the world to continue their struggle to be disciples, and to make disciples wherever they go, his continuing presence. From the pages of Matthew's gospel, we can discern a community of disciples struggling to be faithful in the face of many trials, a community which fits well Paul's description of the young church at Corinth, where 'not many wise, not many great, not many noble are called' (1 Corinthians 1:26). Humanly speaking, Matthew's church is up against it. The promise remains, for them, for us, for all disciples: 'Remember, I am with you, always'. The presence of Jesus remains with his people. In him, God has drawn near – to stay.

Study

By yourself

Reflect on your journey through the gospel of Matthew. In what ways has it taught you more of Jesus or changed your view of him?

Ask yourself now the question from the Introduction: 'What about Jesus excites, scares, perplexes, challenges, reassures me?' (See 'How to use this book – some suggestions', in the Introduction).

For group work

It's a long road through Matthew's gospel. If you've made it to the end, well done! Endurance in discipleship is dear to Matthew's heart. Take time now to have a celebration meal together. Share with each other what you've learnt of Jesus on the way and what lessons you've gleaned for your own discipleship journey today and for the life of your faith community.

By way of preparation for your sharing together, ask each member of the group to bring with them to the meeting an object which speaks of their journey. It can be either of their own creation or simply something 'off the shelf'. Each member in turn can then introduce their object to the others.

End with this prayer, said together:

> Jesus, we thank you for your words of truth and love,
>> we bless you, that from beginning to end, you are the word of
>> truth and love for us.
> We thank you for those who have kept company with us on
>> our journey of exploration,
> we bless you for those who journey with us in our community of faith.
> Above all, we cherish your promise
> that you will be with us, always.
> May we see you, discern you and know you
> through your living words, through your presence in friend
>> and stranger,
> and through our walking your way together in the midst of the
>> world, now.
> We ask this for your own name's sake.   Amen.

Chapter 40

EPILOGUE:
WITH US ... ALWAYS

Matthew's gospel is born out of pain and struggle. The pain has twin foci – on the one hand the Passion of Jesus and on the other the trials of Matthew's community's costly emergence from its womb in Judaism and coming to terms with life with Gentile Christians. At times, the wounds of Matthew's painful struggle show through and disfigure Matthew's story, unlike the wounds of the risen Christ, which remain his glory (see John 20:24–9). It has been said that the raw materials for the later development of the doctrine of hell are contained within Matthew; certainly, occasionally a picture of God as Gerard Hughes' 'Uncle George' – see the quotation in Chapter 27 p. 277 in the comment on the parable of the wedding feast – comes to view. There is, in Matthew, fuel for an unhealthy judgementalism; worse, as we have seen, elements of the gospel and particularly 27:25 have been used to stoke the fires of anti-semitism which have been such a recurring blot on Christian history. On the other hand, from Matthew's gospel there issues a stream of words of insight and encouragement for both individual believer and the community of faith to hold on in tough times to Jesus' way of forgiveness, compassion and love from below. The words of the Sermon on the Mount (5–7), Seventy times seven (18:21–2), and the Sheep and the Goats (25:31–46) will forever cast their luminous light on all who seriously embrace the discipleship way.

Matthew is always the teacher who has shown us Jesus as the one who both speaks words of truth and is in himself the word of truth. That combination of word and action is dear to Matthew; he constantly pillories hypocrisy on the one hand, while on the other his ideal disciple is the person of humble integrity and compassion who simply gets on with living the faith life. Ever at the disciple's side is Jesus, the revealer of the mystery of the heavenly kingdom come to earth. Jesus offers a double revelation. Underneath the peasant's cloak, the teacher's garment, the bloody body, faith discerns the lineaments of the heavenly king. The heavenly king is also discerned, met and ministered to when he is seen and cared for in the hungry, the thirsty, the stranger, the naked, the sick, the prisoner. Present whenever two or three meet in his name, 'with us always', Jesus is forever with the fragile community of faith seeking to live its life in the midst of the struggles and ambiguities of the world. We can also see Matthew's gospel as a manual of discipleship, a guide to seeing and going with Jesus on the way of faith, which is always the way of the cross and the way to Easter.

We could sum up thus. Matthew tells us of the way in which, through Jesus Christ, God has come to meet us and will never leave us. The sense of 'God with us' is well conveyed in the following Advent meditation by Gerard Hughes. Let it banish all notions of 'Uncle George' and go with us as we continue on the quest that Matthew sets for us – to be down-to-earth disciples of Jesus in the midst of our world of today.

The God who holds us now in being every second of our lives is the God who manifested Godself to us in Jesus 2,000-plus years ago. We are not living in an in-between time between two Comings: we are living in the same NOW as we remember 2,000 years ago, and the second Coming will be in the same NOW. God is as near to us at this moment as God was present to Mary 2,000 years ago. If this leaves your head spinning, let it spin; just hear God calling you by name and telling you, 'I am with you always, even till the end of time'.

During Advent, it is good to keep reminding ourselves 'God is come'. If that jars grammatically, try, 'God has come and is now here, wherever and however I happen to be. The Spirit, who lived in Jesus and raised him from the dead, now lives in me.' Just keep listening to the phrase being spoken to you. Don't argue with it. Tell God your felt reactions; God who, in St Augustine's words, 'is nearer to me than I am to myself'.

In this way, you are allowing yourself to meet God in God's continuous Coming and letting God be your teacher: 'He who is your teacher will hide no longer, and you will see your teacher with your own eyes. Whether you turn to right or to left you will hear this voice behind you saying, "This is the way, follow it"' (Isaiah 30:21).

And God is come not only to me, but is present in every single human being. The way we relate to one another is the way we meet God in his Coming. (Gerry W. Hughes SJ, in *The Tablet*, 26 November 2005 p. 17)

BIBLIOGRAPHY

Auden, W. H. (1968), *Selected Poems*, London: Faber & Faber.

Berrigan, Daniel (1996), *Isaiah: Spirit of Courage, Gift of Tears*, Minneapolis: Augsburg Fortress Press.

Bonhoeffer, Dietrich (1959), *The Cost of Discipleship*, London: SCM Press.

Bonhoeffer, Dietrich (1967), *Letters and Papers from Prison*, 3rd edn, London: SCM Press.

Bornkamm, G. (1995), 'The authority to "bind" and "loose" in the church of Matthew's Gospel', in G. M. Stanton (ed.), *The Interpretation of Matthew*, Edinburgh: T&T Clark.

Brown, Raymond E. (1993), *The Birth of the Messiah*, New York: Doubleday.

Carter, Warren (2000), *Matthew and the Margins: a Socio-political and Religious Reading*, Sheffield: Sheffield Academic Press.

Church Hymnary, 4th edn, Norwich: The Canterbury Press, 2005.

Common Order (1994), Church of Scotland Panel on Worship: Edinburgh: Saint Andrew Press.

Crawford, Thomas (1990), *Boswell, Burns and the French Revolution*, Edinburgh: Saltire Society.

Davidson, Robert (1998), *The Vitality of Worship: A Commentary on the Book of Psalms*, Edinburgh: Handsel Press.

Eliot, T. S. (1969a), *Collected Poems*, London: Faber & Faber.

Eliot, T. S. (1969b), *The Complete Poems and Plays*, London: Faber & Faber.

Forrester, Duncan (2005), *Theological Fragments*, London: T&T Clark.

Fraser, Ian (2006), *The Way Ahead: Grown-Up Christians*, Glasgow: Wild Goose Publications.

Fung, Raymond (1992), *The Isaiah Vision*, Geneva: World Council of Churches.

Galbraith, J. K. (2005), *The Economics of Innocent Fraud: Truth for our Time*, London: Allen Lane.

Godwin, Gail (2001), *Genealogy and Grace*, Robertsbridge: Plough Publishing House.

Hays, Richard (1996), *The Moral Vision of the New Testament*, New York: HarperCollins.

Herzog, William II (1994), *The Parables as Subversive Speech: Jesus as Pedagogue of the Oppressed*, Louisville: Westminster John Knox Press.

Herzog, William II (2000), *Jesus, Justice and the Reign of God*, Louisville: Westminster John Knox Press.

Holloway, Richard (2002), *On Forgiveness*, Edinburgh: Canongate Books.

Hughes, Gerard W. (1997), *God, Where are You?*, London: DLT.

Hunter, A. M. (1965), *Design for Life*, London: SCM Press.

John, Jeffrey (2001), *The Meaning in the Miracles*, Norwich: SCM/Canterbury Press.

Jones, W. Paul (2000), *A Season in the Desert*, Brewster, MA: Paraclete Press.

Josipovici, Gabriel (1988), *The Book of God*, New Haven/London: Yale University Press.

Käsemann, Ernst (1969), *Jesus Means Freedom*, London: SCM Press.

Kierkegaard, Søren (1941), *Fear and Trembling*, Princeton: Princeton University Press.

Kingsbury, Jack (1986), *Matthew as Story*, Philadelphia: Fortress Press.

Leach, Kenneth (1985), *True God: An Exploration in Spiritual Theology*, London: Sheldon Press.

Lewis, Alan (2001), *Between Cross and Resurrection: A Theology of Holy Saturday*, Cambridge: Eerdmans.

Luz, Ulrich (2005), *Studies in Matthew*, Cambridge: Eerdmans.

MacCaig, Norman (1990), *Collected Poems*, London: Chatto & Windus.

McIlhagga, Kate (2004), *The Green Heart of the Snowdrop*, Glasgow: Wild Goose Publications.

MacLeod, George (1985), *The Whole Earth Shall Cry Glory*, Iona: Wild Goose Publications.

Mayne, Michael (2001), *Learning to Dance*, London: DLT.

Miller, John (2002), *Reflections on the Beatitudes*, Edinburgh: Saint Andrew Press.

Nhat Hanh, Thich (1988), *Interbeing*, Berkeley, CA: Parallax Press.

Nouwen, Henri (2000), *The Only Necessary Thing*, London: DLT.

Pray Now (annual), Edinburgh: Saint Andrew Press.

Rohr, Richard (1997), *The Good News According to Luke*, New York: Crossroad.

Romero, Oscar (1988), *The Violence of Love*, Robertsbridge: Plough Publishing House.

Sacks, Jonathan (2003), *The Dignity of Difference: How to Avoid the Clash of Civilizations*, London: Continuum.

Sacks, Jonathan (2005), *To Heal a Fractured World: The Ethics of Responsibility*, London: Continuum.

Schweizer, Eduard (1976), *The Good News According to Matthew* (London: SPCK).

Sheffield, Julian (2001), 'The Father in the Gospel of Matthew', in A.-J. Levine (ed.), *A Feminist Companion to Matthew*, Sheffield: Sheffield Academic Press.

Smith, Ronald Gregor (1956), *The New Man: Christianity and Man's Coming of Age*, London: SCM Press.

Smith, Ronald Gregor (1969), *The Free Man: Studies in Christian Anthropology*, London: Collins.

Steiner, George (1989), *Real Presences*, London: Faber & Faber.

Steven, Kenneth C. (2000), *Iona*, Edinburgh: Saint Andrew Press.

Thomas, R. S. (1993), *Collected Poems*, London: J. M. Dent/Orion Publishing Group.

Thomas, R. S. (2004), *Collected Later Poems*, Northumberland: Bloodaxe.

Vanier, Jean (1988), *The Broken Body*, London: DLT.

Walker, Alice (1984), *Horses Make a Landscape Look More Beautiful*, New York: Harcourt Brace Jovanovich.

Westhelle, Victor (2006), *The Scandalous God*, Minneapolis: Fortress Press.

Whyte, Iain (2006), *Scotland and the Abolition of Black Slavery, 1756–1838*, Edinburgh: Edinburgh University Press.

Williams, Rowan (2000a), *Christ on Trial*, London: Fount.

Williams, Rowan (2000b), *On Christian Theology*, Oxford: Blackwell.

Wright, Tom (2002), *Matthew for Everyone*, 2 vols, London: SPCK.